MANNISH WATER

Mannish Water:
An Anthology of Social, Political and Cultural Essays by Black Scholarly Men in 21st-Century America—Reflections on their Lives and their World

EDITED BY CARLTON LONG and OLUFEMI VAUGHAN

WITH A FOREWORD BY PENIEL E. JOSEPH

(Award-Winning Author of *The Sword and the Shield: The Revolutionary Lives of Malcolm X and Martin Luther King, Jr.*)

AND AN AFTERWORD BY YOHURU WILLIAMS

(Distinguished University Professor of History, University of St. Thomas)

AFRICA WORLD PRESS

TRENTON | LONDON | CAPE TOWN | NAIROBI | ADDIS ABABA | ASMARA | IBADAN | NEW DELHI

AFRICA WORLD PRESS
541 West Ingham Avenue | Suite B
Trenton, New Jersey 08638

Copyright © 2024

All rights reserved. No part of this publication may be reproduced, stored in a retrieval system or transmitted in any form or by any means electronic, mechanical, photocopying, recording or otherwise without the prior written permission of the publisher.

Cover art: Jerome Lagarrigue, "Self Portrait"
Cover design: Mot Long & Shaggy Flores
Book design: LiteBook Prepress Services
Indexer: Shreya Joshi

Cataloging-in-Publication Data may be obtained from the Library of Congress.

ISBNs: 978-1-56902-859-9 (HB)
        978-1-56902-860-5 (PB)

*To my dear mother, Geneva Turner Long
and for my beloved wife, Monique*

–CL

* * * * * *

*To the memory of my dear mother, Gladys Aduke Vaughan
and for my beloved wife, Rosemary*

–OV

Foreword
Black Men and the Problem of Humanity

Peniel E. Joseph

The police killings of George Floyd and Breonna Taylor in 2020 opened up historical floodgates that cast a spotlight on systemic racism, White supremacy, and Black rebellion in the face of political and personal heartbreak. Dizzying juxtapositions abounded over the course of a year that seemed to encapsulate, with each passing day, the grandeur and travails of American history. Black people form the beating heart of the American story, even as our presence remains viewed, by some quite irrelevant critics, as pathological. In many ways, 2020 and the Age of Black Lives Matter 2.0 represent the answer to W.E.B. Du Bois' "unasked question" of "how does it feel to be a problem?". Black political rebellions that reverberated around the world turned that question on its head, asking instead: What kind of society revels in the public torture, arrest, and execution of human beings who are Black?

The racial disparities accompanying the COVID-19 pandemic disproportionately gutted already vulnerable Black communities beginning in the first weeks of March 2020. Black folk confronted premature death in ways that were both new and terrifyingly familiar as winter turned to spring.

As a Black man raised by a single mother in New York City during the late 1970s and 1980s, I watched the scenes of suffering unfold with the suffocating intimacy of a familial tragedy. From my adopted city of Austin, Texas I watched with increasing horror news of pandemic outbreaks in my hometown of Queens, New York. Black frontline workers employed in warehouses, hospitals, nursing homes, meatpacking plants, postal, emergency services, and other frontline occupations faced the choice of exposure to the virus or the risk of losing their already precarious livelihoods. Black folks residing in America's lower frequencies confronted the pandemic in lost wages, inability to pay the rent, food insecurity, illness, and death.

I counted myself among the most fortunate Black people in America—able to continue my university teaching fairly seamlessly via Zoom classes, a situation that allowed me to spend more time with my pre-kindergartner daughter, whose classes were all online. My entire family, including my mother in New York and my Emergency Room–physician brother in Maryland, were safe.

As the Pandemic Spring continued, I sounded the alarm about the ways in which systems of structural racism, violence, and white supremacy were exacerbating both COVID-19's impact on Black America and a national response—including a federal bailout authored by the Trump Administration, all together amplifying the inequities so deeply baked into the nation's DNA as to have become normalized. Black businesses were more likely to close and less likely to receive government assistance. Black workers across the nation were underrepresented among that segment of the labor force that could work from home (people like me). Black students were more likely to not have Internet access, hence, less likely to be able to attend school virtually. The Black poor were in a double bind, with widespread school closures impacting the ability of millions of school children to access a nutritious breakfast, hot lunch, tutoring, aftercare, and mental, physical, and wellness resources provided by public schools. In my role as a scholar-activist and public intellectual, I argued that America's civil rights legacy—despite its contradictions, shortcomings, and failures—stood at risk in the face of a pandemic that upended myths of racial progress that had endured well into the first two decades of the twenty-first century.

When I think back to the first four months, three weeks, and five days of 2020, what stands out is the silence. Not from Black people, but the nation in the wake of Black death. The carnage the pandemic wrought on Black communities that spring took place within a rapidly transforming historical context. COVID-19 appeared, like a lightning storm, in unexpected places where its greatest harm befell the most vulnerable.

Black men's bodies conjure lure and loathing in the American imagination. Black male athletic prowess is cheered on sports fields, but Black male conscientiousness not so much, as witnessed by the NFL's efforts to silence Colin Kaepernick's peaceful protest against police brutality.

George Floyd's public execution on May 25, 2020 telescoped one hundred and fifty-five years of American history into an agonizing nine-plus minutes that found a Black man being murdered by a white police officer in Minnesota. The viral video, released at the exact moment pandemic restrictions nationwide were easing, helped spark the largest social justice movement in American history. Floyd's murder reminded Black men all around the world of our vulnerability, the depth of racial oppression, and the breadth of state-sanctioned violence against our very existence.

It also triggered breathtaking displays of Black love. Black Lives Matter protests harnessed rage, grief, and love in effervescent displays that included glorious exhibitions of Black bodies singing, dancing, and praying.

The next few days unfolded in a dizzying blur as protests in support of justice for Floyd grew exponentially around the nation and spread to global cities in Europe and Africa. The fact that the death of a previously unknown Black man—rather than of a well-known public figure like Dr. Martin Luther King, Jr., for instance—triggered the largest social justice movement in American history itself represents a kind of bittersweet progress.

Black radicalism is most easily identified with the Black Power–era politics of the 1960s and 1970s, with images of Malcolm X jabbing his finger in the air during a Harlem rally to make a particularly emphatic point. Martin Luther King, Jr. embodies the search for radical Black citizenship just as Malcolm reflects the emphatic demand for radical Black dignity. Malcolm and Martin, so often viewed as dueling opposites, represent dual sides of the same revolutionary coin—Black men who wore dark suits as a kind of political armor in well-publicized struggles to end systemic racism and defeat white supremacy, Malcolm and Martin also showcase the possibilities of a progressive Black masculinity. Their mistakes, shortcomings, and failures have only humanized the breadth of their political genius.

The very phrase "Black Lives Matter" sparked controversy then, inspiring a white supremacist and law enforcement backlash—"All Lives Matter" and/or "Blue Lives Matter"—whose very existence reflected a bad faith adherence to color-blind racism, further infecting the entire national discourse around race. The political rebellions unfolding across the nation reflected centuries of struggle for Black dignity and citizenship. But more than that, they reflected Black men's profound vulnerability in a society that continues to denigrate our humanity.

COVID-19 proved a point a long time in the making. The pandemic impacted everyone differently. The more than a million Americans who have died as of this writing experienced the pandemic in different ways than those who survived. The political rebellions unleashed by the combination of the pandemic, the George Floyd protests, and the violence of racial capitalism were decades—nay, centuries—in the making. But the response proved remarkably coherent, framed by an intersectional political analysis and policy demands authored by a contemporary generation of Black and Queer feminist activists and organizers who represent an important part of the Black radical tradition.

In 2020, terms such as "Abolish Prisons" and "Defund the Police" became mainstream. Movements nurtured for decades, some for over a century, in networks of Black radical and feminist organizations, non-profits, informal policy advocacy groups, churches, schools, and over social media were ready when the time came. The 2016 BLM policy agenda proved key in this regard, offering the most granular policy recommendations for investments in Black people over punishment, reparations for slavery, a universal basic income and living wage, free health care and education and housing for Black communities, and an understanding that in order to build a new world, vestiges of the old order needed to come tumbling down.

The racial and political reckonings of 2020 are deeply rooted in struggles for Black dignity and citizenship that continue in our own time. Malcolm X's notion of Black radical dignity and Martin Luther King Jr.'s conceptions of Black radical citizenship are especially crucial to this particular historical epic. Malcolm defined Black dignity as the recognition of humanity inherently denied in America. From Malcolm's perspective, citizenship could never be realized without Black people's having a deeper understanding of their intrinsic worth, beauty, and intelligence. This required a profound appreciation of history, both in America and before, a project Malcolm spent his entire, short life trying to complete. King defined citizenship as more than just voting rights and racial integration. He defined citizenship as more than merely the absence of racial and economic oppression. For King, citizenship meant redistributive justice that allowed Black life to flourish. Good jobs, a living wage, food justice, health care, and the end to structures of domestic and global violence patially describe the kind of citizenship that King aspired to. Malcolm X's call to transform struggles into an international human rights movement dovetailed with King's call for a Beloved Community free of militarism, materialism, and racism.

As the proud son of Haitian immigrants who came to America in 1965, I watched these events with a profound array of mixed feelings. I participated in numerous interviews, gave countless virtual seminars, wrote the most op-ed essays in my life, and shamelessly promoted my recent dual biography of Malcolm X and Martin Luther King, Jr. Suddenly, Black scholars mattered, perhaps especially those of us who were engaged in the history of the Black Radical Tradition. That tradition proved at once enduring and, in certain instances, malleable. The flexibility of racial capitalism could be seen in its effortless accommodation of once fugitive knowledge production that could be comfortably reinterpreted as intellectual property capable of turning radical organizations and political actors into more comfortable economic elites.

I cried when I watched George Floyd's life slipping away in May and cried all over again during the trial of former police officer Derek Chauvin, whose infamous knee to the neck of yet another Black person made history in 2020. I wept in between these events as well. 2020 changed me as a person, a father, a partner, and a human being.

I have always used history to make sense of the world, a gift bequeathed to me by my mother, who remains the most intellectually curious person I have ever known. My study of history became a vocation under her tutelage, with C.L.R. James' "The Black Jacobins" read in elementary school courtesy of mom's personal library. The histories of rebellion against slavery, Jim Crow, and white supremacy—whether taking place in Haiti or Harlem, New Orleans or Nigeria, Bandung or Brooklyn—always left me feeling more exhilarated and empowered than defeated and depressed.

2020 changed this. The rapidly expanding roll call of Black martyrs dying slow and fast deaths under regimes of brutal, state-sanctioned violence, ritualized political cruelty of elected officials, and the casual malice of quotidian structures of governance left me, in the midst of the pandemic, feeling hollowed out and in need of replenishment. My family nourished my heart, but my normally optimistic political soul needed to recharge its batteries.

Hope dawned, incrementally, as the year progressed. The striking juxtapositions surrounding the search for Black dignity and citizenship in the face of a relentless onslaught of violence, misery, and death were not aberrations. These were integral facets of American history that were being faced in such large numbers and in such a public way for the first time. The lessons we were learning together were rooted in the Black Radical Tradition that I had spent my entire life studying. As a student of this history, I recognized 2020 as a high point in a longer running drama. If the 1963 March On Washington hoped to turn America, for one afternoon, into a mass movement meeting, 2020 went one better: It transformed the American Project into a global seminar on Black dignity and citizenship, complete with soul-shattering public lynchings, life affirming Black-led multiracial demonstrations, intellectual re-imaginings of the very meaning of democracy, and public displays of Black genius. There was so much more. Much of the public now sought, just as I had since I was a boy, to better understand the present by carefully studying the past.

I feel more hopeful and cautiously optimistic now than in the heat of the historical events that unfolded in the wake of George Floyd's death. And this is *not* because I see a clear path toward victory in toppling systems of racial violence and death that reproduce themselves with uncanny sophistication at every level of American society as well as around the world.

Black Democratic primary voters in South Carolina could trace back a genealogy of fighting for Black citizenship that went back to Reconstruction, when Black folks were the majority. In 1895, South Carolina delegate Thomas Miller, at a state convention organized expressly to disenfranchise the Negro vote in the wake of a "redemptionist" backlash, lamented about the "eight years in power" Blacks enjoyed in the state during Radical Reconstruction. From 1868 to 1876, Black South Carolinians led the way in creating a politics that built hospitals, invested in public schools, roads, bridges, and anti-poverty efforts that found a way to bring universal healing to a state scarred by the violence of the Civil War. Considering our current moment, those voters who chose Biden did so with the memory of a not-so-distant past that continues to inform the present.

The January 6, 2021 white riot at the United States Capitol proved to be not an aberration, but a central part of American history. Donald Trump's "Big Lie" in the aftermath of his defeat at the hands of Black America's overwhelmingly supported candidates—Joe Biden and Kamala Harris—continued the "Lost Cause" narrative upholding white supremacy as the nation's true moral guide and political soul. Since the rioters—and the then president—cited voter fraud in Black cities that helped Biden win Georgia, Pennsylvania, Michigan, and Wisconsin, the assault on the Capitol represented a denial of Black citizenship.

Yet instances of Black joy flowered against assaults on Black humanity. The BLM protests inspired local political battles that led to concrete policy changes, including the reallocation of millions of dollars intended towards punishment to be diverted toward restorative justice, education, mental health, and anti-poverty programs.

Black history took center stage over the course of 2020. Black men's physical vulnerability triggered the largest political rebellion in American history. The story of Black men—Black husbands, Black fathers, Black sons, and Black brothers—grappling with their emotional vulnerability is one of the most important--and insufficiently studied—aspects of the current historical moment.

Mannish Water represents a profoundly important historical and literary intervention by offering narratives—jumpstarted by George Floyd's murder—of Black male voices too often left out of the national conversation. Black men from various journeys and backgrounds—Silent Generation, Baby Boomers, Gen-Xers, and millennials—share their stories of survival and loss, love and failure, fear and hope. In so doing, they remind us of the undiscovered country between personal vulnerability and political engagement that contours the lives of so many Black men living in America.

My hope lies in the recognition that more people than ever, led by Black people, including the Black men who share their stories and bare their souls in this book, are engaged in the same search as I was. The aspirational world is large enough to sustain the abolition democracy that W.E.B. Du Bois recounts in his stunning book *Black Reconstruction*. My hope rests, further, in the genius at the heart of Black men courageous enough to mine their personal vulnerability in search of a wider collective good for the entire community. In 2020, the message of Black dignity and citizenship traversed the nation. Like Promethean fire, this message became the flame that lit political rebellions capable of toppling political regimes, Confederate monuments, and a redemptionist political order that refuses to die. The aforementioned miners of these fiery messages—these forthright fellow travelers—may never discover the answers, but in seeking to ask more complex, difficult, and challenging questions, they help us all come closer, I believe, to fashioning the freedom dreams that possess the power to liberate the entire world.

Preface

Carlton Long

"Mannish Water" is the name of a special soup—and we will get to that. This anthology is a collection of very special essays—and we will get to that, too. But let us begin at the beginning, that is, with simply the very idea of a "preface."

A preface is a funny thing, a wonderful, splendid, rapturous thing. It allows a person, in effect, to speak before speaking. Such a privilege strikes me as exceptionally valuable, particularly as a vulnerable spirit that dwells within a fragile "black" body in a Wild, Wild West kind of a place called "America." Let me attempt to explain further. I wonder what it would have been like if a Breonna Taylor, a George Floyd, a Sean Bell, a Trayvon Martin, or a Sandra Bland—or an Amir Locke, a Patrick Lyoya, a Jayland Walker, or any of far too many unnamed others—had been able to offer the entire world some kind of "preface," some kind of clear-eyed and full-throated verbal precursor, prior to their violent deaths. I do not mean by this some kind of statement of dread or premonition; that sort of thing happens a lot, especially among spiritually clear people who are empathic. No, I mean something quite different. What if they were able to narrate for us beforehand, and yet from behind the veil, a blow-by-blow account of their last moments? What if just one or two or three of them were "clairvoyant" and could mount a fulsome, verbal defense of themselves, in the moment of their deaths, for the whole world to witness—to see completely, hear totally, and understand fully? What if such were possible? Beforehand. Before these human beings were trashed or lied about in the streets, within the precincts, in the media, in the courts of law, and in the courts of public opinion. Prefaces from them. Prior to the lies, the spin, the gaslighting, the projections, and inversions. What if the pure, honest, and unsullied truths about their last moments could have been foreseen and foretold fully by them, in their own words? What if their voices, now silent, could speak—with a fullness? Of course, famous television documentary series such as *American Crime Story* and *The First 48* will offer us a bit of something like that. They often tell us that the brutality leveled upon a broken body effectively "speaks" to the nearest prosecutor's office saying: "Look what they did to me", and "Don't miss this. They did this, too." Evidence speaks, to be certain; but, in all truth, it would have been remarkably helpful if, in the aforementioned cases we all know of and in so very many others like them, we could have accessed some form of a preface—some kind of precious, honest presaging statement—regarding the terror to which the Breonnas and Georges, the Trayvons and Seans, the Patricks and Amirs and Sandras (and so very many others like them) and their bodies speak, or spake.[1]

The best that I can offer is this: I do not believe that I shall ever be slain by police officers or vigilantes, and yet I do not know that for sure. There are some things, however, that I do know for certain, and they are quite related to these other points. The things that I do know, with Cartesian certainty, pertain to my character, personality, philosophy of life, my habits and values. I can "preface" whatever happens by sharing with the world my truth.

If cops ever assail my life, I implore you not to let the lies stick. Let them not say that I reached for or brandished a gun. I do not possess a gun to reach for or to brandish. Do not let them claim that I wielded a knife. I hate knives and as my dear wife will affirm, I guardedly wrap the sharp ones in our home in paper towels lest they be seen, tragically, by some wrong and random set of passing eyes. If our sharp knives must be left out and about on the kitchen island for either current or pending use, I wrap and wrap, in pitiful disguise, both blade and handle.

Do not let any cop allege that I ran from the cops; I have never run from cops. Do not let them say that I attacked them physically. My last physical fight was when I was in the third grade. Do not let them say that I made quick or threatening movements; I am deliberative to a fault and have seen far too many visuals of trigger-happy cops to even think of making a quick or threatening move upon them, or even within their presence. Do not let them say I refused to place my hands upon the wheel. They were at 10 and 2, or at worst, at 9 and 3. Do not let any of the lies stick if/when they rain down, torrentially, at a rate of 24/7. Tell it for me. I was an innocent man. And not that it should matter, but I was also good.

If vigilantes ever assail my life, do please simply begin or end each sentence about them with these two words: "the vigilantes."

And pray for me, yes, a little bit—but save the lion's share for yourselves. "Lion of Judah!" Save the lion's share of the prayer for yourselves.

And for my country, if not a prayer, then at least perhaps a "preface" can also be invoked, soon, to succour the suckers in America where fascism and white power continue to seek comfort.

I do not believe that my country will fall, at least not in my lifetime, and yet my globalist self takes note of the fact that Margaret Thatcher once claimed, with youthful conviction, that Britain would never elect a female prime minister, at least not in her lifetime. So, I am cautious when I suggest that our institutions will hold and our democracy, such as it is, will prevail. But if it does not, it will not be because the "black" people did not customarily come to the rescue.

We were there in the Continental Army, and in every war since. We fought on the beaches. We marched in the streets. We bled on the bridges when we were not being hanged from them—hanged by our fellow Americans. We registered. We voted. We integrated. We took the ideals and promises seriously, more seriously than most, even while such dreams were observed, for us, mostly in the breach. We resisted. We said we would never surrender. And we meant it. Let no one lie and say that we, as a people, did not toil and did not stay vigilant. Perhaps a tattered preface for a battered America can nonetheless provide us all right now some kind of peace of mind. This book project is in many ways all about what Lauryn Hill once intoned as "some kind of peace of mind." It is possible. A discordant America produces restlessness. Truth has a certain sound and meaning has a certain rhyme. This book is all about those tensions as black scholarly men search for, and speak to, their truths and the intermittent rhyme in it all.

In fact, when we allow ourselves to think in terms of personal truths and rhyme, certain ideas and projects can tend to make sense somewhat instantaneously. I am, for example, forever grateful to the people of the island country of Jamaica for the extraordinary term "Mannish Water." It is the name of a famous soup in Jamaica, but the phrase applies beautifully here as well in the name of this book. Powerfully poetic, "Mannish Water" in many ways symbolizes the essence of this scholarly endeavor. I rush to add, in all transparency, that I happen to be from the US, indeed from Gary, Indiana, although my wife's family is from Jamaica.

And if you think about it, "Mannish Water" could sound, after all, like something of an anthology of writings done by men. It is that, here and now, but it is also—and was first—the name given to a particular dish known synonymously in Jamaica as "Goat Head Soup." The celebrated dish is popular among men for its flavors, taste, and nutrients, but also because it is said, rather euphemistically, to make men "strong." The same soup exists in Nigeria and other parts of Africa and the African Diaspora. Famously served to grooms on their wedding night, it can be found, under the name "Mannish Water", not only in Jamaica, but nowadays in the United States, in Jamaican and other Afro-diasporic households and restaurants. But more than an Afro-diasporic aphrodisiac, Mannish Water—truly Goat Head Soup—represents a medley, a compilation of meat and vegetable, carefully raised and harvested, apportioned, chopped, diced, seasoned and stewed to taste. It is flesh and bone. It is sacrifice. It is from the earth. And it is power which is prepared with care, with great attention to detail, and which is served up, usually on a Saturday afternoon or evening, at the end of a long work week, to make us strong, to rejuvenate us.

The biographically-driven, or "autoethnographic", essays in this rare collection routinely speak honestly of life, hope, struggle and the quest for meaning. They reveal in their own distinctive ways, journeys of aspiration, pain, struggle, and resilience whilst ushering the readers toward earnest and forthright critiques of love, life, community, manhood, kinship, and responsibility. The essays often reveal a strong but tender regard for all things sacred—past, present, and recurring. Nestled in memoir, and an appreciation of purpose and historicity, the chapters in this anthology, all written by mature "black" men, collectively showcase, like the peacock, a breathtaking imprimatur of boundless creativity and imagination. At the same time, the men who speak through these pages are fully human enough to allow themselves to be vulnerable. The writers in these pages boldly visit, as well, the gardens of their mothers. Therein they stumble upon, at times serendipitously, their wives, sisters and daughters. The men find healing in that fragrant place, one which they leave and enter humbly, but unafraid.[2] Black men on manhood, as revealed here, is, in other words, a fully communal endeavor. Their stories, struggles, and hard-gained wisdom—as much as their pains, pangs, doubts, and fears—engage for the reader that which is America, today. Through their exploration of kinship, society, politics, purpose, and spirit, the men in this anthology go a very long way in attempting to make and share meaning.

In the 1970s, the famous Chicago BAM (Black Arts Movement) poet Carolyn M. Rodgers asked in her piece, "For Sapphires," an aching question. It was: "I wonder what woman does Daddy see" when he looks at Mama.[3] Much of the world seems to be asking today, "I wonder what America do black men see?" What world do we see whilst we perform our masculinity, indeed our manhood, in the face of it all. Do black men, like Rodgers and the sisters of whom she speaks, "try to make too much sense out of a world of pain?"[4] Or are the issues deeper still?

The black men in this collection unpack it all in scholarly fashion, even though they wear a rich variety of hats, e.g., civic leaders, businessmen, activists, theologians, politicians, writers, griots, poets, entrepreneurs, photographers, educators, journalists, fathers, sons, lovers, husbands, and friends. The contributors to this anthology have humbled me with the power, genuineness, and honesty of their life stories. It is not hyperbole to say that I have been transformed by their words, and for this I am forever grateful.

The arc of this book has been blessed from the start and it has been steeped in years of priceless and precious relationships. I learned of the soup "Mannish Water" through my wife's dear family, and it was through creative conversations with my beloved wife that the title and much of the earliest conceptualizations of this book took form. And Olufemi ("Femi") Vaughan, the best co-editor I could possibly have dreamt of, educated and labored with me tirelessly for the past two years in the shaping and re-shaping of the scope and depth of this book project. Throughout the pandemic, Femi and I met weekly via teleconference. In hindsight, these often hours-long conversations probably should have been recorded, as they were extraordinarily rich and incisive in their own right. They marked not just the robust and steady launch of this book project, but they also represented a deep strengthening of a true brotherhood. Not only that, the rigorous conversations also represented a reunion of sorts. Femi and I had been graduate students together at Oxford University years ago and it was there that we first became friends. Although we did not reside in the same of the many Oxford colleges (I was at St. Catz and he St. Antony's), we also shared in England many friends in common. Moreover, with our both being concerned with politics and social justice even back then, Femi and I enjoyed being part of an extended family, a "beloved community" of our own, right there in Oxford. Life took over and we lost track, as college friends often do, for years. But in recent years we reconnected and have embarked, with God's grace, on making—as John Lewis would say—some "good trouble."

This project is blessed, then, through many blessed relationships—not least of which are the very great bonds that Femi and I have either made or strengthened with the many talented men in this anthology. We do not all think the same way, nor do we all express ourselves in the same way. The men in this volume do, however, bring honesty and personal conviction to the telling of their stories. Femi and I welcome them, applaud them, and thank them for sharing their truths and their vulnerabilities.

To let you in on just one of the myriad provocative ruminations that Femi and I have knocked around since the 2020 start of this book project, please consider for a moment the concept of "kinship." This was one of the highly recurring themes of ours throughout this initiative. Femi and I have talked a lot about close blood lines, and also bonds which may not be so close "by blood" but which nonetheless feel or operate like close blood lines—or at least operate as one might expect close blood lines to operate. Add to this the epistemological mysteries of biological lineage and personal narratives, and one really then is facing a veritable puzzle. Femi and I often made ourselves laugh. "Did my well-traveled, American maternal grandmother, who was born in 1897 ever meet, or perhaps just walk past your well-traveled, Nigerian grandmother who was born about the same year?" When my haplogroups DNA report came back "Carlton Long, a Nigerian man", such conversations for me, a multi-generational Hoosier and Garyite, became infinitely more complicated. "I don't know my brothers" has thus real meaning, it seems, for all of humanity, myself included. This book has helped me to understand my literal and figurative brothers and sisters more. "Kinship," it seems, is a bit of a head-spinner. I find it astounding nowadays to observe how people either "unpack" or simply ignore it. As you may have gleaned by now, it has been a tremendous joy for me to work through the copious themes of this book with Femi. And I know that I speak for us both when I proclaim that it has been an honor for us both to read what our "brothers" in this volume wish to share with us—and indeed with the world.

This *Mannish Water* anthology, in summary then, aims to go back and fetch—with God's grace—many valuable stories, thoughts, memories and understandings of beliefs, values, experiences, and kinship ties. It uncovers the nearly erased and works to rescue the unknown and the forgotten. This book aims, in some ways, to redeem the future from the past, to aid the good in all who are "still alive" and "still here"—and, in so doing, make us stronger. A council of elders has assembled herein to help the whole community, ourselves included, to prosper from such an abundant harvest. May it feed sister, brother, people, nation, and world.

ENDNOTES

1   The catalog of quickly high-profiled, publicly and suspiciously slain African-Americans includes, simply by way of example: Sean Bell; Sandra Bland; Michael Brown; James Byrd, Jr.; Philando Castile; Stephon Clark; John Crawford, III; Terrence Crutcher; Amadou Diallo; George Floyd; Eric Garner; Atatiana Jefferson; Amir Locke; Patrick Lyoya; Trayvon Martin; Tamir Rice; Walter Scott; Alton Sterling; and Breonna Taylor]

2   For detailed discussion see, Alice Walker, *In Search of Our Mothers' Garden: Womanist Prose* (New York: Harcourt Brace, 1983).

3   See Rodgers' "Poem for Some Black Women" in her collected works, as noted *infra*.

4   Rodgers was a luminary of the Black Arts Movement. See her celebrated poetic works in two major anthologies: Carolyn M. Rodgers, *Paper Soul* (Chicago: Third World Press, 1968) and Carolyn M. Rodgers, *Songs of a Blackbird* (Chicago: Third World Press, 1969).

Contents

Foreword — vii
    Black Men and the Problem of Humanity — vii
        Peniel E. Joseph — *vii*

Preface — xiii
        Carlton Long

Contributors — xxiii

Introduction — 1
        Carlton Long and Olufemi Vaughan — *1*

CHAPTER ONE — 19
    Psalm 124: "If It Had Not Been for the Lord" — 19
        Oral Moses — *19*

CHAPTER TWO — 35
    Journey to the Job of a Lifetime — 35
        Hugh Price — *35*

CHAPTER THREE — 59
    Deconstructing Faith: A Letter to My Grandson — 59
        Thomas M. Jackson — *59*

CHAPTER FOUR — 73
    Illuminations: Pandemic Reflections on Racial Justice, Hope and Love — 73
        James Henry Harris — *73*

CHAPTER FIVE — 89
    This Just In: Peace Is Not More Important than Truth — 89
        Shannon Travis — *89*

CHAPTER SIX 103
Paused on Fast-Forward: Memoir in Unrequited Anxiety 103
F. Keith Slaughter 103

CHAPTER SEVEN 119
Picturing Freedom 119
Cecil Williams 119

CHAPTER EIGHT 123
Observations from the Porch: A Story of Death, Life, and
the Railroad in Between 123
Austin L. Scott 123

CHAPTER NINE 137
Learning to Forgive 137
Rodney J. Reynolds 137

CHAPTER TEN 153
Walking 153
Norm Jones 153

CHAPTER ELEVEN 163
"...the Child that's Got His Own" 163
Jason Scott Manuel 163

CHAPTER TWELVE 179
Getting a Handle on Things 179
Darryl W. Aaron 179

CHAPTER THIRTEEN 191
Once You Are Converted, Strengthen Your Brother 191
Vernon G. Smith 191

CHAPTER FOURTEEN 205
Faith has Prepared Us for this Moment 205
Askia Davis 205

CHAPTER FIFTEEN 221
When I Was a Boy 221
Daniel Black 221

CHAPTER SIXTEEN — 227
Miguel Se Fue — 227
Tony Medina — *227*

CHAPTER SEVENTEEN — 233
For You...I Give — 233
Taroue W. Brooks — *233*

CHAPTER EIGHTEEN — 247
My Sardonic Self — 247
Hank Grimes — *247*

CHAPTER NINETEEN — 267
Ancestral Calling: An Afro-Rican "WandaVision" Novela: A True Barrio Story — 267
Jaime "Shaggy" Flores — *267*

CHAPTER TWENTY — 283
Becoming Lazarus — 283
Lazarus Louis Baptiste — *283*

Afterword — 297
Yohuru Williams — *297*

Epilogue — 301

About the Authors — 303

Index — 315

Contributors

Oral Moses, *a sharecropper's son who becomes a classically trained international singer and educator, shares his inspirational journey of hope, faith, and spiritual discovery.*

Hugh Price, *celebrated leader of the National Urban League, contextualizes his famous life and work and his family's contributions deeply within the history of the American republic.*

Thom Jackson, *lawyer, entrepreneur and educational leader, pens a 21st-century, Baldwinesque exhortation to grandson.*

James Henry Harris, *preacher, engages the sui generis problem of American racism and injustice within the broader context of two urgent problems—televised police murder and violence and the COVID-19 pandemic.*

Shannon Travis, *Emmy-award winning journalist, reflects upon his personal and professional search for peace and truth against a complicated backdrop of love, pain, and "family" secrets and lies.*

F. Keith Slaughter, *chaplain, seminary professor, and Baptist preacher, unpacks head-on the boldness of racial oppression and certain raw struggles and strategies for hope and resistance during the global pandemic.*

Cecil Williams, *celebrated museum owner and Civil Rights Era photographer, casually discusses his iconic photography and its enduring cultural relevance.*

Austin L. Scott, *missionary, educator, and healthcare professional, charts his redemptive journey from childhood abandonment to adolescent rescue and new life in Christ, highlighting along the way an understanding of the structural intentionality of American racism.*

Rodney J. Reynolds, *New York journalist and media company owner conveys the struggles of growing up as a talented athlete and the son of a loving, supportive, and protective mother and an alcoholic, mercurial, and too-often disengaged father.*

Norm Jones, *senior-level educational administrator, reflects on his world and family values as well as his academic and intellectual journey as a black, middle-class son, husband, father, and friend.*

Jason Manuel, *entrepreneur from the New Jersey Tri-State area reveals an enduring Christian faith amidst the complexity of having been deeply loved by his mother but resoundingly rejected by his father, all while navigating a strangely cruel and racialized world.*

Darryl W. Aaron, *Baptist preacher, husband, and father, wrestles with the terror of the Trayvon Martin slaying and the breathtaking implications that arise through witnessing and fearing racist events both personally and societally.*

Vernon G. Smith, *Hoosier educator, elected official, and minister, exhorts multi-generational audiences to draw upon biblical wisdom and other ancient precepts and examples to combat the perils of racism and the risks of personal failure.*

Askia Davis, *New York educational leader born in segregated, rural Georgia, charts powerful paths which include his time as a valedictorian, community leader, Black Panther, political prisoner, school superintendent, family man, and much more.*

Danny Black, *educator, novelist and musician, who identifies as "black, male, queer," shares heart-rendering and soulful testimonies about his passage to manhood, self-knowledge, and love.*

Tony Medina, *Afro-Latino poet, professor, and griot, recalls giants of the Black and Nuyorican world, centering the life and legacy of Miguel Algarín, and the impact of literary giants on Medina's own life.*

Taroue W. Brooks, *filmmaker, lifestyle architect, and HBCU college trustee, shares valuable lessons and insights gained from his nurturing neighborhood in Gary, Indiana, and the application of those lessons on his celebrity-laden philanthropic work in the broader world.*

Hank Grimes, *world-traveled polyglot and ESL instructor shares, with humor, his Odyssean insights, critiques, and hard-earned truths as a "black, gay, non-theist" from the United States of America.*

Jaime "Shaggy" Flores, *Afro-Rican poet, spoken word artist, and Santero, relays his exceptional journey of survival, physical and intellectual hunger, and unexpected life-altering discoveries.*

Lazarus Louis Baptiste, *Haitian-American photographer and New York creative and independent entrepreneur, reveals, with great wit, a marvelous and inspirational journey from boyhood to manhood, a trek spanning Haiti, Canada, and the US.*

Introduction

Carlton Long and Olufemi Vaughan

The *Mannish Water* anthology hails from an America where the work is far from finished, where the people are, of course, imperfect, and where the agonies and triumphs of the past continue, veritably, to breathe tell-tale life into each present and passing moment. Black men communicate segments of their life stories in this anthology, but their words are not exclusively about black men. Their courageous and reflective autoethnographic essays speak, also, to family, community, society, and self in society and to the soaring ideals of the American republic as well as the crushing realities of its quotidian offerings. These black men speak, in their own ways, to the multiple current crises in America. But they also speak to the yearnings of Black people—indeed the majority of people—in America.

Democracy and human rights are, after all, clearly imperiled in the US as well as abroad in this third decade of the twenty-first century. For the first time ever, the International Institute for Democracy and Electoral Assistance (IDEA), the highly respected, global policy institute based in Stockholm, Sweden, has listed the United States as a "backsliding" democracy, a decline which the think tank marks as having begun in 2019. Many Americans—increasingly represented as white male folk with long guns—at the same time seem to be dying to kill, sometimes with impunity. Meanwhile, outright fascists, "white power" advocates and sympathizers, as well as racist politicians, waging racist political campaigns under the guise of 21st century "cultural wars," seem to be proliferating in state houses, in the US Congress, on television, and on the political stump locally just as Americans have geared up for the critical battles of the 2024 presidential election.

This anthology arrives, then, at a crucial time in the life of the American experiment. It comes when not much seems sacred, or soaring, anymore. Injudicious norm-busting has landed the US with a norm-busting, radicalized, reactionary US Supreme Court. On local levels, school books and reading lists are attacked. America's Toni Morrison, one of our great literary patron saints and, perhaps more than anyone else, the black world's beloved, truth-speaking

Cassandra, has been assailed, after her death, by a vocal minority of persons who are proudly, woefully, and willfully ignorant of what the name "Toni Morrison" means on these shores and in the broader world. Contemporary America is struggling with "being" and "nothingness"[1] and many of the essayists in this volume seem keenly aware of the existential crises which seem to be facing not only America, but also Black America.

Against this multi-layered backdrop, therefore, we, the editors, wish to be clear in stating quite explicitly what this book is not (or at least what it is not intended to be) versus what it is, or what we greatly hope you will find it to be. This work, by "black scholarly men in America," is not about being "my brother's keeper." It is not at all intended to be a journey of black men talking only to black men about being black men. It is not "for us by us", if the "us" in such a phrase is meant to mean exclusively "black men" or even interchangeably "black males." The overarching goal in soliciting and sharing these essays has never been either to advance a concept of black male exceptionalism, or one of American exceptionalism, or to reassert, buoy, or reify the black man's presumed role in some extant schema of global patriarchy. Instead, our goal in this *Mannish Water* anthology is to center the voices of black men in America, for purposes of group sharing and self-knowledge, to be certain, but also for the goal of revelation—to the self and to a community of many others. Our communitarian goal is, thus, for the black men in this anthology to share their individual and collective truths not only with black men and black boys, but also and equally with black women and black girls, indeed with black people globally, however they are identified, by self and/or society, through the overlapping and intersecting lenses of race, gender, sex, and class. Our expectation is that just as the men in this volume quite sincerely and humbly visit, in their writings, the gardens of their mothers, grandmothers, aunts, sisters, and other women of biological or fictive kin, so too shall their essays reflect the deeply valued lives of these women and girls, the heart and heartbeat of the essayists' first community.[2]

It is now possible, therefore, to define the project further. In the current critical time of "racial reckoning" in the United States and throughout the world, this scholarly project is, we believe, essential. In this "inflection" moment, when increasingly layered and complicated conversations surround the politics, history, nature, and exigencies of "race" in America (including the existential implications of "race" and state power *vis-a-vis* the black body in an historically self-gaslighting "white settler nation"), an anthology of biographically-based essays written by black, scholarly men from the United States is especially relevant and timely. After all, the contemporary crisis of racial reckoning in the United States wildly and viciously centers the black man and the promise of black manhood, so much so, in fact, that a few simple names ("Ahmaud Arbery," "Daunte Wright," "George Floyd," "Trayvon Martin," "Eric Garner," and "Sean Bell" amongst too many others) evoke enormous sentiment, commentary, debate, and editorializing. These hapless, helpless, involuntary martyrs have come to represent a universe of meaning which is itself grounded in a rather tortured—familiar and yet strange—idea of "America."

It stands to reason, then, that thoughtful men who live in, or have emerged from, such a peculiar historical, social, and cultural milieu can offer meaningful reflections on lived experiences, submitting new knowledge and wisdom to ongoing national and global conversations and narratives. Literature on "race" is, of course, already voluminous, especially in the context of 21st-century scholarship. However, an anthology of essays written by and drawn from black men in America today will also begin to fill a gap which exists in current scholarship and writing on "race" and identity, in the United States.

More specifically, much of value has increasingly been written about "blackness" and "maleness" in the United States. Subjects, topics, and themes related to black men feature within feminist and womanist scholarship and in multiple other domains, including Women's Studies, Gender Studies, Men's Studies, Queer Studies, and more. The *Mannish Water* anthology will likely not fit squarely within these disciplinary homes, but rather enjoy overlapping spaces with each of them, whilst anchoring itself in a pro-womanist space of maleness and blackness. In this project, the "black man" or "black male" is not themed as a sociological problem (*Tally's Corner*); an epiphenomenon of broader patriarchy overall or some twin to white male hegemony (*A Black Man's Worth: Conqueror and Head of Household*); or as an afterthought to conversations which center white maleness (*The Way of the Superior Man*).

Further, this project does not blend fiction and non-fiction (*Brotherman*). It does not attempt to make the black male's minority sexual identity status or his "intersectionality" its overarching theme. Finally, neither does it attempt, as an anthology, to amass short stories—or any other form of fiction—related to the singular experience of a black man concerning being a black male (*The Awkward Black Man*). Given its autoethnographic impulse, it is not even, strictly speaking, a collection of memoirs, the intentional deference to memory in the essays notwithstanding.

Instead, this non-fiction anthology presents works which, like buckshot, hit that which is surrounded. That is, these essays land on themes and perspectives that might be found intermittently in the aforementioned disciplinary homes. At the same time, in circumventing stereotypes and indeed de-centering the domains of popular entertainment and sports, whilst privileging academia and scholarly writing, this rare collection of new, previously unpublished essays allows black men as "black men" to unpack and reveal themselves in contexts, ways, and definitions that may defy popular imagination or may simply not be immediately recognizable. This work as a whole thus achieves something different overall. It enlists the contributors in the use of memoir, but also the social sciences and the humanities generally, in the variegated telling of their stories. The talented and diverse "black scholarly men" in this anthology thus employ richly diverse analytical tools from their respective academic disciplines as they excavate narratives and engage the broadly proscribed, overarching themes of the anthology.

Kinship and historicity, for example—and not merely the celebrated, Western notion of the "individual", or the concept of history as something dead, gone, distant or tucked away—feature among the various salient foci of the essays in this anthology. The writers who have contributed to this anthology are diverse professionals who are accustomed to the rigors of academic analysis as well as the protocols of professional presentation.

If successful, our work in this compilation will begin to represent, all told, something of a long overdue corollary to womanism. We center black men, yes, but as members of an indivisible and broader black, and indeed human, community. At the same time, and this bears emphasis, the black women and girls in our approach are not rendered invisible, distorted (remember Melissa Harris-Perry's discussions of the "crooked room"), or otherwise marginalized—at the very least not intentionally. As the men in this anthology reveal from working through their own trauma, terrors, and triumphs from boyhood to manhood, it is a sobering, reassuring, and incontrovertible fact that our women and girls are very much there with us, as indeed we hope they desire to be, "through every line of pain and glory."

From a broader philosophical point of view, the men in this collection confront and struggle to unpack, rather like Fanon, the purpose and meaning of their lives, and indeed the fact of their blackness. Many, no doubt, would share Fanon's observation: "I came into the world imbued with the will to find a meaning in things…and then I found that I was an object in the midst of other objects."[3] Healing of the black communities not simply in the United States, but throughout the African Diaspora (or "The Black World"), must be communitarian. In our view, there is no other way up or out of our struggles and our pain. Let this anthology be, therefore, a modest step forward in the development of "Mannish Studies"—an academic area of focus which centers the voices of men and boys who are "raced" and raised as "black" and whose voices and lives embrace not simply self and same, but also the broader, communitarian totality of black women and black girls, i.e., all people who are "raced" and raised as "black."

The question of "racing" is no small matter. In this project, we, the editors, problematize "race" as a social construct, assessing it, in the manner that many scholars do, as unrooted in biological reality, as clearly and obviously fabricated, reified, continuously imbued with active and ongoing social meaning, in the modern world.[4] We are clear in our assessment that, in terms of phenomenology, "race" resides largely in the linguistic and socio-conceptual modern world within a tragically confused and confusing Schrödinger's Box. To underscore the problems of the concurrent reality and unreality of "race," we have routinely applied editorial quotation marks to the word when it is used as a noun in this anthology. Charles Husband popularized this convention over a generation ago in Britain, but the bold convention remains, at the moment, sadly, observed more in the breach, in most social science literature, than in any universal, or even near universal, adoption. Rather than reinforcing the existing "commonsense" or pedestrian concept of *race*, our project, in a Husbandian tradition, seeks, for pedagogical reasons and accordingly as an "object lesson," also to problematize it as "race."

If successful, still, this collection will bring to mind a powerful black intellectual tradition and the transformative works of a great many leaders therein. The essays in the *Mannish Water* anthology often are either intentionally or intuitively in spirited and honest dialog with Baldwin, Morrison, DuBois; Aime' Cesaire, Alice Walker, James Cone, Angela Y. Davis, C.L.R. James; Patricia Hill Collins, and, of course, Marcus Garvey, Booker T. Washington, MLK, Malcolm X, Franz Fanon, Fannie Lou Hamer, and many, many towering others.

To connect even more effectively, then, the real-life experience of the contributors in this anthology to broader themes in the struggle of Black people for self-actualization, we have encouraged the writers to explore their works through an ethno-biographical conceptual lens, and in so doing critically interrogate their thoughts on the complicated issues of Blackness and Black maleness in American society. This methodological approach has a rich history in Africana intellectual tradition, not only in Black Atlantic studies, but also in African and African diaspora oral discourse (see, for example, *The Caribbean Oral Tradition: Literature, Performance, and Practice*, edited by Hanetha Vete-Congolo, Palgrave Macmillan, 2016). This scholarly genre is reflected, for example, in the brilliant personal narratives that have enriched our understanding of the experience of enslaved Africans and their descendants across the Atlantic world (*The Oxford Handbook of African American Slave Narratives*, edited by John Ernest, Oxford University Press, 2020). Additionally, this ethno-biographical conceptual approach is reflected in the African American literary tradition in which first-person narration articulates quotidian experiences of Black life in American society and history (see, for example, James Baldwin's seminal book, *The Fire Next Time*).

In other words, the contributors to this anthology are not only thoughtful and discerning, but they also build upon a long-established intellectual and literary tradition. Their narratives, like those of their forebears, are intellectually honest, provocative, and unapologetically self-assertive as they reflect upon their lives and their world. For example, in much the same way that Aimé Césaire centers, with revolutionary beauty, the idea of blackness, goodness and hope for humanity, as witnessed in his landmark work (*Return to My Native Land*),[5] the essayists in the *Mannish Water* anthology proclaim, on their own terms, in their own ways, at their own choosing, a jubilant "hooray" for the souls of Black folk and the resilient spirit of black people in America and in the world.[6] At the same time, their comments and claims, *en masse*, are carefully parsed, searingly analytical, sharply critical, and refreshingly self-aware. Under their watch, no one escapes scrutiny or critique—self, family, kin (biological and fictive), friends, enemies, community, neighbors, strangers, country, world—no one. They do not all approach "God" or the *idea* of "God" in the same way—and sometimes, not at all, or not very much at all. Some theses are full-throated, others not. Indeed, the writers often vary significantly in their cosmological approaches, understandings, and convictions. To be sure, certain Judaeo-Christian assumptions and undercurrents prevail. Even so, such voices here, by and large, tend to be more personally declarative than evangelical or proselytizing. All in all, there is a perceptible Judaeo-Christian river, however, that flows unapologetically through many chapters of this book. The essayists' great breadth and depth of thought, experience, and training resonate between the lines, irrespective of individual ideology, thus driving and inviting spirited inquiry throughout this important collection of essays. It is valuable, also, to view the twenty chapters herein from a bird's-eye view. Such an overview is provided immediately below, through chapter synopses, which follow *infra.* and *ad seriatum.*

Panoramically, the chapters contained in this anthology are loosely organized around the striving of Black people for fulfillment and well-being in American society, especially since the end of the Second World War. For many Black men—indeed all Black people—the Civil Rights/Black Era was a watershed moment of self-actualization and self-affirmation in American society.

ORAL MOSES

In the opening chapter, accomplished musician and activist Oral Moses takes the reader on an extraordinary life journey that interlaces a native home in the segregated American South, the struggle for Black liberation after the Second World War, and Moses' encounter with Africa after independence in the 1970s.

As one of ten children born to sharecroppers in the small farming and hunting community of Coward, South Carolina, Moses shares a vibrant coming-of-age story steeped in the challenges, fears, and losses of the Civil Rights Era as well as his own hopes, aspirations, dreams, and courage.

HUGH PRICE

Tracing his lineage directly to the American Revolution, Hugh Price, former CEO and President of the National Urban League, similarly, details a unique family history that is richly interwoven in the fabric of America—a history that touches the life of George Washington at Valley Forge. Against this remarkable backdrop, Price underscores the preparation for and rise to a remarkable life in public service and media. With his work deeply rooted in the struggle of black people for civil rights, social justice, and economic well-being, Price provides a candid analysis of the challenges and opportunities of working with local, state, and federal officials in the decades immediately after the Civil Rights Era. Such an enterprise, Price perceptively asserts, is complicated even among politicians and policy makers attentive to the plight of poor people, including many who are black and brown.

THOM JACKSON

Analyzed in the context of the contested discourse of the rights of Black people and the American legal system, attorney and entrepreneur Thom Jackson shares an essay penned primarily as a letter to his progeny. This autoethnographic essay candidly examines the failed promises of American law and constitutionalism vis-à-vis the black man and his kin. Through a profound genre of storytelling, Jackson queries conventional understandings of the "moral arc of the universe" as it relates to faith and racial justice in the United States, exhorting his grandson (as James Baldwin admonished his namesake nephew, James, about two generations ago) to attend shrewdly to the lessons of the American past in the present, underscoring raw, painful and sobering cautionary tales.[7]

CECIL WILLIAMS

In a vignette essay, celebrated photographer Cecil Williams reflects upon the power of the past in the present moment from his iconic collection of Civil

Rights Era photographs. Williams discusses his photography from perspectives both in front of and behind the lens. He writes, in a warm and desultory way, of his early fascination with cameras, of the socially and politically restless environment in which he mounted his photography campaign, and also of the distinguished African-American and other subjects whom he was fortunate enough to capture on film.

Austin L. Scott

Austin L. Scott's autoethnographic essay discusses his experience growing up in the Ridgeview section of segregated Hickory, North Carolina—"a section of the city that seemed suspended in time." Scott's keen awareness of the structural inequalities of his childhood community assumes an explicitly racial insight—and a fine point—in one glaringly poignant encounter that occurred for him literally along the railroad tracks of his hometown, deeply polarized in black and white. Like Fanon's racially polarized world of the colonizer and the colonized,[8] Scott proceeds in his discourse to unpack philosophically, sociologically, and theologically the problems of racial segregation, deprivation, and discrimination. He calls, accordingly, for a Christian renewal of mind, heart and spirit within the Black communities that suffer on "the other side of the tracks."

James Henry Harris

Much of what provided the immediate impetus for this anthology was the rupture from the twin devastations of the COVID-19 pandemic and the public lynching of George Floyd in 2020. Not surprisingly, several notable essays captured the trials, tribulations, and triumphs that accompanied this turbulent moment, especially for vulnerable Black communities. Theologian James Henry Harris takes the reader on a literal walk through his world in a moment of trauma and uncertainty. Harris is fully aware of the zeitgeist in which he, and his black body, live, move and have their being. He reveals the theological and philosophical influences that shaped his worldview (for example, from Samuel Dewitt Proctor, Fannie Lou Hamer, and Martin Luther King, Jr., to Walter Benjamin and Ludwig Wittgenstein) in a time of despair. He elevates for scrutiny, query, discussion, and meditation the phenomena of pain, struggle, suffering, hope, and joy. Focusing on sermonic meditations and discourses on love, justice, and hope, Harris seeks the meaning of—and responds to—the exigencies of the COVID-19 pandemic, police and vigilante violence against black people, and the stark realities of a "divided nation." Referencing biblical scripture, as well as other ancient and modern canonical texts, notably Shakespeare, Dante, Countee Cullen, Richard Wright, etc., Harris equips the reader with affirming thoughts on love, hope, and social change. He exhorts African-Americans to understand and embrace the meaning, purpose, and application of love. In the end, Harris offers a way up and out, after having lamented "the sins of our oppressors."

F. Keith Slaughter

In his chapter, theologian and radio talk show host F. Keith Slaughter continues with the subject of COVID-19 and social justice in the Black community. He explores in deeply human terms the existential threat of the COVID-19 pandemic for marginalized Black people. Despite the anti-Black racism of the Trump presidency and the structural inequalities exposed by COVID-19, Slaughter underscores the creative ways in which the congregation in his church actively responded to the multitude of crises of the day. At the same time, he lays bare the profound losses, told and untold, which many poor Black Americans are expected to bear.

Shannon Travis

Black men, like people everywhere, strive to reconcile the ambivalence—and pain—of family life. Emmy award winning journalist Shannon Travis confronts a problem "[as old as] Adam and Eve…in the Garden of Eden"—the human indulgence in secrets and lies." Travis frames his personal narrative within the larger context of American history, "the "lies and secrets," for example, that drove and infused the brutality of US slavery. He notes how the Civil Rights Movement's resistance to white racism assumed its own often clandestine nature. Travis confronts, layer by layer, the secrets and lies within his lived experiences, notably family secrets, shame and betrayals, trials and triumphs, some of which flirted with death and led to powerful moments of reconciliation and revelation.

Rodney J. Reynolds

In his chapter, Rodney J. Reynolds conveys some of the challenges related to growing up without a father. Tracing the problem of fatherlessness through the arc of Midwestern childhood ambitions and spirited athleticism, Reynolds notes the effects of his father's destructive alcoholism on the family. Having acquired along the way role models and adopted father figures, Reynolds highlights, in general, a life of vulnerability, talent, drive, intervention, and resilience. Ultimately married and the father of two grown sons of his own, Reynolds demonstrates, moreover, how he has found a way, through love, hope, and faith, to transcend the pains of the past.

JASON SCOTT MANUEL

Jason Scott Manuel expounds on the poignant subjects of fatherlessness, human agency, and redemption. His chapter is a commanding and sobering pathway to Black manhood. With the support of a devoted mother to his credit, Manuel underscores the roles of male relatives as surrogate fathers, filling the vacuum left by an absent biological father. Both as a child and as a young man, he finds the "voice of a father" from an unexpected place and exposes the perils of false starts in his family. Manuel solemnizes, too, the loving presence of fictive kin—an "Uncle Clyde"—in his life, defining him ultimately as "the man I [have] modeled myself after almost entirely." Manuel's essay pulsates with transformative life lessons and cautionary tales for black and brown boys growing up in urban America where troubles lurk, some officially authorized yet hiding, as the essayist reveals, in plain sight.

DARRYL W. AARON

Similar to the redemptive message of Manuel, several essays in this anthology explore the many layers of black men as a father, fictive kin, and mentor. Highlighting persistent anxiety over his son's safety, theologian Darryl W. Aaron shares some thoughts on the precariousness of black life in American society. With threats all around, he insists even as a black Baptist preacher—and perhaps particularly as a black Baptist preacher—that prayer in itself is not enough. Aaron points, with alarm, to the enduring problem of white supremacist behavior and thought in America as manifested in "Trumpism." He rebukes the scourge of racism in the life of the republic as well as in the firsthand accounts that he poignantly recalls.

VERNON G. SMITH

Vernon G. Smith's chapter exhorts the moral and ethical responsibility of black men to uplift Black American—and indeed the wider—society. Smith frames his exhortations against the narrative of personal biography, one which reflects a large, Christian, middle-class Black family that has worked to make ends meet in his native Gary, Indiana. He invites the reader to be clearer on identity ("know who you are"); to believe in self; to have a vision; to understand the limits of essentialism in history; to dare to be different; to think for oneself; and to do everything possible to support those whom one can reach.

TAROUE W. BROOKS

Another native of Gary, Indiana, entrepreneur and visionary Taroue Brooks, in his chapter, charts a journey of personal growth that begins in Gary and carries him into a world of elite event planning, celebrity life, educational leadership, and documentary filmmaking. Brooks communicates how he was encouraged, successfully, to overcome childhood challenges through sheer resolve. He illustrates, further, how his mother's wisdom prepared him mightily for the unexpected challenges that he would later encounter in life. He also reveals how the wisdom of the grown men and women from his neighborhood "on 14th Avenue" further equipped him formidably for life. Using a gumbo creation metaphor throughout, Brooks compares his coming into his own as a similarly complex and careful process. Honoring, too, the complexity and humanity of black men and boys universally, Brooks celebrates his collaborative film "What About Me?" as representative of a number of black men and boys who live "positive" lives and do not fit the stereotypes which commonly have been advanced in popular mainstream narratives of black males.

NORM JONES

Norm Jones, a former college administrator, invites the reader to reflect on the assorted meanings of status, work, achievement, education, and credentials. He engages questions of duty, responsibility, and motivation with regard to the self and the collective. In direct language, Jones discusses his own academic journey, including his ultimate discovery of himself as an "intellectual." Drawing upon the strength, examples, and urgings of his family, kin, and others, Jones celebrates the peace that he has made with himself as an "introvert." He prompts the reader to think deeply about individual purpose and he concludes with a salute not only to "black excellent men," but also to the presence of love, family, marriage, and fatherhood in a life.

Daniel Black

Writer Daniel Black's chapter is an unapologetic affirmation of a world that is at once black, African, and African diaspora. He reveals—with confidence, pride, and a tell-tale love of the African world—his long journey of discovering and accepting himself as "Black, male, queer" and still made in *Imago Dei*. Black chronicles, moreover, a young life longing for love, acceptance, and even admiration. With powerful juxtapositions of his teen years at play, Black paints for the reader a coruscating portrait of his life—rife with color and tensions, competing aspirations and simple tragedy. For all its strife, Black's is a whole-hearted and earnestly pursued odyssey from boyhood to manhood. He poignantly underscores the perils of growing up queer, black, and male as well as young, gifted, and Daniel Black, meaning also religious, inquisitive, honest, and searching. Black condemns the condemners—the broader society's dispensers of judgment and intolerance—noting that many Black Americans also feature in that number. He ends the essay by recollecting an impressionistic, nearly surreal, encounter that apportions him room for profound self-reflection, self-discovery, and, perhaps, a rare chance at true friendship, understanding, and love.

Tony Medina

This dynamic black and African world, infused with contingent movements of minds, materials, spirituality, and culture is further underscored in poet and literary scholar Tony Medina's chapter "Miguel Se Fue." Medina confronts the sombering impact of death and loss on his world, especially as they relate contemporarily to the devastating COVID-19 pandemic. He contemplates as well the countervailing brilliance of memory, what it endures as black and brown people press on in a search for meaning, even in the presence of unspeakable loss. Medina remembers—and takes the reader on the equivalent of—a New York City subway train ride through Manhattan/Harlem and the Bronx as he glowingly expounds upon Nuyorican culture "back in the day when back in the day was back in the day." With reflections, recollections, and interpretations that invoke not only the hugely impactful life of Miguel Algarín, celebrated founder of the Nuyorican Poets Café, but also the rich lives of many other black and brown artists, intellectuals, and activists, including Amiri Baraka, Ntozake Shange, Pablo Neruda, Lenora Fulani, and Paul Beatty, Medina underscores what it means to be alive, connected to the past, and concurrently building the present society, the future, humanity and the arts.

Jaime "Shaggy" Flores

This wondrous world of Black men in the United States' Black diaspora is further explored in Jaime "Shaggy" Flores' chapter. A spoken word artist, poet and scholar of the African Diaspora, Flores guides the reader through a difficult and complicated family history in which truthful words—something he demonstrates that he has valued since childhood—have not always been spoken to him. As the narrative shows, as a child he longs to negotiate his way around not only lies, verbal abuse, and physical attack ("I was [the] favorite punching bag"), but also through an aching hunger for both food and books. Accordingly, in his compelling autoethnographic essay, Flores brings to light not only a family's pain, dysfunction, and struggle, but also its invested hopes of finding something better—in, for example, migration from Spanish Harlem to Puerto Rico to Western Massachusetts. In his matter-of-fact rendering, Flores reveals the substantial perils of poverty, racism, and family problems. Having overcome challenges from his natal family, Flores, long since married and with a family of his own, responds in 2021 to an unexpected and powerful "ancestral calling," one that reveals to the *santero*, in the midst of the COVID-19 pandemic, an edifying and unanticipated new reality.

Hank Grimes

In this Global Age, the Black American male world is seen to be fully global in educator, polyglot, and "ex-pat" Hank Grimes's chapter, "My Sardonic Self." Drawing on insights from over thirty years of traveling the world, Grimes invites the reader to accompany him on a revelatory journey of domestic and transnational recollection. Offering colorful memoirs and vivid snapshots of conversations which are, from the outset, honest and direct, Grimes confesses that he is "unapologetically… a black, gay, non-theist who hails from the United States of America." In his rich narratives, which start in Indianapolis and eventually circle the globe, Grimes appears early on as a frank and earnest child, a rather precocious and at times mischievous schoolboy, whose mother, conveniently or not, teaches right down the hall in his elementary school classroom. In this powerful essay, the reader witnesses a restless and "mannish" little boy who eventually burgeons into an angsty teen full of youthful self-awareness. In short order, the essay reveals an educated, well-traveled, worldly man who operates in a sophisticated way intellectually, culturally, and interpersonally. We are a "fly on the wall" as Grimes journeys through China, Japan, Morocco, Saudi Arabia, and elsewhere. His desultory, thought-provoking observations provide insight into one black American man's extraordinary personal experiences of the epochal Democracy Movement days in China's Tiananmen Square and many of Grimes's other memorable encounters with individuals and groups outside of the US. His dry wit and sardonic humor are noted stateside by a cherished encourager who qualifies also as "fictive kin," but also by people abroad. Grimes's essay ultimately also portrays an inquisitive and reflective globetrotting denizen who returns home with new and complicated questions and answers about what it means—and perhaps does not mean—to be "African-American" and/or "Black" today.

Askia Davis, Sr.

In Chapter Fourteen, educational leader, community activist, and former Black Panther Askia Davis, Sr. shares insights into his life of remarkable achievement, service, courage, and risk in the essay "Faith Has Prepared Us for This Moment." Charting his earliest days in Swainsboro, Georgia (remarkable in their own right) to his exceptional rise in educational leadership in New York City (with far-reaching national impact), Askia Davis, Sr. reveals the unshakeable sources of his strength and the nature of his faith not only in his personal potential and growth, but also in the potential and resiliency of Black people in America.

Lazarus Louis Baptiste

"Becoming Lazarus," the final essay of this anthology, is penned by photographer, entrepreneur, and writer Lazarus Louis Baptiste. In his resplendent account, Baptiste takes the reader through a rapturous, witty, and colorful life story which begins in Haiti ("in one of those historic Haitian Gingerbread-style houses in the Bois Verna section of Port-au-Prince"), proceeds to Canada ("a boarding house run by nuns in Montreal"), and ultimately lands, with enthusiasm, in the USA ("I was going to live in New York City and be an actual New Yorker…*(You can't tell me nothin')*… I was eleven then, and even at fifty-one, I still write love poems to the City of New York").

As Lazarus comes forth in this essay, it becomes increasingly clear that his narrative, like all the others in this very fine collection, speaks to the almost unfathomable potential that human relationships possess when the matter comes to moving individuals or groups toward either "life" or "death." In this vein, Lazarus's contribution reveals that not one of us, as a human being, can "make it" on our own, and every human existence relies heavily upon many, many others. Take note of the extraordinarily special relationship and understandings that Baptiste shares with his father, his grandmother, and his magnetic Cousin Junior. "Becoming Lazarus" is spectacularly vibrant and rich with color. The relationships with people are what causes everything else to shine and shimmer brightly, to burst with color. The relationships make accessible and positively memorable, even spectacular, the phenomena of which Baptiste so eloquently speaks—e.g., the kites, the chickens and cherry trees, the boarding house, new homes, old homes, laughter, playful childhood bloodiness, well-intentioned mischief, school, sports, and all aspirations.

Taken as an individual essay, standing as an island on its own, the chapter represents Baptiste's exceptional and rapidly spinning world—a space where he effectively processes, deciphers, and interprets a cornucopia of complex and often nuanced social, political, and cross-cultural experiences, attitudes, and perceptions. It is where he, as an individual, shares and reveals, with humor and great style, profound feelings of love, friendship, alienation, belonging, and human aspiration.

Seen, however, as a culminating and collective metaphor for all of the spectacular individual essays in this anthology, "Becoming Lazarus" becomes something more, something even greater. Like the biblical Lazarus of Bethany in the Gospel of John, all of the essays in this volume, taken as a whole, can represent an opportunity for renewal, rebirth, and new life. Lazarus is called from the dead not simply because he is Lazarus, but perhaps also because he is loved. The Gospel proclaims "Lazarus, whom you loveth" has died. Relationships matter for us all. Let this book summon all of us, individually and collectively, from that which is dead. And let the many narratives herein chasten us, cause us to reckon with ourselves, quicken our spirits, and cause us to "come forth"—individually and collectively—with life.

* * *

On a secular note, Aime Cesaire told us all in his writings "the work of man [and woman] is not finished." This *Mannish Water* anthology hopefully goes some distance, ever so modestly, to prove and reprove that point. We, the editors, buoyed by our essayists, and all of our sacred kin (living, dead, and unborn) certainly agree: the work of [hu]man[ity] is not at all finished.

There is *gravitas* in knowing that the great work of humanity is not finished. There is sometimes tragedy, too, in sensing (or even "knowing") that you are "right" in your assessment. As the editors of this important anthology, we are not at all gratified to find that some of the central themes of this book are repeatedly vindicated as time goes by. The epidemic of state violence, brutality, and murder upon the black body recurs in this country like the ticking of a clock;

or, if one leans upon the messages of DuBois (in *The Souls of Black Folk*) or Baldwin (in *The Fire Next Time*), the ticking recurs rather like a time bomb. As Morrison, too, reminds us (in *Paradise*), the bomb of state violence can explode upon the black body at almost any time. With regard to the black body, of all types, the US continues to promote an undying need for jails and cemeteries—the latter, apparently, increasingly preferred over the former. For example, whilst putting the finishing touches on this anthology over the last few months, we have found ourselves, tragically, updating the roster of the dead -- and not simply "the dead" -- but the somber names of young dead, often the young black men who are murdered of late by the unfettered unleashing of state power, of state power run wild, run amok. Some time ago, during one round of edits, we found ourselves adding the name "Patrick Lyoya." Nonetheless, before we could produce our final edits prior to publication, we have found ourselves including, yet again, another name: "Jayland Walker." And there is no conceivable end in sight. So our arguments are, sadly, vindicated. But we, as scholars, as "black" men in America, as human beings in a troubled 21st-century world, we are not at all vindicated. As we go to press, we stare up "in yellow surprise at the sun," rather like Richard Wright's character who grapples to understand that which exists "between the world and me." We return, with dread and fury, to inane conversations and are asked, stunningly, to participate in vacuous and asinine dialogs about tasers and handguns (*"But did he have a gun?"*…*"Was there a flash from his car?"*… etc.) We look over our shoulders, towards the *longue durée*, past and present, and sense ahead of us the possible crumbling of American democracy. The US will never see itself, it seems, as engaged in routinely violent excesses of the state, carried out in civic spaces by the constabularies, the long arm and iron fist of the state. Agents of the state, who not only wield power and no small measure of presumed authority, but who also enjoy immense presumptions of innocence, cool-headedness, sound, civic-minded judgment, superhuman equanimity, good intention, and such, and who also enjoy manifestly broad, blue protective cover, a more than healthy dose of journalistic benefit of the doubt, and, of course, very often, paid leave and unassailable pensions. Meanwhile a radical, reactionary Supreme Court majority elevates gun rights "for all" while shooting down the "penumbras" of *stare decisis* precedents which have, for two generations, safeguarded privacy rights, civil rights and civil liberties—or did so, at least, in the halcyon days of a better, or at least more recognizable, America. Tick tock, and now: In what country, on what planet, in what universe is it acceptable to riddle a human body with over sixty bullets, for about eight police officers to unload their weapons, pumping nearly 100 bullets at or into a human body? And we are so numb, so insensate, that the question we ask is: "Did he have a gun?" during the traffic stop. Were this to occur in Leopold's Belgian

Congo, in Stalin's Soviet Union, or in Pinochet's Chile, our calls, it seems, would be about "barbarity." *Mannish Water,* then, continues to ask, it seems, "Where is the equal protection under the law?" ... "For whom is that genuinely a prerogative and a Constitutional protection?" ... "For whom is equal protection a right, or even a privilege?" The names of our murdered citizens keep coming, and, it would appear, so also do the same tired replies to our fevered and anguished queries. Americans, it seems, want desperately to believe in the myths of America. How strange is this "double consciousness" which asks the brutalized and even massacred black body to beg the pardon of the executioners! The names keep coming, and if they cease after this book has gone to press, what a miracle that might be! We believe in miracles, but we are not fools. Tragically, if we are not ready to explore—seriously—structural change, the names will keep coming even as the pages of this book keep getting turned. This is America. And it very much seems that the work here, in written and lived form, is very far from finished.

ENDNOTES

1 See the classic discourse on existential struggle in: Jean-Paul Sartre. (Being and Nothingness: An Essay on Phenomenological Ontology). London: Routhledge, 1956.
2 For detailed discussion see: Alice Walker, *In Search of Our Mothers' Garden: Womanist Prose* (New York: Harcourt Brace, 1983).
3 See Frantz Fanon. (Black Skin, White Masks). New York: Grove Press, 2008
4 For detailed discussion see, V. Y. Mudimbe. (The Idea of Africa). Bloomington: Indiana University Press, 1994. See also, George M. Fredrickson. (Racism: A Short History). Princeton: Princeton University Press, 2003.
5 See: Aime Cesaire, *Return to My Native Land* (New York: Penguin, 1969
6 See W. E. B. Du Bois. (The Souls of Black Folk). New York: Barnes and Noble, 2003
7 See James Baldwin. (The Fire Next Time). New York: Modern Library, 2021.
8 For detailed analysis see: Frantz Fanon, *The Wretched of the Earth* (New York: Grove Press, 2005).

CHAPTER ONE
Psalm 124: "If It Had Not Been for the Lord"

Oral Moses

I was born into a family of ten (five boys and five girls) to Otis Moses and Elveta Lewis. My father made his living, and accordingly provided for his family, as a sharecropper. Added to that was his fishing and hunting to make ends meet as a black man in the South. My mother was a housewife, and one who cared well for our family. We lived in the small farming community of Coward, South Carolina, a place where most everyone survived by working close to the earth. More specifically, my family and I belonged to a small community called "New Hope"" or "Olive Grove," fourteen miles southeast of Florence at the railroad crossing just off of Highway 52. This area consisted of: Olive Grove Baptist, the local black church; Olive Grove Segregated School for Negro Children; a baseball field for "Negroes"; and a store owned by Manly Huggins, a white man who was known as the archracist of the community. His wife, Bertha Mae, was known, however, to have helped several blacks quickly get out of the community.

We were seen as basically a poor, black family trying to make a living sharecropping for and interacting with white men. Blacks in "New Hope"/"Olive Grove" never seemed to make enough to support a family well, yet, in the case of my father and other black men in that area, we managed.

My father had been born "out of wedlock" to a single mother—Sarah Thomas—and a young man, Townsend Johnson. Sarah Thomas eventually married Chester Moses. However, by this time, the young boy who would become my father was seven years old. He already knew his own biological father and all of his biological—or "real"—father's relatives. Still, as children growing up, we were "Moseses" and yet we had all of these cousins who were "Johnsons" and "Hawkinses." It never seemed to bother any of us. We loved all our people.

My mother was the great granddaughter of "Carolina Kelly Cooper," as he is noted in the 1880 census. In the 1860s he owned more than 400 acres of land. His youngest daughter, Louisa (pronounced: "Lou-I-sah") Cooper married Moses Lewis and they produced six children, of whom my grandfather, Isaac "Pa" Lewis, was the eldest. Isaac married Vermal McCant and together they had thirteen children, of which my mother was the seventh child.

Knowing one's family was very important. One would often hear people ask: "Don't you know your people?" We knew our cousins and lived among them as though they were our sisters and brothers to some extent. Our house was oftentimes filled with cousins from all sides of our family—the Lewises, the Moseses, and the Johnsons. As a young boy, I knew these people and loved and respected them all. This was what made us strong and wedded us all together as a close-knit family. This is also where I learned how to properly address family members as aunts ("ants"), uncles, cousins, and Mr. and Mrs. (pronounced "Miss"). Most of all, it was here where we all learned to attend church and worship.

As a boy, I found that my life was happy, idealistic, and carefree. As part of the younger, "Moses" set of children, I played, sang songs, and just enjoyed being in the Moses household. I never knew what "sick" was until I heard my mother say my father had simply "stepped out of the house" and just dropped. All I came to know was that after he just "fell down," my father never walked again by himself. This was devastating for my family. Daddy had provided for us. He had challenged white men who had insisted that his older sons stay out of school and help plow the fields. My father would say to them, "When you keep your sons out of school, I'll keep my boys out of school." Of course, this meant he had to move, but he never backed down or relented.

Once my father became ill and bedridden, we all came to understand that he had suffered a stroke. He was told, "Otis, you have to move." That "move" was not a reference to his physical mobility, but rather to our physical home. Here we were, a poor, black family, with no money, with, at that time, eight children. Because my father was well-respected in the community, people—black and white—came to our rescue. One white man, L. J. Gause, for whom my father had worked, said, "Otis, I have a house you can move into." So, there we moved to this old, weather-beaten, four room house in which no one had lived for years; but, it was home for us -- for my sick father, my mother, and their eight children. This old house, which stood about a tenth of a mile off Highway 52, was surrounded and shaded by an old pecan tree, a black walnut tree, and an old oak tree. The old oak gave shade to an old pump that gave some of the best and coolest water around. This was all buffered by a lane road that led right past our front door and parallel to a ditch that separated land ownership. Here we lived, in this old house, which provided one large living room area, a kitchen, a large bedroom and a small backroom. In the one large room we crowded four beds, and in the smaller room we placed one. This became home.

Home was all surrounded by a cotton field just beyond the front yard, a dirt road to our right, a tobacco field to our left, and in the back were: a corn field, my mother's garden, and, of course, the outhouse. Here we lived with my mother now in charge, caring for my father and eight children. How, I do not know, but God provided. In these early days I was, yes, a happy child. I was the typical boy. I was often off into many things and, being more than two-and-a-half years older than my younger brother, I felt some privilege all the while. And so I climbed on top of the chicken coop, tested a razor blade by cutting into a new leather chair, and refused to let my sister climb the apple tree. These were just a few of my tricks. For such things I was properly "whipped" and made to sit by my father and not move. My life was most memorable.

As a child in school I worked and did my lessons. For me, school was fun and I excelled consistently, despite a setback in second grade. Miss Wingate, who had taught my father, was now my teacher. Without a doubt, what Miss Wingate said was law. As second graders, my classmates and I were told that we were going to have a party and everyone in the class had to bring something. ("Oral, you are to bring an onion for the hot dogs.") My family didn't have an onion or money to buy one. I don't believe I even knew what an onion was. Well, I did not bring the onion. When I received my report card, which showcased all A's and B's, the grades had all been changed to F's—all F's. Miss Wingate had literally taken her ink pen and marked over every A and B with F's. So, for not bringing an onion to school, I was kept back in second grade. I had to repeat second grade all over again. Such days I remember well. All of my friends had moved on to third grade and I was still in second grade. I was not the only child this happened to. Some parents went to school and made Miss Wingate change the grades back to the original ones. My parents did not do so; why, I do not know. Miss Wingate is still a legend in my community.

One of the ways in which we were able to survive was that my oldest brother became a school bus driver. This brought some assistance to my mother. When it came time for him to graduate from high school, my mother asked him what he wanted to do, hoping he would say he wanted to be a farmer. My brother replied, "I want to go to college." My mother responded that she was disappointed, but respected my brother's choice. Now my mother was faced with caring, on her own, for the rest of us children and a sick husband. These were the days I most vividly remember: my mother's simply sweeping the floor, praying, and crying that God would have mercy and help. I recall her singing and crying the hymn, "Am I a soldier of the cross, a follower of the lamb?" I hear her words so vividly: "Must I be carried to the cross on flowery beds of ease?" I also recall my asking her, "Mama, what's wrong?" This was my mother, a young woman in her 30's, pleading to God for help. How my mother and father made it in those days, I do not know, but there was always food on the table, a clean house, and there was, in general, happiness. In the midst of all of this, two more children were born and we were now a family of ten.

There soon would come, however, the days when I would first experience death. I went to bed one night and was awakened by all this crying and praying. I had never heard this before. My mother's friend and neighbor, Miss Blanche Hall, was there praying and calling on the Lord to have mercy. I looked around, awakened out of my sleep, peered across the room, and saw that there lying in my mother's bed was my little brother, Thaddeus—lying still with a thin white cloth covering his face. I still had no idea what was wrong since I had never experienced death before. My little brother lay there still. I kept walking by the bed, thinking that maybe he would get up soon and start playing as he usually did. This two-and-a-half-year-old baby was always running around making fun. He was funny, and everybody loved Thaddeus. He never moved.

That was the first of several deaths I would experience in that house. My brother had caught typhoid fever and had died overnight. Before this, I had never witnessed such extreme crying, wailing, praying, and calling on Jesus for help. Then my baby sister died and, finally—and most devastating—was the death of my father. By now, as a nine-year-old boy, I had become accustomed to death, dying, funerals, coffins and, of course, all the ghost stories and thoughts. However, when my father passed, I witnessed a whole new level of dying. My father had been completely bedridden for two years and had been slowly passing away. He had suffered a stroke with his first fall, had gotten up and continued along to the field to work. He continued his life using a cane, sitting in a chair. He had gotten worse and was taken to the hospital, Sanders Memorial for "colored people." He had lain in the hospital for about two weeks only to be brought back home after no improvement because, as was said, there was no medicine to help black people. So they brought him home and he was home until his death. This was the time when many cousins, relatives, and friends came to see him. Among these people was the undisputed matriarch of our family, my father's mother's sister, or Aunt ("Ant") Lula. Grandmama Sarah was long since dead and Aunt Lula was there as her surrogate. Aunt Lula was also the community midwife and earth healer. She possessed deep knowledge about medicine and was well respected by the local doctors. Our house was well protected by the presence of Aunt Lula. It seemed that she was always there, especially during my father's last days. When my father began to breathe heavily in his last hours, Aunt Lula told us that these were "death rattles." Sure enough, shortly thereafter my father was gone. After he passed, I saw many things that I did not understand. There were church men who went around our house making strange movements, gesticulations, or "signs" which I never understood. I later learned that my father was a respected Mason. On the morning of his funeral, we stood around my father's coffin, in the sitting room of our house, and watched my mother place my father's Masonic ring on his finger. He had been suited up and he wore his

Masonic apron. When it was time for the funeral, several men dressed in their Masonic ware carried my father's coffin from our house and down the walkway, walking under the swords which all other Masons held high as the coffin was borne carefully to the long black hearse. This was my first time seeing such pageantry. Men were in their suits, white aprons and gloves, and red hats. Women were in their white dresses and head coverings. As the hearse and lined procession approached the church, I heard the sudden peal of a bell. This loud, sad sound still rings in my memory today. I shall never forget the tolling of the bell for my father.

After my father's death, life became different for me. I was now the oldest boy at home, not that this meant much. I was still just a child and thus acted like a child…except for one thing. It became my job to get wood, always, to warm the house. My mother would regularly send my younger brother and me to the woods to gather wood for fire. My brother Fred and I, with a dull ax, would go and find these small trees that we could cut down and bring home for fire. This became a chore that I have hated to this day—and did not do well back then. My mother was always on me to "Go get wood for fire." My job, then, was school, come home, go get wood for fire, and hopefully to have brought in enough wood for warming the house and for cooking. How my mother made it, "I do not know." There was always food on the table, a warm, clean bed, and clean clothes. For my mother, no matter what we did not have, we went to school. We were never forced to stay at home to pick cotton or work in the fields. We always had to "go to school." Although we did not have money, my mother kept us involved in the community. As members of Olive Grove Baptist Church, we took part in community activities. My brother and I were Boy Scouts, we attended Vacation Bible School, Sunday School, the Kiddy Club, and sang in the children's choir. It was in these early days that I became interested in the piano and began trying to play. However, singing seems to have attracted me more. For us, the Olive Grove Community became our safe haven. I attended the Olive Grove segregated school and was taught and nurtured by teachers who were, to my family, either our relatives, neighbors, or friends. Report cards were always shown with pride. Everybody wanted to do well in school. Although the books we were given, or which we bought, were second-hand and oftentimes missing pages, we students were encouraged to do well.

As I grew older and became more aware of my surroundings, and more keenly aware of who I was, I began to feel out my place in this segregated society of 1950's Coward, South Carolina. I was very aware that I was a "Negro" and had been taught to behave in a certain manner in the presence of white people. As a little boy, I was aware that my playmate was the son of the man for whom my father had sharecropped. My family and I were always aware that we were black and "they" were white, and perhaps no more so than when hearing about the death of a little boy, my age, in Money, Mississippi. Emmett Till, this little black boy, had been lynched. I remember very well that when my mother and I worked around white people in the summer, she kept me very close to her side. I remember how very much she guarded and monitored every word that came out of my mouth. And she would not let me get "nowhere" close to a white woman. She cautioned me, "Keep your mouth shut." I remember those scary days. This lynching awakened me to life in a way that I had never known before.

Not long after the Emmett Till lynching, maybe months or even a year later, I recall one Sunday my mother's sister's husband, Uncle Bell, came to take us, my mother and at that time all five children, to spend the day in Lake City at their home. To get to Lake City, we had to pass my oldest sister's house. She was married and lived in this little "redneck speed trap" called Coward. We stopped, got out of the car, and went in to stay just a few minutes because my mother wanted to get to her sister's church, which was called "Central Holiness." As we were coming out of my sister's house, a car pulled up to the house next door, filled with white men. Two of them got out of the back seat of the car and pulled out this black man, Henry Burgess, who lived next door to my sister. We noticed that Henry could not walk and appeared unconscious, with long white strings of slime or phlegm coming out of his nostrils and mouth. He looked dead. My mother and Uncle Bell quickly ushered all of us children into the car and quietly drove away without saying a word. This scene I have never forgotten in all of my years of living. That day, there was no conversation about any of what had happened. The next week my sister told my mother that on that particular Sunday morning, Henry had gotten up and, as usual, gone out onto his front porch to relax before breakfast. That carload of white men had pulled up to his house and one of them, who was the local sheriff, named Cal, had asked, "Hey Henry, how would you like to go for a ride with us?" Henry, who spoke with a slight stutter, had replied, "A-a-a-okay." They took him down into the woods and beat him unconscious for no reason at all, and then brought him home, took him into his house, and laid him in his bed. His wife and children said nothing and did nothing. Henry lived in this community to be more than seventy years old and nothing was ever done about this crime. This incident has stayed in my consciousness all of these years and certainly has helped to shape my thoughts and views on who I am as a black man in America.

There were other stories that the older people talked about, of black men such as my Uncle Vander, a person who fought white men and had to be slipped out of the community and sent North. Many times, such departures occurred with the assistance of other white people. So, as a boy of twelve, I found that these incidents, among others, had well begun to inform me of how to live among white people in anything that resembled "community."

Olive Grove Church was the center of my community. It was here that we were taught how to treat our fellowmen, where we convened for meetings of all kinds, had church services, held Sunday afternoon programs (wherein I learned how to speak before the public and sing), and learned about our civic duty. It was here that we were taught how to get a voter registration card and were told, in the same breath, "Don't tell a soul." My mother was the only woman among a mere seven in the entire community who dared to get a voter registration card. This was our family secret.

Olive Grove Church was also where I had my first religious experience. September revival was a tradition. This awakened me to "getting religion." Since I was a twelve-year-old boy, it was considered time for me to "give" my life "to Jesus." So, during revival, when the minister made the "call," I stepped forward and went to the "mourner's bench," got on my knees, and prayed to God, asking Him to forgive me of all my sins, wash me clean, and save my soul. I felt nothing, but when I got up, I was declared "saved." The following Sunday I, like all the others who claimed religion, was dressed in all white, wrapped in a white sheet, taken to the baptismal pool and submerged in water—"in the name of the Father, Son and The Holy Ghost." I felt then that I had been washed clean, that I was different, and that I now belonged to more than my family. I felt that I belonged at the same time to the broader Christian community. This ritual embedded me into the community and the church like no other act had done in my entire young life. This religious experience also made me aware of other churches in our general living area. My mother was always a devout Christian and since the time of my father's death had really become very active in the church. This was not unusual because she was born into a very devout A. M. E. Church family. My great, great grandfather (Carolina Kelly Cooper) had started Jeremiah A. M. E. Church in the late 1800's.

In 1962, my mother walked out of a second marriage with her last three children in tow and moved to Bridgeport, Connecticut. One day, I was in Carver High, a segregated school in the deep South, and the next day I was in an integrated school up North. I had never been in the company of so many white people. However, I don't recall its having had much of an effect on me. It was different. These whites were very different from whites in the South—so I thought. We were now different. Little did I know that I would soon encounter simply a different form of racism from that of the South. My first encounter of racism in this new, Northern environment, unbeknownst to me at the time, was rather administrative. In that new school I was carefully guided into a general curriculum. The school curriculum was based on a "four track" system, offering various distinctive tracks of study: Business, Mechanical, General, and College Prep. I was carefully guided into the general curriculum. I had always been a fairly good "A" and "B" student, but the college curriculum, which obviously would have prepared me for college, was not offered to me. The guidance counselor made sure that I stayed in the general curriculum. I remember the look on Mrs. Rose Barone's face, smiling yet firm: "Now make sure you stay in the general plan." After graduating from high school, I learned that I had not been prepared for collegiate study. Naturally, this was disappointing. As an 18-year-old black man, I had undergone several life experiences which had been preparing me spiritually and emotionally for one of two occupations: a preacher or a school teacher.

Because of all the civil unrest and racial divide of the times, I felt that we were still living in a segregated society. I had left South Carolina and never wanted to return. In 1963, we woke up on Sunday for church and heard that a church in Birmingham, Alabama had been bombed. The attack had killed four little girls attending Sunday School. I don't remember if I was numb or devastated. That Sunday was a dark and bleak day in Connecticut. By now, I was the official musician at a little C. M. E. Methodist Church. The Pastor, Rev. Broadnax, and his wife had helped my mother and her children get settled when we had first moved to Connecticut. On that Sunday evening, we were invited to an ecumenical church service at this very large white church, Park Street Congregational Church. I had never before been in a white church with all white people. What an experience! As I sat in the back pew in the rear of the church, I was lifted to a whole new experience of church worship. This service highlighted the ugliness and hate of the bombing of the church, but it also shed new light on music and opened a new door for music appreciation for me. For the first time in my life, I heard the peal of a pipe organ and was carried away by its awesomeness. I cannot recall right now exactly how I felt back then as a fifteen-year-old black boy, except to say that I felt "safe." I was now in Connecticut, hearing this wondrous pipe organ, and this horrible, horrible thing had just happened in Alabama.

Yet I knew even more that I was black and that the same thing could still happen to me. It was just that my mother, a praying woman, had gotten us this far. I looked back then, as I do now, on the power of prayer. I actually heard my mother pray all throughout my childhood, quite memorably after my brother's death, and at other times. I recall my mother's praying another time, very much in particular. It was on the occasion of one of South Carolina's severe hurricanes—Hurricane Jane, I believe. It all started as a very peaceful day in the tobacco season of the summer. The cotton and corn fields around our old house were in full growth. Mr. L. J.'s tobacco field was the most beautiful crop he claimed he had ever had. Everybody marveled at how even it was, all across the entire field.

He prided himself in this year's crop. Then the storm came. When the storm hit, we five children were all cloistered in our old house with my mother. The wind was so fierce that my mother took a chair and pushed it against the door. Then she said, "Come on, children, let's pray." My mother called so hard on God to help us, to save us against the forceful winds! She cried and called on God to protect us from the hurricane. The winds whipped and howled, thunder and lightning and pouring rain menaced all around our old, beat-up house—with us, all the while, pushing against the door. Finally, after an eternity, the storm and winds subsided. When all was over, my mother carefully opened the door to see what damage had been done. To our amazement, no trees around our house had been blown down or limbs broken. The old oak tree which shaded the pump was still there, the huge pecan tree was still there, the old outhouse was still there, my mother's garden was still there. Crops around our old house were beaten down, and Mr. L. J.'s beautiful tobacco field looked like God had taken His hand and just laid it across the entire field; all of the tobacco lay flat on the ground. When Mr. L.J. saw his tobacco field, he broke down and cried. His beautiful crop of tobacco had been destroyed. Here we were in this beat-up, old house that barely kept us warm in winter, with tattered wooden floors, and yet my mother's prayer had protected us and kept us. Little did I think about this incident at the time. I was just a boy, 12 or 13 years old, but now in my adult years when I think about this, I am moved to tears—moved to tears when I think of my mother's prayer. As I reflect on this part of my life, I am even more convinced of, and moved by, the awesome power of prayer.

This brings to mind the "prayer band" to which my mother belonged. This was a group of women in the community who would go from house to house once a week, or whenever someone requested, and hold a prayer meeting. Many people came out and gave their lives to God and were filled with the Holy Ghost. I was among those who found themselves on the threshing floor calling out to God to save them from a sinful life. I found myself caught up in the prayer meetings at a young age. I was mesmerized by all the praising of God, the calling out to Jesus to "save me," the shouting and laying claim to salvation which was also shown among these women.

At age 18, I was notified that I would be drafted, so I enlisted in the US Army. I knew I would probably end up in Vietnam, like every other black man my age. However, I was sent to Germany. While in Germany, I heard about the Seventh Army Soldiers Chorus. When it came time to audition, I did so and was accepted. This was a chorus of thirty soldiers chosen at the request of General Polk to foster friendship between Germans and Americans. However, we traveled, in fact, to all the European NATO countries, singing to bring goodwill to all those victims of World War II. I found myself in an elite group of soldiers, singing and performing for the heads of state as well as the military of the German, Italian, and Dutch governments. Every day was a new learning experience. But every day I found myself falling back on what I had learned from my mother in the beat-up, old wooden house and in the church. It was in this group, too, that I was inspired to continue my education. Every single soldier in the chorus, except for me, had attended college. I had felt this lack and had been challenged by some in the second tenor section, which I led. I saw the need.

One of my Army buddies said to me, "Moses, you should go to Fisk." The Army had been my great challenge because of Vietnam. In Germany, I had found a new freedom. Among my German friends I was treated differently from how I was treated in the US. In 1968 Martin Luther King, Jr., was assassinated and I found myself with tears in my eyes as I witnessed all the burning and looting occurring at home. I recall sitting out on the balcony of the barracks crying because I was not at home and then, again, perhaps not wanting to be at home. This was a hard time for me. I had during this time my first thoughts of wanting to leave America and never return. But there was always the thought in the back of my mind: "You need to go to college." This thought brought me home. When I returned home after two and a half years in Germany, I found myself hating being back home. In Germany, I had found a new life, new friends, and new ways of thinking. Here at home, in Connecticut, I was in the ghetto. Broken glass everywhere, burned trees, burned buildings from the riots. I was so disappointed that I wrote to my friends in Germany, crying and telling them that I wanted to return to Germany. Yet and still, I felt bound here by the fact that I did not have a college education. So, I decided to return to a post-secondary program to take college prep courses and accordingly fill in the gaps of my education. This I did. I took SAT exams, applied to Fisk University, and was accepted. And yet, although I had been accepted to Fisk University and had been able to secure a student loan, I still did not have enough money for room and board. The Army buddy who had first suggested I attend Fisk said, "Moses, I know this professor who keeps a student in his house. Maybe he will let you stay at his house." I was accordingly introduced to Dr. John R. Cottin, who replied, "Write me a letter asking me if you might stay in my house." I wrote him a formal letter and he agreed to let me live in his house while attending Fisk. I had a student loan, a promise of a place to live, and what little money I had saved, and I was off to Fisk University. I did not know what to expect living in Dr. Cottin's house except that I had a nice place to stay and I had to make sure that I did what I was supposed to do: "go to school." I soon learned that I lived in the home of a well-respected professor who had taught at Fisk University for 44 years and had graduated from the University of Michigan in 1922. As one of his former students said, and who also taught at Fisk, "Moses, you go to Fisk over there, but this house is the university." I would soon come to know and understand exactly what that meant. I spent many hours sitting with and listening to Dr. Cottin talk to me on many subjects. He talked of knowing and working with W.E.B. Du Bois, Alain Locke, and James Weldon Johnson, just to name a few significant black scholars who were a part of his world. Dr. Cottin also spoke of having met George Washington Carver when Cottin was a young boy. I sat for hours quietly listening to this man speak the wisdom of living. He said to me in one of his long evening talks, "Moses, everything you see in this house is what I asked God for." He said, "Whatever you want in life, write it down on a piece of paper and say, 'God, for these I thank you.' Believe it and then as God blesses you, check off the list each item you receive." He said, "Moses, make your list and see that God will bless you with all you ask of Him." That night I started making my list and to this day I still have my list, and, sure enough, God has blessed me with everything I asked for and much more. Living in the home of Dr. John R. Cottin still remains undoubtedly one of the most impactful opportunities of my entire life thus far. He taught me how to live. Fisk University was a life-changing experience. I excelled in my classes and, of course, had many days of sitting and listening to Dr. Cottin. I became a Fisk Jubilee Singer and immersed myself in the gallant history and tradition of the Singers at Fisk. But then when I heard stories of the Singers directly from Dr. Cottin, these stories were all the more inspirational and engaging.

After four years of study at Fisk University, I graduated magna cum laude and was the recipient of a Thomas J. Watson Fellowship, a most welcome prize, which allowed me to return to Germany for another year of study. As the years have passed, I have been blessed enough to complete my terminal degree. Indeed, I have also taught in higher education for more than thirty years.

In 1998, while I was waiting in line to meet the well-known Nigerian playwright Wole Soyinka, a Nigerian man whom I did not know asked me, "So where are you from?" I replied, "Oh, I'm American." He replied, "No, you're not. You'd better hurry up and go home." I was taken aback. His statement shocked the very core of my soul. I knew immediately what he meant. Out of all the traveling I had done, people I had met, places I had seen, I had never been to Africa and had never even thought that this was such a serious omission in my life. Yet it was here, hitting me in the face. By 1999, I had become part of a cultural study trip that would travel to Ghana, West Africa. Boy, was I pumped! What to expect?

"Welcome to Accra, Ghana." Drums were playing, people were rushing, we were being ushered through customs as V.I.P.'s. Our baggage was all being handled separately, and then... out to our awaiting bus, which would be our mode of transportation for the next several weeks. Boy, did I feel special! As we traveled to our hotel, I saw a city that was in some ways different from, but in many other respects typical of, other big cities I had known. The main difference was that there were black people everywhere. This was a new feeling, a new sight, a new view of the world. Boy, was I blown away, just by the sight of seeing my people, everywhere! We traveled from Accra to Kumasi. This is the cultural seat of the Ashanti People. When we arrived in the city of Kumasi, I suddenly had a deep shock to my system. I felt something deep within my body that I had never felt before, something I have never been able to explain. It was as if there was a spiritual connection that did something to my soul. I saw people who were connected to things I had always seen growing up as a child, things that I felt I knew from somewhere else. It did not frighten me, but made me feel comfortable, and "stilled,' deep within. This was a moment in my life I cannot explain and I shall never forget. I felt connected to Kumasi.

A few days later, as we stood in the Ashanti palace waiting to meet the Ashanti king, I was emotionally moved by how this historical structure had been so pillaged by the wars of the past. Western countries, the Portuguese, the Dutch, and finally the British had waged wars in attempts to gain cultural dominance over the Ashanti people. The European pillagers had left this royal palace stripped of all of its riches in gold, its cultural artifacts, all the while laying claim to its title, "the Gold Coast." When my fellow travelers and I entered the courtyard where the king might be found, there he was, seated among his royal court of chiefs, all dressed in their Adinkra Cloths. To their right sat all the common people and visitors. Directly in front sat His Majesty the King, Otumfuo Osei Tutu II, under this giant umbrella, all dressed in the royal Kente Cloth which only the king may wear. Before I realized it, tears were rolling down my cheeks. I was witnessing something that I could not have previously imagined I would ever see in my life. And then in this setting I hear, "Dr. Oral Moses from Georgia." I moved forward, being careful not to stumble, bent my body at the waist in my best, most respectable bow, and then I carefully backed away, being just as careful not to stumble. After meeting the king, you must back away as if in a movie picture played in reverse because proper etiquette is that you never turn your back to royalty.

As we arrived in Cape Coast, I was struck by the awesome majesty of the landscape and the sheer beauty of the view of the Atlantic Ocean in Ghana. As a child growing up, I was fed, as much as my peers, such negative stories about Africa that it did not matter then if I ever saw it. But now, here in this beautiful land, my whole attitude and mind were being reshaped in a 180 degree turnaround. This was a whole new epiphany. A gestalt. No doubt my most emotional moment came when we visited the slave castle—Elmina—a guarded fortress where Europeans had kept captive Africans. This was the holding place where prisoners of war, sold into slavery, were kept in less than human conditions until they were taken through the "Door of No Return" and packed in slave ships for transport to North America.

I don't know what I felt! Maybe I tried not to be there, not to be a part of this history. But this was my history, this "Door of No Return" is my ancestry. This is the passageway through which I entered North America? Now I felt the hurt, the agony, the brutality, and the horrific treatment of my people. This was *my* pathway.

I left Ghana with a new vision and a new outlook about Africa. At the invitation of the Department of Music at University of Cape Coast, I was invited to spend a semester teaching "Voice and African American Music." So, on March 7, 2003, Independence Day in Ghana, I arrived at UCC for the spring semester. The chair of the department asked me what I wanted to do in addition to teaching my regular classes. I responded, "I want to sing a recital of spirituals at the slave castle." They gladly agreed. So, at the end of the semester, in May 2003, I presented an evening of spirituals at the Cape Coast Castle along with several choirs from the surrounding areas. As I stood on stage singing "Deep River," the crashing sounds of the waves of the Atlantic Ocean battered and splashed against the wall of the slave castle. This percussive sound became a rhythmic counterpoint to the smooth legato rhythm of the melody. The audience's thunderous applause brought comfort and excitement to this evening. As I sang "Witness," the audience kept time to this very rhythmic rap beat. As I sang, "You read about Samson from his birth……he killed ten thousand of the Philistines," the audience suddenly erupted into great thunderous applause and cheers. I was so shocked by this response that I nearly lost my concentration. What a welcome reaction this was! Ghana had given me confidence and a new love of self, of me, of my blackness. It had made me feel at home in my blackness and stronger in my intellectual abilities. The evening ended with lots of singing and dancing around the castle courtyard. This was an evening I shall never forget. In fact, in 2010, I returned to Ghana once again to sing another concert at the Cape Coast Castle. This concert was just as moving and spiritually invigorating as the first one. We sang, we danced and enjoyed the evening once again, but what made this evening different was that for the first time I also visited Asin Manso, "The Last Bath." This was the river to which the captured were taken after having been marched for days and weeks. This was the last place they stopped and it is where they were allowed to bathe themselves prior to being marched another 40 or 50 miles to Cape Coast Castle, or Elmina Castle. "Asin Manso," for many of them, was as far as they got. Some died, some killed themselves. Here one can feel the spirit of these people who suffered greatly. For me, this was a strange place; one could feel the spirit of all those innocent souls who came to this place on this horrific journey and could go no farther. Here they took their last breath. This is a sad place. As everyone quietly walked away, I stayed behind. I wanted to have time to myself. Here I looked and tried to imagine what it must have been like being in a group of captured Africans, not knowing what would become of you, your life, your fate.

As I walked away, two little boys were there just beyond the gate with a soccer ball in their hands. They just sat and watched me. That night I awoke in the middle of my sleep, in the midst of an interesting experience. I felt as if I was being thrown across my room. I had never had such a feeling in my entire life. It was frightening. I have never shared this experience with anyone. Ghana made an indelible impression on me, one that made my traveling to Germany for concerts become quite secondary. When I think, deeply, of why I am here, it is because of the prayers of my mother and the music of my people, the songs of strength that sprang from deep within their souls, against the horrific and brutal torture that they endured in slavery. As they endured hardships far beyond what any human being could truly stand, beautiful poignant melodies flowed from their lips, expressing their anguish and their longing—melodies that spoke of an enduring faith in God, a hope for deliverance, and a deep-seated belief that they would, one day, be "going home." This music is a protest song for freedom, a cry for deliverance from bondage, a call out from deep within the soul, and one that proclaims, "All I want is a little more faith in Jesus."

ENDNOTES

1   For a classic text which engages similar themes of kinship, culture, and faith, see James Baldwin's *Go Tell It On the Mountain* (Random House Publishing Group, 1995; first published in Great Britain by Michael Joseph, 1954).
2   For an impressive, scholarly account of the involvement of African-American men in "Masonry" or the fraternal organization commonly referred to as "the masons", see Peter P. Hinks and Stephen Kantrowicz, eds., *All Men Free and Brethren: Essays on the History of African American Freemasonry* (Cornell University Press, 2013).
3   For a more detailed exposition of this seismic and horrific lynching, which helped to galvanize the Civil Rights Movement in America, see Timothy B. Tyson's very insightful *New York Times* bestseller, *The Blood of Emmett Till* (New York: Simon and Schuster, 2017).
4   A powerful and authoritative oral history of the Civil Rights Movement can be found in Howell Raines' *My Soul Is Rested: Movement Days in the Deep South Remembered* (London: Penguin Books, 1983).
5   Rich and provocative accounts and analyses of African-Americans' fulfilled and unfulfilled hopes and dreams as they relate to the famed Great Migration can be found in Isabel Wilkerson's authoritative *The Warmth of Other Suns: The Epic Story of America's Great Migration* (New York: Vintage Books, 2011).

6   It may be difficult to understand and appreciate fully the talent and work of the Fisk Jubilee Singers without some understanding of the genius of Harry T. Burleigh. A brilliant account of his life and work can be found in Jean E. Snyder's contemporary classic *Harry T. Burleigh: From the Spiritual to the Harlem* Renaissance (Urbana, IL: University of Illinois Press, 2016).

7   For a more expansive discussion of such history and impacts, see James S. Guseh and Emmanuel O. Oritsejafor's *Governance and Democracy in Africa: Regional and Continental Perspectives* (Lanham, MD: Lexington Books, 2019).

8   The lingering impact of social and economic history is evidenced in the political cultural upheaval which Ghana had to endure in its own journey beyond colonialism. For an extraordinary, personalized glimpse into "post-independence" life and struggle in Ghana, see John Dramani Mahama's profoundly engaging memoir, *My First Coup D'Etat and Other True Stories from the Lost Decades of Africa* (London: Bloomsbury, 2012).

9   For a dependable foundation to aid one's understanding of not only Ghana, but also of West Africa more generally, see Eugene L. Mendonsa's *West Africa: An Introduction to Its History, Civilization and Contemporary Situation* (Durham, NC: Carolina Academic Press, 2002).

BIBLIOGRAPHY

Baldwin, James. *Go Tell It on the Mountain*. New York: Random House Publishing Group, 1995. First published in Great Britain by Michael Joseph, 1954.

Dramani, John. *My First Coup D'Etat, and Other True Stories from the Lost Decades of Africa*. London: Bloomsbury, 2012.

Guseh, James S. *Governance and Democracy in Africa*. Emmanuel O. Oritseja for Lexington Books. Lanham, MD: Lexington Books, 2018.

Hinks, Peter P. and Kantrowicz, Stephen, eds. *All Men Free and Brethren: Essays on the History of African American Freemasonry*. Ithaca, NY: Cornell University Press, 2013.

Mendonsa, Eugene L. *West Africa: An Introduction to Its History, Civilization and Its Contemporary Situation*. Durham, NC: Carolina Academic Press, 2002.

Raines, Howell. *My Soul Is Rested: Movement Days in the Deep South Remembered*. London: Penguin Books, 1983.

Snyder, Jean E. *Harry T. Burleigh: From the Spiritual to the Harlem Renaissance*. Urbana, IL: University of Illinois Press, 2016.

Tyson, Timothy B. *The Blood of Emmett Till*. New York: Simon and Schuster, 2017.

Wilkerson, Isabel. *The Warmth of Other Suns: the Epic Story of America's Great Migration*. New York: Vintage Books, 2011.

CHAPTER TWO
Journey to the Job of a Lifetime

Hugh Price

Introduction

Sunday, July 24, 1994. Indianapolis, Indiana. Annual conference of the National Urban League. Early evening. After an enthusiastic introduction by the chairman of the board of directors of the National Urban League, I left my seat at the dais, stepped to the lectern, and looked out over the crowd of approximately 3,000 Urban Leaguers and onlookers in the cavernous hall of the Indiana Convention Center. A phalanx of TV cameras from local stations, network affiliates, and CSPAN, along with radio and newspaper correspondents, among others, was positioned about midway from the front.

This opening event of the annual conference, known as the Keynote Session, traditionally serves as the occasion when the president and CEO of the League lays out his vision, agenda, and exhortations to the leaders, staff, and volunteers of the sprawling Urban League movement. This year—1994—the high-profile event also marked my introduction to the Urban League movement and indeed the nation as the seventh president of this venerable and revered 84-year-old organization.

Founded in 1910, the National Urban League, which is the mother ship of the Urban League movement, has long been a leading civil rights advocate and champion of empowering our people to enter the economic mainstream. More than once I heard the legendary Vernon Jordan say that running the National Urban League was the best job he ever had. The Urban League grew out of the Great Migration in the early 20th century which saw millions of Black people gravitate from the rigid segregation and racist violence of the South mainly to cities in the North, Midwest, and West Coast. This prompted the creation of local Urban League affiliates in cities from coast to coast, all devoted to addressing the basic food, clothing, shelter, and employment needs of the new arrivals.

While the keynote session in 1994 marked my national debut as president of the National Urban League, in actuality it was the culmination of my journey to the job of a lifetime. Many ancestors, adults, and colleagues had steered and accompanied me on this journey. Most, but not all, were Black men. They, along with my beloved wife and daughters, inspired and indulged my restless quest to serve our people and, as my alma mater Amherst College puts it, to lead a life of consequence.

The DNA Made Me Do It

While I'm certainly no geneticist, I have little doubt that several of my ancestors planted the seeds for my professional journey. Let's start with the forebears on my mother's side.[1] My great-great-great-great grandfather, Nero Hawley, lived in Trumbull, Connecticut. Born a slave in 1742, he was persuaded by the promise of freedom, plus a signing bonus, to enlist on April 20, 1777, in the Continental Army. At the time, he belonged to a sawmill owner named Daniel Hawley. A scout, Nero joined other ragtag troops who camped at Valley Forge during the brutal winter of 1777–1778 under the command of General George Washington. He earned an honorable discharge in April 1781, after which he became a free man.

Nero's story gives the lie to two troubling impulses in American race relations. For centuries, white racists have cast aspersions on the loyalty and credentials of Black people as bona fide Americans. Meanwhile, some Black leaders have occasionally espoused returning to Africa. Nero Hawley hailed from Trumbull, deep in the heart of New England. He fought for America's independence, risking his life so that Americans could exercise the very freedom of speech that emboldens some racists to say we should be sent back to Africa. Let them return to their ancestral lands. Black folk long ago earned the right to stay put as full-fledged US citizens. It's a hard-won entitlement we'll never relinquish.

Then there is the Latimer branch of my family tree, also on my mother's side. On October 4, 1842, my great-great-grandfather George W. Latimer and his wife, Rebecca, who was pregnant with my great-grandmother Margaret, escaped slavery in Norfolk, Virginia, and headed North. They stowed away on a ship during the first part of the daring journey to Baltimore. They traveled the next leg via train to Philadelphia, I believe, as master and slave since George was fair-skinned and Rebecca was darker-hued. They completed the trip to Boston as husband and wife.

Shortly after arriving, George was spotted by a former employee of his slave owner, James Gray. Gray arranged for Latimer's arrest and incarceration in the Leverett Street jail. He then initiated legal proceedings to compel Latimer's return to Virginia. Free Blacks in Boston held a vigil to prevent George from being spirited out of the city. After a flurry of negotiations, an abolitionist minister purchased him from Gray for $400 and he was finally freed.

Historian Asa Davis maintained that Latimer was "the first fugitive slave whose emancipation guided and influenced the American abolitionists of the 1850s." The incomparable Frederick Douglass and the noted abolitionist William Lloyd Garrison rallied to Latimer's side. The saga even inspired John Greenleaf Whittier to write a poem about George's odyssey, entitled "From Massachusetts to Virginia." The episode transformed him into a celebrity. Gratified but not satisfied, abolitionists successfully lobbied the Massachusetts legislature to enact laws forbidding judges, justices of the peace, and officers of the commonwealth from aiding in the arrest, detention, or delivery of any person claimed as a fugitive slave.

George and Rebecca had four children, the youngest of whom was Lewis. In 1864, Lewis fibbed about his age and enlisted in the Navy. After receiving an honorable discharge when the Civil War ended, he secured a menial job with the patent law firm of Crosby and Gould. Through research, practice, and observation, Lewis taught himself mechanical drawing and won a promotion to draftsman. Alexander Graham Bell, who was affiliated with the firm, retained Lewis to perfect his patent application for the telephone so that it could be filed first in the US, beating out a rival inventor.

Later, as a mechanical draftsman for Hiram Maxim, who founded the U.S. Electrical Lighting Company, Lewis drew on his knowledge of electric power and lighting to perfect the light bulb that Thomas Edison originally invented. Lewis devised and patented the carbonized conductors for incandescent lamps which enabled them to stay lit significantly longer, thus revolutionizing the electric light bulb industry. By 1918, he had garnered such acclaim that he became a charter—and the only Black—member of the esteemed Edison Pioneers.

Lewis Latimer's impressive accomplishments illuminate another chapter in the Black experience which isn't fully understood or appreciated, namely the notable contributions of Black inventors who created some of the indispensable conveniences that we take for granted and which contributed to America's dynamic growth and prosperity. What's more, Latimer was an unabashed "race" man. Alarmed by overt segregation and lynching of our people, he joined in calling for a national convention to strengthen the organized Black voice on behalf of justice and equal rights.

Turning to my father's ancestors, Robert Gunnell was his great-great-grandfather on his mother's side. Gunnell purchased his freedom in the mid-1830s. Soon thereafter he bought a six-acre farm in Langley, Virginia, just across the Potomac River from the Georgetown section of Washington, DC. He married a slave named Harriet Lee and they had eight children. Gunnell registered his entire family as his personal slaves in order to prevent them from being seized and sold in other Southern states. In 1862, Congress freed the slaves within Washington's city limits, where the Gunnells resided. He was paid $2,168.10 in compensation for the liberation of his slaves.

Around 1866, local Black people began conducting religious services at the Gunnell's home. This was the first place where they could worship in Fairfax County, which encompasses Langley. The Gunnells subsequently built the first schoolhouse for local Black children on their land. In 1879, they donated a half-acre parcel for the site of a church which, once completed, became known as Gunnell's Chapel Methodist Church. Thus, my ancestors helped build the infrastructure for Black worship, education, and advancement in their community, a lesson never lost on me as a youngster.

My father's paternal grandfather was Robert Price. Born into slavery, he and his wife Julia belonged to the remarkably resilient generation of ex-slaves who purchased farms, thereby enabling them to provide for themselves and their families. Mind you, the Hill Top community where they lived in Charles County, Maryland, was unabashed Ku Klux Klan territory. Contrary to the frequent image in early movies of Black people as servants and slackers, my resilient Price ancestors, like so many of their neighbors, strove for and achieved self-reliance, another aspiration and attribute passed down to me through the generations.

My Parents--My Rocks

My father, Kline A. Price, Sr., was a native Washingtonian. His own father, who was a farmer, died when he was just three. Although trained as a schoolteacher, his mother could not find a teaching job in DC. So she worked as a handmaiden for wealthy white women, most notably a vaudeville performer named Nora Bayes. Since his mother traveled frequently with Ms. Bayes, my father lived from age two until sixteen with his mother's sister, Mary Jones, and her family on Third and T Streets NW in the Le Droit Park neighborhood, near Howard. Dad's roommate during these years was his first cousin Frank, who was ten years older. Those who knew my father as a youngster say he was highly self-reliant, if something of a loner.

Dad took such enormous pride in my accomplishments that it grieves me still that he did not live to see me ascend to the national stage. Despite his reserved personality, he was given to hooting for joy when I won an academic prize at a school assembly. He would have lost his cool entirely watching me deliver a keynote address before thousands of Urban Leaguers, seeing me appear on *Meet the Press*, or hearing about my travels in the company of President Bill Clinton aboard Air Force One.

My father attended the renowned—and segregated—Dunbar High School. He received a superb education there from its first-rate faculty, many of whom held PhDs but were unable to land teaching jobs at mainstream colleges and universities. Following Dunbar, he enrolled at Howard University. Graduating with a BA in 1928, he opted to become a physician. Howard medical school was a struggle. Not academically, mind you, but financially. With scant help from his family, dad supported himself by working lengthy hours as an elevator operator at the old Methodist Building. He persuaded congressmen who lived in the apartment building to secure books from the Library of Congress for his required reading. He prepared his assignments during lulls between elevator runs.[2]

Dad finished medical school in 1933. By then, his cousin, or Uncle Frank as we called him, had become the first Black physician to earn certification from the American Board of Urology. Dad followed his cousin into urology and joined his practice. By 1943, my father felt prepared to seek American Board certification. He journeyed to Chicago to take the test. One white examiner tried to foil Dad by asking him to provide a diagnosis based on an x-ray so faint that it could barely be read. Fortunately, a test supervisor intervened and instructed the examiner to give Dad a more legible x-ray. My father passed the grueling exam and became only the second African American certified by the American Board of Urology.

Dad reveled in family and close friends, but definitely could do without the socializing associated with big-city life. Although never a public person, he touched and deeply influenced—and indeed saved—the lives of countless men, women, and children. He was totally comfortable in his own skin. All sons should be reared by such a profoundly inspiring, yet utterly grounded role model.

My mother, Charlotte Schuster Price, was born in New Haven, Connecticut and grew up in nearby West Haven. After high school she attended Howard, where she first met my father. However, she left after a year and went back home to work. Mom returned to DC after their marriage in 1935. During the World War II years, she returned to Howard to complete her undergraduate degree.

A traditionalist about the paramount role of wives in the home during children's formative years, my father believed mom should not work if our family could afford for her not to. She acquiesced but compensated by volunteering almost full-time each week with various civic causes close to her heart. In the early 1950s, she became active in the League of Women Voters and participated in their rallies to secure voting rights for Washingtonians. She also joined the Americans for Democratic Action, which pushed aggressively for integration.

Once my brother and I were grown, Dad encouraged my mother to pursue a graduate degree and professional career. At the age of fifty-eight, she transformed herself from activist to archivist by earning a master's degree in library science. This belated career move proved fortuitous because my father died barely two years later. Thus, she was well equipped intellectually and professionally for widowhood at a comparatively young age.

Energetic and indefatigable, Mom lived for forty more years entirely on her own. She moved from Washington to Plymouth, Massachusetts, where, at the age of sixty-one, she worked as an archivist at Pilgrim Hall, the historical society there. In 1975, the board appointed her acting executive director. While I've never confirmed it, chances are she was the first African American to run a mainstream historical society in the US.

Although Mom could have held the directorship on a permanent basis, she decided to move to the home she and my father had built years earlier on Cape Cod in anticipation of retiring there. Up until her late eighties, she provided archival assistance to the Wampanoag Native American tribe of Mashpee and served as archivist at the Falmouth Historical Society and the Woods Hole Historical Museum. Perhaps not surprisingly, my mother, the prototypical Energizer Bunny, lived to be 101.

The Remarkable "Village" That Raised Me

Howard University served as the *de facto* intellectual and geographical hub of Washington's Black community when I was growing up. A mere fifteen-minute walk north of Howard lies my old neighborhood—and my family's first house on New Hampshire Avenue NW, near the intersection with Park Road. My parents' close friends, neighbors, and professional colleagues comprised the "village" that raised me. Most lived within walking distance. All of them were strivers. Indeed, many were the first integrators in their fields, hell-bent on breaching the barriers to integration and opportunity in the American mainstream.

Virtually all of these "villagers" were born between 1890 and 1910, merely 25 to 45 years after the Emancipation Proclamation and scarcely a generation after the tragic end of Reconstruction. They grew up steeped in the travails of their parents and grandparents, who had been born into slavery and/or had escaped the violence and degradation of post-Reconstruction in the Deep South. They all lived and raised their children in rigidly segregated DC. Most of them had graduated from Dunbar. Many were also grads of Howard University and/or its medical school. The physicians among them typically taught full-time or, like my father, part time at Howard medical school while holding positions at its teaching hospital, Freedmen's.

Come to think of it, the village that raised me actually began forming when my father was a child. When he and his cousin Frank were growing up in Le Droit Park, the Smith family lived across from the Jones family on T Street. Two of the three Smith sisters—Hilda and Otwiner—were contemporaries of my father and attended Dunbar around the same time. The much younger sister, Ruth, would become the mother of my future wife. My father operated on the Smith sisters' father and thus my wife's grandfather. Hilda, who became one of mom's dearest friends, was my fifth- and sixth-grade teacher at Bruce Elementary School.

Hilda's husband, Dr. Montague Cobb, was one of the most distinguished and civic-minded members of our village. My principal booster for Amherst College, he even started recruiting me when I was in his wife's class. He was both a physician and the first African American PhD in anthropology. Dr. Cobb devoted his research and advocacy to disproving scientific justifications for racism. For many years he led the fight for the admission of Black physicians to practice in Washington's white hospitals and organized national conferences on hospital discrimination and integration. Active as well on the broader civil rights stage, he served as president of the board of the National Association for the Advancement of Colored People (NAACP) from 1976 to 1982.

My village included two other illustrious Dunbar and Amherst alumni. One was Dr. Charles Drew of Howard medical school. He attained international fame during World War II by discovering blood plasma, pioneering improved methods for blood storage, and developing large-scale blood banks. His innovations enabled medics to save the lives of thousands of Allied soldiers. Dr. Drew was appointed director of the first American Red Cross Blood Bank in 1941. Yet he resigned the following year after the armed forces ruled that while blood from Black soldiers would be accepted, it must be stored separately from that of whites. In 1961, my brother married the late Dr. Drew's eldest daughter, Bebe, and they remain so sixty years later.

The other Dunbar/Amherst villager of note and slightly earlier vintage was Charles Hamilton Houston. Under his hard-charging deanship, Howard law school was the intellectual and strategic epicenter of civil rights litigation action. Houston was the prime architect of the legal strategy to dismantle segregation. School desegregation in DC was propelled by a protest which truly bubbled up from the ground. In 1947, a Black barber named Gardner Bishop launched a boycott of Browne Junior High, an overcrowded Black school attended by his daughters. The boycott lasted for months. At one point, Bishop approached Houston for help. They filed lawsuits aimed at forcing Washington to equalize Black and white schools. Supporters formed the Consolidated Parents, whose ranks included my mother and her close friends Marie Smith and Burma Whitted. The group raised money for the lawsuits.

These luminaries weren't the only villagers who blazed new trails for Black folk. Marie Smith's husband, Dr. Alonzo deGrate Smith, was the first Black physician in the US to receive national board certification in pediatrics. In addition to teaching at Howard medical school, he was a researcher and child-health activist. Todd Duncan, a pioneering opera singer, was George Gershwin's choice to perform the role of Porgy in *Porgy and Bess* in 1935.

Other nearby neighbors of note included Sam Lacy, the baseball Hall of Fame reporter for *The Afro American* newspaper who crusaded relentlessly for the integration of baseball. Directly across New Hampshire Avenue from us lived Arthur Carter, another crusading journalist and future executive editor and publisher of *The Afro*. From my childhood perspective, what was most memorable about Mr. Carter is that he arranged for his son Chip and me to have our picture taken with Jackie Robinson, the transcendent Black hero of that era. I was an impressionable eleven-year-old at the time. The photo appeared in *The Afro* with the very 1950s caption, "Small Fry Meet Dodgers' Big Guy."

A well-known member of the extended village was E. Frederic Morrow. He and his wife Catherine were close friends of my parents and frequent visitors to our home. A former field secretary for the NAACP, Mr. Morrow served in the Eisenhower administration and was the first African American to hold an executive position in the White House. His responsibilities included advising how the president should deal with the virulent reaction by Southern racists to the *Brown v. Board of Education* school desegregation decree. Mr. Morrow chronicled his experiences in his memoir, *Black Man in the White House*.

These pioneering villagers weren't posters on a wall of heroes in my segregated elementary school. They were flesh-and-blood relatives, neighbors, friends, colleagues, and contemporaries of my parents. All were "race" men and women, devoted to using their education, positions, and leverage to help advance the cause of our people. While I wasn't versed in every detail of their accomplishments and breakthroughs, I knew enough from my parents to be inspired by their examples and accomplishments.

Coming of Age by Becoming Aware

Prior to the landmark *Brown* decision in 1954, Washington's public schools were rigidly segregated. I attended Blanche Kelso Bruce Elementary School. It truly was a neighborhood school. My parents knew many of my teachers from church, civic clubs, social events, and, of course, Dunbar and Howard.

Since mom was always eager to break free of segregation, once I graduated from Bruce, my parents sent me way across town for seventh grade at Georgetown Day School. It was a private day school where many integration-minded parents, including my mother's colleagues from her various causes, sent their children. Thus, up to that point, my pre-adolescent life, mainly if not exclusively within the social constraints and geographical confines of segregation, was pleasant and trauma-free.

The *Brown* case, which was brought by the NAACP Legal Defense Fund under the direction of Houston's protégé and successor, Thurgood Marshall, altered the course of American history on May 17, 1954. That year was a game-changer for the nation, not to mention for me. As housing segregation began melting, our family moved to the northeast section of the city. We now lived in the zone for the previously white Taft Junior High School. Therefore, I became one of the first contingents of Black students to integrate the DC schools that fall.

No more villagers and longtime friends of my parents on the faculty. From an entirely Black student body to a member of a vastly outnumbered minority. Some teachers were supportive; others indifferent. A few white classmates were friendly; some were downright hostile. There was little if any socializing after school or visiting each other's homes across color lines. And, certainly, no interracial dating as teenage hormones began awakening. School transitioned abruptly from a blithe childhood experience to a dutiful mission to excel, avoid conflict, and stay out of trouble. The lessons about focus and resilience that I had absorbed from my parents and the villagers started sinking in and sustaining me.

I continued on much the same trajectory and faced similar challenges at Coolidge High School, another previously white public school with sparse Black enrollment. High school taught me my first, unforgettable lesson about the subtleties of institutional as opposed to in-your-face racism. In the summer of 1958, between the eleventh and twelfth grades, I was selected for an internship with a US Defense Department subcontractor known as the Operations Research Office (ORO). Those, like me, who were chosen excelled in math and science. In fact, I was the first Black student ever selected for this prestigious opportunity. Some busybodies at ORO, who were white, took it upon themselves to administer a battery of tests designed to gauge our potential. I was mystified as to why they even bothered, since we interns had already demonstrated that we were strong students with bright futures. We would not have been selected otherwise.

I shall never forget the prognosis when the ORO staffers debriefed me on the test results. "You probably will go to college," they solemnly opined, "but you shouldn't count on getting into graduate or professional school." I walked, silent and fuming, out of the room. Fortunately, I already knew that my preliminary SAT scores, school grades, and class ranking probably were plenty strong enough to qualify me for admission to Ivy League universities and their small-college equivalents. When I reported the episode to my parents, they told me to pay ORO no heed.

Even so, the encounter triggered a kaleidoscope of emotions. It confused, embarrassed, and humiliated me. For the first time in my life, adults had called my scholastic ability, intelligence, and potential into question. Based on my parents' assessment and the encouragement of villagers like Dr. Cobb who knew me well, I had set my sights on applying to top colleges and universities. Was I naively overreaching? Should I now lower my sights for college and beyond?

The assessment left me wondering if I had suffered an early encounter with what came to be known as institutional racism. I refer to those barely discernible, seemingly innocent decisions by "gatekeepers" that are designed to stifle hope, hold people of color back, deny us deserved opportunities to advance, and sow doubt about our potential and our rightful place in the American mainstream. I discovered as an adolescent that racism can be subtle, as if written with invisible ink. The lesson I derived from ORO test taught me volumes about the way the world works. It underscored the need to set my personal radar to detect any signs of racism or hypocrisy.

In retrospect, I realize it helped chart the course of much of my career, with its recurring focus on cultivating youngsters' academic and social development, recognizing their undetected or "misunderestimated" potential, affording them second chances to straighten out their lives, and guiding them onto constructive pathways. The experience also underscored how indispensable caring adults—parents, older brothers, "villagers," and homeroom teachers like Ms. Anderson, my white homeroom teacher at Coolidge—are in the lives of kids.

My scholastic success at Coolidge enabled me to set my sights on some of the top colleges and universities east of the Mississippi River. ORO's middling assessment notwithstanding, I did get to go to college, to Amherst in fact. Harvard and several other topflight institutions also admitted me.

When I entered Amherst in 1959, students focused their energies mostly on campus life—courses, sports, dating, and BS-ing the hours away. This was particularly true up North, far removed from the burgeoning civil rights movement below the Mason Dixon Line. We were the last quiescent generation. For instance, although I was upset that Amherst tolerated on-campus fraternities which would not admit Black students, I did not call out the college administration, much less attempt to organize the miniscule number of Black students and any white sympathizers to take over a campus building or picket the offending fraternities. That wasn't done back then. Instead, I stewed about the affront, yet dutifully joined an integrated frat.

Courageous students in the South began staging sit-ins at lunch counters to break the back of segregation. They followed the Reverend Martin Luther King, Jr. in the marches he led. Impatient with the pace of change, young activists formed two vigorous new organizations—the Student Nonviolent Coordinating Committee (SNCC) and the Students for a Democratic Society. These groups boisterously challenged the status quo. This wasn't just some college students skipping classes to demonstrate. Some were dying or being bludgeoned by Sheriff Bull Connor of Birmingham, Alabama, and his racist ilk.

This surge in student activism gradually awakened my social conscience. My consciousness was further aroused by President John F. Kennedy's memorable inaugural address in 1961. My generation felt he was speaking directly to us when he issued his soul-stirring challenge: "Ask not what your country can do for you; ask what you can do for your country."

I attribute my gradual awakening to an authentic commitment to justice but also, frankly, to my growing guilt that I was not as engaged as my braver contemporaries in righting society's wrongs. Also, my mother's activist genes probably were slowly kicking in. In the spring of my senior year, I joined busloads of students from New England colleges and universities who descended on Washington to picket in front of the White House. JFK, who talked a good game about civil rights but had delivered little, loomed as our target. The demonstration went off without a hitch, although there was little sign it changed his mind.

During the summer following graduation, national civil rights leaders delivered a vastly louder wake-up call to JFK and the nation when they organized the March on Washington for Jobs and Freedom, which was held on August 28, 1963. Crowd estimates ranged from 250,000 to 500,000. I volunteered to serve as a marshal for the march. Our job was to contain any disturbances by encircling the antagonists with our arms extended and ushering them away from the crowd and toward law enforcement officers standing by.

Malcolm X derided the 1963 march as "the Farce on Washington." Stokely Carmichael, the fiery black nationalist from SNCC, dismissed it as "only a sanitized, middle-class version of the real black power movement." By contrast, James Baldwin captured the emotions and cautious optimism of many hopeful attendees, including me, with an eloquence we could never emulate: "That day, for a moment, it almost seemed that we stood on a height, and could see our inheritance; perhaps we could make the kingdom real, perhaps the beloved community would not forever remain the dream one dreamed in agony." The March on Washington ranks as one of the epiphanies of my life. A visceral experience of bearing witness to history, the March on Washington made an indelible impression on me. The contours of my life's calling began taking shape that sweltering summer day.

The Formative Years Professionally

Since attorneys like Charles Hamilton Houston and Thurgood Marshall played pivotal roles in the struggle for civil rights, the idea of attending law school after Amherst strongly appealed to me. My top choice was Yale. In addition to being ranked consistently as the best law school in the country, what made Yale feel just right for me was the ethos of public service that pervaded the institution.

In the fall of 1962, I took the LSAT, basically the law school equivalent of the SAT. I butchered the test. Nevertheless, Yale admitted me. Clearly, the dean of admissions, who was white, had placed a bet on me. Many years later I received an honorary degree from the University as well as the Award of Merit from the Yale Law School Association. The latter is the highest honor bestowed by the alumni association, and past awardees include President Bill Clinton, Secretaries of State Cyrus Vance and Hillary Clinton, and several US Supreme Court justices. ORO obviously flunked its assessment that I probably should not count on getting into professional school.

My wife and I got married over the Christmas break of my first year in law school. My career plans began coming into sharper focus a month later when President Lyndon Johnson, in his annual State of the Union address, declared war on poverty and vowed to eliminate it within our lifetimes. I believed him—probably because I wanted to and surely because I didn't know any better.

Our first daughter was born a year later. To help support our young family, I worked part time as a social worker and mentor for a group of teenage boys who perpetually got in trouble with the law. The program was run by Community Progress Incorporated (CPI), the local anti-poverty agency, whose executive director was a very wise and well-connected white man named Mitchell Sviridoff. Fresh out of law school in 1966, I commenced my zigzag journey to the job of a lifetime. The first stop was the New Haven Legal Assistance Association. I represented clients charged with crimes or coping with unscrupulous slumlords.

During the mid-1960s, riots erupted in cities around the country. August 1967 was New Haven's turn. In the aftermath of the riot, the leaders of various Black groups created a new umbrella organization called the Black Coalition of New Haven. Its mission was to restore faith in the city, exert influence for Blacks, and orchestrate the physical and spiritual rebuilding of communities devastated by the disturbances. In the spring of 1968, I was hired as the first executive director of the Black Coalition. The job thrust me smack into the center of the local political and policy action at the tender age of twenty-six. I relished the work and, to be truthful, enjoyed the public exposure.

Two of the Coalition's founders, Henry Parker and Al Tindall, became indispensable mentors at this energizing yet vulnerable stage of my fledgling career. Fortunately, activism never morphed into idiocy. Years later, I learned from an article in the Hartford Courant that the New Haven police considered me dangerous but had never managed to catch me doing anything illegal. I knew that our phone was wiretapped and that the Coalition had been infiltrated by police informants. More importantly, I could have told them my parents and our "villagers" didn't raise a son who was dangerous or dumb enough to flout the law.

Around this time, I encountered an African American scholar, Dr. James Comer, who would have a profound effect on me throughout the remainder of my career. My wife and I had purchased our first home in a predominantly Black, working-class neighborhood of Newhallville in New Haven. It was right across the street from an innovative new elementary school named after Martin Luther King. We heard they were going to try a new educational approach conceived by a Yale professor named Comer. When my wife and I first met Dr. Comer and his wife, we naturally played the "Who do you know?" game. We learned that he had graduated from Howard medical school and that my wife's mother, an anatomy professor there, had taught him. As had my father.

Dr. Comer's vision was to engage all the key adults involved in the education and upbringing of children—from the principal, teachers, and front office staff to the parents and caregivers—in a collaborative effort to foster the healthy academic, social, and emotional development of students. We enrolled our eldest daughter in MLK school and she thrived there. I became a devotee of the Comer philosophy from that day forward.

While we lived in New Haven, I followed the tradition of my father, brother, and Uncle Frank by pledging the Alpha Phi Alpha fraternity, the oldest Black Greek-letter frat in the nation. I was reasonably active in the beginning, but my involvement tapered off once we moved to New York and the volume of work-related travel escalated dramatically. Even so, I've remained an Alpha man at heart and was delighted that I could help with a monumental Alpha initiative many years later. In 1968, following the assassination of MLK, the fraternity proposed creating a memorial in his honor in DC. Nearly thirty years later, Congress approved the project and authorized the fraternity to fundraise and make it happen.

Harry Johnson, the former national president of Alpha, became president and CEO of the MLK National Memorial Project Foundation, which spearheaded every phase of its development. Toward the end of the fundraising campaign, the project was several million dollars short. Harry and Russell Simmons, the rap music mogul, approached me about helping to round up additional funding. As an Alpha and a devotee of King, I was delighted to do what I could. I served on two Fortune 500 corporate boards at the time and persuaded those companies to donate over $3 million between them. I also pitched an African American foundation executive I knew, who in turn persuaded his foundation to contribute $3 million. I'm pretty certain he then approached a colleague at another foundation, which put up another $3 million. All told, I was directly and indirectly instrumental in generating between $6 million and $9 million dollars for this most cherished of Alpha causes, which, hopefully, helps me atone for being otherwise inactive all these years.

Following the Black Coalition, I joined an urban affairs consulting firm, also in New Haven. The work broadened my professional horizons right away. Mike Sviridoff, the former head of CPI, was now vice-president of the Ford Foundation. He presided over its vast domestic program division. Mike, who had spotted me in New Haven as an up-and-coming attorney and advocate, became like a professional rabbi or godfather to me.

He contracted with me to conduct evaluations of some of the foundation's major grantees. Through these assignments, I met role models whom I had admired from afar. Leaders like Whitney Young, Vernon Jordan, and John Jacob, my illustrious predecessors as president of the National Urban League. Franklin Thomas, head of the Bedford-Stuyvesant Restoration Corporation and later the first Black president of the Ford Foundation. John Lewis, the revered future congressman who ran the Voter Education Project, and Roy Wilkins, head of the NAACP. I visited the Reverend Leon Sullivan of Philadelphia, a towering figure intellectually and physically, who gave 13 stemwinding speeches about community development that made true believers of all who heard him. I observed how these men comported themselves. They were smart, buttoned-up, committed "race" men who comfortably navigated the white as well as Black worlds. They epitomized who I wanted to become professionally.

True to my peripatetic nature, I worked at Cogen Holt for five years, followed by two more as Human Resources Administrator for Frank Logue, the mayor of New Haven. Then, one day in the fall of 1977, I received an unexpected call from Max Frankel, the Pulitzer-Prize winning journalist with the *New York Times* who now headed its editorial page. He was calling to let me know I was under serious consideration for appointment to the editorial board of the *Times*. As flattering as it was to be approached, I could not fathom how I had popped up on the newspaper's radar screen. It turns out that Jack Rosenthal, the deputy editor, and Mike Sviridoff were longtime friends. Mike had put my name in play.

At *The Times,* I wrote editorials on an array of topics—urban policy, criminal justice, the fairness doctrine, and deregulation of the telecommunications industry. Inspired and informed by Dr. Comer's work, education was a major concentration of mine. About five years into writing editorials for *The Times,* I began, yet again, to get antsy. Writing for the "journal of record" truly was a privilege. But I was anxious now to get mind and body back into running, making, or "doing" something, as opposed to writing about it. Having zigged into a reflective role, it was time again to zag into an operational one.

I swung into search mode by alerting several strategically situated friends, starting with Sviridoff, that I was amenable to moving on. Several months into this low-key prospecting, Jay Iselin, the president of WNET/Thirteen, the public television station in New York City, called to invite me to lunch. The position Jay wanted to discuss was senior vice-president in charge of the Metropolitan Division. This entailed oversight of the local program schedule, acquisitions for local broadcasts and programming, on-air pledging, and direct-mail solicitation. I knew *nada* about any of this, which made the idea of accepting the position all the more tantalizing. I accepted the offer and began work in November of 1982.

The challenge and enjoyment increased exponentially in 1984, when I was asked to take charge of the National Division, which produced and distributed such award-winning PBS series as *Great Performances* and *Nature.* This division also co-produced the *MacNeil/Lehrer NewsHour.* The unit was fresh from creating two renowned documentary series—*The Brain* and *Civilization and the Jews.* On my watch, our award-winning producers conceived, produced and/or co-produced such new series as *American Masters, The Mind, Childhood, Dancing,* and *Art of the Western World,* among others.

Less noticed and appreciated at the time was that I was part of a triumvirate of senior African American executives, all appointed by Jay, who made public television history. George Miles, as executive vice-president and chief operating officer, was the highest-ranking Black executive in the history of PBS. He went on to become the first Black president of a major PBS station, namely WQED in Pittsburgh. Melvin Ming served as senior vice-president and chief financial officer, another high-water mark for us in public television. Mel subsequently made even more history by serving as the first Black president and CEO of Sesame Workshop, producer of *Sesame Street,* the pioneering and hugely popular children's television series. And as senior vice-president and director of the national division, I ran—depending on the volume of production in a given year—the largest or one of the two largest production enterprises in all of public television.

George, Mel, and I were not reticent about using our leverage to advance Black programming on public television. In those days, local stations got to vote on which programs they wanted PBS to fund. The balloting was by weighted vote based on the size of each station's market. Since WNET served the most populous market in the country, our vote carried the most weight and was highly influential.

When Henry Hampton, the gifted Black executive producer, originally proposed *Eyes on the Prize*, his new series on the history of the civil rights movement, the initial reaction among many local station leaders was lukewarm. Some wondered why it couldn't be one documentary film instead of a six-part series. George, Mel, and I were annoyed by the equivocal attitude toward the series and the clear implication that the history of the epic civil rights movement wasn't worthy of six hours of airtime. Backstopped by the largest and most coveted market in public television, we helped rally support among local station managers by casting our station's vote enthusiastically and publicly for the series. *Hampton* and *Eyes on the Prize*, which ultimately consisted of two seasons spanning fourteen episodes, went on to garner the most prestigious awards in the broadcast industry.

During these years I was invited to join the Westchester Clubmen, a social organization comprised of African American professionals who resided in suburban Westchester County, north of New York City. At one point, the membership included such celebrities as Sidney Poitier, Cab Calloway, and Gordon Parks. The Clubmen traditionally blended socializing with supporting programs for young people. When it came my turn to be president, we were casting about for a way to help teenage boys who were struggling in school and, given their current trajectory, unlikely to do well enough to qualify for college or land a good job. Citing Dr. Comer's philosophy and my own mentoring experience while in law school, I helped persuade the group to devote our collective financial contributions to hiring youth workers and tutors who could "be there" with such boys five days a week after school.

Our program, aptly known these days as "Higher Aims," was launched in 1992 and is still going strong nearly three decades later. In an effort to broaden the young fellows' horizons, members of the Clubmen occasionally took the fellows to mind-expanding places like the Metropolitan Museum of Art. I brought them to WNET/Thirteen so they could tour the studios and control rooms. The youngsters were surprised and delighted to meet George Miles and Mel Ming, and to learn that the three of us ran much of the station. George, whose commanding presence and booming voice always reminded me of Paul Robeson, told the rapt youngsters that whenever somebody said there was something he could not do or accomplish, that was exactly what he was going to do in order to prove the doubters wrong.

Just as cable television was coming of age, Jay Iselin stepped down as president of WNET ,in 1987, after fifteen remarkably productive years. I decided to make a run for the presidency, figuring I had a good shot. Between the local broadcast side and the national production operation, I had overseen about two-thirds of the organization. At a minimum, I assumed the selection committee would take a serious look at me.

Was I ever wrong! The committee granted me a perfunctory twenty-minute interview. As I left the room, I shook my head in disbelief. My ego was crushed, smashed to smithereens on the proverbial glass ceiling. I took scant consolation in the fact that the committee treated the three other inside candidates just as cavalierly. Evidently, the search committee was intent on enlisting a veteran commercial TV executive as the new leader.

I badly wanted the presidency for many reasons. I had grown to love public television, with its lofty mission and international scope. The appointment would have made history because I stood to become the first African American to head a public TV station in the United States, and the largest one at that. With prominent blacks such as Clifton Wharton, Franklin Thomas, and Vernon Jordan shattering assorted glass ceilings, the egotist in me wanted to join their ranks in yet another previously unpenetrated realm of American life.

The rejection put me in a funk. Our eldest daughter snapped me out of the doldrums several months later. I was standing in the kitchen with my by-then accustomed hangdog look. She suddenly said, "Don't worry about not getting that job. You're being saved for something more important." I finally put the rejection behind me and regained peace of mind.

As good fortune would have it, a friend named Peter Goldmark was appointed president of the Rockefeller Foundation around this time. I sent him a congratulatory letter that also included some thoughts about the state of urban America. Peter got the unsubtle hint that I was available. He asked me to become vice-president of the foundation. I put my detour into public television behind me and returned to my life's work of empowering poor and minority people to enter the American mainstream.

The Rockefeller Foundation felt just right. A perfect example of how we leveraged our resources was the National Commission on Teaching and America's Future. My colleagues and I conceived of the commission during a strategic discussion around my desk. To direct the commission, I recruited Linda Darling-Hammond, a distinguished professor at Columbia Teachers College who was and remains one of America's foremost experts on K-12 education.

I delighted in the fact that Linda, who is African American, had been an undergraduate student of mine at Yale. Leading the commission instantly catapulted her into position as the country's pre-eminent and highest-profile expert on this critical subject. I also took the initiative to expand the reach of Dr. Comer's School Development Program to many more school systems. The foundation's backing paid gratifying dividends. Our grants expanded the reach of his work and boosted his national profile.

The Job of a Lifetime

I enjoyed foundation life immensely and felt no particular itch to move on. Then in 1993, John Jacob, the longtime president and CEO of the National Urban League, announced that he was stepping down. I also learned that Charles Hamilton, a League board member and prominent attorney, chaired the search committee. Working with him was John Gibbs of the global executive search firm of Spencer Stuart. I knew both of them and in fact all three of us once belonged to the men's organization called the Westchester Clubmen. Not that these relationships did me any good, since the search took about a year to play out as the committee considered an array of high-profile candidates.

The job I had dreamt of my entire professional life finally materialized, suddenly, if not entirely out of the blue. Charles Hamilton invited me to join John Gibbs and him for breakfast. They said I was on a very short list of candidates. Trying my best not to hyperventilate, I indicated that I was very enthusiastic about the prospect of taking the helm.

Now that the League had initiated the courtship, I vowed to do my level best to consummate it. In response to their request, I sent several memos detailing my major positions, brief histories of several key initiatives I had been instrumental in conceiving, and my analysis of the major challenges facing both Black people and the Urban League. At the risk of overkill, I wanted to be crystal-clear how keen I was about the presidency and how well prepared I was to take the helm.

The board of trustees convened on May 23, 1994 and seemed to meet forever. Late in the day, the call I had been waiting for my entire professional life finally came. I had been selected as the seventh president in the history of the National Urban League. I excitedly called my wife, our daughters, and my brother. My mind flashed back to that conversation with our daughter seven years earlier, when I was in a funk after losing out on the presidency of WNET/Thirteen. This obviously was the "something more important" that she predicted I was being saved for.

The keynote session at the annual conference in late July marked my official unveiling, if you will, in front of the movement's leaders from across the country. Throughout my career prior to the League, I wrote every speech I had ever delivered. The same would be true this time. No stemwinding orator, I use speeches to teach instead of preach. My forté was laying out facts, insights, and analysis, and then advocating concrete actions listeners could take to make conditions better. I often spotted people in the audience scribbling notes on program books and scraps of paper. This was gratification aplenty for me.

To judge by the deluge of press coverage, my inaugural keynote address made a big splash. We released an advance copy to the *New York Times* in the hope that if it paid attention, other media would as well. On the morning of my speech, the *Sunday Times* ran a front-page article headlined, "A Rights Leader Minimizes Racism as a Poverty Factor." C-SPAN broadcast it live and repeated it for weeks on end. Early the following morning, I was interviewed by Bryant Gumbel on NBC's *Today* show. The *Wall Street Journal* weighed in with a major article titled, "New Chief of Urban League Outlines Ambitious but Practical Plan for Cities."

Nationally syndicated columnists commented extensively on the speech as well. Within days, Bob Herbert of the *New York Times* wrote a column titled, "Blacks' Problems, Seen Plain: Hugh Price of the National Urban League tells the truth, courageous and unadorned." William Raspberry of the Washington Post devoted two consecutive columns to my speech during the week after I delivered it. E. J. Dionne Jr., also with the Post, focused on my remarks about Black-Jewish relations in a column titled, "Hugh Price's Radical Alternative to Farrakhan." Some coverage came in an unexpected form. Several newspapers ran sizable excerpts from the speech without our even submitting it for their consideration. For instance, the *Boston Globe* titled its excerpt, "Revising the social compact: The new head of the Urban League urges a new way of looking at our society." The foregoing is just a small sampling of the astonishing amount of media coverage, and that's not even counting the TV and radio appearances that ensued.

Once the deluge subsided, I climbed back down from the ego mountaintop and got to work on implementing the agenda I had optimistically articulated. The centerpiece of my administration was the League's Campaign for African American Achievement, which aimed to spread the "gospel of achievement" among our children and their families and in our communities. We designated September as Achievement Month. On the third Saturday of the month, Urban League affiliates across the country staged block parties, rallies, and street festivals to herald the annual resumption of school and celebrate youngsters for

"Doing the Right Thing"—namely, striving to excel in school. Each year, these events drew upwards of sixty thousand young people and parents.

The capper when it came to recognizing academic achievement was our National Achievers Society (NAS). We took a Florida model known as the McKnight Achievers Society to the national level with the blessing of its founder, Dr. Israel Tribble, head of the Florida Education Fund. Urban League affiliates across the country created NAS chapters and inducted Black students who had earned B averages or better in school. The ceremonies typically were attended by hundreds of parents, grandparents, siblings, and well-wishers.

The Academy for Educational Development (AED) evaluated our Achievement Campaign. According to AED, the young people reached by the Achievement Campaign cited a number of benefits, notably a clearer sense of what it meant to achieve. Young people reported that exposure to the Campaign is implanting and reinforcing the message that, regardless of the career path they choose to pursue, academic achievement will make it easier. One focus group respondent put it succinctly: "A rapper that knows how to read and write stands a better chance of holding on to his loot than one who can't."

The AED evaluators wrote glowingly of the League's community-based honor society. The NAS helped to establish a common bond among young people in the same community but not necessarily of the same background. Within the same focus groups, participants often hailed from disparate backgrounds. They spoke of the positive peer influence that they exerted on each other as one of the benefits of the Campaign. They also mentioned how, collectively, they are changing the often negative perception of African American youth in their communities.

The issue aside from education that captured the most of my attention was the criminal "injustice" system. At the height of the tension over baseless police brutality and killings, racial profiling, and widespread abuse of civil liberties, I basically orchestrated the effort by national civil rights organizations to pressure President Clinton, who was MIA, to take on this issue. We staged multiple press conferences at the National Press Club spotlighting parents whose children had been unjustly killed by police. I wrote an open letter to Mr. Clinton and the League purchased space to publish it in the *New York Times*. We convened a massive press conference featuring high profile members of Congress and leaders of Black, Latino, Asian American, Jewish, and Italian American organizations.

The escalating pressure finally got the president's attention. He deployed the Justice Department to ratchet up pressure on renegade police departments. The tension between minorities and police gradually subsided in much of the country. Sadly, unwarranted police killings of African Americans continue. And so, too, must the protests, litigation, and pressure for change.

We tackled other contentious issues. Endless skirmishes over affirmative action kept me busy. My overture to the Jewish community in my inaugural keynote address prompted a response in kind. When Black churches in the South were torched by arsonists, we teamed up with the Anti-Defamation League to help rebuild them with funds coming primarily from the Jewish community[3]. A conservative named Charles Murray published a notorious book, titled *The Bell Curve*, which, among other outrages, resurrected the specter of eugenics by casting doubt on the intelligence of Black people. Unwilling to let the book go unchallenged, we staged a policy forum, carried by CSPAN, featuring noted science historian Stephen Jay Gould, eminent psychologist Edmund W. Gordon, and other scholars, who attacked Murray's research and conclusions. We certainly did not prevail in all of these battles. For a wonk like me, leading the National Urban League in these policy wars was indeed a dream come true.

Once an Urban Leaguer, Always an Urban Leaguer

Taking the helm of the National Urban League drew me into a multilayered kinship network unlike any other I had known. Throughout its 111-year history, there have only been eight CEOs of the organization. Remarkably enough, for just shy of twenty years—namely, from 2003 when Marc Morial succeeded me until early 2021 when Vernon Jordan passed away—half of the CEOs in the entire history of the League were upright.

During that nearly twenty-year stretch, Marc typically convened us annually, often at the League's headquarters. The purpose was straightforward. Keep the bonds among us strong. Update us on contemporary priorities, challenges, policies, and programs of the League. Share "war stories" from "back in the day." And, probably most meaningful for all of us, drop in unannounced on training sessions for visiting Urban League staffers, and meet and mingle with them as well as headquarters staff.

Some African American board members were so devoted, indispensable, wise, and generous with their time that they easily qualify as members of this unofficial kinship network. I speak of two senior vice-chairs—Bernard Watson, president of the William Penn Foundation, and Charles Collins, CEO of the YMCA of San Francisco, whose father founded the Bay Area Urban League. Charles Hamilton, the distinguished attorney who first joined the board as a college student, and who chaired several CEO search committees, certainly belongs.

Running the National Urban League drew me closely into another informal contingent of the kinship network. I have in mind the seasoned and savvy CEOs—mostly, but not exclusively men—of local Urban League affiliates. Such long-distance runners as John Mack of Los Angeles, Henry Thomas of Springfield, MA, T. Willard Fair of Miami, James Compton of Chicago, Maudine Cooper of DC, James Buford of St. Louis, and J.T. McLawhorn of Columbia, SC. Mildred Love, the revered director of affiliate relations for the National Urban League, qualifies as an unofficial member of this network, since she was the den mother of us all.

These wise Urban Leaguers "schooled" me about the ethos of the movement. They were a vital support network for me and, as longtime colleagues, key supporters of one another and other affiliate leaders. They routinely journeyed, at their own expense and even after they had retired, to reunite with other Urban Leaguers at the annual Equal Opportunity Day gala in New York City.

Retirement

After almost nine years, I announced in November of 2002 that I planned to step down as CEO the following April. In my statement, I said there is never a *good* time to leave the job of a lifetime. But there inevitably comes a *right* time. I always considered leading an organization like the National Urban League akin to a relay race. You run your laps as hard and as fast as you humanly can. Then you pass the baton to the next runner before tiring, stumbling, and falling on your face. This ensures that organizations continue to be headed by younger generations of leaders with contemporary skill sets, abundant energy, and cutting-edge strategies geared to fighting the next wars, not just the last ones. I believe this is the recipe for organizational resilience and relevance.

My mission as change agent for the National Urban League was largely accomplished. In my view, it had successfully evolved from a 20th-century organization to a 21st-century one. My journey to the job of a lifetime was complete.

Notwithstanding racism and the resurgence of white supremacy, the relentless, unwavering trek by Black people to the American mainstream continues, undeterred. In his little-known Emancipation Speech in 1962, Reverend Martin Luther King, Jr. quoted a slave preacher who said of our collective journey:

Lord, we ain't what we oughta be. We ain't what we want to be. We ain't what we gonna be. But, thank God, we ain't what we was.

Amen.

ENDNOTES

1   For a more extensive or luxuriated account of my family history and my life's journey, see: Hugh Price, *Hugh Price: This African-American Life* (Winston Salem, : John F. Blair, Publisher, 2017).
2   Black experience within the history of Washington, DC is fascinating and, in many ways, a source of real pride. See Chris Myers Asch and George Derek Musgrove, *Chocolate City: A History of Race and Democracy in the Nation's Capital* (Chapel Hill, NC: University of North Carolina Press, 2017).
3   For more on Black and Jewish cooperation, see Gabrielle Simon Edgcomb, *From Swastika to Jim Crow: Refugee Scholars at Black Colleges* (Malabar, FL: Krieger Publishing Company, 1993).

BIBLIOGRAPHY

Asch, Chris Myers and Musgrove, George Derek. *Chocolate City: A History of Race and Democracy in the Nation's Capital.* Chapel Hill, NC: The University of North Carolina Press, 2017.

Edgcomb, Gabrelle Simon. *From Swastika to Jim Crow: Refugee Scholars at Black Colleges.* Malabar, FL: Krieger Publishing Company, 1993.

Price, Hugh B. *This African-American Life: A Memoir.* Winston-Salem, NC: John F. Blair Publisher, 2017.

CHAPTER THREE
Deconstructing Faith: A Letter to My Grandson

Thomas M. Jackson

I. Faith[1]

Would it be unfathomable to you if I told you that I lived a shielded childhood? I am the third child of a single, Black American mother, who bore five children before she was 25 years old—one of whom was quasi-adopted. I say "quasi-adopted" because my mother allowed one of my younger brothers to be raised by a local Black American husband and wife who could not bear children of their own, but with the precondition that my brother would know and be permitted to grow up with his sister and brothers. Indeed, four of the five of us were actually half-siblings. However, because we "grew up under the same roof," it was irrelevant to us that all but my sister and I share our mother but not a father. This was not uncommon, but it is not what shielded my childhood experience.

Economically, we were poor, though not "working poor." Our level of poverty was unapologetically penurious. We lived in public housing or moved, often involuntarily, from one rented, privately-owned apartment to another as frequently as the seasons. Sometimes, when landlords would refuse to rent to us or the potential arrangements were notoriously untenable for my mother, we lived for short stints with a close relative (typically, an aunt or a cousin) or one of my mother's girlfriends, the latter of whom quickly became our "Aunt So-and-So." When my mother did not work, we anxiously awaited "mother's day"—the first day of each month when her welfare check would arrive. We often went hungry, going days without eating (or just living off of "sugar sandwiches"—two pieces of Wonder® white bread with white sugar on them). There is no pain like hunger: It gnaws at you from the inside out, starves your ability to focus on anything else, and drains every sense of hope from your spirit.

I was born in 1960, which meant that by 1965 I was 5 years old and just old enough to be an early beneficiary of President Johnson's "Great Society" welfare reforms. Federal programs, such as the Food Stamp Program, were aimed at bypassing local, racially-driven decisions which excluded Black women, like my mother, from receiving the welfare benefits to which she was entitled based on her lack of income. I recall the caseworker, typically a middle-aged White woman, stopping by our apartment often unannounced. She would knock on the door, my mother would ask "Who is it?" and as soon as we heard the caseworker's voice, the winds in our home would shift, like the ominous "dunt dunt da" in a dramatic television series when the plot surprisingly thickens or when things were about to go decidedly wrong for the main characters.[2] The adoption of "play relatives" was common among many Black families during my childhood. In this instance "Aunt" or "Auntie" denotes an affectionate, fictive kinship as distinguished from the diminutive and disparaging uses of the word "auntie" and "uncle" by white slave owners and which, until recently, were replicated by such household brands as Uncle Ben's Rice and Aunt Jemima's pancakes and syrup. Ethnographic research documents that fictive kin are important members of the informal networks of African American families….Fictive kin are defined as "individuals who are unrelated by either blood or marriage, but regard one another in kinship terms….Fictive kin are accorded many of the same rights and statuses as family members and are expected to participate in the duties of the extended family."[3] My mother had no choice but to give access to the caseworker, who would walk through our home with the precision of a termite inspector, checking to see whether "the house is properly kept" and whether my mother had a man living in the house. I would later learn that such "white glove" tests were unconstitutional. However, the more devastating impact of such inspections was that they kept Black women, like my mother, and Black boys, like my brothers and me, from having the benefit of a Black man, who loved and respected my mother, consistently and predictably in our lives.[4] It also reinforced and perpetuated the very cycle of brokenness, dysfunction, and poverty that poor families, like ours, wanted to escape.

    I recall overhearing conversations about racism, but they seemed abstract. Looking through a child's lens, my poor white friends, who also resided in public housing, lived no better than we; and, in some instances, they lived under circumstances that appeared depressingly worse—unkempt apartments or rented shacks, mothers who drank and chain-smoked unfiltered Camel cigarettes all day, an absent or abusive father, and, like me, going to elementary school mostly because it might be the only meal either of us received that day. My daily, closest, recurring memory of poor "White people" left me later wondering, "Did they really think that their situation was better than ours?" I later learned that the privilege of being born White was not in where and how they lived, but the relative ease with which they could get out. During the thirteen-year period between 1959 (the year my sister was born) and 1966 (one year after my youngest half-brother was born), the poverty level for both Blacks and Whites declined, again, largely due to President Johnson's War on Poverty. "The poverty rate… declined for both whites and nonwhites, but the gap between the two racial groups remain[ed] exceedingly wide."[5] However, the benefits from these programs were rarely sufficient to both pay rent and ensure that poor Black and Brown kids (and even poor White kids, for that matter) had adequate food and clothing. This was contrary to Governor Ronald Reagan's politically motivated, racially-tinged mythological trope about the "Welfare Queen" who used her food stamps to buy a prime steak and her public assistance payments to buy a Cadillac.[6] More often, poor parents like my mother had to choose between food, clothing, and shelter—food was never steak, clothing was always the last choice, and shelter, as I said, was transitional.

I remember the Civil Rights marches of the mid-1960's, but, to be transparent, I remember that time through the eyes of a child, growing from about 5 years old until 9 years old. I remember my mother's marching in our small, southwestern Ohio town and the speeches by her 20-something peers—again, my play "aunties" and "uncles"—but the speeches, although passionate, were not real to me. No more real than the Baptist sermons through which I squirmed every Sunday morning. My mother would explain that she and her friends were marching "today, so that you don't have-to tomorrow!" However, neither she nor any of her 20-something peers would ever share with any of us kids their true "why." Why was it so important for them to march? What experiences in their lives served as the impetus to their "I am Spartacus" moments? They, like so many in their generation, wanted to protect us from the emotional impact of knowing their personal confrontations with racism or even the individual personifications of institutionalized racism that laid the foundation for our then-current penurious circumstances. They shielded us from the pain of their experiences while marching for our future.

I write you, my son, because, if I have succeeded in one of my seminal objectives, I suspect that your life is both sheltered and shielded, and I am now a mythological figure in our family's proud but fragmented genealogy. Family lore, in an effort to cement pride and build hope, often omits reality. For that reason, I am concerned about the impact of my success and the ensuing naivety of your soul.

As Oscar Wilde observes: The things people say of a man do not alter a man. He is what he is... A man cannot always be estimated by what he does. He may keep the law, and yet be worthless.[7] He may break the law, and yet be fine. He may be bad, without ever doing anything bad. He may commit a sin against society, and yet realize through that sin his true perfection.

It is the soul of a man that gives him the courage to stand even when he is standing alone. Your soul, my son, will be shaped by your understanding of our history (the unshielded experiences of those who have come before you), your clear-eyed view of your context (what is happening around you and whether you have the courage to stand and do something about it), and your faith. This letter is intended to remove the shield and gird you for the reality of being a Black man in a country that demands your patriotism while blithely institutionalizing your extinction.

II. The evidence of things not seen...

Before proceeding further, I need you to understand three basic principles on the nature of all human beings. First, human beings are not rational, we rationalize. Our ability to rationalize is replete among our most basic survival instincts. We can rationalize our way to inflicting the most inhumane atrocities or to summoning our highest ideals. Whether it is slavery in the United States, genocide in Armenia or Germany, or human trafficking in Haiti or Thailand, each is supported by its own series of rationalizations, whether rooted in history, science, pseudo-science, or the thirst for political power. Indeed, in many instances, our rationalized atrocities are rooted in our warped sense of righteousness. Christians often twist themselves and their scriptures into pretzels to support their rationalized deviations. The seminal story that becomes, as one author describes it, "the foundational test for those who wanted to justify slavery [or racism in the US][8] on Biblical grounds," is the story that depicts one of Noah's three sons, Ham, as mocking his drunken father's nakedness while his brothers, Shem and Japheth, respectfully cover their father:

> And Noah awoke from his wine, and knew what [Ham, the father of Canaan] his younger son had done unto him. And he said, "Cursed be Canaan; a servant of servants shall he be unto his brethren.' And he said, 'Blessed be the Lord God of Shem; and Canaan shall be his servant. God shall enlarge Japheth, and he shall dwell in the tents of Shem; and Canaan shall be his servant." (Genesis 9:24-27)

Christian slave owners rationalized, without any real historical evidence or support, that Ham was Black and his brothers were White, which defies logic when you consider that all three shared the same father (Noah) and mother (Emzara), and when you consider further that Noah and his wife were more than likely related. Yet, human rationalizations often suspend the trilogy of fact, history, and logic to reach their inhumane end. This is, in some respects, because of the second basic principle of human nature—fear...or, more precisely, fear of the stranger: xenophobia.

We human beings seem to be inherently afraid of "the other." Our primordial fears are the root cause of many of our "isms"—whether racism, sexism, or gender-orientation or religious bias. We have not evolved beyond our innate fear of outsiders, which, from the broadest ("macro") perspective is made manifest in our fear of other countries and from the most narrow ("micro") perspective is evidenced in our fears of other individuals and their beliefs. As observed in the short essay, "Why Xenophobia Works":

> All evolution's children got xenophobia. We've all got the fear of outsiders in our genes. In the natural environment it was adaptive. It contributed to group cohesion and, thus, to "Most human attitudes and behaviour have both a genetic and an environmental component. This is also true for our fear of others who are different to us—xenophobia—and intolerance of their viewpoints—bigotry. Hardwired into the brain's amygdala region is a fear reflex that is primed by encounters with the unfamiliar."[9],[10] But in a world of huge, plural societies and devastating weapons, xenophobia has obviously become a danger to the human species.

The intersectionality of our ability to rationalize, rather than be rational, with our innate xenophobia is staggeringly obvious. It is how a megalomaniac such as Adolph Hitler can convince millions of Germans that their hyperinflation and economic collapse were caused by an ethnic infiltration of a single "race"—the Jews. Similarly, it callously justifies the decision of early American colonists (British soldiers, to be exact) to lace the winter blankets of Indigenous American men, women, and children with the smallpox virus despite the known, indiscriminate brutality of the disease. By this inane intersectionality, structural racism, ethnic cleansing, and war are separate, indelible coordinates in the evolutionary plane of human existence.

While institutional racism in the US may feel unique in its origin, impact, and longevity, it must be viewed as part of the straight line in the evolution and adaptation of humankind. It is "in our DNA." It is part of who we are, driven and ruled by our fears; and it is virally communicated across families, continents, and generations. Its irrationality deliberately overlooked or ignored, the seductive logic of Biblically-supported racism appears as axiomatic as the "transitive property of equality":

A. We are created in the image of God. God is on our side. Transitive property of equality is a fundamental algebraic principle that tells us that if we have two things that are equal to each other and the second thing is equal

to a third thing, then the first thing is also equal to the third thing. The formula for this property is if A = B and B = C, then A = C. The genocide of Indigenous Americans by British soldiers and White Americans is a human rights tragedy that cannot be understated in our country's history. The tactic of giving smallpox-infected blankets to Indigenous Americans, "however callous and brutal, is only a small part of a larger story of brutality in the 1600s and 1700s. During this period British forces tried to drive out [Indigenous] Americans by cutting down their corn and burning their homes, turning them into refugees… that rendered them far more vulnerable to the ravages of disease than a pile of infected blankets."[11]
B. They do not look like us. God is not on their side.
C. We are, therefore, performing the will of God by abusing them, demonizing them, discriminating against them, enslaving them, or ultimately, extinguishing them.

This is the mantric syllogism of the tribes of humanity, and one that reverberates throughout our history. To be clear, I am not saying that you should hopelessly accede to this twisted syllogism or any of its historically tenacious corollaries. I am saying that, because it is innate to humanity's (and, therefore, America's) "DNA," you must do more than appreciate it—you must anticipate it. It is the reality of the proud pillars on which many of this country's greatest achievements were built, and the raw, recurring, and certain context in which you will live.

III. The substance of things hoped for…

We were the "children of the dream"—the epitome of Dr. King's proverbial "four little children," who would "one day live in a nation where they will not be judged by the color of their skin but by the content of their character." Our mandate was unequivocal. We were Black children, who, regardless of our economic or familial circumstances, would grow up and prove that we deserved "a seat at the table," and not just any table. Not, for example, a seat at the table in any of our Black neighborhoods; the special significance of those tables was presumed, but taking seats there—in our own communities— did not prove our worth. Neither did taking a seat at the table of our Asian, Indian, Indigenous American, or LatinX brothers and sisters. Those tables, at the time, were not viewed as relevant to the uniqueness of our struggle. We were collectively and explicitly charged with getting a seat at the *White man's* table. Only when seated at *that* table could the dream be realized and our illusive freedom come about.[12]

Being "children of the dream" required sacrifices that we never admitted we were making. Integration, for example, ripped the Black middle class out of our otherwise stable, economically diverse, predominantly Black neighborhoods. While we applauded and desired to emulate the success of those who "got out," our neighborhoods became even poorer, our schools even more segregated, and our families even more vulnerable. We willingly sacrificed this for the dream.

Not surprisingly, where there was one of us in the classroom, there were all of us. We often were "the first real Black person" our White classmates and, later, our White college-mates had ever seen—outside of television. We uniformly accepted the fact that we would have to work harder and be "ten times better"—that was, if you pardon the pun, the table stake of our putative success. It was drilled into us by everyone who cared about us, like the heart-throbbing mantra of an African drum. We even embraced the fact that we were forced to play by a different set of rules and, thus, would have to force our way to the table by attending the right schools, excelling in our academics, dressing for success, and overachieving in our professions. The working conclusion to our accepted premise: they would *have to* give us a seat at their table if we followed their rules and proved ourselves worthy.

However, while focused on Dr. King's clarion call to accompany him on his dream, we missed James Monroe Whitfield's ominous, albeit poetic, warning of a pernicious reality. Ignoring the many requests by my White primary, secondary, and post-secondary classmates to feel my hair, I feel compelled to share my conversations from the fall of 1978 with my two White college roommates, one from Illinois and the other from Indiana. After looking through my clothes in my school-assigned closet and chest-of-drawers, they exclaimed, "Where are your platform shoes?" They were under the admittedly naïve impression that all Black people dressed like the character "Huggy Bear" in the then-popular television series, "Starsky and Hutch," which featured a Black, pimp-like snitch, known as much for his exaggerated colorful attire as his broken English, the latter of which was intended to approximate the dialect of the 1970's California ghetto. Their expectation was that I would be representative of my entire "race." My point is that, like our shoes and clothes, everyone expected us to wear our entire "race" wherever we went. Rumbling throughout US history, Black hope—unwittingly welded to White fear of Black equity—is always dashed. Speaking of the Black soldiers who returned home from fighting in America's Civil War, Whitfield wrote:

> The thought ne'er entered in their brains
> That they endured those toils and pains,
> To forge fresh fetters, heavier chains

> For their own children, in whose veins
> Should flow that patriotic blood,
> So freely shed on field and flood.
> Oh no; they fought, as they believed,
> For the inherent rights of man;
> But mark, how they have been deceived
> By slavery's accursed plan.
> They never thought,
> when thus they shed
> Their heart's best blood,
> in freedom's cause
> That their own sons would live in dread,
> Under unjust, oppressive laws:
> That those who quietly enjoyed
> The rights for which they fought and fell,
> Could be the framers of a code,
> That would disgrace the fiends of hell!
> Could they have looked,
> with prophet's ken,
> Down to the present evil time,
> Seen free-born men, uncharged with crime,
> Consigned unto a slaver's pen—
> Or thrust into a prison cell,
> With thieves and murderers to dwell—

Whitfield's poem captures the utter shock and disbelief of a generation that never conceived that the sacrifice of nearly 200,000 Black Union soldiers to win America's Civil War would give way to 80 years of Black Codes, false imprisonment, convict leasing, lynching, and other forms of racial violence, as well as an intricate web of Jim Crow laws. Whitfield's warning would find its reprise in the astonishment of 2.5 million Black Americans who served in World War II only to return to an America replete with segregationist laws throughout the North and the South, and unable to capitalize on federal laws, such as the G.I. Bill, designed to rebuild America's middle class.[13]

My generation, too, would live Whitfield's poetic warning over and over, with the predictive repetition of a scratched album, as our gains from the so-called "Civil Rights Movement" of the 1960's gave way to the backlash against affirmative action in the 1970's; as the War on Poverty gave way to countless other and often misguided efforts to "curb abuses" in the welfare system in the 1970's through the 1980's; and as jobs programs, such as the

Comprehensive Employment Training Act (CETA), which successfully kept young adults and even teenagers like my friends and me off the streets in the summers, were replaced with… well, nothing. President Reagan ended CETA with exaggerated allegations of abuse and corruption, but failed to replace it, giving way to a surge in drug-related crimes in neighborhoods like mine around the country. The teenagers after me never had a chance. Instead of receiving good-paying summer jobs and a reason to stay off the streets, they became cannon fodder for urban gangs and drug kingpins. (How is it that the rich are permitted to abuse federal programs with impunity for billions of dollars, but the poor are not afforded such a luxury? The slightest hint of abuse by the poor—Black or White—results in termination of the program, notwithstanding its greater good.)

More to the point, we, the "children of the dream," perhaps more than any other generation, graduated high school and flooded colleges and professional workplaces across America at levels historically unseen in this country, yet we still faced the inescapable trope of the Black man as a lazy, irresponsible criminal. We were convinced that our hard work and academic and professional successes, like the life-threatening sacrifice of Black American men acclaimed in Whiteman's America, would, as my great-grandmother often said, "amount to something." Our simple premise, whether we said it out loud to each other or not, was that assimilation was the path to cementing civil rights—that they would see us differently if we lived like them, sounded like them, and even spoke like them.

I am now convinced, my son, that civil rights for Black Americans, and particularly Black American men, has never been a "movement." It is an odyssey, an eternal journey. For us, the long arc of the moral universe bends, but ever so slowly and not without retraction, before ever finding justice as its mark. And even when it lands, it seldom falls forward. One need only trace the history of the many so-called "civil rights movements" throughout US history to understand why I feel compelled to illuminate for you this slow-walking, selectively blind turtle that is American justice, and why you must temper Dr. King's Dream with Whitfield's poetic warning.[14]

In the 102 years between 1866 and 1968, there were no fewer than ten separate federal Civil Rights Acts and two amendments to the US Constitution, each of which was accompanied by its particular moment of social conscience and all of which were designed, in some measure, to protect the rights of Black Americans. However, none of these efforts ever succeeded in demolishing America's unsavory addiction to racism embodied in its recurring discrimination and violence, particularly toward Black Americans, and even more so towards Black men: The list that follows distinguishes anti-slavery movements and the ensuing legislation, such as the 19th century's abolitionist efforts that brought about the Emancipation Proclamation in 1863 and the adoption of the 13th Amendment to the US Constitution in 1865, from the civil rights movements and ensuing legislation. In short, the anti-slavery movements recognize the natural rights of Black Americans to be treated as human beings rather than property, while civil rights movements are aimed at recognizing that Black Americans, as citizens of the polity known as the United States of America, are entitled to the same inalienable rights described by Thomas Jefferson in the Declaration of Independence and guaranteed under the US Constitution.

I. The Civil Rights Act of 1864 was enacted to grant equal rights under the law to all people within the jurisdiction of the United States.

II. The 14th Amendment to the US Constitution was ratified in 1868 and granted Black Americans, among other things, both citizenship and equal protection under the law.

III. The 15th Amendment to the US Constitution was ratified in 1870 and granted Black American men the right to vote.

IV. The Civil Rights Acts of 1870 through 1871 (the "Enforcement Acts") were three federal acts that gave the federal government substantial authority to prosecute those who violated the civil and political rights of African Americans, especially members of the Ku Klux Klan.

V. The Civil Rights Act of 1875 was enacted to guarantee Black Americans equal treatment in public accommodations and public transportation and prohibited their exclusion from jury service.

VI. The Civil Rights Act of 1957 was enacted to create a Civil Rights Division in the Justice Department and to protect the voting rights of Black Americans.

VII. The Civil Rights Act of 1960 was enacted to strengthen the government's power to protect voting rights. The Civil Rights Act of 1875 was declared unconstitutional by the US Supreme Court in a collection of five so-called "Civil Rights Cases." The Court's ruling emboldened the state legislatures' passing Jim Crow laws and cemented the premise of "separate but equal" throughout the United States until the passage of the Civil Rights Act of 1964. The US Constitution did not afford women, including Black women, the right to vote until the adoption of the 19th Amendment in 1920.

VIII. The Civil Rights Act of 1964 was enacted to prohibit all forms of racial, religious, gender-based, or ethnic discrimination and purported to desegregate schools and any other public institution.

IX. The Civil Rights Act of 1965 (the "Voting Rights Act")

X. The Civil Rights Act of 1968 was enacted to prevent housing discrimination. Notwithstanding the five Civil Rights Acts between 1864 and 1957 and the two Constitutional Amendments, racially motivated White Southern Democrats, backed by both the federal and state judicial systems, still enacted Black Codes, which permitted convict leasing, sharecropping, and peonage. It is now axiomatic and very well admitted that, during this period, over four thousand Blacks, mostly Black men and boys, were lynched, and their body parts, including their privates, were amputated and either auctioned or kept, or sold as good luck charms or souvenirs.

Who would have thought that the adoption of two Constitutional Amendments in under two years' time would lay the groundwork not only for over 100 years of institutionalized racism, but also for the mass incarceration of the very same people whom the constitutional amendments were designed to make free? Fast forward.

Imagine the frustration of the four Black students who decided to stage a sit-in in 1960 at a "Whites Only" restaurant counter in a Woolworth's store in Greensboro, North Carolina, knowing, while they were being punched, kicked, and spat upon, that they should have been protected by no fewer than four federal Civil Rights laws i.e., the Civil Rights Acts of 1864 – providing them equal rights under the law; and the three Enforcement Acts of 1870 and 1871 – [15] protecting them from racial violence and the full weight of the US Constitution. This same Constitution should have protected my mother from the unauthorized home entry and "white glove" inspection of the case worker, and should have protected my friends and me from the dilapidated and negligently, if not intentionally, underfunded schools we attended as well as the many times that we were stopped by the local police and state patrolmen for manufactured issues, such as missing headlights or for being in neighborhoods where we "didn't belong."

Each time we heard of the unconstitutionally protected manslaughter of a Black man, our premise for success was indicted. Rodney King's brutal beating on national television indicted us. Trayvon Martin's late-night murder by a self-righteous neighborhood vigilante, who was set free, indicted us. The brazen killings of Manuel Ellis, Daunte Wright, Tamir Rice, and so many more not only indicted us, but obliterated every notion that we, the "children of the dream," had our hard work, attendance at the right schools, and professional success as all we ever had to possess or obtain in order to be accepted.

Again, I say, civil rights for Black Americans, and particularly for Black men, has its moments, but it was never a "movement." A movement is transformative and its results are scalable, stackable and sustained over time. In America, civil rights for Black men is an odyssey, my son, a never-ending, never yielding, slow crawl to a mythical land where "justice roll[s] on like a river, [and] righteousness like a never-failing stream" (Amos 5:24, New International Version)! Like Theodore Parker, the 19th-century abolitionist and Unitarian minister, I cannot[16] pretend to understand the moral universe. The arc is a long one. My eye reaches but a little way. I cannot calculate the curve and complete the figure by experience of sight. I can divine it by conscience. And from what I see, I am sure it bends toward justice. For us, however, the long arc of the moral universe bends, but ever so slowly and not without a sure, episodic retraction, before ever finding justice, as its true mark; and even when it achieves its mark, when the arrows of justice fall, they seldom fall forward. Sometimes, they even ricochet.

And so, my son, do not be deceived by the success you have achieved or inherited, or by the cleverly gratifying feeling of progress. Protect your soul. The perception of progress is no substitute for the demand of an unequivocally equal justice, no more than knowledge is a substitute for wisdom. You are the descendant of a people of great faith, but you will encounter those who are equally the descendants of a belief that your natural and inalienable rights are unearned gifts bestowed on you by them. They, like pied pipers, will spew rationalized admonitions to the tune of: "Be patient. These things take time. Look at how far we have come." Our path ignored Frederick Douglass' admonition that "Power concedes nothing without a demand. It never did and it never will." Our willful assimilation ignored the urgency of now in James Baldwin's exasperated retort:

> What is it you want me to reconcile myself to? . . . It has taken my father's time, my mother's time, my uncle's time, my brothers' and my sisters' time, my nieces' and my nephews' time. How much time do you want for your 'progress'?[17]

The staggering reality of this point rings clear in the words of a White, Yazoo Delta planter, who in 1866, proclaimed: "I think God intended the niggers to be slaves. Now since man has deranged God's plan, I think the best we can do is keep 'em as near to a state of bondage as possible. . . . My theory is, feed 'em well, clothe 'em well, and then, if they don't work . . . whip 'em well."[18]

Do not accept our path. Demand your own.

If you tarry, my son, you, too, will be left asking, "How much longer 'til freedom comes?" and you will write the next letter.

ENDNOTES

1 In a widely interpreted passage in Hebrews 11:1, the author defines "faith" as follows: "Now faith is the substance of things hoped for, the evidence of things not seen." (King James Version) Deconstructing Faith: A Letter To My Grandson

2 "Poverty is the constant stress of not having enough to eat, of not knowing where you're going to sleep tonight, [and] of knowing you are one emergency away from sleeping on the streets." Poverty Myths, ATD Fourth World," 4thworldmovement.org/overcoming-poverty/poverty-myths/?gclid=EAIaIQobChMIsLCLvbS58QIVawaICR0F8wqmE AAYASAAEgKo3PD_BwE.

3 Robert Joseph Taylor, et al., "Racial and Ethnic Differences in Extended Family, Friendship, Fictive Kin, and Congregational Informal Support Networks," *Family Relations*, vol. 62, no. 4 (2013), pp. 609–624;, doi:10.1111/fare.12030.

4 See, for related discussion and critique, Daniel Geary. (Beyond Civil Rights, The Moynihan Report and Its Legacy). Philadelphia: University of Pennsylvania Press, 2015.

5 President Johnson's "War on Poverty" was launched in his State of the Union Address on January 8, 1964. "Welfare Expands in the 1960s." Soc 315 Social Welfare, people.eou.edu/socwelf/readings/week-2/welfare-expands-in-the-1960s/.

6 See, for expanded context, George Fredrickson (Racism: A Short History). Princeton: Princeton University Press, 2002.

7 In 1966, after 6 consecutive years of economic expansion, 41 percent of the nonwhite population was poor as compared with 12 percent of the whites." "Welfare Expands in the 1960s." Soc. 315 Social Welfare, people.eou.edu/socwelf/readings/week-2/welfare-expands-in-the-1960s/.

8 Wilde, Oscar. The Soul of Man under Socialism. Mint Editions, 2021.

9 Tom Oliver Professor of Applied Ecology." "Is Racism and Bigotry in Our DNA?" The Conversation, 18 Mar. 2021, theconversation.com/is-racism-and-bigotry-in-our-dna-135096.

10 Emzara was the daughter of Rake'el, the granddaughter of Methuselah, the wife and cousin of Noah, and the mother of Shem, Ham, and Japheth. But see, Chaffey, Tim. "Who Was Noah's Wife?" Answers in Genesis, Answers In Genesis, 25 Aug. 2015, answersingenesis.org/bible-characters/noah/who-was-noahs-wife/ (exploring the different names given to Noah's wife throughout history). Genesis 19:18–27 (King James Version)

11 Kiger, Patrick J. "Did Colonists Give Infected Blankets to Native Americans as Biological Warfare?" History.com, A&E Television Networks, 15 Nov. 2018, www.history.com/news/colonists-native-americans-smallpox-blankets.. 10 "Why Xenophobia Works." Psychology Today, Sussex Publishers, www.psychologytoday.com/us/blog/evolution-in-daily-life/201812/why-xenophobia-works. Deconstructing Faith: A Letter To My Grandson 7

12 NAACP: The 1963 March on Washington; https://naacp.org/find-resources/history-explained/1963-march-washington (July 2021).
13 Whitfield, James Monroe, et al. The Works of James M. Whitfield: "America" and Other Writings by a Nineteenth-Century African American Poet. Univ. of North Carolina Press, 2011.
14 See Richard Kluger's classic discussion of the problematic journey to and through the Brown decision, a legal high mark for the Civil Rights Movement. (Simple Justice). New York: Knopf Doubleday Publishing, 1977.
15 "Journey to Freedom." EJI Reports, 15 June 2020, eji.org/report/reconstruction-in-america/journey-to-freedom/#chapter-1-intro.
16 Chughtai, Alia. "Know Their Names: Black People Killed by the Police in the US." Al Jazeera Interactives, Al Jazeera, 7 July 2021, interactive.aljazeera.com/aje/2020/know-their-names/index.html.
17 Thorsen, Karen, director. James Baldwin: the Price of a Ticket.
18 Mancini, Matthew, and David M. Oshinsky. "'Worse Than Slavery': Parchman Farm and the Ordeal of Jim Crow Justice." The American Journal of Legal History, vol. 42, no. 4, 1998, p. 444., doi:10.2307/846060. 21 "Ten Sermons of Religion/Of Justice and the Conscience." Wikisource, the Free Online Library, en.wikisource.org/wiki/Ten_Sermons_of_Religion/Of_Justice_and_the_Conscience.

BIBLIOGRAPHY

George M. Fredrickson. (Racism: A Short History). Princeton, New Jersey: Princeton University Press, 2002.

Daniel Geary. (Beyond Civil Rights, the Moynihan Report and Its Legacy). Philadelphia: University of Pennsylvania Press, 2015.

Richard Kluger. (Simple Justice: The History of Brown v. Board of Education and America's Struggle for Equality). New York: Knopf Doubleday Publishing Group, 1977.

CHAPTER FOUR

Illuminations: Pandemic Reflections on Racial Justice, Hope and Love

James Henry Harris

Introduction

Let me begin this essay with a little story about my own experiences as I continue to walk and exercise in my neighborhood. It demonstrates the dual pandemics of everyday Black life and the ravages of the coronavirus. The characters are a white dog, an old white lady, and me. So, here we go:

Even the little dog looked at me like I was an anomaly, a threat, a spectacle. As I walked past them on a quiet tree-lined street—the dog and his owner, an aging white woman with long stringy hair—his little black beady eyes followed me intently with quiet suspicion. I felt that even the little shaggy white dog had been taught to poke and stare at a Black man walking past a white woman in the early morning, an hour or so after sunrise. The gaze of the beady eyes following my every motion caused me to feel "some kinda way." Just guilty of being "Black while walking." I felt like a thief, like I had broken the law. At that moment, I began to imagine that I could be arrested, and suddenly I could not breathe. I was choking on fear that was more than a notion. It was bombarding me like a waterfall and I was losing my grip as I remembered the execution of the Martinsville Seven—seven young Black males executed for the supposed rape of a white woman in 1949. All seven were executed in the Virginia State Penitentiary in Richmond, VA, in February of 1951. I also thought of the wrongful conviction of the Central Park Five, and then, like a streak of lightning, Emmett Till's face flashed before my eyes as fear almost caused me to holler for help.

I am James Henry Harris, born and raised in the sweltering racist climate of the South. Virginia is the place where the governor and the state legislature chose to close all the public schools rather than integrate them. The racism is historical and deep-seated. I am a Black preacher and a scholar—a dialectic that often seems anathema to a lot of folk, except folk like my theological mentors Samuel DeWitt Proctor, Fannie Lou Hamer, and Martin Luther King, Jr. Some may wonder why I put Fannie Lou in this mix. The simple answer is that she was a powerful thinker and activist who had an "honorary doctorate" in the "ways of Black folk."[1]

This piece is inspired by several philosophers as well. Methodologically, the short sermonic meditations are written in an adaptation of the form of Walter Benjamin's *Illuminations* and Ludwig Wittgenstein's *Tractatus*.[2] My point is that all human beings are dialectical in nature, such that there is good and evil, love and hate, right and wrong, strength and weakness embedded in the mind and body of all humans. And the preacher, like all others, is human. The following words express my pain and struggle with the dialectic of suffering and hope and joy and sorrow as I seek to inspire and encourage Black folk while scolding them about their unwillingness to take the vaccine. The sermonic meditations below are discourses on love, justice, and hope. These are the things of which I must speak because I cannot be silent.

Every morning while walking, a pandemic ritual as strengthening to me as weightlifting, I experience something graceful and encouraging. It's a pantheistic panentheism that allows me to see the sunshine and rain clouds with renewed hope and love. Every morning I am arrested by the beauty of the towering white oaks, the splendor of the cedars, and the shade of gum trees. I can only think that God is bigger than the specter of the coronavirus. God is the painter of the glorious array of trees, flowers, grasses, rocks, and dirt. During the hopelessness of the pandemic and its variations of lockdowns, our wearing of face masks, and getting vaccinated, I have learned of my own fears and faith and the quest for hope yet unborn, hope unrecognized and unattainable without faith and the power of the Holy Spirit.

The most baffling and distressful reality of the global pandemic has been the persistent reluctance of Black folk in my church and community to take the vaccine. They fear taking the vaccine more than they fear death itself. I have used all the logic and rhetoric I know to convince Blacks of all educational and socioeconomic levels to get vaccinated. And yet, I hear so many reasons based on conspiracy theories and the politics of Trump as to why they don't trust the vaccine. Folk who suddenly want to see "more study" of the vaccine to those who say "there is a government chip" in the vaccine to track Blacks. The irony is that all of these people are getting their information from their cellphones, which is a much more likely tracking device than a (0.3-mL) vaccine.

When I see burnt orange and the brown rusty speckled leaves of fall and the lush green foliage of spring and summer, I feel the lure of life's promises as the wind breezes through the tree leaves even on a hot summer day. Some days I cannot walk slowly enough to take in the beauty of nature and the smells of summer fragrances floating from the flowers and the trees and the grasses covered by the freshness of noonday rain showers. It's too much for my eyes to behold, and yet I see and hear the symphony of birds singing and leaves shaking and wind blowing as the natural orchestra of nature is conducted by the God of all things. The psalmist is spot-on with the words, *"The earth is the Lord's, and all that is in it, the world, and all those who live in it"* (Psalm 24:1, NRSV).

In this essay, I seek to interpret my understanding of surviving during the most difficult and challenging time of my life. Before the pandemic, I was a people person, a traveler, a visitor to hospitals and nursing homes—a community leader and pastor to Black people. I was lecturing and preaching around the country and abroad. I was honored to deliver the Hampton University Ministers' Conference lectures twice in a three-year period. I had lectured on Black Suffering in Pretoria, South Africa and traveled to Paris with members of the Society for the Study of Black Religion.

This was a Black Paris educational tour, and it was my first time visiting the iconic city. I was staying at the Mercure Hotel in Montmartre in Northern Paris. I enjoyed the beautiful weather and the sounds and smells of Turkish and Lebanese cuisines mixed into a fusion of horizons. I thought of my ancestors who found some semblance of acceptance in Paris as they sought to escape the blatant racism in America. Folk such as Josephine Baker, Richard Wright, James Baldwin, and Countee Cullen. Josephine Baker became a wealthy star in Paris after getting started at the Theatre Des Champs-Elysees in the 1920's. I visited the small café in the Montmartre District where it is said that James Baldwin wrote *Go Tell It On The Mountain* and where Malcolm X ate his last meal during a stopover on his way back to America from Africa before being assassinated in New York. Richard Wright, like Marvin Gaye, loved Paris and Paris had a strange love for Black skin. I was awestruck when I saw the home of one of my favorite writers and intellectuals and the plaque on the outside wall stating Richard Wright had lived there on the 5th floor from 1948 to 1951. *Black Boy* became even more real to me at that very moment. It was like a baptism by illumination and revelation. Also, jazz was introduced to Paris by Black musicians from the United States. I visited the Tabou Club in Paris, where Chester Hines performed. I digress too long about my love of Black history and culture and what a joy it was to be in Paris for ten days with my wife Demetrius, oldest son Corey, and youngest son Cameron, who was able to join us on the last day. I reflect, *in medias res*, in order to contrast my pre-pandemic happiness and world travels with the stifling reality of being on the brink of sadness and depression throughout this awful pandemic.

One reason why I often feel the fear and trembling of hopelessness is grounded in my "no confidence" in the ability of doctors, lawyers, and politicians to speak truth to the people. Every element of the American government from the White House to the CDC and FDA has become politicized. And the millions of Black folks who refuse to get vaccinated, putting entire families, communities, cities, and states at risk, are in effect Trump supporters. Mr. Trump's cavalier attitude regarding the coronavirus has effectively been embraced by millions of Black millennials, Generation Xers, and those categorized as Generation Z—those who believe the vaccine conspiracy.

I. A Living Hope

> *Blessed be the God and Father of our Lord Jesus Christ! By his great mercy he has given us a new birth into a living hope through the resurrection of Jesus Christ from the dead and into an inheritance that is imperishable, undefiled, and unfading.* (I Peter 1:3-4, NRSV)

These are difficult and dangerous times. It seems that we are being bombarded by a barrage of ominous and stunning statistics every single day about the coronavirus, the infection that is attacking our bodies and our spirits. To be under attack by the very breath we breathe and the wind that blows and the invisible presence of germs that can destroy us is an awesome and awful reality.

We cannot help but be saddened and fearful during this pandemic, which for Black folk is made more burdensome by the oppressive reality we face as a people. We continue to be a part of the global South, though we live in the Northern Hemisphere and in the richest country in the world. This is a richness that continues to escape most of us because, though the nation is rich, Black people remain poor and in poverty, sickened and stymied by racism and injustice, strapped and strained by the structural power and presence of disparities on every hand. In a relatively recent National Public Radio report (June 24, 2021), I was troubled to learn that the life expectancy of Black folk had decreased by nearly four years. This is catastrophic and oppressive. Racism and disparities in the health care of Blacks are alarming as we enter the second year of the coronavirus pandemic.

The letter by the Apostle Peter quoted above addresses the critical situation in the lives of the people. There are people who have been abused; their social and cultural life has been under siege, and they have become marginalized because of Jesus Christ. Black people understand deeply what it means to be on the margins, on the fringes, on the boundary of disease and despair; on the boundary of feeling saddled by the strong and stifling hands of hopelessness and heartache.[3] And yet, that's not the only thing that I understand and experience because that's only one side of the equation. There is another side to this situation, this human existence, and that's hope—"A Living Hope," according to the scripture text. *"Blessed be the God and Father of our Lord Jesus Christ! By his great mercy he has given us a new birth into a living hope through the resurrection of Jesus Christ from the dead"* (I Peter 1:3).

We have been born into a new birth by the great mercy of God. The text says, *"by his great mercy he has given us a new birth"* Wow! We have a new birth. We are new creatures. We have been born again. Whatever was is gone. The old self, the old attitudes, the old habits, the old behaviors and actions have been overwhelmed, overtaken, and replaced by newness. A new birth, all because of the great mercy of God. Not just mercy, which is beautiful and bounteous by itself, but *"by His great mercy"* He has given us a new birth. This is powerful. This is what God has given us. It's a new birth given unto us by His great mercy. Not just mercy, but by His great mercy. This is mercy extended. This is mercy on steroids. This is hyper-mercy. This is great mercy that's given, not earned. Given. Not deserved, but given to us. This is the gift. This gift of mercy, great mercy, has given us a new birth. Today is a new day for a new "you" because of the great mercy of God. This is an Easter mercy. A resurrection mercy. Hallelujah!

Then the scripture text says that this new birth is into a *"living hope through the resurrection of Jesus Christ from the dead."* We live in hope by the power of the resurrection and through the resurrection. So, we are no longer hopeless. Yes, we are still poor. Yes, we are still oppressed. Yes, we are still disenfranchised and dejected. Yes, we are still suffering and in pain. All of these things are still existential and real-life experiences that befall and beset us every day. But now we are bearers and beneficiaries of a "new birth" into a "living hope" through "the resurrection." The resurrection is the new life. The resurrection is the new birth. The resurrection is the foundation of our new hope. Hope for me is all about the present understanding of the future. Hope is the "now" that can feel, understand, and experience the presence of the "then." Then, "I saw a new heaven and a new earth" (Revelation 21:1, NRSV). This is the power of the resurrection of Jesus Christ that is instantiated in us with every breath we breathe.

II. A New World Order

"And do not grieve the Holy Spirit of God, with which you were marked with a seal for the day of redemption. Put away from you all bitterness and wrath and anger and wrangling and slander, together with all malice. Be kind to one another, tenderhearted, forgiving one another, as God in Christ has forgiven you" (Ephesians 4:30-32, NRSV).

Today, as I look around my social and geopolitical environment, I see that there is so much vitriol and venomous talk and actions that seem to engulf us.

We are bombarded every day with personal experiences and reports of injustice and evil. Seemingly, the world, and the United States in particular, are in the business of grieving the Holy Spirit—making God ashamed of God's own creation. God is not pleased with the callous and reckless actions of this nation's former president who lied and cheated his way into the presidency and convinced the people that it's okay to have the blood of nearly seven hundred thousand people dead because of the coronavirus, and a disproportionate number of them Black and Latinx. This is a global disaster and an American tragedy. And I, for one, am angry and stressed about it. I am also gripped by fear!

This also makes me sad, somber, and silent because the pain of suffering and struggle almost shatters the flicker of hope that remains in my heart, soul, and spirit. The invisible tears are still evident in my words and my speech, in my sermons, and in my songs as I invoke the spirit of James Baldwin in *The Fire Next Time*, and the spirit of the Psalmist who declares "The earth is the Lord's and all that is in it, the world and those who live in it" (Psalm 24:1).

I need to read and re-read these words to convince and persuade myself of our frailty and weakness, to remember that despite all the callousness and corruption of the politicians who are driven more by the mighty dollar and vulgar capitalistic greed than by caring for the lives of people, Black and poor people, in particular, continue to live in hope.

The scripture text encourages and admonishes us to get rid of the old social order, the old behaviors and actions, the old understanding of the meaning of church and community driven by anger, lies, and falsehoods. And instead "put this old stuff away" because there is a new world order emerging in the Black church and among the people of God.

So, I am compelled to put away negativity. Bury it. Lay it aside. Pack it up and seal it in an airtight container where it will never again show its ugly face. Put away from you "all bitterness and wrath." Stop being sharply unpleasant and evil. Stop being vengeful and indignant, always angry with the world, the people in your orbit, in your circle, your family, your cohorts, etc. Such actions are perfidious and treacherous.

Put away all bitterness, wrath, anger and wrangling. Wrangling has to do with arguing with one another, which is prevalent in families and Black churches. Put it away, along with slander and malice. Let the evils of your life go into a stash of banned behaviors and practices. Whatever it is. Then the text pivots to a positive directive: "Be kind to one another." Kindness doesn't cost us anything. Smile and be respectful. Kindness. Good morning, kindness. Hello, kindness. Please, kindness. Thank you, kindness. I'm sorry, kindness. Be forgiving of one another. People are going to be people, saying and doing ugly and evil things. But we don't have to reciprocate in that way. As the vicars of Christ, we can be kind.

III. A Time to Grow

"Rid yourselves, therefore, of all malice and all guile, insincerity, envy, and all slander. Like newborn infants, long for the pure, spiritual milk, so that by it you may grow into salvation--, if indeed you have tasted that the Lord is good" (I Peter 2:1-3, NRSV).

I have been thinking that during this worldwide coronavirus pandemic, we all have been given an unexpected opportunity. It's an inopportune opportunity to recalibrate our faith, our commitment. It's an opportunity to reconsider the value and importance of our lives and the baggage we carry around daily. Because of this global pandemic, this coronavirus, we have been confined to certain limited and prescribed social spaces such as the house, the backyard, and our cars or trucks. In a sense, we are indeed "home alone" because that has been the safest place for us to practice social and physical distancing. Under normal circumstances and conditions, we would be running and ripping, coming and going at a fast pace by shopping and sightseeing, "malling around," getting ourselves into debt, buying more and more stuff to feed our insatiable appetite, ego, and our greed. Yes, we all are guilty of getting in our own way, stagnated by routine and wrongful actions. This is the first time in the past 100 years that Second Baptist Church, organized in 1840, has been closed, shutdown on Sundays—not by a hurricane, a cyclone, an earthquake, or a world war, but by a virus that has been more deadly in one year than the Vietnam War, which lasted for seventeen years.

This virus, circulating among us for nearly two years, has done more damage more quickly than anything since the 1918 Flu Pandemic. And yet, I believe it is a time for us as Black folk to work on ourselves, our attitudes, and our behaviors. Too often, we spend our time crafting ways to deceive and trick one another. We have been in church for years and years and we are still envious and resentful of our fellow brothers and sisters. We tend to want what someone else has. That's envy. And it doesn't stop there, because we often spread false rumors, or slander someone with our evil words. We gossip and say things that we know are not only wrong, but untrue. We behave like this throughout the church and its community. This is a time for us to look in the mirror, since we have been home more than usual. We are compelled to look at ourselves in the mirror and examine our behavior.

The above scripture captures our need for spiritual growth. We have been given a golden opportunity to figure out how sacred we want our lives to be. And this is the directive. This is the imperative for spiritual food in order that we can grow. This is a time to grow. The scripture says, in I Peter 1:1-2, NRSV: "Rid yourselves, therefore, of all malice and all guile, insincerity, envy, and all slander. Like newborn infants, long for the pure, spiritual milk, so that by it you may grow into salvation...."

I encourage all of us to spend this time away from public, in-person worship—away from congregating together—to cleanse ourselves, to rid ourselves of these negative behaviors and debilitating attitudes and actions because we all have more time to ourselves, more time to think, to pray, to grow spiritually. Let's adhere to this scriptural directive: "Rid yourselves, therefore of all malice, all guile, insincerity, envy, and slander." Get rid of it. Dispose of it. Discard it. Eliminate it. Eject it. Expel it. Trash it. Dump it. Rid yourself of all this baggage so that when the Church reopens, our spiritual growth will have been so phenomenal that we will be unrecognizable to ourselves and others. In other words, the pandemic would have transformed us such that we become new creatures. We will have gotten rid of so much baggage; malice, guile, insincerity, and envy that our church and community will never be the same. That the coronavirus will have helped us to become better human beings and Christians in ways that the sermon, the Sunday school, and the officers could have never achieved. The text also says, "Like newborns, like infants long for pure, spiritual milk, so that by it you may grow into salvation--, if indeed you have tasted that the Lord is good" (I Peter 1:2-3, NRSV).

Like infants, we grow, too, after we rid ourselves of malice, guile, and insincerity; we can now grow into salvation. Salvation here is a growth process. You can't claim salvation without emulating Jesus Christ and longing for spiritual nutrition. God's word is the pure spiritual milk we need in order to grow. This is the time to grow. This is the time for all of us to become saved again. We are growing into salvation. We are constantly being saved over and over again as we grow stronger in the Lord. Our salvation is incomplete, which means that we can never stop growing because to stop growing is to die.

IV. In Defense of Hope

"Always be ready to make your defense to anyone who demands from you an accounting for the hope that is in you, yet do it with gentleness and respect" (I Peter 3:15-16, NRSV).

Today, right now, during this persistent pandemic, this worldwide attack of the virus on the human species generally and on Black people more viciously, it is normal for us to feel that the walls are caving in on us. That the curtain of certainty and the tumult of time are affecting us in ways that we cannot fully understand or describe. In a sense, for the first time in many years. I feel helpless and hopeless, gripped by the hands of despair. Hopelessness seeks to be the order of the day for me. Every day on CNN, NBC, CBS, Fox News, and on the Internet, this pandemic is the lead story and often it is the only story. We learn more and more about what, when, and how we got ourselves as a nation and state in this crisis; a health crisis that is also an economic crisis and a crisis of leadership at the highest levels of government and business. And the propaganda and the false narratives are overwhelming.

For years, Republicans and Democrats have been trying to topple the federal government, advancing policies of less regulation, corporate coziness, cutting this social program and that economic stimulus package and saying that Washington is broken. Well now it is broken "for real, for real", when there is no wisdom coming out of the White House or Congress because it has become a "swamp," a bunch of bumbling rich white Trump-sponsored Beverly Hillbillies banding together to destroy the fabric of the democracy, the republic. The riots and insurrection of January 6, 2021, testify to the racism and White supremacy that prop up the nation and the current Republican elected officials.

Clearly, this is about power, greed, and egoism at the expense and pain of the American people. Every time I see a "breaking news" story I also see how the CDC, medical doctors, and other health officials stand in fear of business interests, and former President Trump's bullying them to the point of their trembling, acquiescence, or inertia. For the longest time it had become harder and harder to get a straight answer from the leading infectious disease specialists because they were afraid to speak truth to power because their boss was an obnoxious liar surrounded by sycophants. This has been an American tragedy. These politicians sat on the data about the virus while it spread from China to Europe and to the US. In this country alone, it has killed nearly a million people. This is a disaster of epic proportions, and people want to go back to beaches and bars because the sun is shining and the temperature is rising. Well, Black people must look out for themselves. There can be no more singing in church choirs, no more meeting and greeting, no more hugging and holding hands in Black churches and in classrooms. Anything less than this is a formula for even greater catastrophe, more senseless pain and sorrow. And the Biden Administration suffers from some of the same egoism and irrationality as its predecessor.

Today, we stand on the brink of a budding new world, on the brink of developing a new approach to life. A life of careful observance of self and others. Today, we are caught in the crossfires of health and hope, caught in the middle of tension between science, business greediness, and superstition. Today, Black people, poor people, sick people, church people, faithful people, are caught between a rock and a hard place. Between science and the tsunami, all because we as Blacks have helped to turn the country over to a bunch of hoodlums with law and business degrees from every major American institution of higher learning. And most of them have succumbed to politics and greed. Seldom has politics sunk so low as to wager and gamble with the lives of millions and millions of Black and poor people. Don't get me wrong, we have had some awful, terrible, and incompetent leaders regardless of political party, but this recent group has taken us to a "danger zone" almost unmatched in American history. Remember, my beloved, the concept and practice of states' rights have never been kind to Black people and that's where we have ended up today, with no national policy on a national pandemic disaster. And the recent presidents say that each state must fend for itself. This is a hopeless situation. And yet as Black people, we do have hope beyond this current deadly crisis, because we have endured slavery, Reconstruction, Jim and Jane Crow, the Civil Rights Movement, and a national resurgence of Black voter suppression.

The scripture says, "Always be ready to make your defense to anyone who demands from you an accounting for the hope that is in you." This is the essence of Christian faith in this text, which boils down to Black hope. Usually there is a triangle, a three-part element to our practice of Christianity. In other texts, hope is paired with love and faith. They are the three "stooges" or "three amigos," but here hope stands alone without its cohorts, without its friends, without any props.

It is not faith, like it is in the Book of Corinthians. It is not love, as it is in the gospels. But here, it is just hope. Alone, standing naked, unconquered and unaccompanied by anything. Hope to aspire. Hope to expect. Hope to dream, to plan. Hope to anticipate, to gaze, and to desire.

Be ready, my friends, to tell anyone why you smile in the midst of sorrow and sadness. Be ready to acknowledge that God, through Jesus Christ, has done great things for us. That's accounting for the hope that is in you and me. Be ready to defend your testimony. And be ready to testify about your defense. So, my beloved, we have a hope in us that cannot be quelled; it cannot be curtailed. It cannot even be contained because it is grounded in the God of Sojourner Truth and Frederick Douglass. This God is the ground of our hope.

VII. Living in Love

"Therefore, be imitators of God, as beloved children, and walk in love, as Christ loved us and gave himself up for us, a fragrant offering and sacrifice to God" (Ephesian 5:1-2, NRSV).

When I look around and observe the culture, the atmosphere, the social and political climate, the spirit of the people, and the high-octane vicious rhetoric and logical fallacies being spewed out of the mouths of politicians and lawyers, there seems to be no love anywhere to be found. We are imitating everybody except God and Jesus Christ. The White evangelical church and the largest online evangelical university in the country are reeling from the recent sex scandal of the Liberty University president, while demanding that the students embrace standards and practices that they, the leaders, don't really practice. Stormy Daniels ain't got nothing on these "Bible-toting," Word-of-God, church-going, Trump-supporting White evangelicals.

Black folk have a lot to lose and if we didn't know it before, we should know it now. The nation is divided; the world is in a pandemic. We are still in a global crisis and some folks are not capable of "social distancing" because no matter how poor and uneducated, White folk and some Blacks will put your lives at risk by standing too close, not wearing a mask, and not washing their hands. Nobody is coming to rescue Black folk from this raging fire, this inferno that continues to kill poor struggling Black people at disproportionate rates. Again, we are approaching a million deaths in this country alone, mainly because of the "goons" who don't believe in science, Congress, and the worthless doctors who are too capitalistic to speak truth to power. Language such as "Ain't nobody going to tell me what to do" or "You can't take away my freedoms" characterize White privilege, no matter how poor the speakers might be.

And the coronavirus pandemic is accompanied by the pandemic of racism and white supremacy, which is used to create and stoke fear in soccer moms of suburbia and made the 2020 election about guns and violence, which is to say "law and order," implying that Black people are lawless and violent, which is a boldface lie. A hoax. I have said again and again that Black people are not violent. If they were, Black men and women would be up in arms, carrying AK-47s on their shoulders, walking down the streets of Milwaukee and small-time America like that young white boy. The police now believe that the "Black Lives Matter" protests are violent and threatening the White folk in the suburbs. The message actually switched from the botching of the response to the coronavirus to if you elect Joe Biden, you won't be safe, and some folks were buying it. This is absolutely incredible. But it didn't work because Biden was elected with the help of the overwhelming Black vote.

Well, in today's scripture text, the focus is on love. Not the vitriol and hate speech we hear every day. Not the culture wars or the racism that we see every time a Black man or woman is shot by White police. Not the police offering the white boy a drink and asking him if he was okay while shooting an unarmed Black man in the back seven times. Can't you see this for what it is or do we "love White people" so much that we are blind to our own suffering and oppression? The text says, "Be imitators of God, as beloved children." We have the standard—be imitators of God. Not to flatter God, because God can't be flattered or duped. God has no need for an ego or for our approval. Imitate God and act according to God's will. And live in love. Wow! Live in love.

Living in love is to say "live in God" because God is love. Living in love is to realize that every day, every breath, every step, every instance of happiness, every opportunity to praise God is a reflection of the love that God extends to us. Living in love is living in the power and presence of God whose love for us is seen vividly in Christ, who likewise loved us and gave Himself for us. Living in love is living in the power of the Holy Spirit and in the hope of the resurrection. Every breath, every step, every prayer, every testimony, every hope, and every dream is empowered by the love of Christ.

Our love for one another, for the church, for the community, for humankind, for those who love us and those who hate us, those who embrace us and those who repel us—this living in love is the beautiful gift of God demonstrated in Christ Jesus. Love has no equal.

VIII. Love's Obedience

"Now that you have purified your souls by your obedience to the truth so that you have genuine mutual affection, love one another deeply from the heart. You have been born anew, not of perishable but of imperishable seed, through the living and enduring word of God" (I Peter 1:22-23, NRSV).

There is no human entity, no invention, no understanding of aesthetics, of beauty, of wonder, of knowledge, of compassion, or of sacrifice that equals to or even compares to a mother's and father's love. It is simply indescribable or incomprehensible. It cannot be fully articulated or described by the limitations of language, spoken or written. It is beyond language's capacity. Take, for example, the early 14th-century poem *The Divine Comedy*, where Dante, in the second part of *Purgatorio,* writes:

> And tell me if the man I see here is the one who published the new poem, beginning "Ladies, you who have the knowledge of love." I said to him, "I am one who, when love breathes in me, take note. And in whatever way he dictates within, that way I signify." (Dante, *Purgatorio,* Canto XXIV)

Now we may not be familiar with Dante or Shakespeare or even the poetry of Langston Hughes or Patricia Smith. But we know the poetry and songs of Smokey Robinson or Bruno Mars and Missy Elliot, not to mention the old school music of Marvin Gaye, Aretha Franklin, The O'Jays, and the Supremes. All of these people could croon and poeticize about love. And others like

Elizabeth Barrett Browning ("How do I love thee? Let me count the ways") or John Donne ("Go Catch a Falling Star" or "Drinking Alone in The Moonlight"). We have heard Sonnet 18 by Shakespeare, ("Shall I compare thee to a summer's day? Thou art more lovely and more beautiful"). Or Paul Laurence Dunbar's poem, *We Wear the Mask*:

> We wear the mask that grins and lies, It hides our cheeks and shades our eyes—This debt we pay to human guile, With torn and bleeding hearts we smile....

All of these words speak so eloquently of love as a type of romance or a type of longing, an emotional roller-coaster type of reverence. But all these poets and singers speak with a "thinness" and superficiality, a tragic weakness of words often as hollow as the rotten and decaying trunk of an old oak tree. They don't compare; they can't compare or compete with the salient love of a mother for her children. The wordless expression of admiration and inspiration that emanates from a smile, a glance, a hot meal, a touch on the head or a nod of approval is the embodiment of love. These gestures by mothers and fathers all over the world speak of a love so profound that they make words, however powerful, almost seem profane. Words, however poetic, seem paltry, puny, and patronizing. I implore us all to see and understand love from a different vantage point, a more expansive yet particular point of reference.

So, the scripture text issues forth this new imperative, this new authoritative commanding and essential immediacy to do something now. It's urgent. It's a call to arms. A call to action, like "come here now." It's critically important. Don't lollygag. Don't procrastinate. Don't linger. Don't waste my time. It's imperative. The text says, "Now that you have purified your souls by obedience to the truth"; clearly, the purification of the soul is a daunting task that can and must be done as a preliminary step toward truth and love. We all have to get away from negativity. If your friends, family, or colleagues, and folk on your job are always negative, get away from them as fast as your feet will move. Don't entertain negativity either, actively or passively.

Being positive is important to the purification of your soul, which works together with your body. You must clear your mind—purify your mind. You can't do that by "wining and whiskeying" yourself too much. And lay off the beer and the blunts during this season of isolation and social distancing. Let today's communion and its symbolism and meaning help to change your habits. Drink water. Do something good every day. Be good and kind to others. Always say "Thank You" and don't gossip about people. Meditate and pray during this time of isolation. Walk outside with your mask on, read a book, read a novel, read history and science. Read a comic book. But, for the sake of sanity and spiritual growth, read *something* every day!

Whenever the church re-opens, let's be more purified than we were before the coronavirus forced us to shut our doors. Let us return whenever it's safe as a more spiritual, pure-hearted, and purified people than the whole time we were in church, taking it all for granted. Let our love for the church, the people and the place, the sanctuary at Second Baptist, Idlewood Avenue, be made stronger so that when the doors open again after the dangers of this virus have faded into oblivion, we will be forever grateful for the church that God has given us and never again will anyone have to beg and barter with us about going and coming to church. I know that you love God, and you love God's church because we all have determined that the work of ministry and the work of the church must go on and I thank God for what you have done and continue to do.

And now the text says, "Now that you have purified your souls by your obedience to the truth so that you have genuine mutual affection, love one another deeply from the heart" (1 Peter 1:22, NRSV). It is not enough for me to love you, but you must love me, too. Mutual love is a "quid pro quo" love. It is a "you scratch my back, I scratch your back" kind of love. It is reciprocal love. This is a love that goes in both directions. It is not a "one way" love. Mutual love is when people feel the same way about each other. "Love one another deeply from the heart." Wow. This is godly love. Mutual love is deep. Mutual love is a joy-filled love. Mutual love is truthful love. It is the deep love of a mother and father. It is the love of God; a love that gave us Jesus Christ. The love of a mother and father is the closest thing I can think of to the love of God. It is the perfect analogy and correlative to the agapeic love of God.

IX. On Love

"Above all, maintain constant love for one another, for love covers a multitude of sins" (I Peter 4:8, NRSV). I've been thinking that the spirit of American chattel slavery lives on not just in the South, but across this country, from sea to shining sea. The recent murders by police of Ahmaud Arbery in Georgia, Breonna Taylor in Louisville, and George Floyd in Minneapolis have helped some Black people to acknowledge and understand the fact that racism is alive and well and living everywhere we breathe. It is as dominant and ever-present and as deadly as the coronavirus.

Now, I've been saying this in sermonic messages and academic lectures for thirty years and I've had difficulty in getting our people to understand and accept this. As a matter of fact, it has been Black people who have said to me that they don't want to hear any more about Black pain and suffering. Well, it cannot be avoided, and it can't be swept under the rug any longer. The evidence is ubiquitous.

The continued senseless murders of Black people by police is a national crime and a public health emergency—a continuation of the slavocracy. Derek Chauvin appeared to get a "charge," a satanic and demonic satisfaction, from publicly killing, murdering a Black man. This was done in broad daylight while cellphone cameras were rolling and people—including children—in the street were begging him to stop. This police lynching, causing a forty-six-year-old Black man to call on his mama and to say "I can't breathe," makes me so aggrieved and angry that I become speechless. All the police officers, all four of them and hundreds of others, need to be charged with and convicted of murder.

For so long Black people have been docile and silent while the smoldering embers of anguish and anger continue to burn and the rage against racism has been quelled by our abiding love. Well, no longer can the lid be held on the pot. The pressure cooker cannot contain the heat, so the only language we can speak during this oppression is one of revolt and riots. Nobody seems to have been willing to listen to the pleas of our people. Black people are dying at alarming rates from the coronavirus and myriad diseases. We are the ones working and laboring in impossible places where there is no protection, no social distancing, no regard for our poverty, our struggles in schools and on the front lines. This man, George Floyd, Black and beaten down, had lost his job and simply wanted a pack of cigarettes purchased with a "so-called" counterfeit twenty-dollar bill. Four White cops responded to a call about a counterfeit twenty-dollar bill, and he is killed, murdered on the spot. This is crazy because his death is, in fact, about something else. It's about power and violence and it's about White supremacy and racism. It's about injustice and hate and the continued sovereignty of white folks.

While the scripture encourages us to "maintain constant love for one another, for love covers a multitude of sins," I can only think that we as Black people have been and are a loving people. And we have allowed our love for this country and our love of Whites to keep us quiet and docile for too long. We have allowed our Sunday-school religion and the slave masters of the airways—from Oral Roberts to hundreds of Black conservative evangelical preachers and teachers—to keep us quiet and content, suffering more and more, and wrongfully comparing it to Christ's as a justification for its continuation.

Well, our love has covered the sins of our oppressors for too long. And their sins have been multitudinous. We know how it feels to be discriminated against, to be harassed, to be second-guessed and overlooked. We have borne the heat of the night and the heat of the day. We have felt and seen sorrow and sadness. "We've been 'buked and we've been scorned.'" And there was something about the expression of "hedonistic pleasure" on the face and in the body language of the murderous police officer that made me realize again that this White man sees himself as a "sovereign" god who can take the life of a grown Black man at will. The slavocracy lives on in the police and in the justice system. Critical Race Theory must be taught in every Black church and every Historically Black College and University in America.

This scripture text—"above all, maintain constant love for one another"—should help us understand that the protests we see, taken together, are in fact acts of love for one another. No longer can we sit back in silence while our people are treated like dogs. These protests against police murders of Black people can only be seen as showing love for one another in a way that we haven't done before. The pain and the suffering can no longer be contained. We know that Black people love Whites, but now we are beginning to show that we love one another.

ENDNOTES

1   For more on Fannie Lou Hamer's extraordinary life, see Kay Mills's *This Little Light of Mine: The Life of Fannie Lou Hamer* (Lexington, Kentucky: University Press of Kentucky, 2007).
2   See Walter Benjamin, *Illuminations* (New York: Schocken Books, 1968) and also Ludwig Wittgenstein, *Tractatus Logico-Philosohicus* (London: Routledge and Kegan Paul, 1963).
3   Black people's renewed or sustained hope was, of course, demonstrated mightily in the struggles of the Civil Rights Movement. See Taylor Branch's *Parting the Waters: America in the King Years 1954-63* (New York: Simon and Schuster, 1989).

BIBLIOGRAPHY

Benjamin, Walter. *Illuminations*. New York: Schocken Books, 1968.
Branch, Taylor. *Parting the Waters: America in the King Years 1954-63*. New York: Simon and Schuster, 1989.
Mills, Kay. *This Little Light of Mine: The Life of Fannie Lou Hamer*. Lexington, KY: University Press of Kentucky, 2007.
Proctor, Samuel D. *"How Shall They Hear?": Effective Preaching for Vital Faith*. King of Prussia, PA: Judson Press, 1992.
Proctor, Samuel D. *Samuel D. Proctor: My Moral Odyssey*. King of Prussia, PA: Judson Press, 1989.
Wittgenstein, Ludwig. *Tractatus Logico-Philosophicus*. London: Routledge and Kegan Paul, 1963.

CHAPTER FIVE
This Just In: Peace Is Not More Important than Truth

Shannon Travis

No one community holds the title for keeping the biggest secrets or telling the biggest lies. Ever since Adam and Eve shattered their state of innocence and bliss in the Garden of Eden, human beings have kept their forbidden fruit off trees of community knowledge. But despite all "races" being well versed in keeping secrets, the African-American community has a unique history with it. During slavery in North America, Africans and their descendants harbored secrets to avoid plantation brutality and even escape from it. In the Civil Rights era, activists used secret meetings and clandestine codes to register to vote and otherwise organize against White oppression. And in modern politics, black politicians and supporters deploy covert tactics as political strategy. What's more, the need to confront societal pressures, avoid negative impressions, and cope with weighty expectations has caused African-Americans to develop and maintain a culturally-specific style of keeping things on the hush.

My journey—and that of my family—highlights these truths. My father, mother, brother, sister and I were taught (and deeply tied ourselves to) that most revered African-American tradition: what happens in the family, stays in the family, even if the trauma of silence plunges you into darkness or breaks you into pieces. As for me, my road to success—in the Ivy League, in the highest halls of journalism, and in the rarified air of entrepreneurship—while spectacular, wound through some dark alleys where secrets and lies thrive.[1]

In most cases, my actions bore only personal consequences. But there were times when my work as a political reporter, covering the three branches of government and their most senior members, clashed with my craving to operate as my true self. There were even times when the consequences of this behavior risked national security.

I know others whose actions are similarly extreme. Some deploy smoke screens to shroud things at the core of their identity, concealing their innermost feelings and desires from people who believe they know them best—family, friends, loved ones, colleagues. Others use public personas to hide private behaviors. Still others go to great lengths to shield their shame. In nearly all cases, they convince themselves that a cloak-and-dagger life is necessary to maintain a relationship, career, family ties, or positive public opinion. But I have learned that most secrets are not bombshells. Instead, the keepers of secrets often traffic in them out of personal indulgence. For, as highly evolved as the Black community is—on economic, political, cultural, historic, artistic, and other issues—it can be downright primeval in the practice of openness and acceptance.

I have studied my past to see how these issues play out in my own family. One story involves my grandmother's boyfriend, Phillip. He was a hard-nosed Southerner who, like many Chicagoans, had migrated north to the city. I remember his being regularly drunk and somewhat abusive. And I remember he would touch and "tickle" me inappropriately when no one else was around. To be honest, my youth and the passage of time render the memory opaque, so there is much I cannot remember. I was around three years old at the time. I cannot recall exactly where it would happen in my grandmother's house on the Southside of Chicago. Or how I'd react and what he'd say to quiet me. But I am clear on one thing: my hazy memories of Phillip's inappropriate touching are not anxieties I seeded in my own spirit.

According to psychologists, this is not uncommon. "Recovered memories" is how the International Society for Traumatic Stress Studies puts it. Many adults somehow recall their sexual abuse from the perspective of very young victims (particularly between ages 1 and 3.) Whether or not they remember specific details of the trauma is an open question. But what's often true is they are certain it happened—as I am. My own explanation is that a child's tender brain often can't assign events the magnitude they deserve. How could a child remember the significance of something if he or she is too young to know what's normal and what's not? I also believe that predators, like Phillip, innately understand this—that youth offers the perfect opportunity to keep a secret unseen, unspoken, or unbelieved.

While this is disturbing, in my mind it's still not the most distressing thing. That an older man would victimize me, as a child, is one thing. That I, as an older man now, would still find it hard to reveal and discuss this with my family is more tragic. As an adult, why have I carried shame over something that happened to me as a child—something I had no choice in or control over? Perhaps this too requires psychological explanation. But, here again, I'd offer my own theory: recalling trauma to relieve the pain is something my family shuns. "The past is the past" or "Just pray on it" are admonitions I've heard countless times. This same reluctance applies to another, more memorable trauma that, to this day, is mostly off limits for family dissection.

My father, Marshall, was a stoic, humorous man with a wide smile, hearty laugh, and outsize personality. Just about everyone who met him liked him. Socially, he was the life of the party. And in our family, he was a happy warrior in times of ease and struggle alike. He'd grown up in Louisiana, surrounded by siblings and extended family, but his mother passed away when he was a teenager. So his aunt, who'd been living in Chicago, came to move his brother, sister, and him to the city so that they could live with her. From what I understand, the experience was mostly good for him.

In Chicago he met my mother and after a few years of courtship, they married. He was 19, she was 18. Not long afterwards, my brother and sister were born. By the time I came along, they were seven and four years old, respectively. At one point, my father started running marathons in races around the city. He was a steady provider for his family, spending nearly 30 years as a blue-collar worker, mostly for General Foods. I can still recall my excitement when he'd bring home gallons of barbecue sauce or new flavors of Kool-Aid that the other kids on the block would have to wait to try. Purplesaurus Rex Grape was my favorite. From everything I know, we were a solidly middle-class family, at times struggling to make ends meet, but relatively happy.

Except for the darkness. I don't know when it started or how old I was, but specific scenes endure. My father would come home—from work, from drinking, from wherever—and verbally and physically abuse my mother. Never us, his three children. Only her. Each nightmare seemed endless. I still hear the boom in his voice and the terror in her screams—sounds that often woke me from my sleep. It happened mostly at night.

I hated this version of him. I was a typical "mama's boy," incessantly sympathetic to anything happening to her. Once, after years crying from a distance, I'd had enough. I was a teenager by then and a rush of adrenaline convinced me that my wiry frame could stop my father's impending attack. So I went to the back porch, where the fight was unfolding, and told him—quite clearly—to "Stop!" I prepared myself to make him do so. Shocked but emboldened, my father looked at me with wild eyes. "Shannon, I will fuck you up!", he shouted. I retreated. At some point, the fight ended, as they always did, and the episode was over.[2]

In those years, I didn't understand that drug addiction was his demon. But, as a young man, I watched him transform his life. Not only did he join Narcotics Anonymous to free himself from drugs but, as part of his own recovery, he helped other addicts do the same. Countless others. He would travel throughout Chicago and parts of the country "sponsoring," mentoring, and guiding those who were saddled with the same demons. He would speak at NA National

Conventions. Men would travel to our home and thank him tearfully. They would tell us, his family, how much he'd helped them get their lives back.

Let me explain why I feel so comfortable writing about something so private: my father was not ashamed of his past. Instead, he was extremely public about his journey. He would often refer to himself as an "addict" to remind us, and perhaps himself, that you're never truly free from the disease. He would proudly tell people, sometimes strangers, of his struggles. I remember his avoiding foods such as Bourbon Barbecue sauce, beer-battered chicken, or tequila-grilled shrimp, to guard his sobriety. Even a trace of liquor, he would say, could reignite one's addiction. He was determined to stay clean, and I trust with my entire spirit that he did.

Sometime before his death, I was on an insignificant visit home. He'd asked me to clear some morning time so we could go have breakfast, just he and I. We went to the IHOP near our house in suburban Chicago, where he and my mother had moved after they retired. I was in my 30's, and I loved this Dad—caring, sensitive, reflective. We'd have normal father-son outings. We especially loved going to the Army Thrift Store to find old things that were new to us. But for this particular breakfast, I had no idea what was about to happen.

Over coffee, pancakes, bacon, and eggs, my father asked for my forgiveness. He went further than he'd ever gone before in detailing the darkness of his disease—things he'd done for drugs, things that he was ashamed of, secrets he'd kept, lies he'd told. But he especially wanted to acknowledge—atone for—the abuse he'd served up to his family all those years. It was a significant step in his recovery, and one that was years in the making.

"Shannon, I'm sorry. I'm asking if you can forgive me," he said. I could hardly muster words through choked-up tears. Even in this powerful moment, I still didn't want the waitress or other customers to know what was going on. Of course I could forgive what had happened, I calmly told him. But it was hard to forget. Certain scenes still haunted me. He understood. We commiserated, together. In the end, what I critically needed him to know was that I was extremely proud of the man he'd become.

He'd been through the depths of drug-induced despair. He'd cleaned himself up through sheer determination, family support, and faith in God. He'd helped others battle their demons and take back their lives. He'd traveled the country teaching about addiction. He'd apologized to his family for the things he'd done. He never left us, was always a provider. He'd given his life to God. As for my mother, I'd watch him respect, protect, and dote over her in ways that even true gentlemen might study. They remained together until his death, for nearly 30 years.

To me, my father is a hero. How many people could do what he did? His story is worth discussing, disseminating, celebrating, perhaps a tool to inspire. So why does my family resist even talking about it? Why do some view it more as a cause for shame rather than celebration?

One weekend in 2005, while I was visiting home on a random trip from New York, the diabetes he'd long battled took his life. He died unexpectedly in the bed he shared with my mother—but in my arms. It was the middle of the day. Mom stood behind me in the doorway, screaming hysterically. I fanned out my body to cover him, to shield her eyes from what was happening—Dad, in my hands, passing from this world. He took his last breaths as I held his head.

Because he was a God-fearing Christian, I truly believe my father made it into heaven. But I also tell myself that it's because he'd released the secrets of his past. When my time comes, I hope the same is true of me. But, to do that, I believe, requires similar efforts of atonement and letting go of shame in my own life. That would include traveling back down those alleys that wound through my professional life.

For 12 years, I was a Black man working in the highest echelons of journalism. This is noteworthy because newsrooms chronically suffer from a lack of diversity. According to one study by the American Society of News Editors, only about 7 percent of newsroom employees are Black, although other studies put that number somewhat higher. My own experience suggests that only a small number advance from local news and lesser-known publications to work at the most recognized and respected outlets—the print news trifecta of the *Wall Street Journal*, the *New York Times*, and the *Washington Post*; the three mainstream news outlets of ABC, CBS, and NBC; the most highly rated cable news channels, Fox News, MSNBC, and CNN; and the biggest online news sites.[3]

I arrived at CNN not even weeks after graduating from the Columbia University Graduate School of Journalism in 2003. A recruiter named Kelvin Davis had seen potential in me during a random meeting at an on-campus career fair. I was 32 years old at the time, having already spent nine years as an engineer in New York City. Transitioning into news would be a dramatic career change. But journalism, I believed, was my true calling, a love affair that began after I first saw Ed Bradley's awesome reporting aura on *60 Minutes*.[4]

I'd been chosen for the CNN Masters Fellowship, a 6-person work experience composed of graduates and students from top journalism and business schools. Three fellows would dive into the business of news, media, and entertainment, rotating throughout units at CNN and TBS, while two others and I would rotate throughout the news and editorial units at CNN and HLN. It was a 12-week summer fellowship. Although the experience would be immersive, there would be no specific guarantee of a job at the end of the program.

I eagerly left my $60,000-per-year job—more than I'd ever made at the time—to earn $1,000 per week for 12 weeks. "What if I'm not offered a job?" I thought. My reassurance: I'd give the universe veto power over my decision and return back to engineering, if necessary. The fellowship was at CNN's flagship Atlanta headquarters. I'd never lived in the South, so that, too, was a bonus. Shortly after my parents watched me walk across the stage on Columbia's Butler Lawn, I confidently packed up and moved in early June.

Atlanta was an exotic and magical place—big enough for one to disappear in, yet small enough for the waitress at the popular Thumbs Up Diner to remember your name. It also offered the chance to write a new professional chapter, wherein I could ignite my new career toward an unexpected high. And the city represented still other things: an immersion in African-American history, art, cuisine, music, sports, politics, and general black excellence.

Near the end of my fellowship, I was offered a job. The President of CNN himself, a truly gracious man named Jon Walton, arranged it. I'd met him in various meetings and events designed to expose the CNN Fellows to upper management. I believe he eyed my potential and promise. One day, I was in a one-on-one meeting with him, talking about my professional background and goals; days later, Human Resources offered me a job. I happily took it. I would be a writer for two shows: *CNN Live Today* for three days of the week and *CNN Saturday/Sunday Morning* for the other two. Daryn Kagan and Leon Harris anchored the first show. My weekend show had a rotating crew of anchors, including Anderson Cooper in his early days at the network. Both jobs were on the graveyard shift, roughly 2 a.m. to 10 a.m. The more impressive and experienced writers worked on dayside programs, so these hours offered the opportunity for new writers like me to stand out. But there was a price: the sacrifice of my Friday and Saturday nights.

I survived on pots of cheap coffee and grit. My job was to write scripts for air: show opens, reporter intros, news packages, 30-40 second news "tells," "Coming up" teases—all read or steered by the shows' anchors. As a writer, your Executive Producer expects you to get news to air first or fast, but truth and accuracy were king. At any given moment, hundreds of thousands of people watched CNN, if not millions. As the "most trusted name in news," the network was a place where facts, breathed to life by an anchor's words, had to be bulletproof. Knowing how to gather complicated, sometimes voluminous, facts; breaking them down to digestible chunks of information; making sure every word was accurate and doing this at record speed were skills few writers possessed.

Within the pressure-cooker newsroom environment, you earn your stripes by meeting these must-haves. But you earned real praise by being creative. Nearly everyone took notice of a memorable turn of phrase in a script, a creative on-screen news headline, or a colorful and concise show open. I excelled at these things. My bosses regularly offered, "Excellent intro, Shannon," "Great banner," and "You wrote that news script fast and creatively." I appreciated the praise, and my career began to take off, especially after the US found a disheveled dictator deep in a ditch.

In March of 2003, three months before I arrived at CNN, the United States invaded Iraq. US political leaders and the military/intelligence complex said that Iraq possessed weapons of mass destruction. This was two years after the 9/11 attacks. With the country still reeling, President George W. Bush's administration settled on some swaggering diplomacy. It vowed the US would not tolerate tyrannical regimes possessing chemical, biological, and possibly nuclear weapons. The invasion was America's promise to destroy the supposed stockpile and "decapitate" Iraq's leadership, according to administration officials. But instead of finding troves of dangerous weapons, American, British, and partner coalition troops were met by insurgents who began a protracted battle bathed in blood. "Mission Accomplished," the president's early overreach on May 1st, was farce in the face of the realities on the ground — bloodthirsty fighters using crude tools of war, such as explosive vests and suicide cement trucks; and the bodies of US and coalition troops piling up, a phenomenon the administration had not expected. Meanwhile, Iraq's feared and notorious leader, Saddam Hussein, was nowhere to be found, despite being America's number one target.

It was the kind of fast-moving, multi-layered story custom-made for cable news. And there I was, still early in my tenure, working day and night along with my colleagues, mastering each day's developments to inform my writing and making a name for myself.[5] Then, on a relatively warm Atlanta night in December, Hussein was pulled from the earth.[6]

It was overnight and I was hungover. I loved my job, but I hated the hours. I was young. Sacrificing my Friday and Saturday nights was not something I did happily. So I'd often go rogue, forgoing my 6 p.m. bedtime to hit Atlanta's many nightclubs. After hours of partying, I'd head straight to work. On a slow news night, you could sleep a bit in the near empty newsroom or, at least, rest easy. But there would be no rest when one of the world's most wanted men was finally captured.

Our internal news alerts blared Hussein's capture near 4 a.m. US troops found him in a hole, about six-to-eight feet underground and just wide enough to lie in. Early reports, and subsequent pictures, showed the towering dictator a shell of his former self. The troops found him near Tikrit, his boyhood home. Our team on the ground in Iraq relayed word Hussein was dazed and confused when found. Though he'd had a gun, he did not resist. President Bush wasted little time seizing the moment. "In the history of Iraq, a dark and painful era is over," the president declared on air.

It was a milestone in America's fight for Iraq. And it presented a milestone in my news career at the network. That early morning, despite being tired and hungover, I sprang into action, doing some of my best work ever. Verifying facts. Writing with clarity and passion and purpose and impact. Updating scripts as developments warranted. Packaging the story with the weight and momentousness it deserved. This continued in the ensuing days and weeks. Soon after, I was taken off the "graveyard shift" and assigned to write for the more desirable and talent-discriminating dayside shows. This included *Late Edition with Wolf Blitzer*, the most important show before the primetime lineup.

Though my career elevation was going according to plan, my romantic life was stalled. I was a new face in a new town with a world of dating and sexual opportunities. And yet, my world was a marble. I spent my days plotting and celebrating career success and my nights charting a path through a solitude borne of secrecy.

You see, I was rising to a level of career success that few in my community have ever—and most likely will ever—see. But privately, I was keeping my own secret. At that point, I was attracted to both women and men. I'd long known this, and long hid it from those close to me. I understood that the African-American community was not fully embracing of bisexuality. Many Blacks frown on it in ways they do not frown on infidelity, children born out of wedlock, mental and physical abuse of a partner, economic irresponsibility, or lack of drive toward realizing one's full personal potential. For many in the Black community, being attracted to the same sex is the most unforgivable sin. Back then an ambitious, not fully mature, not fully enlightened Shannon was not about to publicly embrace his truth—and let his job, his family, and others desert him.

In this light, Atlanta offered me something deeper—the chance to explore a side of myself I'd long denied. There were many chances to connect while operating in the shadows. Duggans Sports Bar was a favorite, as were various restaurants-turned-nightclubs in Phipps Plaza and elsewhere. Discreet men like me were not so easy to spot. But no other city I'd lived in offered me the chance to move so freely while maintaining my secret. And then, *he* came.

It was nearly a month after I'd arrived in Atlanta. We made contact via an app quite popular at the time. Though I can't recall our initial discussions, I'll never forget our initial meeting.

It was at a gas station on Peachtree Street. I'd just bought a shiny new toy—a sleek, jet-black Infiniti FX SUV with chrome accents and an all black leather interior, joining other Atlantans in flaunting my success in the streets. I'd just graduated from the top journalism school in the country. I'd obtained the bragging rights that came with CNN employment. And I was a new commodity in the city. So, I must admit, humility was not my strong suit. But when this handsome, masculine, tall, funny man with more charisma than I'd ever known pulled up next to me, I was utterly nervous.

"What's up, man?" he said enthusiastically while jumping in my car. I was interested, but aghast. "Did this man really open my door and jump right in, uninvited?" I thought. "Should I put him out? What if someone sees us?" Yes, we agreed to meet. We did not agree to invade the comfort of each other's cars. And yet, there we were, at the pump not pumping gas, acting as if we'd finally found exactly what we needed.

He was magnetic. His laughs were huge, his compliments flowing with sincerity. When he smiled, it was as if God gifted him pure joy. I was instantly drawn in.

In the immediate days after meeting, we poured into each other. He'd drive to the house I was renting with a roommate off Interstate 20 and Moreland Avenue. I'd go to his new apartment, still absent of furniture, in Buckhead. Each time we met, time would fade. I vehemently did not want to like him. I'd just moved to Atlanta. I enjoyed moving around as an enigma. "It's too soon for a relationship," I told my best friend. And yet, there we were, spending hours sharing, laughing, talking, commiserating. One night, I remember we sat in his apartment on the bare floor, smoking marijuana, feeling the air for particle proof that this was all real.

Years before, I'd read author E. Lynn Harris' seminal work, *Invisible Life*. It was groundbreaking: peeling back the curtain on the lives of otherwise straight men as they grappled with their bisexuality, navigated a complicated existence, and battled the demons that self-torment befriends. The lead character in the novel, Raymond Winston Tyler, Jr., is a conservative, career-driven college senior who dates women, when fate intervenes. He meets Kelvin, the handsome, gregarious, rule-breaking star football player at their university. Though he initially resists, Raymond is drawn to Kelvin.

There is one scene in the book so romantically charged and yet so tragic that, upon reading it, I cried. Raymond and Kelvin, with limited places to meet, retreat to a wintry field on campus. Falling snow and the wide-open space offer cover. Giddy at the chance to be together, they fall on the ground and roll around together in the snow—a moment of bliss before each returned to an individual state of woe. Their actual lives did not allow their infatuation to flourish.

It was as if the book were prophecy. I, too, was a conservative, career-driven Black man whose life took a detour on the road to self-discovery. I, too, was forced to nervously navigate this new existence at Columbia University and in New York City, as the lead character eventually did on his journey. I, too, met a man—my personality polar opposite—who represented something so taboo I couldn't turn away. I was Raymond. My new companion was Kelvin. We, too, were African-American men with secrets to keep. And though we never rolled around in a snowy open field, we, too, sought out safe spaces for short-lived moments, knowing that our infatuation could not flourish under the weight of being Black men.

There were times we would hold hands in the car and drive in silence. Other times, we'd eat at a restaurant, barely looking away from each other. In these moments, our secret was safe. We were safe. Once, we attended an Atlanta Hawks basketball game. We'd been arguing about something, so the tension had followed us. I was trying to keep our voices down, ever the control freak. But in his anger, he yelled something at me. I remember the twin pangs of shock—the sting of his words and knowing that others seated next to us knew they were watching a lovers' fight. I'll never forget the fear I had of strangers' judgment. For a moment, I felt what it was like to be "invisible" no more.

On balance, we grew to something neither of us truly predicted or understood. Although our affair was brief, it informed our entire romantic lives. More importantly, it informed our lives as Black men charting worlds of expectations, demands, assumptions, and beliefs.

I recently spoke with him about the kismet that briefly took over our lives some 20 years ago. He listened as I recalled the most important, private moments. Then, after a brief silence, he offered the most profound response. "Shannon, imagine what might have been, if we had only been brave," he said. It took my breath away. Where we might have been with each other. Where we might have been as African-American men, living our truths, fulfilling our lives.

Looking back, it feels like I denied myself a once-in-a-lifetime rite of passage. In my attraction to men, he was my first true love. It was the first full exploration of a side of myself I'd long kept secret and suppressed. We spent every possible public and private moment together, but we did our best not to be seen. We believed we were strong Black men, and yet, we couldn't pass the ultimate test of strength: being true to ourselves without fear and the weakness it brings.

I can think of no other scene from my past that more clearly proves life's paradox—that I could experience something so intensely beautiful and yet so mournfully tragic. And where should the blame lie—with cowardice and my own limiting fears, or with draconian notions against male-on-male intimacy that I learned while growing up and that are weighted in African-American homophobia?

In his book, *The Mismeasure of Man*, author Stephen Jay Gould writes this: "We pass through this world but once. Few tragedies can be more extensive than the stunting of life, few injustices deeper than the denial of an opportunity to strive or even to hope, by a limit imposed from without, but falsely identified as lying within."

I moved on from Atlanta after two years and made some impressive achievements: being promoted to Senior Writer, Producer, Senior Producer, then National Political Reporter; being on a team that won an Emmy for covering the 2012 presidential election between President Barack Obama and Republican nominee Mitt Romney; traveling with Vice-President Biden for half a year aboard Air Force Two; visiting 47 of 50 states to cover all manner of stories; hosting and co-producing a high-profile CNN documentary; being invited to speak at Harvard, Georgetown Law, Temple University, and other esteemed venues; being accepted to graduate school at Harvard; founding and succeeding in a startup built by my own sweat; being named a Top Entrepreneur to Watch in the US in *Entrepreneur Magazine*. But more success bred more secrecy. I continued to live my personal life out of view. That is, until another dark experience finally brought a stark reality to light.

It was July of 2017. I was standing outside a room in the intensive care unit at the University of Chicago Hospital—afraid to enter. Two sets of sliding glass doors separated me from the inside. I'd made it past the first doors into the anteroom where approved visitors disinfect and put on hospital gowns. But I wasn't sure I could muster the emotional strength to go further. Fear of what I might see—what I might encounter—reduced a 45-year-old man to a frightened little boy. Just on the other side of the glass was my mother, fighting for her life.

In the hallway, a nurse said to me, "Your mother is a very strong woman. I mean, physically strong. She's slowly coming from under the anesthesia. And she's kicking and grabbing very hard. We had to lightly constrain her to the bed."

My mom, Catherine, had just emerged from an over eight-hour surgery to remove a tumor from her brain. During her procedure, every minute in the waiting room—especially the hourly updates—was fraught with fear. But that was nothing compared to the dread of seeing her post-surgery. I walked in.

The room was dimly lit, but aglow with medical equipment that danced and buzzed with watchful light and sound. She lay there prone, with all manner of wires attached to her body and a tube stuck down her throat. She was unquestionably still. For a while, I watched in silence. Then, I took to a chair and began to pray.

Out of nowhere, she awoke. Not in the regular sense of alertness, but in a post-anesthetic haze. From somewhere, she drew strength and almost lunged forward in the bed. She didn't scan the room, as if searching for anyone. She looked directly at me, as if already knowing I was there beside her. With a garbled tongue, but clear message, she spoke words that changed my life.

"*Shannon, let me fight. Let me fight!*" Each time her words slightly louder. She repeated it a few times, as if consciously pushing the most important point she'd ever made.

It was the closest thing to a miracle that I had ever witnessed. She should not have been able to speak at all, and definitely not so pointedly. She knew I was there. She knew the state she was in and declared she was ready for battle. I stood there in shock. What experience do you draw from to deal with a situation like this? What should you do when your mother—who, according to the nurses, is still fully anesthetized—rises from her bed like a messiah?

I grabbed her hand, her grip like a vise. "Yes, Mom. I will let you fight. I will let you fight! I love you. Fight!" Tears streamed down my face. "Jesus, I know you are here with us!", I said over and over.

With this, she calmly retreated, lay back down, and slipped back into whatever slumber she was supposed to be under. It was yet another time I'd been visited by a macabre moment that, also, was strangely beautiful. My mother who'd experienced so much death—of her husband, son, daughter, siblings—vowing not to join them, just yet. A son, who'd gone to Chicago and put his entire life on hold to care for her, vowing to let her fight—and to fight on, with her. All of this just moments after God allowed doctors to save her life.

I have never publicly recounted this scene. In five years, there have been only a few times I've even allowed myself to remember it. And yet, it's a memory with powerful symbolism.

My mother could have left this earth without knowing the full truth about my life. We were the last remaining members of our five-member nuclear family. My 27-year-old sister had died in 1993 from leukemia, even after I'd undergone a harrowing yet hopeful bone marrow transplant which temporarily saved her life. Four years later, my 31-year-old brother died from dermatomyositis, an incurable degenerative inflammatory disease whose symptoms include rashes and the gradual loss of all muscle function. Combine this with God's choosing my father after a years-long battle with diabetes.

My mother and I had lost the core of our family. Now, here I stood, facing the potential of losing her. In that moment and the days after her sensitive brain surgery, a procedure with an unfavorable percentage of success and full recovery, I wondered: would I go to my grave—or see yet another loved one go to theirs—guarding secrets? It was an awakening. If the true impact of secrets and lies was the building of foolish fortresses between my loved ones and me, then I wanted no more of it. After waiting awhile for my mother to fully recover, which she did, I revealed my secret to her.

She was instantly accepting, but far from ecstatic. She'd prefer I not reveal this to others. I am 50 years old now, not exactly in need of parental permission. But I am respectful of her wishes. I have not told other members of the family, her friends, or others close to her. "I feel like that's your personal business," she often says to me. In other words, keep your secrets close.

There is a scene from the TV show *Pose* that might offer guidance. It is, of course, the Emmy-winning and groundbreaking show on FX about the struggles of Black and Brown members of the LGBTQ community in 1980s/90s New York—and their underground ball culture. In the scene, the protagonist "Pray Tell" returns home to Pittsburgh to reveal to his mom and family that AIDS will rob him of his future within about six months. Throughout the episode, he rails against the Black church that, he believes, drove him away from his family into an underground existence. He scolds his mother for forcing upon him an intense religious adherence that had prompted self-hate. He taunts her for turning a blind eye when he revealed that her husband—his stepfather— had molested him.

The drama builds to a crescendo that finally ends in an honest moment between the mother and son. While watching television in her bedroom, Pray Tell says, "You know what I love about you people? Every one of you has a secret that you think the other people don't know about. But everybody knows everything."

The mother wastes no time responding: "Because peace is more important than truth."

It was a sublime moment of art imitating life. Is there any question that many African-American mothers, fathers, or families value peace—and, might I add, privacy—over truth? Is there any question that this carries a price? As an Emmy winner myself, I'd offer a script change: sometimes your truth *is* your peace. And that is more important. Until more of us accept this, or at least attempt to understand it, I fear we'll continue to value secrecy and embrace darkness over sanity and the sanctity of light.

ENDNOTES

1   For a provocative conversation regarding the success of black people in traditionally or ostensibly "white" spaces, read Randal D. Pinkett and Jeffrey Robinson, *Black Faces in White Places: 10 Game Changing Strategies to Achieve Success and Find Greatness* (Nashville, TN: HarperCollins Leadership, 2018).
2   It appears that young sons often want to rescue their mothers who are abused, but are seemingly rarely successful in such endeavors. In this vein, see also Will Smith's powerful memoir, *Will* (New York: Penguin Press, 2021).
3   For very helpful additional background, see Hank Whittemore's *CNN, The Inside Story: How a Band of Mavericks Changed the Face of Television News* (New York: Little, Brown and Company, 1990).

4   The role of the media vis-à-vis people of color in general, and black people in particular, is a fascinating history in itself. A well sourced historical treatment can be found in Juan Gonzalez and Joseph Torres's book, *News for All the People: The Epic Story of Race and the Media* (Brooklyn, NY: Verso, 2012).

5   See, for reference on writing and revision, Richard Lanham's very useful text, *Revising Prose* (New York: Pearson Longman, 2006).

6   For additional insights into powerful firsthand accounts surrounding this pivotal moment in relatively recent US geopolitical history, see the book by Lt. Col. Steve Russell, *We Got Him! A Memoir of the Hunt and Capture of Saddam Hussein* (New York: Pocket Books, 2012).

BIBLIOGRAPHY

Gonzalez, Juan and Torres, Joseph. *News for All the People, The Epic Story of Race and the American Media*. Brooklyn, NY: Verso, 2012.

Lanham, Richard. *Revising Prose*. New York, NY: Pearson Longman, 2006.

Pinkett, Randal D. and Robinson, Jeffrey. *Black Faces in White Places: 20 Game Changing Strategies to Achieve Success and Find Greatness*. Seattle, WA: Amazon, 2018.

Russell, (Lt. Col.) Steve. *We Got Him! A Memoir of the Hunt and Capture of Saddam Hussein*. New York, NY: Pocket Books, 2012.

Smith, Will, with Mark Manson. *Will*. New York, NY: Penguin Press, 2021.

Whittemore, Hank. *CNN, The Inside Story: How A Band of Mavericks Changed the Face of Television News*. New York, NY: Little, Brown and Company, 1990.

CHAPTER SIX
Paused on Fast-Forward: Memoir in Unrequited Anxiety

F. Keith Slaughter

Lately, I have been engulfed in an ocean of despair. The pandemic has taken its toll on me. My weaknesses and frailties have been exposed. My mind is not trustworthy. My body argues with my spirit. I lurch toward death while desperately holding on to the future—tomorrow—a tomorrow that never comes. It is as if the world is paused on fast-forward. I feel thrust and hurled into a frightening and horrific present, but it appears no one is afraid but me.

The Coronavirus Era

I had intuited the ominous premonition of impending doom since the beginning of the Trump Era. I could feel the zeitgeist demand movement toward a more uncertain future as I consumed and analyzed news, social media, and other forms of information. With Trump came a bolder and more bizarre atmosphere in America. Whites were emboldened to be more intense and expressive of their hatred of Black people. Republicans, led by Kentucky senator Mitch McConnell, advanced an anti-Black, white supremist agenda. "Alternative facts" were introduced as an antiseptic explication of the justification of whites' deception of themselves and the world. Many Black and anti-racist white people, who embraced ideals of democracy and justice, informally united under the contrived and complicated banner of Black Lives Matter. The rise of white militia hate groups was evident throughout the country. There was a 100% increase in gun sales in the US from November of 2019 through March of 2020. Apparently, I was not the only one to notice the conflictual state of our country, as some whites openly expressed fear of "Black Lives Matter" protesters (whom the data show were responsible for zero deaths of persons) while unarmed Black people were being mowed down by white police and white vigilante gunfire. According to a *Washington Post* article dated May 13, 2021, "Although half of the people shot and killed by police are White,

Black Americans are shot at a disproportionate rate. They account for less than 13 percent of the US population, but are killed by police at more than twice the rate of White Americans. Hispanic Americans are also killed by police at a disproportionate rate."[1,2,3]

In March of 2020 I felt the cataclysmic shift that I dreaded would come. I did not know exactly what was on the horizon, but I knew that this country and our world were about to change. The educational journey to Brazil into which my doctoral students and I had invested two years of preparation was unceremoniously canceled. My sons were college students—one a freshman at Clark-Atlanta University and the other a senior at Morehouse College. I climbed the stairs, interrupted their video game, and began to share my grave concerns about the future of the world with them. I told them that the world as they knew it was about to change forever. "We must be strong and protect each other," I said with a sense of gravitas, "because we are on the precipice of some dangerous times." They began to laugh mockingly as if I were an anencephalus moron. Clearly, neither believed my prognostication. They know that their father is given to hyperbolic excursions into what may be considered the absurd. However, they soon discovered that the "old man" was not "trippin'" or "cappin'" this time.

> March 9, 2020: Confirmed and presumptive cases of virus in Georgia increase to 17. Fulton County announces schools and offices would close the next day.

> March 10, 2020: Georgia races to respond to coronavirus as number of possible cases rises to 22, including the first case reported in South Georgia.

> March 11, 2020: The World Health Organization declares coronavirus is now a global pandemic.

> March 11, 2020: NBA suspends season as player tests positive for coronavirus. Savannah cancels St. Patrick's Day festival and parade.

> March 11, 2020: After President Donald Trump announces restrictions on travel to Europe, Atlanta-based Delta Air Lines prepares for a big hit to business.

> March 12, 2020: News breaks on several fronts. As Georgia reports the state's first death from COVID-19, the Georgia Legislature suspends its session. Additional metro Atlanta schools suspend in-person classes. And

the NCAA cancels the Atlanta Final Four basketball tournament. Gov. Brian Kemp orders most state employees to work from home.

March 13, 2020: Gov. Brian Kemp announces he will declare a public health emergency and call for a special legislative session to marshal the state's response. In Augusta, the Master's golf tournament is postponed.[4]

March 16, 2020: Gov. Brian Kemp orders Public K-12 schools and colleges closed through the end of March. Atlanta Mayor Keisha Lance Bottoms issues executive order limiting gatherings to 50 people. Major League Baseball delays the start of its season.

March 17, 2020: TSA closes some checkpoints at Hartsfield Jackson after a screener tests positive for coronavirus.

March 19, 2020: Atlanta Mayor Keisha Lance Bottoms orders the closing of all in-person dining in restaurants.

Then came the shut-down of America. Everything stopped. Everything. One Saturday in mid-March, a few of the members of our church met to determine how we would respond to the fear, uncertainty, and dread that the pandemic brought. We were aware of the fact that public schools were now closed. That meant that school cafeterias were closed. Our church was, in fact, closed; but, because of our commitment to care for our community, we decided that we could be most helpful in this crisis by serving meals to the children in our neighborhood.

Our church had a thriving pre-pandemic food pantry. Many of the residents in the historic Pittsburg community of Atlanta knew of the food ministry that our church had operated for the past five years. We had garnered a reputation for sharing and hospitality. Since its inception, our church had provided 25-lb boxes of fruits, vegetables, meats, canned goods, desserts, and beverages each Sunday after our worship service. The food pantry was created for everyone—not just the unsheltered and people who would be considered poor. The idea was that all of us are poor. We are the Beloved Community. We all need help financially, so the boxes of food were given to everyone in an attempt to show grace and hospitality to all. None among us could walk into a supermarket and walk out with a 25-lb box of food without spending some money. There is a way in which the Beloved Community Church gave offerings *to* the people without expecting an offering *from* the people.

Because businesses were shut down, people were out of work, and children were out of school, we expanded our food sharing ministry to include larger boxes of food, and emergency boxes for anyone who requested one, any day of the week. I was aware of the shame, discomfort, and vulnerability that Black people feel when we must receive help from outside our homes. There is a vulgar admixture of gratefulness, anger, and humiliation associated with receiving something that we did not work for. I think the vestigial psycho-forms of enslavement make shame a prominent feature of Black self-consciousness.[5] So I insisted that we serve our people with respect, gentleness, and care. Our church began to serve lunch and dinner to the children of the community, three days a week, until it became apparent that the adults needed the hot meals as well. We began to serve lunch and dinner, from 12 to 5 pm each day, to all who graced us with their precious presence. We became "essential personnel" in the war on "Covid." In an instant our church was transformed from a Sunday and Wednesday gathering place into a daily operation. The volunteers in the food pantry and I were stretched to capacity as we responded to the need around us.

Like other churches, we halted all other meetings, except those considered to be "essential"; and the only thing deemed "essential" was feeding our people. I serve a small congregation, but there are many people who benefit from our ministry. After a few weeks of quarantine, I invited our church band to come and make music on Sundays. I wanted to give them an opportunity to continue to play together and to give them a "love gift" that I knew they missed and needed. Informed by my chaplaincy training and experience, I understood the power of the "ministry of presence" in crisis. I wanted community members to know that the church was open to serve. There is a way in which I wanted to convey a commitment of Black consistency in a community gripped by the destabilizing force of young, white gentrification of "one of Atlanta, Georgia's oldest neighborhoods established by African Americans." In 5 years, we had become a trusted ministry in the Pittsburgh community.

The band played and we worshiped until the spring weather became warm enough for us to worship outside. "Open Air Worship" service began as we gathered on the church parking lot in the safety of our cars. The band would play, the choir would sing, I would preach, and we would pretend that all was well. Those who were afraid of coronavirus exposure stayed home and eventually fell away from the congregation. Many members and curious on-lookers came out armed with hand sanitizer, rubber gloves and N95 masks—and some without. Our faces and expressions were concealed. We stopped touching each other because we were socially distanced. The absence of touch and nearness, coupled with the anonymity imposed by the mandatory masking tested my intuition and discernment. I could no longer read the human texts with which I had been familiar. It was a strange and eerie time. The initial uncertainty that I felt was exacerbated by the deceptive and unscrupulous behavior of the then US president. Every day he told a different lie. The *Washington Post* reports that

Trump told an average of 39 lies per day in the last year of his presidency.[6] This character even suggested that people should inject bleach into their bodies as a possible cure for Covid-19. I felt confused and frustrated, afraid and disordered, as I attempted to make sense out of the chaos that existed in and around me.

The seminary where I had spent almost every day of my life for the past 20 years was now closed and the classes that I taught were shifted from in-person to virtual. This was a devastating blow to my routine and my sanity. I had grown accustomed to being in my office space, sharing with my colleagues and students *in vivo*. I now was faced with the grief of losing face-to-face contact with my friends while being barred from the holy ground that I have loved since my foot touched it. I am a "Baby Boomer," born on the cusp of "Generation X." I was an adult when personal computers became commonplace, essential appliances. I was in my mid-30's when the Internet was invented. My business, academic, and interrelational style would be considered "old school."

I grew up in an era where doors were left unlocked and yet the community was secure. As a child, I gleefully skipped down rock roads respectfully greeting the elders who sat in wooden rockers on their rickety front porches. I sat and talked with them and blessed them with my company, and they reciprocated the grace by giving me maybe a slice of watermelon or a nickel to buy candy at Mr. Roosevelt's neighborhood house store. Consequently, I pride myself on my ability to connect authentically with those with whom I work and serve and live. I prefer to walk to my colleagues' offices and discuss work and concerns as opposed to emailing my thoughts. I feel surveilled and intruded upon when I am forced to immediately commit my thoughts to an inerasable, irretrievable format that others outside of those to whom I wish to speak may be privy. It is as though we were thrust into a virtual "panopticon," a space where "the idea that it was possible and desirable to achieve social control through the anonymous and automatic operation of power survived and was embraced." When "Covid" came, my colleagues and I were immediately forced to add technological adroitness to our already difficult areas of expertise. We met via "Zoom" and pretended that we had magically become savvy in the delivery of curriculum and content overnight. It was clear that that was the expectation.

As March turned into May, the academic year concluded with no celebration and no real graduation because everybody was stuck in front of a device. The pandemic lingered and strengthened as people around the world began to die. Then my friends began to die; loved ones passed away without the dignity of a funeral. The therapy and resolution died. This added to my anguish, sadness, and psychological instability. During the summer session I created a course called "Black Thanatology: Death, Dying and Bereavement" wherein I invited my students to address their grief in response to the mortality that we were experiencing.[7]

Meanwhile my family began to suffer. The presence of my 84-year-old mother made me sensitive and hyper-vigilant with reference to who accessed my home. My children were generally uncooperative with the quarantine restrictions. They seemed to think that they enjoyed a type of "Covid immunity" associated with their youth. "Only old folks are dying," they would say, as I reminded them that their mother, my mother (their grandmother), and I are "old." My youngest son suffered most. He no longer lived on campus. The autonomy that he had longed for throughout high school was stifled during the second semester of his freshman year in college at CAU. The elevations and depressions of his personality became more disparate and intense. His undiagnosed bi-polar self was on full display for the family to observe. We were all shaken and confused by his behavior. His mania was irritating, but harmless. His depressive episodes were frightening and disturbing. My wife, my mother, and I seemed to join him on a circuitous journey of sadness, fear, disgust, and relief. We each took our turn expressing our sickness. My elder son became a virtual member of the household as he sought "sane space" in his girlfriend's apartment. The pathology associated with the pandemic obviously followed him into her space. Their arguments were epic. I was just as afraid for my elder son as I was for the younger.

May 25th was the day that began a cosmic social explosion. The epicenter was Minneapolis, Minnesota but the reverberations were felt around the world. On May 25, 2020, I lost a friend and brother that I had never met. His name was George Floyd. On that day the world witnessed via the cell phone video of a Black teenaged girl, Darnella Frazier, a Black man's execution at the hands of police. In a sense, I died with Floyd, while he was resurrected in me.

The execution of Floyd was made all the more palpable and real on the next day, the 26th, when viewers of the video became aware that they had actually witnessed the murder. This was "white police terror snuff porn" at its finest. Initially it was presumed that what we saw was a barbaric arrest wherein murderer Derrick Chauvin kneeled on the neck of George Floyd for 9 minutes and 29 seconds. Major media announced that George Floyd died later from the injury, or from a heart problem, or from an illegal drug that he had induced. The truth is that we all saw with our own eyes his murder by suffocation. The news networks showed his death, over and over again; reminiscent of how Black preachers crucify Christ afresh each Sunday morning. It was not a lynching, but was indeed a crucifixion without benefit of a trial. His trial would come later, after his death; and he would be found not guilty. It was a sacred death that shocked and transfigured many whites into temporarily empathic human beings, and they flooded the streets in protest alongside Black people, responding to a visceral call for justice in America. "Covid Summer" had begun.

"Covid Summer"

After that day in May I began to weep often. Relationships in various and different spheres of my life began to suffer. I began to mentally mutter the lament of Floyd, saying, "Aagh, aagh, I can't breathe, Momma, I can't breathe" intermittently, throughout the day. I didn't give voice to the audition, but I screamed on the inside, "Please, please, please, I can't breathe," in a gruff and raspy mimicry of honor. Floyd's words bounced off the backboard of my brain like a missed shot at the hoop nailed to the wall of my granddaddy's junk house. By the first Sunday in June I was able to preach about it. The sermon is the language that I speak most fluently. Heretofore, I have written extensively about my belief that some of the pain that Black people feel and some of the suffering that Black people experience can be mollified by Black preaching. For me, Black preaching is a group therapy session, a conjure, a healing session, a juju experience with deep bio-psychosocial implications. In the midst of my anger and anguish, I wrote:

> This is not really a sermon, but rather, this is an exhortation—a communication of encouragement for you to rejoice, keep on fighting and realize that you are blessed even when you feel confused and broken and ineffective, unloved and unappreciated. (That's a word for somebody right dare…come on talk to me). My dear beloved sisters and brethren, God has granted us the grace to gather on this day to celebrate God's omnipresence, God's influence, and God's power. I think that it is fair and quite accurate for me to state that the whole world has changed, right before our eyes, as we have all been impacted by a silent, but lethal agent that has killed over 101,000 people in America, caused over 2000 deaths in Georgia and over 250 deaths here in Fulton County. And the numbers continue to climb as we struggle to be safe, keep healthy and stay alive during this latest expression of hell and damnation.

> And, o, my sistren and my brethren, while we find ourselves in the existential struggle to stay alive in the midst of Covid-19, we continue to encounter bloodthirsty crackers who push and beat and punish and murder and exploit us as if we were still enslaved by them. This is nothing new. They been making us sick every since we invited them onto the shores of our motherland, Africa. They been killing us, we just started videoing them while they do it and putting it on the Facebook, the Twitter and the Instagram for the whole world to see. This is nothing new for us; what is new is that our enemies are now totally exposed in their pathologically murderous practices. What is new is that white folks and scary negroes

of every variety now find it appropriate to comment on Black suffering (albeit, with very careful word choices to express their discomfort with the slow-motion torture and murder of another unarmed Black man in a public lynching on national tv). See, I ain't no scared negroe. What's new is that the same message that I have preached, every Sunday for the last 20 years, can now be heard by scary-ass, greedy-ass, comfortable-ass, politricking-ass middle class negroes who think that white supremacy can't touch their privileged Black behinds. What's new is the fact that nothing is really new at all. They been killing us, whenever they get ready, since 1415, and been getting away with it with no payback. What's new is that people finally charged the right price and ain't scared to wait for the receipt.

Let me say this; and listen to me, to what I'm saying, Beloved. Something is changing, but it's not a political change; what we are witnessing is a spiritual transformation. What is changing is Black people's understanding of who we are in God. Black people are coming to understand that God created us to be free and that it is a sin against God for us to sit quietly as subordinate beings beneath the hand of white oppressors and genociders. Black people are learning our value—that we deserve to live, to deserve to be paid for being victimized by white murder and terror in service to the continuance of white supremacy/patriarchy and Black genocide.

Why is it, why is it, why is it that people all over the world are emerging from their places of convenience and comfort to join us in the marching and the protests and other acts of resistance? Why is it that whites who hate and pity us now speak up on our behalf—on behalf of justice and liberation? Why is it that everybody wants to beg our pardon now? It must have become apparent to the world what was proclaimed by sweet Black Jesus, our elder brother—in the 5th chapter of Matthew in the sermon on the mount—and that is, we are blessed! (Point at somebody and tell um, 'we blessed.')

Let me show you what the text says. 'When Jesus saw the crowds, he went up the mountain; and after he sat down, his disciples came to him. 2 Then he began to speak, and taught them, saying: 3 'Blessed are the poor in spirit, for theirs is the kingdom of heaven. 4 Blessed are those who mourn, for they will be comforted. 5 Blessed are the meek, for they will inherit the earth. 6 Blessed are those who hunger and thirst for righteousness, for they will be filled. 7 Blessed are the merciful, for they will receive mercy. 8 Blessed are the pure in heart, for they will see God. 9 Blessed are the peacemakers, for they will be called children of God. 10 Blessed are those who are persecuted for righteousness' sake, for theirs is the kingdom of heaven.

11 Blessed are you when people revile you and persecute you and utter all kinds of evil against you falsely on my account. 12 Rejoice and be glad, for your reward is great in heaven, for in the same way, they persecuted the prophets who were before you.'

It is as if our elder brother sat there on 'the mount of the beatitudes', on the Korazim Plateau, and gazed two thousand and twenty years into the future, saw our situation and pronounced these supreme and superlative blessings on us for such a time as this. (Can y'all feel this?) In essence he says, 'If you broke down, you blessed, if you sad and depressed and drunk and sick and unstable you blessed. If you HIV+, if you got the diabetes, the cancer, the gout or the coronavirus, you blessed. If you homeless, you blessed. If you in the rooming house, the bando or the shelter, you blessed. If you got a home, can't afford it, and won't never own it, but gone pay for it til the day you die, you blessed. If you walking, you blessed, if you wrecked your car and it was your fault, you blessed. If you can catch a ride, the bus, the lyft, the uber or with somebody you got to give some gas money, you still blessed.'

I need you to listen at Jesus suggest to us that because of the fact that we are economically oppressed, because we have been under- and-mis-educated to the point where we must be reeducated; because the people in charge of the world that we live in are dirty, pathological, murderous and deceitful liars, WE ARE BLESSED! Because the police kill us whenever they get ready and get away with it, because we are the last hired and the first fired from a bullshit job where they was already disrespectful and exploitative in the first place, because we have been hated by the haters, killed by the killers, sold by the sellers, enslaved by the slavers, abused by the abusers, we now find ourselves being blessed by the Blessor. (Nigh throw up the power sign, look at somebody 6ft away from you and shout, I'm blessed!).

I got to leave you here. I didn't want to hold you long, it's hot out here and I don't want to bore you, but I just needed to hold you long enough to tell you that God loves us because they hate us, and we are positioned at this moment in time to change the course of history if we could grab a holt of the reality that we are blessed. God loves us. White folks hate us, but they ain't God. We're blessed. We really are. Can I tell you how I know that we are God's blessed, beloved creation? Can I tell you? Well, in verse number 11, I heard Jesus saying, "Blessed are you when people revile you and persecute you and utter all kinds of evil against you falsely on my account." In other words, Jesus is saying, when you are hated without a reason and your enemies try to kill your body and your soul, when people create a lexicon of lies to describe your character, Rejoice, get happy, get glad because your reward will be great; you will be remembered, because we remember those who fight and stand and die for righteousness—right thinking and right action.

Finally, I was in a discussion the other day, with some other pastors and scholars and activists who asked me what I thought Jesus would say if he were right here, right now; and I said that I believe Jesus would say: "Kill me…ain't nothing new…kill me, like you killed Breonna Taylor, kill me, like you killed Sean Reed, kill me, like you killed George Floyd, Stephon Clark, Botham Jean, Sandra Bland, Philando Castile, Nicholas Thomas, Anthony Hill, Samuel DuBose, Jamarion Robinson, Jordan Davis, Tamir Rice, Alton Sterling, Terence Crutcher, Freddie Gray, Michael Brown, Akai Gurley, Laquan McDonald, Eric Garner, Tamir Rice, Amadou Diallo, Martin Luther King, Malcolm X, Medgar Evers, Emmett Till, and millions of other unnamed souls, ancestors, children of Oludumare and servants of Jah, the most high god. Kill me, and I will rise again. The moment we lose our fear of death is the moment we begin to truly live. Kill me, and I will rise again."

I preached this message as an acknowledgment of my belief that we were all standing in a new world. It was actually a message of hope for those who believe in resurrection. I sensed possibilities for revolutionary change in America as the citizenry seemed to be united around ending police terror directed against Black people. Within a week after sharing these words with my congregation, Rayshard Brooks, an unarmed Black man, was murdered by white Atlanta police. His blood was carelessly spilled just 5 blocks away from where our church is located. I passed the site daily on my way to work at the church. I stopped to pray, to pay respect to his spirit and to comfort some of the mourners and protestors who occupied the blood-stained parking lot of the burned-out Wendy's where he was murdered. The streets were flooded with protestors or people who were simply quarantine-fatigued. Each day I was traumatized all the more by the terror and carnage inflicted upon Black people in America.

The noose of the pandemic seemed to strangle my mind. The deaths were unceasing. My best friend, Jeff Moore, my friend and fraternity brother Mike Murrell, my cousin, my uncle, my aunt—classmates, former colleagues, former students, fathers and brothers and mothers of my friends. My grief was unacknowledged. I received no consolation. My soul was mortally wounded. I preached the same sermon at every socially-distanced memorial service, not out of sloth or disrespect, but because I could not focus or concentrate long enough to complete a coherent thought. I preached or rather, re-preached sermons from my homiletic archives like old albums snapping and popping on the turntable reminding me of a different time.

"Covid Winter"

A new academic year began and my students and I were left behind. The technology was perfect because devices are machines. People are not machines. I was unable to connect with my students. I felt like a failure. And then came "Covid Winter." It was the longest winter that I have ever experienced. My church began to suffer immensely. Many of the relationships in which I was deeply invested were strained and broken like a promise of eternity to a one-night stand. In my mind it lasted from October 2020 til May of the following year. It didn't snow in Atlanta, but it was uncharacteristically cold. I stopped my healthy eating regime, I stopped exercising, I couldn't sleep, I felt totally inadequate, insufficient, compromised, and bloated. I cried every day. "I can't breathe, I can't breathe, Momma, please, please, please." My self-medication regimen rendered me zombie-like. My soul was absent. I sent a shell of myself to church, Zoom meetings, and other spaces that I once fully occupied. I often thought of taking my own life. So much for the ministry of presence.

Trump, the 2020 elections, and police murders of Black people dominated the headlines as the new year began. My world was still at a standstill. I could not discern a difference between Democrats or Republicans. After Biden and Harris won, I was relieved, but skeptical, as I nursed an active hermeneutic of suspicion with reference to whites and politicians—especially, white politicians. After the election, Joe Biden credited the Black vote and Black people for his victory. On January 6, 2021, white Republican Trump supporters launched a treasonous domestic terror attack on the US Capitol Building to express their dismay with the outcome of the presidential election and to deter vice-president Mike Pence and the US Senate from certifying the presidential election results. White people actually impaled US capitol police with weaponized flag poles affixed with American flags. Rabid, white Trump sycophants beat, kicked, stomped, tasered, crushed, suffocated, and otherwise assaulted the police like they were niggers, as they (the police) cowered under the force of white privilege and white entitlement fueled by presidential prodding and radical, fanatical right-wing, white nationalist, white evangelical racism and white supremacy. The world looked on with horror and amazement as American democracy was again imperiled by the narcissistic pathological behaviors associated with what Dr. Bobby Wright called "the psychopathic racial personality." And the pandemic continued to rage with no end in sight.

I think that we tend to classify whites on a graduated continuum of good-to-bad, while they all practice, overtly or covertly, or at least benefit from white supremacy as a global system of oppression. I am angered by Black and white theologians, academics, and politicians who co-create a false narrative of the white capacity for compassion. Generally speaking, white Europeans (colonizers and otherwise) are the enemy of Black people, Black freedom, Black liberation, Black health, Black wealth—in a phrase, Black "beingness." I resent being "mindfucked" into thinking that I am somehow wrong to hate white people (who systematize and operationalize hate towards me), while it is quite permissible for me to hate myself and others who look like me and indeed to participate in my own self-destruction and the genocide of my own people. I am not deluded. Gil Scott Heron said it's "Winter in America":

> "And now It's winter
> Seem like winter in America
> The time when all of the healers done been killed…"[8]

(Gil Scott Heron said more, by the way, about people not fighting, and brutality; and, simply put, it is worth reading or listening to "Winter in America" in its entirety). The introduction of a Covid-19 vaccine was a central phenomenon of "Covid Winter." The new Biden-led government assured the American public[9] that a vaccine for the virus would soon be available for everyone.[10] But this is America. Elites, politicians, physicians, and other preferred whites received the vaccine first. Many Black people who wanted the vaccine couldn't access it. Many didn't want it—and many still refuse to take the vaccine that is now readily available to most Americans. I don't trust whites, in general; and I certainly don't trust government agencies, like the CDC, or privately-owned pharmaceutical companies or "big pharma." As leader of our church, it fell upon me to craft a statement explaining the "religious rationale" for our refusal to take the vaccine in any of its formulations: "Because of our interpretation of the Principles and Virtues of Ma'at, which are stated and published Guiding Ideals of our faith, we espouse the religious position, belief and practice, based on an ethical stance and moral conviction, against the receiving of certain chemicals in our bodies for the purposes of non-immediate or non-emergency life support or preservation." In this statement I assert our freedom as Black people to control our Black bodies, honor our skepticism and suspicion of whites, and express our ability to make decisions based upon Black truth and reality. One question guided my decision to take this stance on this critical issue: if whites have lied to Black people about everything else, why should they be trusted to be truthful about the coronavirus vaccine and its potential impact on the health of Black people? As Chuck D of Public Enemy proclaimed, "Can't Truss It." [11]

More than a year had passed since the pandemic began. By May 17, 2021 restrictions were being lifted as the data show 157,827,208 (almost 50% of persons in the US) had received at least one dose of vaccine, while 123,828,224 (roughly 38%) of Americans were totally vaccinated. As the number of persons vaccinated increased and the number of persons contracting the virus diminished precipitously, many people in the US embraced a new sense of "freedom." The "vaccinated ones" were told that they could return to life without masks or social distancing, while the "non-vaccinated" were advised to stay masked, distanced, and afraid.

The academic year ended and I escaped to sanctuary in Florida for a few days of respite. It was still a little chilly, but the drive and the change of scenery were much needed and appreciated. On my first evening away, my phone rang and I responded to my wife's solemn tone. She said she had bad news. My heart dropped, fearing that something dreadful had befallen a family member. I am in constant fear for the welfare of my sons. She said, "Kool, from across the street, is dead." I felt a sickness in my chest and stomach; and I wept for him.

Kool was a young brother who ran a rooming house across the street from our church. She said that he had gone to a club on Sunday night and was murdered by a 15-year-old boy. As I reflected on the death of my friend, who was like a son to me, I was overcome by a rush of irony and guilt—a sort of survivor's remorse, by proxy. My elder son graduated from Morehouse College within the same 24-hour span in which Kool was murdered. My mind was tangled like thick, nappy hair. I could not brush over the reality that my son and a few hundred other African American men were embarking on the rest of their lives following their dreams; while another brilliant, enterprising young Black man's dreams were eradicated and his life terminated by a Black boy-child as "Covid Winter" came to an end.

Following are the words that I shared as I eulogized my friend at a funeral home on the east side of Atlanta:

"I am filled with emotion at this moment. Many emotions flood my mind; chief of which are sadness, pain and anger. I have found that it is important to name one's emotions, because it is helpful to the grieving process to attach an identification to the way that we feel. Actually, I am traumatized by this murder of my friend. Kool was my friend. He was like a son to me. He called me 'pastor', but he was my counselor. He called me 'OG', but he was really the 'big homie.' Our community, our city, our hood, our block is hurting; and so I can't even begin to imagine how this family must feel. I hurt for each of you and I am clear that there are no words that I could say to make this loss more bearable.

Kool was like his name—cool. He was an early riser and a hard worker. He was an early riser and a hard worker. He was a businessman, because he was 'bout that business, man! Whether he was designing and creating clothing and apparel or creating a masterpiece out of a crumpled wreck, he used his gifts and talents to make things better—to make people better. He took his love for music and added his business acumen to create opportunities for young artists to shine. ('Cause, like Jay-Z said, 'he was a business, man!') He was generous, diplomatic, respectful and diligent, because it was good for business. He was confident, competent, and optimistic; and there was no limit to his commitment to Black excellence. Candidly, I will share that my young brother always treated me and the members of our church with respect. He was obviously raised right. But whether he was dealing with the spirit or the streets, he was professional, because he was building an empire—it was about that business, man.

This may sound strange, but it is true that Kool provided all manners of service for members of our community. Kool was not a 'trap star'; he was a businessman. Now you can look at me and see that I am old; and you know (and I know) that old people need medicine (you follow me)? So I asked my enterprising young neighbor about the quality and potency of the medication that might be available. He assured me of the power and efficacy of the medications and that he stood by his medicine with absolute confidence. Kool was a businessman, but he was my friend. He never overtaxed me—'cause that wouldn't be good for business.

So now we must lay him to rest. We got to set him free; we can't hold him back from taking the next steps of his journey. Time is short, my young sisters and brothers. The whole world has gone mad and damn fool crazy. There is no place to hide because death can find you anywhere. You can be walking among thousands on the strip in Vegas, or lying alone in your bed at night. Death is imminent and unrelenting and it will catch us all.

This past Covid Winter took its toll on me. I almost didn't make it through because the big beast of depression jumped on my back like never before and was riding me down to the ground. The last time I saw Kool, I was pulling up into the church parking lot. I called out his name and he walked over to greet me. 'Good morning, pastor', he said, shaking my hand firmly and looking me in the eye like the businessman that he was. 'How you doing?', he asked, and I told him I was feeling low. He said to me, 'Keep looking up, pastor; it's going to be a great day. We don't have bad days, 'cause it's just good to be here.' He smiled his brilliant white toothy grin as we pulled each other close for what would be our final embrace. His words lifted me and we walked away laughing, returning to the work that was before us."

Conclusion

We all live in a new historical epoch. History will refer to the year 2020 as the year that the "Coronavirus Era" began. White politicians are attempting to rewrite history under the ice-cold gaze of the public eye. They refuse to admit that twice-impeached Donald Trump was denied a second term as president by Black people who operationalized the franchise. They have enacted new legislation aimed at suppressing the Black vote in future elections. They fear the stark truth contained in The 1619 Project, so they pass new laws to ban its being taught in public schools. They reject Critical Race Theory out of hand, without a clear understanding of the methodological parameters and academic utility of this necessary approach to understanding reality. They deny reality and make the steadfast claim that America is NOT a racist country[12] while passing into law the Juneteenth Holiday to commemorate the end of slavery in America. The hypocrisy is staggering. It is believable. I have seen it all before as if I were paused on fast-forward.

June 21, 2021.
F. Keith Slaughter
Interdenominational Theological Center

ENDNOTES

1   https://www.washingtonpost.com/graphics/investigations/police-shootings-database/
2   https://www.statista.com/statistics/1107546/monthly-year-over-year-sales-growth-of-firearms-us
3   Kellyanne Conway, US Counselor to the President under the Trump Administration, deployed the term in defense of the "lies" told by White House Press Secretary Sean Spicer, concerning the attendance numbers at the Trump inauguration in January of 2017.

4   https://www.urbandictionary.com/define.php?term=cappin&utm_source=-search-action

5   https://www.ajc.com/lifestyles/timeline-the-day-period-when-coronavirus-really-changed-life-georgia/mI1Be5ZTZn2onEZgDU3u3O/

6   https://www.washingtonpost.com/politics/2021/01/24/trumps-false-or-misleading-claims-total-30573-over-four-y ears/ 6 (Richard) Moriba Kelsey, *Pittsburgh: A Sense of Community, Historic Reflections of An Atlanta Neighborhood* (Atlanta, GA: Publishing Associates, Inc., 2012), p. 11.

7   Michael White and David Epston, *Narrative Means to Therapeutic Ends* (New York: WW Norton and Company, 1990), pg. 74.

8   Gil Scott-Heron & Brian Jackson. 1973. "Winter in America". Released May 1974. D&B Sound. Silver Spring, MD.

9   F. Keith Slaughter, *Therapeutic Dimensions of Black Preaching* (Mableton, GA: Avant Garde Books, 2019), pp. 54- 57.

10 Bobby E. Wright, *Psychopathic Racial Personality and Other Essays* (Chicago, IL: Third World Press, 1985).

11 As Chuck D told Melody Maker in 1991: "'Can't Truss It' is about how the corporate world of today is just a different kind of slavery. ... The Number One institution that teaches you how to deal is the family, but slavery f–ked that up. So the song is about the ongoing cost of the holocaust." Sep 15, 2020 https://chrissmithauthor.com/2020/09/15/protest-100-public-enemy-cant-truss-it/

12 https://www.theguardian.com/news/datablog/2021/may/06/tim-scott-america-racist-data-racial-disparities

BIBLIOGRAPHY

Slaughter, F. Keith. *Therapeutic Dimensions of Black Preaching*. Mableton, GA: Avant Garde Books, 2019.

White, Michael and Epston, David. *Narrative Means to Therapeutic Ends*. New York: W.W. Norton and Company, 1990.

Wright, Bobby E. *Psychopathic Racial Personality and Other Essays*. Chicago, IL: Third World Press, 1985.

CHAPTER SEVEN
Picturing Freedom

Cecil Williams

Wow! Was I surprised when a friend called in April 2020 to inform me that a picture of me on social media as a young man drinking out of a "White Only" water fountain had gone viral; with even people like Snoop Dogg adding to the hype.[1]

I was not surprised about the image, but about the timing—middle of the COVID-19 Pandemic, with so many important health concerns—that, for the third time, the picture had resurfaced. I am very flattered that my image had been seen and had given a large segment something to take their minds off of "the given" -- the rising death toll around the world.

There is an interesting backstory to the image.

As a stringer correspondent for JET, a popular (but now defunct) weekly news magazine that kept Black America informed, I was photographed at the fountain by a friend who accompanied me on a news assignment to the South Carolina Lowcountry. Even though forbidden by a rigid, racially motivated society, very simply, I drank from the "White Only" water fountain because I was thirsty. During this Jim Crow period of the 1960s, signs and symbols such as this were commonplace in restrooms, restaurants, doctor' offices, and movie theaters.[2]

As a child of segregation, growing up in South Carolina, the heartland of the Deep South, my perspective will no doubt ring out quite differently from others featured in this unique publication.[3]

Hopefully, by writing a brief synopsis about my unique experiences, I can inspire readers to pass the torch. In 1946, a time before many of you were born, I discovered that my Kodak Baby Brownie allowed me to capture images much faster and more accurately than I was able to draw and sketch. And so, at 9 years old, I began a career in photography and journalism that enabled me to capture a large number of the most important events and people of the second half of the 20th century. In sports, I met and photographed Joe Louis, Althea Gibson, Jackie Robinson, John F. Kennedy, Arthur Ashe, and Althea Gibson. In entertainment, Lena Horne, Jackie Wilson, James Brown, Sam Cooke,

Sidney Poitier, Roberta Flack, Gladys Knight, and many others were captured by my more technically advanced camera technologies. My greatest passion came from the events and individuals involved in societal changes, such as with *Briggs v. Elliott*, *Brown v. Board of Education*, Voting Rights, Civil Rights Movement, Rev. Martin Luther King, Jr., Andrew Young, Jesse Jackson, Harvey Gantt, John F. Kennedy, Barack Obama, and hundreds more. In relating to these experiences across the span of 7 decades, I'm hoping my passion for freedom, justice and equality will inspire a new generation of leaders who will make this world a better place.[4]

And, yes, I think a few of the things I did might have had some impact on the racist society I grew up in. Twice, I was arrested by state police while taking pictures of students involved in protesting segregation. While being booked by arresting officers, I borrowed a dime from an incoming protestor and notified the Associated Press that I was in jail and could not perform freelance reporting for them. While visiting relatives in 1960 in New York—camera dangling from my neck—I walked into the Roosevelt Hotel, where newspapers had announced that my hero, Senator John F. Kennedy, was to appear. Looking around, it was clear that I was the only person of color in a room full of journalists. Hotel security escorted me out, but JFK intervened and, besides befriending me, made me his favorite cameraperson. Later, in 1984 and 1995, this political experience led me to launch campaigns to run against one of the staunchest segregationists of the era, US Senator Strom Thurmond. I lost both times, but my cashless campaigns motivated thousands to register and vote.

During the Civil Rights Movement era, JET and Ebony Magazine dispatched me to Clemson University, where, with my most treasured camera, a medium format Hasselblad, I photographed Harvey Gantt, achieving, "integration with dignity." Over decades, in incident after incident, I used injustices of the time as inspiration to depict some of the most impactful moments and icons of the 20th century. Today, besides my five documentaries, my images appear in over 60 history books.[5]

Before the advent of digital imaging, using "film" in cameras resulted in my having a large collection stored in my archives. About five years ago, out of frustration with scanning film, I designed and marketed a rapid film scanning device I named The Filmtoaster. Today, the passion I developed for history has motivated me to establish the first and, so far as I know, only Civil Rights museum in South Carolina. Picture that!

ENDNOTES

1 For a classic, masterful, and gritty message regarding the power of photography to impact a person's life, read Gordon Parks's autobiography, *A Choice of Weapons* (New York: Harper and Row, 1966). While discussing or debating photography as art, see also Katherine Hoffman, *Stieglitz: A Beginning Light* (New Haven: Yale University Press, 2004).

2 See, for example, William R. Ferris's book, I AM A MAN: Photographs of the Civil Rights Movement, 1960-1970 (Jackson, MS: University Press of Mississippi, 2021).

3 See Cecil Williams, *Freedom and Justice: Four Decades of the Civil Rights Movement as Seen by a Black Photographer of the Deep South* (Macon, Georgia: Mercer University Press, 1995).

4 Lives committed to excellence in photography are, after all, a tradition within the African-American community. See, for instance, the life of James Van Der Zee as communicated by Deborah Willis-Braithwaite and Robert C. Birt in *Van Der Zee: Photographer, 1886-1983* (New York: Harry N. Abrams, Inc., in association with National Portrait Gallery, Smithsonian Institution, 1993).

5 It should be noted that photographers have captured remarkable images of extraordinary black women as well, placing their important images and backgrounds before the American public and the world. See, for example, the impressive work in Brian Lanker's classic *I Dream a World: Portraits of Black Women Who Changed America* (New York, New York: Stewart, Tabori and Chang, 1989).

BIBLIOGRAPHY

Willis-Braithwaite, Deborah and Birt, Robert C. *Van Der Zee: Photographer, 1886-1983*. New York: Harry N. Abrams, National Portrait Gallery, 1993.

Ferris, William R. *I AM A MAN: Photographs of the Civil Rights Movement, 1960-1970*. Jackson, MS: University Press of Mississippi, 2021.

Hoffman, Katherine. *Stieglitz: A Beginning Light*. New Haven, CT: Yale University Press, 2004.

Lanker, Brian. *I Dream a World: Portraits of Black Women Who Changed America*. New York: Harry N. Abrams / Stewart, Tabori and Chang, 1989.

Parks, Gordon. *A Choice of Weapons*. New York: Harper and Row, 1966.

Williams, Cecil. *Freedom and Justice: Four Decades of the Civil Rights Struggle as Seen by a Black Photographer of the Deep South*. Macon, GA: Mercer Univ. Press, 1995.

CHAPTER EIGHT

Observations from the Porch: A Story of Death, Life, and the Railroad in Between

Austin L. Scott

A child does not easily understand the complexities and motives that govern human behavior. He or she tends to accept people and circumstances as they represent themselves because, to the child's mind, people present basic and clear realities and truths. As a child, I lived in the Ridgeview section of Hickory, North Carolina with my grandmother, father, and siblings in a section of the city that seemed suspended in time. Directly across the road from my grandmother's house on South Center Street was the abandoned, rusted, and decrepit Joann Fabrics manufacturing plant, amidst overgrown trees, vines, and other vegetation which had clawed their way to reclaim the territory decades after the mill's closure. To the southeast, one block away from my grandmother's house, is a McDonald's adjacent to US Highway 70 and its car dealerships. A block in the opposite direction—southwest—is the ironically-named "Sunny Valley" housing project where I worked "off the books" in the sixth grade, answering phones to earn money in order to participate in my middle school's trip to Washington, DC. North of that housing project are other ones like it and some shuttered businesses which also blight the landscape.

During my upbringing, the most advanced thing we had in my section of town was the public library and the Brown Penn Recreation Center, a hot spot for young children and hormonal teenagers who sought to socialize, play basketball, and pursue a wide variety of other sports and games. "The Penn" was well-known to us in my community as a multi-purpose facility, good for family reunions, church functions, sporting events, and most any other kind of get-together that one could imagine. But that was it. Take any street north, south, east, or west, away from the Brown Penn and the public library—both less than a hundred feet from each other—and you leave the bubble and step back in time. I could never comprehend the stark contrast between these two buildings and the rest of my section of town. Something appeared to have gone gravely wrong with this place, for every day felt as though some pervasive yet nameless evil had seized control and depressed everything. Everyone seemed aware of this tragedy, but somehow never discussed it. Yet the evil had depressed the housing, closed the businesses, and pretty much restricted our breathing space to a fast-food restaurant, basketball court, and the library. Community members kept the presence of this "force" a secret, the same way they kept family traumas secret, and the same way that unwritten expectations of silence worked to preserve family respectability. It was as if everyone had taken a solemn oath. The parties then took the secrets to the grave, the memories of the event(s) faded over time, and generations of their descendants inherited the pain of those traumas with no knowledge of their family origins. Despite the silence, I learned the secret in the most accidental way. In the South, a person previously unaware of the rules that govern social norms quickly becomes aware of their existence once the rules are enforced, whether through legal or extralegal means. I have known both. However, my discovery came from experience with the latter.

When I lived in Hickory, my dad habitually compelled me to go outside whenever he felt I was spending too much time "sitting up under" him in the house.[1] So, one day, being an avid bike rider, I mounted my bicycle and proceeded north. Once I reached the top of South Center Street, I stopped just shy of the railroad tracks which ran perpendicular to my home street—the de facto line of demarcation that separated "My Town" from "Uptown." As I peered across the tracks, waiting for the level crossing signals to lift so I could ride on, I saw, approximately twenty feet away from me, about six or seven men dressed with sheets covering their heads and torsos, walking up the railroad tracks on the opposite side of where I waited. As busy as this intersection usually is in the morning, this day was different. Eerily, during this encounter, no cars seemed to be driving past and no pedestrians seemed to be walking along the sidewalks. I was alone. Ignorant as to the nature of what the men represented, due to my youthful inexperience and lack of historical perspective, I simply said to myself, "This has to be the dumbest thing I've ever seen. Sheets are supposed to go on the bed."

In hindsight, I have come to believe that such moments in the presence of evil are often divine appointments. Time slows, one develops this inexplicable sense of fear and warning as the intuition alerts the body to a mortal threat that the rational mind may be unaware of, and the people who should be there either to witness the event or to intervene are not present. Simply put, I was supposed to be there, and yet under the protective hand of God. The episode ended less than five minutes after it began. The klansmen made their way up the tracks, the railroad arm signals lifted, and I rode on. It would take years of study, travel, and other lived experience before I would understand fully what I had beheld that day, the manifestation of mankind's original sin in the form of racist behavior.[2]

If the message that "Blacks" are the menacing "other" is not successfully communicated by passive aggression, the offending party seems to graduate to aggression. This reality was evidenced on that particular day I rode my bike north and stopped on my side of the tracks. The message of the Klan marching along the perimeter of "White Hickory" was clear: somebody forgot their place. And I am convinced that my encounter with the hooded patrol at the Uptown/South Center Street checkpoint was to ensure that I did not forget mine. Therefore, a question similar to that of King Solomon arises, "What is the Black man to do on his side of the train tracks?" Is the entire purpose of the Black experience in America (and around the world) to breach the boundaries of "White heaven" and enter? I do not think so. The wealthy of my "race" who have crossed the tracks and entered this "paradise" often appear more to have been sentenced to, rather than admitted into, their place in such communities. Much is too often contingent upon their ability to be routinely entertaining and likable. But their song and dance of assimilation, of integration, and White cultural appropriation together have not managed to effectuate a sustained improvement of the brothers and sisters on the other side of the tracks—in the "My Towns" of the world.³

Instead, I believe it is better for us to build the wealth of our community than to covet the generational wealth which White people globally obtained *en masse* by fraud. For this reason, I dare say I see, in a way, the divine providence of God in the concerted and flawed human effort to confine our people to the other side of the tracks. It has compelled us to look to one another and to look to God as we have aimed, as any group would, to help ourselves. It forces us to promote, remember, and recover that spirit and vision of Christian ingenuity that built our churches, our K-12 schools, our Historically Black Colleges and Universities, our voluntary associations, and our civic groups that helped carry us from the past to the present with hearts still strong and full—or at least capable—of love.

When my elders would share with me the history of Black achievement, survival, self-help, community-mindedness, and resilience, there was never a hint of hatred towards Whites, despite the weariness in my wise elders' faces following years and years of abuse at the hands of Whites. My people's achievements were rooted, of course, not in hatred of White people, or even in a space of bitterness toward them, but rather in the love for God and a love of and hope for the Black community. To me, this gift to love capaciously, no matter what, is the beauty of Black Christianity that lives on my side of the tracks. We can love our people, our heritage, and our community without hating anyone else. Sadly, too many of our White brothers and sisters on the other side of the tracks have not been able to figure that one out. We, as a historical pattern, would rather pray than slay; build than kill; and, in actual fact, we'd rather earn than burn.

However, while sitting on the porch and listening to the sighs and cries of my elders, or sitting at the kitchen table and hearing their thoughts about the generations that have succeeded them, I can discern that my elders do not believe that their sacrifices have altogether had their desired effects.[4] Therefore, to my earlier point, our preoccupation on this side of tracks must be one thing and one thing only: recovery. I personally preach a return to the emphasis of many of our Afro-Christian ancestors on a new birth in Christ, the fear of God, moral rectitude, responsibility, respectability, discipline, thrift, industriousness, ingenuity, erudition, internationalism, and strong, hetereosexual male-headed Black families. In this way, we will perhaps develop the human capital that can withstand any unjust government policies, unpredictable economic shocks, and ever-increasing hatreds, to build industries with global impact and ones that will create long-term wealth from goods and services which can then be transferred to the next generations of Blacks. As a Christian missionary, I especially hope to see builders who embrace the love and example of Christ. I find true hope and freedom for black men, women, and children in the precepts and examples of Christ.

With regard to manhood, growing up in Hickory, I could sense that there was a longing for more genuinely Christian Black men to work to revive the community. I could see it in the faces of my grandmother and great-grandmother when I heard their stories of abuse and suffering. Like so many old mothers, their childhood years had been stolen by responsibilities far beyond their ability to bear. They had been burdened with caring for homes, siblings, and sick family members, all the while dodging the sexual advances of incestuous fathers, "lowlife" uncles, "perverted" cousins, and licentious ministers. Who can speak of the horrors they experienced when they entertained family at their home, or were entertained as guests at a family member's home, and in the night, they, as young women, teens, or girls, felt their underwear being pulled down, their breasts fondled, and their intimate parts penetrated by some relative? Who can identify with the shame they felt when they tried to tell their parent(s) and were accused of lying? Broadly speaking, who can count the number of children from such encounters, ones that are kept secret from the rest of the family, and are perhaps only discovered at the father or mother's funeral? The same is true for what little Black boys sometimes experience, on our side of the tracks, in the family every day. They, too, are crying out for a new Black man.

Even the hardened drug dealers of my community betrayed the mask and expressed a profound melancholic longing to be made new, sternly warning my peers and me never to be like them. They exhorted us to go to school, get an education, and "stay out of the streets"; in fact, they never allowed us children anywhere near their illegal activities.

I can still remember, by contrast, the weekend I spent at my uncle's house/crack house in the housing projects southeast of where I lived. One night during my visit, two White prostitutes and their pimp were discussing the night's business plan. One of them, a sandy haired woman, stood up against the wall near the front door completely naked. After staring at her for quite some time, I, in my youthful lust, felt emboldened because she was a prostitute and touched her breast. With the humanity that had not yet been taken from her, she slowly shook her head at this middle-schooler. In her glossed-over eyes was a dying hope that I would be a different kind of man—a hope that, no doubt, died, again and again, every night she opened her legs.

Of course, this task of elevating Christ more in the Black community will be arduous. Transformation is, after all, not just a matter of learning truths, but also of unlearning lies. It is a matter of learning correct ways of thinking and shedding every self-destructive thinking pattern. One thing that happens to people living on my side of the tracks is that we often develop an unjustified sense of inferiority. When people live for such a long time in a place that is going nowhere, they gradually conclude that they can go nowhere. It is not always the physical or legal barrier so much anymore that consigns Blacks who live in these communities to this sense of hopelessness, but it is rather a mindset that is developed in response to the stagnation and degradation of our communities over time. Hopelessness seems to lead to resignation, and resignation itself to a certain kind of self-hatred.

For example, one day, after so many years of visiting friends in "White Hickory," while living in "Black Hickory," I was again walking north on South Center Street to "Uptown." After seeing, for the hundredth time, in crossing those old tracks, the contrast of wealth and poverty, development and stasis, opportunity and deprivation, I suddenly began to despise myself. The feeling was the most curious thing. While I was on "their" side of the tracks, no White person had ever disrespected me, nor had a White person ever questioned me explicitly about my presence in "their" area. No business had ever refused me service, and everyone had been very polite to me overall. But my dead-end environment told me, subliminally perhaps, that I was inferior, and I believe the same is true of Black communities across America.

Like someone looking into a mirror, we Blacks over time may come to see our environment (the reality imposed on us and the reality we create) as a reflection of ourselves. Are we transformed into what we behold and listen to daily? Perhaps the situation could be better compared to a feedback loop, in that inputs become outputs and outputs become inputs. Low expectations can beget low expectations, and immoral behavior certainly can foster immoral behavior. In other words, this contained environment arguably creates generational cycles of counterproductive and self-destructive lifestyle choices that, when practiced collectively, by enough community members, can form the dominant culture of that particular environment. The cycle can be seen at work in abandoned mothers whose highest expectations of their children is that they not go to jail, get pregnant, or get somebody pregnant. It is evident in fathers who have no expectations of their children because they were never present in their lives, and do not intend to be present in them, unless or until the courts get involved. The culture manifests itself in Black children who, unnaturally, learn to despise education and any peer who loves learning. Black children reared by married Black parents, who speak Mainstream American English, who love education, who dress respectably, and live in a predominantly Black neighborhood while attending a majority Black K-12 school very commonly experience the tired, unoriginal, and overused insult of being called an "Oreo," are accused of "acting White," and can be generally shunned by students their own age. The ostracized children are often limited to three options when selecting a peer group: 1) Find friends who look and think like them and continue to be disparaged as, "Oreos." 2) Find friends who think like them, but do not look like them, for which they may well be labeled "sell-outs." Or 3) Seek acceptance from those who mock education by suppressing their intelligence.

To this day, I still wrestle with personal insecurity and social anxiety as a result of the harmful influence this culture had on my educational experience from kindergarten through the twelfth grade. The first time I was called "White" was in the sixth or seventh grade, while I was enrolled at what was then "College Park Middle School" and is now "Hickory Career and Arts Magnet School." On the bus to school, the conversation somehow turned to the issue of reading and learning. I joined the conversation, sharing how much I loved to read and other comments to that effect. Once I concluded, as we were nearing the turn to enter the school bus parking lot, a Black girl in the seat horizontal to mine called out to the group, "He's White!" I had no idea what that meant because, despite all the drug use and immorality taking place in my home, we never used that terminology. Nevertheless, I correctly perceived the comment to be a put-down. Later on, in class, the same student called me an "Oreo." These aspersions were only the beginning, as I was regularly bullied by black boys, in great number, during my school career in Hickory. It seemed that there was nothing I could do to gain acceptance. So, unfortunately, I went with the third option, selecting a peer group among whom and for whom I would suppress my intelligence. The lesson? People can truly practice self-hatred if they are taught self-hatred by those who hate themselves.[5] Put simply, many of the people of "Black Hickory" were both the victims and perpetrators of a culture of self-hatred.

The point here is not to highlight the failings of the Black community *per se* or to center and condemn White people. My purpose is to highlight the need for us to unlearn self-sabotaging ways of thinking and being, to encourage the shedding of the destructive elements of "culture," and to move forward—not across the railroad tracks into the White community, but towards greater Christian, academic, and economic growth within our communities. Someone might ask, "How can we all do better if we have not all seen better?" The answer may rest, at least in part, in the idea and realities of internationalization. Since the "My Town USAs" can be found throughout the country, the problem of Black marginalization and isolation is not only a "Black problem," it is a profoundly American problem. Living within the confines of demographically segregated, financially neglected, and politically overlooked communities, many Black residents of these areas hardly believe there is another reality accessible to them outside of their boundaries. Hence, some Black people have never, or only rarely, left their neighborhoods, cities/towns, counties, and states. The people of these "My Town USAs" must experience in person, and not purely via social media, the truth that there exists an entire world outside of America. Through internationalization—the process of Black Americans' becoming physically connected to the international world- and becoming connected, moreover, to ideas, innovations, and cultures abroad—I can envision revitalizing our depressed communities in countless ways. Therefore, in their role the engines of Black empowerment, the Black Church, and the Historically Black Colleges and Universities (which it has established) should work in concert spiritually, academically, economically, and politically, with Christian and other groups internationally who are likewise willing to work with us and keep our best interests at heart. Much good can be accomplished through engaging in joint missionary projects, research, conferences, business ventures, student and faculty exchange programs, study abroad programs, articulation agreements, and dual-enrollment agreements. Blacks must robustly secure passports; be willing, perhaps, to obtain dual citizenships as the opportunity arises; learn as many languages as possible; and become, like many of our historical leaders, global citizens. In this way, we can bring an international store of human capital to bear on the development needs of all of our communities.

My first international experience was in Honduras in 2003 through Wycliffe Bible Translator's "Get Global" program. The program was designed to afford young adults interested in missionary work overseas the opportunity to gain experience through a short-term trip. Initially, I had planned to enroll in a recruitment program with the Charlotte-Mecklenburg Police Department, but I received no response. With what I perceived as no other recourse, and eager to get out of my home, I earnestly prayed to God for an opportunity to occupy my summer, and He answered. Since that mission to Honduras, I have been on four of the seven continents, all except for Australia, Antarctica, and South America. I consider this an incredible accomplishment, given that I never dreamed I would even live to see my current age.[6] We never know what circumstances God will use to push us beyond the comforts of our present context—even when that context is abusive—and move us more accordingly into His will.

Raised in Hickory, orphaned in Charlotte, I always felt my life was confined to chaos, confusion, violence, and family dysfunction. No matter where I turned, whether staying with my father in Hickory, or my mother in Charlotte when she relocated from New York, the first sixteen years of my life were marked by great instability. While I was in utero, my parents tried to kill me. Mother, by using hard drugs and alcohol while pregnant with me; and father, by beating my mother for using hard drugs and alcohol while pregnant with me. He reasoned that if my mother was going to kill me, they should do it together. When I was about the age of four or five, my parents had a major argument, and they decided to split up, leaving me to choose which parent I wanted to live with. I chose my father, and the attempts on my life continued.

From my childhood to my early teens, I was slapped around, beaten, and called every hurtful name under heaven on almost a daily basis by him. One regimen he put me through was particularly humiliating. Whenever I responded incorrectly to questions he asked that he deemed important (often that criterion did not matter), he would call me to stand in front of him, and he would slap me across the face three times in succession. The ritual would go something like this: he would yell, "Come here!" *Slap!!* I would fall back. He would yell again, "Come here!" *Slap!!* I would fall back again. Then the third time, "Come here!" *Slap!!* I would fall for the third time holding my face. He had no reservations about slapping me in front of his friends or anyone who was around. I would tell him frequently throughout the day, "I love you, Dad" because I thought the reason for the beatings was his lack of assurance that I loved him. Nothing I did ever pleased him enough for the hitting to stop. Somewhere between 1999 and 2000, when it became clear that we would lose the house in Hickory, I became his target of choice for venting his frustrations, even to the point of his putting a pistol to his head and threatening to blow his brains out in front of me. I could sense that he was planning to do something desperate to save the property because he had a friend who came by on a motorcycle and he took his gun with him. The morning before he left, I was in his bed while he was getting ready to leave. I said to him, "Dad, don't you want to wait on God?." He replied, "Yeah, son, but I gotta get this money." With that, he left.

Days later he returned and gave me some money, solemnly warning me not to hold onto it. Then, he departed a second time, and I would never live with him again. Two weeks following that second departure, my grandfather relocated me to Charlotte. I prayed that we would lose the house of my bondage, and God answered that prayer. However, I am pleased to report that since my father's release from prison nearly ten years ago, he has become a missionary of peace, healing, and reconciliation to his children and the Scott family. He is a very loving man.[7]

Nonetheless, in terms of my then young and again interrupted life, moving in with my mother, resultantly, was not any better for me. I was bullied by my peers, went for weeks at a time without food and clean clothes, endured my mother's trading sex partners like kids trade toys, and I suffered through all of the destructive consequences of her drug and alcohol abuse. Unloved, by age 16, I was abandoned. My father had been arrested in Florida and given fifteen years for bank robbery, and after so many months of my mom's using the rent money for drugs, we were evicted—for the second time—in my tenth-grade year. We also separated. She checked into a hotel and I remained in the apartment. It was my relationship with the property management that afforded me the chance to get the bolt lock open to retrieve as many possessions as possible before I had to return the key. On what felt like the last day of my life, I opened the door, and the apartment was in shambles. Having nowhere to go, I sat down on the floor—lost, scared, and alone. Later that evening, two of my fellowship members came and prayed for me, then went on with their previously scheduled "Christian activity." I do not fault them for their decision, for every aspect of life revolves around assignments, choices, and preferences. Perhaps they chose their event over me because a speaking engagement is always more preferable than helping someone clean up the train wreck of their lives.

On the day my parents decided to quit their relationship, on the sidewalk, in front of our Poughkeepsie high-rise apartment building, somehow, I knew, even as a child, that I would be better off with my father than with my mother. Maybe I chose my father because of my mother's intermittent absences from my childhood, or because she loved my half-white sister more than me. The choices children make in crisis situations derive more from instinct than "reason." However, a photograph of my mother, sister, and me, in the front yard of our home in Poughkeepsie—a photograph that I have kept for years, has helped clarify my reasoning related to that fateful day of our separation. If *"I love your sister more than you"* were a picture, this image would be the one. In the photo, my sister is in a baby's playpen with my mother on both knees doting over her. My sister had to be less than a year old at this time. I am clearly an appendage or, in art history terms, an "attribute," in the photograph. In the photograph, my three-year-old self has evidently approached my mother for water. Clearly annoyed by my presence, she has turned her head away from me and has extended her right arm, dismissively handing me the bottle of water that is immortalized, through the frozen image, in her hand.

On the day my parents separated, I chose my father, and Mother took my sister, pushing her down the street in a carriage—a metaphor for our relationship to this day. For despite the many visits, phone calls, and dinners, my sister (who lives in an entirely different region of the country than Mother) still holds a higher place in my mother's heart than I. I am not envious of her position, nor do I blame her for our mom's behavior, but the actions Mother took against me during my childhood years, out of favoritism for my sister, have scarred me. For example, I can still recall what happened to me once when my sister and I were both taking a nap and I awoke to read the Bible. At the crinkling sound of the pages turning, my sister said, "Austin, stop making so much noise!" Overhearing my sister's complaint, Mother suddenly burst into the room, snatched the Bible out of my hands, and began beating me on the head with it. I had to stay in the room for the rest of the day and could not join the family for dinner. Mother was willing to get violent with anyone she perceived to be a threat to my sister's comfort. I was, at the same time, simply the child who had been forced upon her by virtue of an unwanted pregnancy.

To be certain, life with both of my parents was marked by severe instability. One day it's a relocation, the next day it's an eviction. One day, your father is robbing banks and being locked away for fifteen years. Another day, drug dealers are visiting the house demanding payment, and your mother's boyfriend/enabler is begging you to, "give them something." All the while, no one seemed to care about what I thought, how I felt, or considered how their decisions would create years of psychological baggage for me to unpack. My voice was muted and my presence was ignored, a slave among slaves.

Yet, during my lifetime I, too, have become guilty of perpetrating gross evil against others. For this reason, I find meaning and hope for redemption--and I feel understood--when Yeshua says, "Truly, truly . . . everyone who commits sin is a slave to sin" (John 8:34 RSV; emphasis added). Hence, we are all slaves; and in a world full of slaves, how do the younger slaves (children), whose voices are all too often muted, respond when thrust into the negative consequences of poor decisions made by the older slaves (adults/parents)? For many, short-term answers are found in gangs, truancy, drug-dealing, drug use, crime, prostitution, self-abuse, and psychiatric residential treatment facilities. The negative behaviors, however, are rooted in prior causes and actions; they are cries for escape—escape from drug-addicted parents, domestic violence, empty refrigerators, unpaid light and water bills, molestation, bullying, and so on.

My first internationalization experience in Honduras was, in fact, an escape for two weeks. I did not want to be home. Nevertheless, I do believe that God uses even adverse conditions to draw people to Himself. For, though I was traumatized by both of my parents, who were themselves the victims of horrific mistreatment during their upbringing, God used my trauma to draw me to the well of salvation. Once I was liberated from enslavement to sin through repentance and faith in Christ, my outlook on eternity changed and my worldview expanded beyond the confines of my cultural, social, and environmental contexts. In other words, Christ not only transformed me and preserved me for eternal life, but also enabled me to see a world beyond my neighborhood, city, county, state, and country. He gave me a vision beyond my side of the railroad tracks, and one that can help the tragic people on my side of the railroad tracks—including some adults who have not grown up very much at all, and children who have grown up far too fast.

In the final analysis, I grew up way too fast. Even as an adult, I find that my adolescent self is still trying to catch up, and thus all of me is never fully present. I often catch myself looking for a childhood that is not there and never will be—longing for it and yet resisting it, as if sparring with a shadow. I saw things I had no business seeing, and experienced things I never should have, including homelessness. But God was merciful to me: numerous Black families, as a common practice, take in children who are not theirs biologically. I was, in that very helpful tradition, informally adopted at age sixteen. Although they had their own dysfunctions, through their good example of hard work and tough love, I understood that no one was going to take care of me. I had to do it myself, with the hand of God providentially ordering my steps, just as they had aimed to do. My experience, like that of so many others, might be seen as a metaphor for much of the Black experience in America. We were born on the other side of the tracks and no one is coming. It is up to the Lord and us. If we do not work together to solve our problems and help ourselves, then no one will. The Bible illustrates this point beautifully. In an origin story that closely mirrors the African-American experience, the Lord, in Ezekiel 16:4-6, proclaims:

> As for your birth, on the day you were born your navel cord was not cut, nor were you washed with water for cleansing; you were not rubbed with salt or even wrapped in cloths. No eye looked with pity on you to do any of these things for you, to have compassion on you. Rather you were thrown out into the open field, for you were abhorred on the day you were born. When I passed by you and saw you squirming in your blood, I said to you while you were in your blood, "Live!" Yes, I said to you while you were in your blood, "Live!"

To my people, hated and thrown to the other side of the tracks, I stand with the Lord, and say, "Live!" Bear fruit right where you have been planted. Through Yeshua, the Christ, live such holy, disciplined, and focused lives that instead of moving away from the problems on your side of the tracks, or depending on outside groups to help to solve those problems, you—indeed, we—can become the solution to the disparities in our communities. What the Lord said to Israel, I say to all our people: "Live!"

ENDNOTES

1   The town of Hickory has a fascinating cultural, city-planning, and even architectural history. For a closer glimpse into the town and its variegated design, see: Kirk F. Mohney and Laura A.W. Phillips, *From Tavern to Town: The Architectural History of Hickory, North Carolina* (Hickory, NC: Hickory Landmarks Society, Inc., and City of Hickory Historic Properties Commission, January 1988). For a broader, panoramic, and certainly politically insightful glimpse into the problem of residential housing discrimination in cities like Hickory throughout America, see also Yelena Bailey, How the Streets Were Made: Housing Segregation and Black Life in America (Chapel Hill, NC: The University of North Carolina Press, 2020).

2   The Ku Klux Klan had been quite virulent and bold in North Carolina, in particular, in the immediate decades prior to my stumbling upon some of them in Hickory. See, for more North Carolina context and history, David Cunningham's *Klansville, U.S.A.: The Rise and Fall of the Civil Rights–Era Klan* (Oxford, UK: Oxford University Press, 2014).

3   A somewhat recent and very incisive critique that examines the politics of racial discrimination and its demographic as well as political-power implications for Northern cities can be found in Brandi Thompson Summer's 2016 book, *Black in Place: The Spatial Aesthetics of Race in a Post Chocolate City* (Chapel Hill, NC: The University of North Carolina Press, 2016). Similarly, one may find it very useful to read, for both its rigor and national perspective, Douglas S. Massey and Nancy Denton's book, *American Apartheid: Segregation and the Making of the Underclass* (Cambridge, MA: Harvard University Press, 1998). Significantly, in terms of noting the impact of segregation and other forms of systemic racism upon both children and adults, Massey and Denton's book grew out of research funded by the National Institute of Child Health and Human Development.

4   See, for example, the various contemporary problems that are given voice in Rashad Shabazz's book, *Spatializing Blackness: Architectures of Confinement and Black Masculinity in Chicago* (Urbana, IL: University of Illinois Press, 2015).

5   To note "self-hatred" as a broader human and theological problem, see also the story of Eva Elle Rose, *From the Other Side of the Tracks: A Memoir* (Bloomington, IN: Author House, 2013).

6   Many similarly situated, bright, young, black (and other) children never survive the stark emotional, material, and spiritual challenges of their youth. Consider, for example, the heartbreaking loss of life and human potential embodied in Jeff Hobbs's nonfiction account, *The Short and Tragic Life of Robert Peace* (New York: Scribner, 2014).

7   The healing that has occurred, and continues to occur, is all the more proof to me that my God actively intervenes, with aid, grace, and mercy, in the horrendous misfortunes and crises that afflict human relationships in today's world. I am, by far, not alone in such thoughts and beliefs. See, for example, the testimonial of Blaire Linne in the inspirational book, *Finding My Father: How the Gospel Heals the Pain of Fatherlessness* (Epsom, Surrey, England: The Good Book Company, 2021).

BIBLIOGRAPHY

Bailey, Yelena. *How the Streets Were Made: Housing Segregation and Black Life in America*. Chapel Hill, NC: The Univ. of North Carolina Press, 2020.

Cunningham, David. *Klansville, U.S.A., The Rise and Fall of the Civil Rights–Era Ku Klux Klan*. New York: Oxford University Press, 2013.

Hobbs, Jeff. *The Short and Tragic Life of Robert Peace*. New York: Scribner, 2014.

Linne, Blair. *Finding My Father: How the Gospel Heals the Pain of Fatherlessness*. Epsom, United Kingdom: The Good Book Company, 2021.

Massey, Douglas S. and Denton, Nancy. *American Apartheid: Segregation and the Making of the Underclass*. Cambridge, MA: Harvard Univ. Press, 1998.

Mohney, Kirk F. and Phillips, Laura A.W.. *From Tavern to Town: The Architectural History of Hickory, North Carolina*. Hickory, NC: Hickory Landmarks Society, Inc., City of Hickory Historic Properties Commission, Jan. 1988.

Rose, Eva Elle. *From the Other Side of the Tracks: A Memoir*. Bloomington, IN: Author House, 2013.

Scott, Austin L. *Between Christ and the Black Man: A Conversation on Race, Politics, and the Church in America*. Monee, IL: CreateSpace, 2021.

Summers, Brandi Thompson. *Black in Place: The Spatial Aesthetics of Race in a Post Chocolate City*. Chapel Hill, NC: The University of North Carolina Press, 2016.

The New American Standard Bible. The Lockman Foundation. 1997.

The Bible. The Revised Standard Version. 2nd ed., Ignatius Press. 2015.

Washington, Booker T. *Up From Slavery: An Autobiography*. New York: Doubleday, Page & Co., 1907.

CHAPTER NINE
Learning to Forgive

Rodney J. Reynolds

Early Years

As I began to write this essay, I knew that I wanted to express my feelings related to growing up without a father in my life. I always felt that just because my parents had divorced when l was young, it didn't mean that my father had to stay out of my life. I guess in later years I just figured it was something that my father specifically chose to do.

As far back as I can remember about growing up in Cleveland, Ohio, my early childhood was pretty normal. I had two childhood best friends, Wayne Winston and Solomon Hill; the latter we called "June". Not a day went by that the three of us were not together. Whether playing catch with a baseball or football on our block of Lancelot, in the Glenville neighborhood, or just hanging out at one of our homes, we were inseparable. Wayne, June, and I even formed a singing group before there was ever a band called "The Jackson 5." June's sister "Jenny" wrote us a song. In my mind's eye, I can still see all of us all suited up one Easter, me even sporting a crushed velvet yellow bowtie, the others looking equally as stylish. I also have fond memories of Wayne, June, and myself running up and down Lancelot, in 1967, chanting "Vote for Stokes"—meaning Carl B. Stokes, who was elected that year the first black mayor of a major city in America. That same night, Dick Hatcher of Gary, Indiana, was also elected mayor. Things were changing.

Other major childhood memories that remain in my mind include even earlier moments of tremendous change. I recall watching the funeral of President Kennedy from a neighbor's home on Paxton Avenue (where we had lived in 1963, prior to moving to Lancelot) and later moments in the 60s as well, such as the riots in the Glenville area that erupted after the assassination of Rev. Dr. Martin Luther King, Jr. To this day, I remember my father's grabbing a gun and leaving the house. There was a family across the street whose sons were said to be members of the "Black Nationalists." I remember at one point the Black Nationalists' purportedly saying that they were going to blow up the gas stations in our neighborhood on a certain date. I was scared, but nothing ever happened. I was only a child, of course, and didn't fully understand what was happening during those turbulent times in our community, neither in Cleveland proper nor across the US in general. I wouldn't come to understand the real impact of those events until I was much older.

Wayne's father often took us to see the "Cleveland Indians" (now, more appropriately, the "Guardians", of course). And as a kid I was afraid of heights. Wayne and June would literally have to walk with me over the bridge to Cleveland Stadium. Before the game, Mr. Winston would stop by Royal Castle where you could buy a box of six small hamburgers, sometimes called "sliders," for what I believe then was a dollar. (Even though I have traveled a lot throughout my career, I am still afraid of heights. Even today, I sometimes have trouble crossing certain bridges in New York—the Whitestone Bridge, for example, and the George Washington Bridge). Once, on a vacation with friends St. Clair and Kimberly Davis in San Francisco, my wife, friends, and I decided to visit Sausalito. As I approached the Golden Gate Bridge by vehicle, I found myself not being able to drive across. I immediately pulled over and promptly told St. Clair that he would have to drive.

So, while, as a child I was afraid to cross the bridge to Cleveland Stadium, once in my stadium seat I was always perfectly able to enjoy watching the baseball game. My favorite player at that time was Duke Sims, the catcher for the Cleveland Indians. His was a position that I would eventually come to play.

Wayne and June both were a year or two older than I. My mother actually "hired" June to walk me to school when I first started attending Iowa Maple Elementary School. Years later, June would always say that I was his first job. My days at Iowa Maple were mostly happy ones. When I was in the third grade I, like many boys in elementary school, apparently, had a crush on a teacher; mine was Ms. Patricia Young. I was chosen one year to attend an academic achievement event at the Pick Carter Hotel in Cleveland. Better still, Ms. Young had been tasked with transporting the chosen students to the event. I was on Cloud Nine because I got to ride with Ms. Young! I was one happy camper.

In my home, however, back down from Cloud Nine, times were not always happy. Sometimes, especially at night, I was not able to do my homework or study because my father would often come home drunk and start an argument with my mother. It seemed as though this went on constantly, but maybe it just seemed that way because I was young. My father drank a lot and his coming home drunk seemed normal. There are several events that still enter my mind on occasion and dredge up old, sad memories of when we lived on Lancelot.

One such event occurred when my mother had agreed to become a "den mother" for the local Cub Scout troop that I had joined. This is where I met my lifelong friend and future college roommate Harold Jackson. We were in the Cub Scouts and Boy Scouts together. For almost any kid, you would think that this would have been a happy time. And it was for a while. However, for some reason that I never figured out, my father made it clear that he didn't want my mother to serve as a den mother. Soon thereafter, my mother resigned. I guess she figured it would be easier to relinquish the position than to continue to go through arguments with my father regarding her participation.

It seemed in general, though, that the more my father drank, the more jealous he typically would become. This jealousy reared its ugly head on numerous occasions. It emerged awfully one day, just before my sister Joyce's wedding in 1968. On a Sunday afternoon, as our family prepared to attend a dinner to meet the family of my sister's soon-to-be husband, my father decided, for some unclear reason, that he didn't want to attend. Maybe it was because he was drunk. Many times when he drank he would get violent, mostly verbally. However, on this day, it went further. Since he wasn't going to the dinner, he didn't want any of us to attend it. He began to threaten us as we left the house, and I remember my sister's carrying a pot of green beans that had been made to take to the dinner. My father pulled his gun out and shot several bullets in the air. I can't be too specific if the shots were directed at us, but I do remember my sister's dropping the pot of green beans as we ducked for cover behind a car. Of course, we didn't go on with the dinner that Sunday afternoon. And as I look back at the incident, I know I was very disappointed over it all—and I was disappointed, as a young kid with a healthy appetite, to see those beans drop in the street, knowing, as I did, that my mother cooked a mean pot of string beans.

The ensuing day of my sister's wedding started off very well. Joyce's wedding was held in our backyard on Lancelot. We had a grapevine in our backyard and some very nice decorations had been placed all around. I was dressed up that day and served as a little usher. I specifically remember walking down the street to June's house and escorting his mom back up the street to the wedding. That was one of the fondest memories I have of Mrs. Hill, who died a year or two later while on a trip to Mobile, Alabama. Mrs. Hill suffered from asthma and had an attack while traveling. June also had asthma and I often worried about him when we were younger.

After the wedding, the family and guests headed to the reception. That is where things got a little ugly. During the reception, a supposedly relaxed, friendly, and celebratory time, my father, who had been drinking, saw another man speak to my mother, and from there things just erupted. The situation deteriorated so badly that my mother and I did not return home that night. For our safety, we stayed with my uncle George and his wife. I remember waking up on Sunday morning feeling like things just didn't seem right. After that incident, I don't think things ever really were.

Going to Indiana

When I was in the 4th grade, my mother and I moved to Indianapolis, Indiana to live with my Aunt Louise and Uncle Bill. I finished the 4th grade at School #60. I always thought it was cool that at that time the schools in Indianapolis didn't have names, but were instead recognized by numbers. Before moving to Indianapolis, my mother had told me that it might be a possibility that my Uncle Walter would purchase me a bike. Wouldn't you know it that I would open my big mouth and repeat what my mother had told me, to my uncle. She was not too happy, and she shared her displeasure with me. My mother and father had separated. I guess she figured she'd had just about enough and that it was time to move. We left Cleveland late one night, departing for Indianapolis. Greyhound got us to Indianapolis safely.

My aunt and uncle's house felt like a safe haven. And boy, could my Aunt Louise cook! My favorite was her chicken and dumplings. And my Uncle Bill was the best popcorn popper in the world! He and I would watch baseball games and eat what seemed to be mounds and mounds of popcorn. The year we spent in Indianapolis was a happy time, even though it had been quite sad to leave Cleveland and to leave behind my friends Wayne and June. In Indianapolis, I had other aunts and uncles around, and therefore many cousins. There was always somebody to play with and, although the majority of my cousins were girls, I didn't mind. I just remember being happy. Happy to not have to endure a lot of arguing and instead being able to see my mother at peace. I felt loved.

After about a year in Indianapolis, my mother and I moved back to Cleveland to live with my father. He had promised her that he would stop drinking. And for about a year he did. One of my fondest memories is how well I was received by Wayne and June when they found out I was back in Cleveland. They were very excited to see me again and it was suddenly as though the three of us had never been apart.

But it wasn't long before my father began drinking again, and my mother and I moved out of the house again, this time to live with my sister and her husband. When my father wasn't drinking, he was the greatest person. But once he took a drink, things changed. I was in the fifth grade when my mother and I moved in with my sister. I attended a school in the area. I would finish out the fifth grade at that school and afterwards my mother and I moved to an apartment off of 71st Street and Kinsman Avenue in the Garden Valley area. I entered the 6th grade at Charles W. Chesnutt. What's ironic is that I often think today about the name Charles W. Chesnutt. On American Legacy Network we're currently streaming a dramatic short film, *The Doll*, produced by Dante James based on one of Chesnutt's short stories.

My First Injury

One day when we were over at Joyce's house, I participated in a pick-up tackle football game in the neighborhood. During those games, no one wore any equipment; it was just hard-nosed, bone-crushing football. Well, at one point when I was running the football, I was tackled and pulled down from behind. Falling backwards with both knees bent, I ended up tearing a ligament in my right knee. And while I didn't finish the game, I did walk home—hoping that the injury had been a minor one. To keep my injury concealed from my mother, because I just knew (or at least thought) she would bar me from ever playing football again if she really knew what had really gone down, I didn't tell anyone what had just occurred. When I arrived back at Joyce's house, I was asked—on top of everything—to go to the store to pick up a loaf of bread. Now, I could either "fess up" and tell my mother and sister what had just happened in the football game or I could soldier on and walk to the store on a bum knee hoping that no one would possibly notice. I chose the latter, and off to the store I went.

Later that night, my mother and I went back to our apartment on 71st Street. After I got into my bed, I figured the swelling in my knee would "just go away." Believe me, it did not! I had convinced myself that everything would be better in the morning. To my surprise (and soon thereafter everyone else's) when I awoke in the morning, my right knee had blown up to about three times its normal size and I couldn't move. I screamed and my mother asked what was wrong. I fibbed and told her that I had hit my knee on the basketball pole during a pick-up game. I thought that if she knew the real deal, she would bar me from ever playing football again, and I just could not imagine that. After all, I was supposed to be the second coming of Paul Warfield, the wide receiver who at the time was with the Cleveland Browns, and would later be traded to the Miami Dolphins. (When that trade happened, I was devastated). So, I couldn't tell my mother the truth. I'd rather be barred from playing basketball. So I thought.

My mother decided to call my Aunt Teddy (my mother's sister) to have Bill, a friend of Aunt Teddy's, come by the apartment and take me to St. Vincent Charity Hospital to be examined. All I can remember is that when Bill went to pick me up, he bent my knee just about an eighth of an inch and I let out such a scream that I'm sure the entire neighborhood heard me. It was probably the worst pain I've ever felt. After I was examined, it was determined that I had suffered torn ligaments in my right knee, but that I did not need surgery. I had to wear a cast for about six months. It was years later, long after my high school playing days were over, that I eventually did "fess up," telling my mother that I had really hurt my knee that day playing football.

During the 6th grade at Charles W. Chesnutt, I started to learn how to play the trumpet. My mother couldn't afford to buy me a new trumpet, but one of my teachers at the school had an old one that she had bought for her son and he no longer used. She was gracious enough to let me use the old trumpet, but I had to promise that I would take good care of it. After practicing the instrument for what seemed to be the entire school year, the day came for the big concert at the school. I was selected to play "Raindrops Keep Falling On My Head" as a duet with a flute player. I had not yet had my cast taken off my right leg so in addition to the nervousness I felt about the pending duet, I also spent time worrying about having to walk up the aisle to the front of the audience while wearing a cast. I was fine, in the end, and actually did a great job.

While my mother had always attended my concerts, both choir and orchestra, I did often wonder about my father's not being there. I believe it's something special for a young boy to look out into the crowd and see his father's face. I didn't necessarily think about the fact that my parents were separated; I just wanted him there. Years later, after having two sons, I would vow to always try to make my sons' important school and church activities, whether they were sports, plays, or conferences. I wanted my sons to know that I was there. And yes, I did make sure I returned to the teacher the trumpet that had been lent to me, and still in mint condition.

A Mother's Prayer Answered

I had graduated from Charles W. Chesnutt and was about to enter the 7th grade when an event happened that probably saved and changed my life forever. My mother had had concerns about my going to the junior high school in the neighborhood where we lived. She had felt it was just too dangerous and she wanted to get the family out of the neighborhood. What happened next was an act of God. My brother Ellis was working at the time for Kraft Foods and lived in the Lee Harvard area, on the second floor of a duplex house with his wife Evelyn and young daughter Erica, my oldest niece. It just so happened that Ellis received a promotion and was to be relocated to Pittsburgh, Pennsylvania. Ellis took that opportunity to ask the landlord if the landlord might consider renting the level in which Ellis lived to his mother and little brother. I don't know all the details, but we were able to relocate to the house where my brother had lived, and I started the 7th grade at Robert H. Jamison Junior High School. My mother's prayer had been answered.

Junior High School and a New Beginning

After we moved to Edgewood in the Lee Harvard area in 1971, I began to make new friends. I would initially forge friendships with two individuals, James "Jimmy" Wade and Brian Eskridge. Both lived in Edgewood and each had a basketball hoop in his backyard. We all would spend many afternoons together during the summer and after school in one of their yards shooting hoops and running up and down the street. We also would play tackle football either on the side grass at Jamison Jr. High School or on the side of the beauty parlor located on East 147th Street. This was the time in my life that I began to see and feel that I had some athletic talent, or so I thought. Brian lived with his mom and dad, and Jimmy, like me, lived with his mom only; but Jimmy spent a lot of time with his dad, who was a prominent individual in Cleveland's black community. While I never expressed it, I was often envious of both guys because their fathers were around. Even though Jimmy didn't live with his dad, it seemed he was always spending time with him—and he attended the same church where his dad was the organist. Jimmy would often tell us that Johnny Mathis was his uncle, although I never believed him. But years later, after seeing photos of Johnny Mathis and Jimmy's mom, I realized they did look like brother and sister. We had a lot of fun with each other and remained friends for years and, in fact, are still friends today. My wife Lillian and I are godparents to Jimmy's daughter, Dasha.

These were important years for a teenage boy. At thirteen I'm sure I thought I knew everything. I was a little rebellious, but my mother kept a tight rein on me. She never let me hang out in the streets, not that I wanted to. Other guys would hang out for hours, but not me. When my mother said "Be in at 10 pm," I was in! Although my father wasn't around and I didn't see him, I was still a pretty happy kid. It was because of all the other positive influences I had in my life. My sister Joyce was always around, and my mother made sure I attended church on a regular basis. Initially we didn't have a car; nonetheless, Mr. and Mrs. Holsendolph would pick me up every Sunday morning to take me to Sunday school. They were really great people and he kept a very clean car, a Buick. Their son Ernest (Ernie), who was much older than I, later became the editor of the *Atlanta Journal Constitution* newspaper. I always thought that was impressive.

My junior high school years are full of fond memories, especially the annual talent shows at Jamison. Groups such as "Earl Gay and the Imaginations" and "The Ponderosa Twins + 1" were the big stars in our neighborhood. Years later, after moving to New York, I would run into an old junior high and high school classmate, Jeffrey Bivens, now known as national radio personality "Jeff Foxx." He and I would often talk about those talent showcases at Jamison and our high school, John F. Kennedy, and reminisce about the groups and people we hadn't seen in years.

Those high school years were also when I really started to notice girls! In fact, my mother must have thought I had become "girl crazy." Once, she had my big brother Ellis speak to me about my fixation with girls, on one of his trips to Cleveland. Since there was no man in the house, she figured he would be the one to have a talk with me. Not sure if it worked, but we had the talk in his car, around the corner from where we lived. I would calm down in later years. Junior high school is also where I met Lincoln Hare and Larry Payton. Both were sports-minded guys and we soon became friends. We were on the track team together. Mr. Kelly was our coach. While I wasn't the fastest guy on the team, I did end up winning the high jump competition in the ninth grade during the district championships at John Adams High School, receiving my first trophy. I still have it, and it's also the first time that I was exposed to the printing industry. Mr. Profitt was my printing teacher and it was from him that I learned to set type by hand and manually print business cards. This was my first entry into publishing. Technology has surely changed the way printing is done today.

And back then, I was changing still. I left junior high in June of 1973 in anticipation of high school and playing football at John F. Kennedy.

The Second Coming of Paul Warfield

I thought I was Paul Warfield. From an early age I wore the number "42" on everything. My first football helmet had "42" painted on it. My heart was broken when Warfield was traded from the Cleveland Browns to the Miami Dolphins. However, it was a good move for Warfield, who went on to become one of the NFL's greatest wide receivers and a member of the historic 1972 Dolphins, who won the Super Bowl and who still today hold the distinction of being the only team to have had a perfect season.[1] I did receive some consolation in high school when Paul Warfield visited our school my senior year. I had an opportunity to touch the Super Bowl ring. What a joy it was for me to meet my sports hero!

In junior high my mind was always on girls, but in high school it changed to sports, especially football, although I did run track. It was also the time I felt, all the more, the absence of a father in my life. I think it's pretty normal for a young man to want to look up in the stands and see his father staring down at him, offering that moral support. That never happened for me. I could never really understand why he was never around. I know that sometimes circumstances prevent someone from traveling or that maybe one of the parents forbids the other from seeing the child, but that wasn't the case.

My mother never once told my father that he couldn't see me or that I couldn't see him.

Anyway, it hurt very much that he was not there in the stands.[2] On the other hand, my mother would often say that she couldn't stand seeing me get hit and hurt, so she never really attended any of my football games until my senior year. And wouldn't you know it, that was when I would get injured in the game? I separated my left shoulder, but remained in the game. I still can't fully rotate that shoulder. My mother did, however, attend my track meets on occasion. I was a much better football player, but I was glad to have her there. Also, although he lived out of town, my brother attended a scrimmage game our high school team had in Barberton, Ohio one Saturday morning. My one big supporter was my brother-in-law George, who attended many games during my high school years. At halftime, George would be standing there to offer encouragement as we came off the field, heading to the locker room. I really appreciated his being there. Throughout all the years I played football and ran track, my father never witnessed any of it. He never made an effort. I missed seeing him there.

High school is also where I forged relationships with individuals who became friends for life. Brain Hall, Sam Scruggs, Howard Drake and I have always shared a special bond, not only because we attended high school together, but also because we became members of Kappa Alpha Psi Fraternity, Inc. together back in 1978. (Those stories I won't be sharing in this essay.) Earl Minter and Bilal Akram also represent friendships that were established in high school that remain in place today. And then there was our group's "adopted sister," Tanya Nokes-Bankston, although she often thought that she was our mother! The times we shared together provide lasting great memories for all of us. While these relationships never replaced the emptiness I felt in not having a father around, they certainly helped. It was good to have people who cared in your corner, and they cared.

The Men in My Life

While I didn't have a father in the house, I realize, as I look back, that there were several African American men who served as role models for me. The first would be my junior high school track coach, Mr. Kelly. He had a way of always encouraging the members of the track team and would sometimes offer little tidbits about life. He surely made us a better team. In high school I was fortunate to have three men whom I could talk to, each about different things. First, there was my football coach, Mr. Roye Kidd. He was a gentle soul off the field, but on the field he could really get in your butt! I respected him greatly. He ended up being my coach for three years. As a sophomore, you generally played on the JV team and all juniors and seniors played varsity football. Well, at one varsity game, the JV team was in the stands and the tight end on varsity was not having a good game. In the stands with my other JV teammates, I was going on about how I could do a better job, etc. The following Monday (after the previous Friday night game) my JV coach, Mr. Mitchell, came to my homeroom and asked me to step outside the door. He let me know that I was being moved up to varsity and to report to the varsity practice after school. I was nervous all day in school. I found out that the coaches had noticed my play during the first couple of JV games and had decided to move me into the starting position on varsity. At my very first varsity practice, in a blocking drill, I was asked to block one of the defensive stars of the team, a senior named Darryl Pugh, a guy who must have been 300 pounds then, in high school (I weighed a grand total of 185 pounds). Of course, "Big Pugh", as we called him, "ate my lunch" and I could hear the laughter. I had been set up. Who did this sophomore think he was? Coming up to varsity! They never let me forget I was a sophomore.

I felt alone, and in my first varsity game, the quarterback wouldn't even throw me the ball. It wasn't until the third or fourth varsity game that I appeared in that the ball even came my way. I had a good game and was pleased when Curtis Johnson, the quarterback, said to me "Good game, JV." I finally felt accepted. I would later find out that another sophomore was on the varsity team, Robert Chisholm. We both were glad to have each other. Throughout my high school playing career, Mr. Kidd was always there for not only me, but the other players as well. He was a great man and really seemed to care for the players on and off the field.

My high school track coach, Harold Kimball, also had a big impact on me. He used to passionately call me "the fat man" because as a football player I was bigger than most of the other guys on the track team. But I was still fast. Mr. Kimball was the essence of "cool." He had attended and run track at Tennessee State and was very proud of that fact. He also had a great heart. I can't tell you how many times he bought track shoes for some of the guys who didn't have them. I don't know what type of salary he earned as an art teacher and track coach, but he was always there for us guys on the track team. We were fortunate to have him as a coach and an unofficial mentor. It really meant a lot to me, given that I had no father at home. His smile could light up a room.

Probably the man who had the most profound effect on my life during my high school years was my printing teacher, Mr. Kenneth Ragland. Mr. Ragland drove a Thunderbird with what we called "gangster doors" and he would sometimes give me a ride close to my house. On those rides, Mr. Ragland introduced me to Stanley Turrentine, a jazz saxophonist. Once, when I was in college at the

University of Cincinnati, "Stanley T," as he was affectionately called, was playing at Bogart's, a local spot near the college. Trying to impress a young lady with my knowledge of jazz, I suggested that we go see Stanley T's show at Bogart's. I thought I was cool.

Mr. Ragland taught me a lot about printing and made sure that not only I, but the entire class, learned the complete printing process. At John F. Kennedy High School, we were fortunate enough to have a couple of AB Dick printing presses and a great camera room. That's where I honed my production skills. I learned everything I could from Mr. Ragland about printing and became an expert at running the presses we had at school—so much so that he often gave me the responsibility of running the classroom when he was away. He must have been in the military because he would always talk in this gruff, military style and his assignments in class were announced as though he were always giving orders to a platoon. He was a character, but we loved him. He also introduced me to Cutty Sark, his favorite drink. He would always talk about going to the Trophy Lounge on Cedar to have a few "Cutty Sarks" after work. He was my main man and I enjoyed being around him. Not only did I learn printing from him, I learned about life. At our high school graduation, he told Jimmy Wade and me in his customary gruff voice: "Life's getting ready to kick you in the ass; get ready." Those were his exact words. I never forgot those words and I'll never forget Mr. Ragland and all that he taught me in high school. Years later, I would find out that he was the uncle of a friend of mine in Cleveland, Donna Berry. When Mr. Ragland passed away several years ago, Donna asked me to write a letter to be included in his obituary. That was one of my biggest honors. I think about him often. In any interview I do, I always find a way to salute Mr. Ragland and what he did for me during those years. I would not be doing what I'm doing today had it not been for him. He deposited so much of himself into me. And countless others. For that I am forever grateful.

Later, after college, three other men would be instrumental in my life: William Hall, Lonzo "Lonnie" Coleman, and Al Quarles. Mr. Hall was the father of my good friend Brian Hall. Mr. Hall and his brother ran a transportation company in Cleveland, Industrial Transport. It continues today and Brian is the CEO. Mr. Hall taught me a lot about business and about how to persevere. Quitting, for him, was never an option. He was always counseling Brian and me about business, conveying to us what we needed to do in order to be successful. Mr. Hall was involved in the Cleveland Business League, itself affiliated with the National Business League, which was founded by Booker T. Washington. Mr. Hall always seemed to state that particular fact with pride.

Lonnie Coleman was also very supportive of me, very encouraging of my business endeavors. In fact, he was one of the very first investors in a magazine

I started years ago in Cleveland. I could always talk to Lonnie about business matters and went by his office many times just to talk to him and to listen to his wisdom. He may not know it, but he had a great impact on me.

Al Quarles has been a mentor and friend for over 25 years. He was there when I started *American Legacy* magazine. I could always count on his counsel, support, and encouragement. As a young man trying to discover what he wanted to accomplish in life, I soon found that each of these men would play a pivotal role in my development. Over the years, I have often wondered what it would have been like if I could have built these types of relationships with my father. I often just wanted someone to talk to. In later years, my brother Ellis and I would grow closer after his retirement. I did have, as well, my father-in-law Henry Freeman, who was a man full of common sense, which he shared to help illuminate for people precisely what was important in life—God and family. One thing for sure, I appreciate what Mr. Kelly, Roye Kidd, Harold Kimball, Kenneth Ragland, William Hall, Al Quarles, and Lonnie Coleman all gave to me. I'm glad they were there.

The Ten-Year Gap

On September 10, 1983 Lillian and I were married in Cleveland, Ohio at Lee Seville Baptist Church, in the presence of God and several hundred family members and friends. Dear friends from high school, college, my fraternity brothers, all came to support Lillian and me on our wedding day. I was especially happy that my cousins Sue and Marsha from Evansville, Indiana traveled to Cleveland for the wedding. But there was one guest in attendance whom I hadn't seen in 10 years, my father. Yes, I hadn't seen my father since 1973, when my brother, sister, and I had visited him in Greenville, Kentucky.

Prior to our very special day, Lillian had taken the initiative to call my father to make sure he was coming to the wedding. For me, it certainly proved to be a day filled with mixed emotions. On your wedding day, you are already dealing with a flood of emotions that relate simply to getting married. I also had emotions stemming from my father's being at the wedding. After the marriage ceremony, just as my father approached me to give me a congratulatory hug, I broke down and cried. Here I was, at the age of 25, crying like a baby! My father-in-law Henry Freeman didn't know what was wrong with me at first until it was explained to him that I was reacting to not having seen my father in so very many years. I was just overcome with emotion. While I was glad that he attended the wedding, I often thought about all of the things he had missed during that ten-year period in which we didn't see each other. Oh, we'd talk on the phone every now and then, but I can't really even tell you when, and what we talked about. I think I thought most about how he had missed my high school years, my playing football and running track. My senior prom. My high school graduation. I always felt short-changed because he was not there. But on this day, all those bad memories seemed to just fade away. For a moment, I had my father around. I was learning to forgive. And you know something, it felt good. It felt so good that I looked forward to becoming a father myself. In the back of my mind, I think I had something to prove. I wanted to be a good father. No exception. And that is something that I worked on constantly.

The Joy of Fatherhood

I guess when you grow up not having your father in your life, you look forward to the occasion of your own fatherhood with great anticipation. For the first five years of our marriage, Lillian and I were unable to conceive a child. Then, in 1988, we were blessed with the birth of our first son, Rodney Jeremiah. And thirteen months later, our second son, Richard Joshua, was born. I will never forget the day that each came into this world.

But more than anything, I was looking forward to fulfilling my role as a father. You always hear people say that they really didn't care if they had a girl or a boy and I'm sure I made similar comments. However, I must admit that I was extremely happy to have two boys! Not that I wouldn't have been just as happy with a daughter, but I had always secretly envisioned playing catch with my sons. I had always vowed to be there for my sons no matter what. Some people might say that I overcompensated in my role because I didn't have a father at home; but, when raising two young African-American boys, I couldn't take the chance. And besides, the boys not only had me, but they had Lillian, who is a fantastic mother. She always tells the story that I never really spanked the boys. And come to think of it, I probably didn't. That was actually her job because most of the time I was traveling. But even though I traveled extensively, I tried to make it to every event possible. Whether there was a little league baseball game, football game, hockey game, school or church program, I'm proud to say that I was there. One event, many years ago, stands out, from when the boys were small. I had been in Kansas City on business and was due to return on Sunday morning for a program of theirs at Antioch Baptist Church in Cleveland. It was a time when I had just begun to teach them how to tie a tie, but still with my assistance.

On that particular Sunday morning Lillian and the boys had arrived at church for the program and my flight was a little late getting back to Cleveland. In the meantime, one of our friends had asked the boys if they wanted him to help them tie their ties. While it wouldn't have bothered me if they had let him assist them, they said "No, thank you" and waited for me to arrive. Upon my arrival, they met me at the back of the church and I proceeded to help them with their ties. There are many situations like this that occurred throughout the years. I just always wanted to be there for my two boys. To talk with them about anything. And I now know that in the back of my mind I always thought about the emptiness I felt in not having had my own father say "I'm proud of you."

My young men hear me say it all the time. I'm proud of what each has accomplished. Rodney Jeremiah played football at Yale, completing undergrad in 2010 and graduating from Yale Divinity School in 2013. And in 2010 Richard Joshua graduated from Boston University, and BU graduate school in 2013. Ok, just let me hold out my chest even more: both are Members of Kappa Alpha Psi Fraternity, Inc. Yes, we have a Kappa house. On some days I'm sure Lillian can't stand it. Not only do I have the joy of being a father of two great sons, we all share another bond that can never be broken. I hope I've set a great example as they enter fatherhood.

The day that I realized just what it meant to be a father was the first Sunday after the horrific events of September 11, 2001. "Nine Eleven" was, of course, a tremendously sad day for all Americans. Rodney Jeremiah happened to have a baseball game in Connecticut that following Sunday. It was a beautiful Sunday afternoon. As another father and I sat in the stadium watching our respective sons play baseball, I thought quietly to myself, "How blessed am I to have the opportunity to just sit here and watch my son play ball after the tragic events of this past week." I will never forget how sitting there, enjoying "America's pastime," made me feel. That's when I knew just how important a role it was that I had played in my sons' lives.

Sometimes I used to complain about getting up early on Saturday morning to take Richard Joshua to hockey practice, especially since he was the goalie, a position which meant (especially when he was little) that I had to help him put on all of those pads, and his skates. But after thinking about it, I realize now that it was pure joy. Those Saturday mornings were special. Joshua knew he could depend on my being there. That made me feel good. That made me proud.

Learning To Forgive

One thing I came to realize was that for me to fulfill the role of a father, I had to forgive my own father and try not to hold onto the feelings that I'd had about his not being around. I must admit, it was extremely hard to do. I used to ask myself "Why?" Why doesn't he visit more? Why doesn't he call more? To be honest, there was never a father/son bond. Sometimes I feel ashamed to say it, but Father's Day could come and go and it really didn't affect me. But I learned how not to be so bitter and how to move forward. I learned how to deal with it. By forgiving him, it allowed me to grow as a man and, more importantly, as a father.

Thank God for restoration. Since the time that my father came to Cleveland in 1983 for my wedding, God allowed us to restore our relationship. I saw my father more, through the years, prior to his passing in 2010. We were blessed to have been able to spend very many great times together, and my sons were able to be with their grandfather on the farm in Greenville, Kentucky. I'm sure there are memories from those times that my sons value and will never forget. My father was a good man. He just had an alcohol problem that ultimately destroyed his family; yet through God's grace, relationships were restored.[3]

One Final Thought

My overall objective in writing and sharing this essay is to say to men that it's important for you to take care of your children.[4] We hear the statistics with regard to the number of households that are headed by women and how these women usually have to chase down men to take care of the men's children. Let me say this: I'm not naive to think that every relationship and every marriage is going to work. What I am saying is that no matter what happens in the relationship or marriage, don't make the children suffer. Men, take care of your children. I could never imagine having a child and not having a relationship with that child. Or not taking the financial responsibility for that child. There is nothing that my wife could have done to me that would have made me not want to be in my sons' lives—nothing.

I recognize that I've been blessed in many ways. I had a wonderful mother who passed away, at the age of 95, in December 2020. She supported me, prayed for me, and wanted nothing but the best for me. The values she taught me when I was a child are ones that I still hold onto today. And for that I thank her. While it is the case that I didn't have a father in the home, I did have, nonetheless, a loving mother who was always there for me.

If any man reading this essay has an estranged relationship with your spouse, ex, or girlfriend, a relationship that is keeping you away from your children, go ahead and make the necessary steps to rectify the situation. The true joys of fatherhood far outweigh any problems that exist between that woman and you, believe me. I am living the joy of fatherhood on a daily basis. My prayer for you is that you will live that joy, too.

ENDNOTES

1   See, for more details and statistics, Roger Gordon, *The Cleveland Browns All-Time All-Stars: The Best Players at Each Position for the Browns* (Lanham, MD: Lyons Press, Rowman and Littlefield, 2022).

2   The painful problem of fatherlessness or paternal absence seems to be a recurring theme in a great deal of memoir writing. A notable and instructive discussion of this social ill, along with some helpful philosophical solutions, can be found in Marvin Olasky's *Lament for a Father: The Journey to Understanding and Forgiveness* (Phillipsburg, NJ: P. and R. Publishing, 2021).

3   Irrespective of one's faith or belief system, or lack thereof, important texts and strategies exist to help children of alcoholics. See, by way of example, Herbert L. Gravitz and Julie D. Bowden, *Recovery: A Guide for Adult Children of Alcoholics* (New York: Simon and Schuster, 1985).

4   Hope exists in this regard, as evidenced in the writings of many fathers, old and young, some famous and some not—all are important. See, worthy of note, the book by celebrity and author Omar Epps, *From Fatherless to Fatherhood* (Morrisville, NC.: Lulu Publishing Services, 2018).

BIBLIOGRAPHY

Epps, Omar. *From Fatherless to Fatherhood*. Morrisville, NC: Lulu Publishing Services, 2018.

Gordon, Roger. *The Cleveland Browns All-Time All-Stars: The Best Players at Each Position for the Browns*. Lanham, MD: Lyons Press, Rowman and Littlefield, 2022.

Gravitz, Herbert L. and Bowden, Julie D. *Recovery: A Guide for Adult Children of Alcoholics*. New York: Simon and Schuster, 1985.

Olasky, Marvin. *Lament for a Father; The Journey to Understanding and Forgiveness*. Phillipsburg, NJ: P. and R. Publishing, 2021.

CHAPTER TEN
Walking

Norm Jones

In Deep

At the age of 46, I find myself periodically contemplating the life of the mind; questioning, in a good way, the contours of my own mind and heart. I was raised by my mother and maternal grandparents. I was three when my parents divorced. My mother and I moved from my birthplace in Phoenix, Arizona to live with my grandparents in Louisville, Kentucky. The story is that my grandfather, a long-time educator, insisted that I attend a private school. I'm fascinated by the generational differences that surely emerged when my likely over-involved grandparents "told" my mother how and where her child would be educated.

My mother spent the majority of her professional life in what seemed to be a frustrating oscillation between social work and teaching sociology. Toward the end of her career, she settled down into a comfortable balance between teaching and advising. I think the advising scratched the social work itch. My theory is that professorship provided more stability, perhaps more status, and certainly more income than social work ever would.

What is it with this thing called status? This thing called work? This thing called education? Credentials? Are they related? Are they step- or half-siblings? Or are they kissing cousins with complicated contempt for one another? I've danced with all four, sometimes in pairs or threesomes, and sometimes in a singular and simple two-step; first one step, then another… just trying to make it to the end of a seemingly endless song.

Until graduate school, I was a very average student. I suppose a more precise statement is that I had average grades. But I know and remember the inextricable connections I made between my grades and who I was as a young intellectual. The truth is that I did not see myself as an intellectual at all. I doubt that I ever even uttered or wrote the word "intellectual" before age 30. But I could certainly perform intellectualism. I was bright. I was charismatic. And I came from a solid academic pedigree as a third-generation college graduate with parents and grandparents each having acquired at least one master's degree. I was also a lazy student, unmotivated or not stimulated by learning, intimidated by math, bored by history, moderately intrigued by—but only peripherally invested in—literature, and absolutely frustrated with "foreign" languages. School was hard and therefore something to be tolerated until no longer required. This meant I was committed to and through college, at least.

I almost went to Hampton. I remember visiting and feeling simultaneously drawn to and disconnected from the place. It felt…rich. I liked that, but I didn't know why. I'd gone to school with rich white folks from Pre-K all the way through high school, a reality that had proven just as annoying as any other adjective I could ascribe. Perhaps my visit to Hampton was my first experience with black wealth.[1] In retrospect, I realized that I'd somehow sensationalized much of what my eyes beheld. But it seemed like everyone drove Jaguars and BMWs, wore designer labels, and walked with great resolve. I'd already been accepted to Morehouse when I visited Hampton. It boiled down to a weird comparison of the pristine aesthetic of Hampton's campus with beautiful water around it and the constant buzz of the Atlanta University Center (AUC). I had never heard of the AUC before visiting Morehouse as a junior. I begged my mother to let me attend Morehouse's Prospective Student Seminar (PSS) which was designed for high-school juniors. You spent a full day in classes, then a weekend learning all about Morehouse and her surrounding institutions, including Spelman College, Morris Brown College, Clark Atlanta University, the Interdenominational Theological Center, and the Morehouse School of Medicine.

By high school I was pretty well traveled, having done an exchange program in Mexico in middle school and having taken annual mini-vacations to not-so-far-off, but interesting, places such as Indianapolis, St. Louis, Chicago, and Virginia. Vacations were always hybrid in nature. There would be no Busch Gardens amusement park unless and until one was subjected to the most immersive tour offered by Colonial Williamsburg, for example. All made worth it when weighed against the endless delight of the all-you-can-eat buffets scattered along the strips and boardwalks of Virginia Beach. A foodie's delight!

I always enjoyed exploration and travel, but I was tired when I landed at Atlanta's Hartsfield International Airport. My backpack felt so heavy. I wasn't just physically tired, I was emotionally spent because of a preoccupation with the unknown. Would Morehouse be as cool as it seemed in the brochures? Would people like me? Would I like them? Was it that deep? My inner dialogues were (and still are, at times) simultaneously annoying and amusing noise in my head. I found it so strange that the subway ran through the airport. It was only after I'd walked what was essentially the length of the airport that I realized I had forfeited the opportunity to ride on the airport trans system. So much for thinking myself "well traveled." I laughed and suddenly felt quite "country."

Toward Friendship

Louisville versus Atlanta became an everyday theme as I made friends at Morehouse. I'd always been proud of the fact that I was from the only "big city" in Kentucky, with its 120 counties! My closest friends—two of whom have become lifelong brothers—were fellow members of the Morehouse College Glee Club. I still remember auditioning for the Glee Club. As I waited to go into the director's office to sing a few bars of whatever music I'd have to read-on-demand, my suspicion about Morehouse was confirmed. I was surrounded by the best of the best. I was swimming in a sea of black men, almost all of whom were, in one way or another, voted the "best" fill in the blank, found to be the first, the only, one of few, etc., etc., etc. At first I harbored some resentment around this realization. I suppose I actually had kind of a love/hate relationship with being the first or only. It was a guaranteed distinction that certainly carried with it a burden, but also a kind of cachet—one that I knew how to amplify and, if necessary, exploit. It was the reason I applied to only historically black colleges and universities.[2] I knew that if I was to have a "black experience," it would have to be in college. It took going to Morehouse to help me understand that my need to feel special was partially rooted in my having been "othered" by so many white people, usually in educational settings. Over time I realized that being one among so many phenomenal black men didn't make me less special, it made me normal. I can't imagine having gone to any other institution.

There isn't a day that goes by that I don't consciously or unconsciously tap into the very necessary reality of black male excellence. I learned that at Morehouse. I've never been (at least in my active imagination) the stereotypical prototype of a Morehouse Man—one who is so self-confident that he cannot be taught, influenced to change his mind, or persuaded by a counter-argument. It is only in my middle age that I better understand these images as societal tropes that, though often presented in humorous frames, are actually an expression of this country's anxious relationship with black men who are very sure about our leadership prowess, our ability to steer a ship (chief among them, our own lives), and, increasingly so, our ability to get in touch with our own male privilege in ways that make more space for the voices of black women who typically hold even better solutions.

I am an Omega Man. I've never been a Que Dawg, though I can certainly play one on TV if the mood hits! Atomic Dog can bring that out of the most reserved of us. Most members of the Divine Nine know the phrase "Friendship is essential to the soul."[3] It is a mantra with which I have a complicated relationship. As the motto of my fraternity, it is wise and revelatory; I can't think of more artful and important words. But my friendships have come in waves and chapters. Very few have been sustained at the level of what I would consider true friendships. And that is why two particular people—both of whom are my Morehouse brothers and, more specifically, my Morehouse Glee Club brothers—represent the best of what human connection offers. They've seen me soar and celebrated me in ways that remind me that greatness is my destiny; that it is where I am intended to dwell. They've also witnessed my downward spirals, some of which probably looked and felt precipitous. They had always been watching me, learning me. It is a dynamic that many friendships lack. It is the thing that allowed them to tell me that I wasn't okay when I wanted them to believe that I was.

We have vacationed together, welcomed each other's children into the world (excited to don the title of "proud uncle"), we've attended each other's weddings, offered toasts to—and, at times, scratched our heads concerning—the institution of marriage and its unapologetic way of showing us the worst and best of ourselves, been there for one another during the loss of loved ones, and so so much more. My crew, my boys have been… necessary air when I didn't know to breathe.

On Time

As I write this memoir-essay, I'm reminded of a book I've always wanted to write. I have no idea what I'll put in the book exactly, but the concept focuses on the interconnectedness of life, the notion that not only does everything happen for a reason but everything, in my opinion, happens at an appointed time. And even if something unexpected or seemingly poorly timed occurs, there's always learning and growth connected to it. In my life, this learning and growth often happens in a retrospective context. I have been journaling for over twenty years. I don't do it quite as much anymore, but I used to enjoy going back and reading old entries as a way of discovering interesting connections. This holds particular salience in my professional life. I can remember sitting in bed, totally baffled by my decision to accept a position as Chief of Staff to the Superintendent of an urban and (at the time) academically bankrupt school district. I was 24. The politics was beyond description and I was absolutely drowning in an ecosystem that I didn't understand.

The superintendent saw something, maybe many things, in me that gave him an assurance that I was the right person for the job. Forgive the term, but that was a "crazy" time. Despite some fairly significant trauma that I will probably have to work through for many years to come, that job grew me up. My smile, my charm, my nice suits that I'd purchased only because they were on sale... none of that was coming to save me from the school board, or angry parents, or unethical vendors willing to "cut me in" if I could help deliver a contract. As scary and unbelievable as it was, this was the real world. My world. And the only way to stay afloat was to get up early and stay up late.

I began to read for content and context. I asked questions. I forced myself to speak up and contribute to conversations even though my introversion urged otherwise. I was more than some young buck the superintendent had recruited (which is how most people saw and treated me). I was the Chief of Staff and I had better act like it if I was to survive. When I left the school district, I likened it to an Israelite fleeing Egypt, except I would like to believe I didn't complain and I certainly had no desire to return. If I were once again to find myself in workplace bondage, it would need to be in a different place and under different circumstances.

Out of Order

The older I get, the less reverence I have for order, in the strict sense of the word. That is to say, I've come to appreciate messiness, finding connection between that which presents as disparate and dissonant. I enjoy, as William Durden, former president of Dickinson College would put it, "living on the diagonal." The idea of finding connection by looking at relationships between things that don't appear connected at all strikes me as the deepest form of learning. It is only at this stage in my career, after about 23 years in education, that things appear to have happened in an "order" that is a bit unexplainable and yet makes complete sense. My plan, since 8th grade, was to be an attorney. Again, I can hear the words of Bill Durden: "I am not a proponent of life plans. Inevitably, they don't tend to work out," he'd say. My ultimate goal was to make a lot of money without having to use math. I held great disdain for math and I have the transcripts to prove it! It's a disdain that haunts me even today.

I'm not entirely sure where my dream of being an attorney came from. I think I probably watched my mother struggle as a social worker and sociology professor. It's not that she struggled to make ends meet, but it seems she was always having to cobble things together to support the life she had created for herself and me. In private school, the unofficial uniform to be worn when one needed to "dress up" consisted of khaki pants (Duckhead brand, of course), boat shoes (LL Bean for many, Sebago for me), and a button down shirt. It was actually an attorney who helped me see that law was not for me.

I remember sitting in his corner office. He was a managing partner. In just about a year and a quarter, I'd risen through the ranks from copier, to legal runner, to paralegal; I attended weekend classes and became certified. I was just as proud of my notary status! Despite my precipitous ascension, my parents were pretty angry with my being so blindly committed to working in law that I'd taken a job making copies. The truth was that my LSAT scores weren't high enough to get me into the law schools I was considering. I'll never forget my shock when the managing partner said "Norm, I don't want to see you here a year from now." He went on to tell me, in his own unique, blunt, yet affirming way, that he'd watched me trying to fit a square peg into a round hole. He told me that he saw my talent and that I needed to dispose of the notion that law was the only respectable career that aligned with my skill set. "I could see you in hospital administration, non-profit leadership, government... your skills could take you any number of places." My mother, still frustrated by this whole "copy" thing, had hounded me about getting a master's of public administration while I was attempting to raise my LSAT score. And it was in that place—graduate school—that I learned of the capaciousness of my mind.

Beyond Belief

I was shocked when I got my first "A" in graduate school. It wasn't that I'd not earned it. I studied hard. But I'd not gotten enough "A" grades throughout school to see them as consistently attainable. Then I got another "A" and another. I got one "B" in graduate school—something which I'm still a bit salty about, as they say. I went through a period of shame and regret. Regret connected to a quiet, but persistent, lamentation that I'd not cared enough, tried hard enough, persisted enough to do better in elementary, middle, high school, and even college. What I came to learn, however, is that knowledge works like time-release medication. I now choose to believe that all learning has contributed to my intellectualism, that all learning includes all of life -- not just formal education—and that my learning includes my teaching, my passing on to others that which I've learned based on my lived experience. My learning is a gift that keeps on giving.

I've come to understand the life of the mind as an oasis of hope. For me, the mind is a container for all I hope for and also the manifestation of all I've experienced. It is the place where a conceptualization or imagination of my best life is cultivated. I've worked hard to bring about the kind of change I wish to see in myself and the world, but I've also come to appreciate the hard realities of change. The mind, when disconnected from the heart, can become the perfect enemy of necessary change. It can become the place where one's intellectualism enters an ugly battle with the unknown; that which resides in the heart but carries with it no empirical evidence or information; a place where logic won't stand up or stick. I think the mind is also the place where we can safely reconcile our intentions with what actually occurs. Most of us have an imagination for how our lives will be constructed, how things will play out. Our growth happens in the spaces where we react to the fact that things have not played out exactly the way we intended. This is also the place where the muscle that is leadership gets developed.

As an introvert, I have a deep and rich inner life. It has taken quite some time to become comfortable with that part of my identity. After reading the book *Quiet* by Susan Cain, I actually began to feel a sense of pride in being an introvert. First off, I'm not very big on labels, but inasmuch as human beings love and need to categorize ourselves, I've found ironiccommunity with other introverts—those who offer no apologies for the attraction to solitude and more sedentary forms of entertainment, relaxation, and intellectual stimulation.

And now, after several deputy positions in both K-12 and higher education, after having focused on issues of diversity, equity, inclusion, and justice as a middle manager, associate vice-president, and vice-president, I find myself recalibrating my thinking and feelings about the things that matter most. One of my revelations is that my intellectual contributions must push past the limits of the academy as a formal bureaucratic structure. Perhaps I speak as an academic administrator, but the notion that the unspoken social contract of some organizations tethers individuals to one space is too confining for me to appreciate at this stage in my life.

For me, the life of the mind is partially about finding those who need and want your messages. Teachers become students and students become teachers when thoughts and ideas are permitted to wander beyond artificial bounds in pursuit of those who are hungry for particular pieces of information—for answers and questions that have come from living life, not just reading textbooks. As a black man, I reject anything that looks or smells like a limit, a line, an artificial and ill-contrived rule. I turn to history to learn more about who made the rule and why it still exists. Even if I didn't want them to be, my thoughts are unbridled and restless. They don't settle until they find their intended dwelling, their home, their companions.

I'm on a quest to actualize and manifest what it means to be a global citizen, to pursue truth actively by looking for it and finding it in myself and others, in food, in music, in prayer, in meditation, in dreams, and in journals. In trees and wind and songs without lyrics. In poems and white papers, data sets and billboards, in rap and opera, in spirituals and hymns, in tapestries and pottery, in cheap seats at a Celtics game (I'm actually a Lakers fan, Massachusetts being one of those frustrating confines), or my son's football practices.

One year, the woman who, over time, became the matriarch of our family gave me a book titled *The Dash* by Linda Ellis. Having grown up with my grandparents, both of whom had multiple siblings, I experienced a lot of death pretty early in life. My grandfather, a man I absolutely idolized, was diagnosed with pancreatic cancer. He died in my arms. I was nine. I'd benefitted from the unending wisdom of elder great uncles and aunts, but I didn't fully appreciate their legacies until that inevitable moment when those gathered read a carefully constructed obituary. I remember how it felt to read line after line about the accomplishments of my kinfolk. Not only their credentials, but their values, the things they care about, and the way they lived their lives. That dash carries with it such a profound opportunity to move beyond individual contribution and recognize that we come into this world to do our little part in perpetuating legacies that pre-date us and will outlast us. I was recently impacted by the death of two individuals whom I didn't know. But I know their loved ones and I grieved beside them and with them. When I learned of each death, less than three weeks apart, I was moved to write this poem. This is the life of the mind… the sense one is given to listen to one's heart with, and to express.

> **The People You Don't Know**
> Feathers in the air
> Have an origin
> Their beauty float on their own merits
> And the beholder knows only what the senses reveal
> The timelessness, the transcendent essence of a lingering feeling
> A feeling. And feelings that have no rational frame.
> People… in their most magnificent abstraction, reflect traditional notions of connection
> The people you don't know, you know all too well.
> And they make our lives more beautiful.

I am the husband of a beautiful black woman and father of two beautiful black young men and one beautiful, young, black baby girl, who happens to be eight but will always be my one and only baby girl. When I see t-shirts and other paraphernalia that promote the quote "I am my ancestors' wildest dreams," I am convicted and convinced, and moved to declare my value and to resolve within myself that any achievement, any act that advances humanity (within and among the black community, in particular), any and every investment I make in the lives of my given and chosen family and all with whom I come in direct or indirect contact is but a drop in the proverbial bucket that is the brilliance and majesty of the African diaspora.

ENDNOTES

1   For broader historical context and insight into black wealth and black upper-class life, see Larry Otis Graham, *Our Kind of People: Inside America's Black Upper Class* (New York: Harper Perennial, 1999) and also, of course, E. Franklin Frazier's classic study, *Black Bourgeoisie: The Book That Brought the Shock of Self-Revelation to Middle-Class Blacks in America* (New York: Free Press, 1997; first published in 1955).

2   In the US context, the rich history and longstanding importance of HBCUs can hardly be overstated. See, for a detailed discussion, Bobby L. Lovett, *America's Historically Black Colleges and Universities, A Narrative History, 1837-2009* (Macon, GA: Mercer University Press, 2015).

3   For very useful and extensive commentary on the "Divine Nine" fraternities and sororities (i.e., the major collegiate and civic organizations known as Alpha Kappa Alpha; Alpha Phi Alpha; Delta Sigma Theta; Iota Phi Theta; Kappa Alpha Sigma; Omega Psi Phi; Phi Beta Sigma; Sigma Gamma Rho; and Zeta Phi Beta), see a couple of very valuable academic resources: Gregory S. Parks, *Black Greek Letter Organizations in the 21st Century, Our Fight Has Just Begun* (Lexington, KY: University Press of Kentucky, 2017) and Lawrence C. Ross, Jr., *The Divine Nine: The History of African American Fraternities and Sororities* (New York: Dafina Books, 2019).

BIBLIOGRAPHY

Cain, Susan. *Quiet: The Power of Introverts in a World That Can't Stop Talking*. New York: Crown, 2012.

Ellis, Linda and Anderson, Mac. *The Dash: Making a Difference with your Life from Beginning to End*. Naperville, Illinois: Simple Truths, 2013.

Frazier, E. Franklin. *Black Bourgeoisie: The Book That Brought the Shock of Self-Revelation to Middle Class Blacks in America*. New York: Free Press, 1997.

Graham, Larry Otis. *Our Kind of People: Inside America's Black Upper Class*. New York: Harper Perennial, 1999.

Lovett, Bobby L. *America's Historically Black Colleges and Universities: A Narrative History, 1837-2009*. Macon, GA: Mercer University Press, 2015.

Parks, Gregory S. *Black Greek Letter Organizations in the 21st Century: Our Fight Has Just Begun*. Lexington, KY: University Press of Kentucky, 2017.

Ross, Lawrence C., Jr. *The Divine Nine: the History of African American Fraternities and Sororities*. New York: Dafina Books, 2019.

CHAPTER ELEVEN

"...the Child that's Got His Own"

Jason Scott Manuel

Of all the many songs that comprise the soundtrack of "the times" of my upbringing, one in particular seems to have played continuously. That song was Billie Holiday's *God Bless the Child*. When I say that the song played continuously, I do not mean that I kept experiencing it audibly throughout the years. I am referring instead to the ability a song has to articulate our conditions, our experiences, our hopes, and our emotions, despite how raw or unresolved they might be. Songs can become a consolidated body of lore that is set to melody, rather like an elegant form of Morse code. So, when I say that the song played continuously, I speak to the lore that the song contained and expressed. I speak, also, to that which also inspired the generation that influenced me. The story that I will share with you is about my having been raised to be that "child" whom the song speaks of, and the hope that led to it.

Part One—The Buoyancy of Hope

Born into this world, no one of us seems to realize how much our early lives float upon the motions of the past and present. The will of God, the intersecting and shifting of human wills, and the timing of events are all winds that blow upon our courses. We are placed into our surroundings as if we were laid into water. This reminds me of the biblical story of the infant Moses. It was the combination of his being placed into the Nile's riverbanks and his encountering another's compassion to draw him out from among the reeds that hid him that, together, yielded a fantastic change of circumstances. In a tragic time of the persecution of his nation, his mother's love and hopes for that child to have a better life prompted her great acts of sacrifice and risk. I witnessed this same kind of love and hope, which flows from one generation to the next, and which also prompts sacrifice and risk. These compassionate acts are similar to those which allowed me to be drawn out of the water and from among reeds, which may have kept me hidden, releasing me into a life that would also benefit from a fantastic change of circumstance.

On July 11th, 1971, I was born in New Jersey, the only son to my mother, Lauren Delores Manuel, a Brooklynite. At a young age, her mother (whom I called "Madre") began to suffer from a severe mental illness that left her incapable of caring for her six children (my mother being the eldest). I was told that throughout Madre's youth she was envied and ridiculed for being light-skinned, educated, and beautiful. Years of enduring this treatment and having the added pressures of caring for a large number of children born in close succession, and with little assistance, absolutely took their toll on her. This ultimately changed the landscape of the family. My grandfather (whom I called "Padre") decided to relocate the family to New Jersey in the hopes that he would find better work opportunities for himself, adequate care for Madre, and stable accommodations for his children. After relocating, Madre would only periodically live in the apartments that Padre rented for them, as her condition fluctuated and over time grew worse. Eventually, as her mental health deteriorated, she would spend much of the rest of her life residing in and out of large mental asylums. (Years later, a government mandate would close some of these facilities for very frightening reasons.) Padre decided that the best solution would be to arrange foster care for his children. He separated them by proximate age ranges into two foster homes within town so that they all could maintain some sense of connectedness and support. He spent the rest of their youth working extremely hard to support a family, which had then become somewhat of a distributed network, now inclusive of the extended relationships of the foster families themselves. He initially worked as a barber. As a former "dandy," he was used to spending a lot of time in local barbershops. After returning from the war, there seemed to be many barbershops in Black neighborhoods, but his situation required more income. He eventually turned to truck driving. Truck driving was good money, but would potentially inconvenience his being accessible to his family. It was a risk worth taking, as options for a man with only a grade school education were limited. Depending on the haul, he was often given portions of the surplus by the companies he drove for. These extras afforded him gifts for his children at times, even food for his own table. Moreover, if you've ever driven cross-country or any long distance, you know there's a lot that you can get off your chest when you are driving a long road and staring at the horizon. He had a lot on his chest. I think these drives were a form of meditation for him. They gave him the solitude he needed to sort out his conflict and guilt over simultaneously sending his wife into institutional care and his children into foster care. I know this because he'd later reveal this to me. His hope was that if he did right by them in this circumstance, perhaps at least the next generation of children would not experience the separation that their parents had. He was correct; none of their children would have that experience—and this was something that gave him peace. Each grandchild born into the family was, for him, a confirmation of his hopes. I was that child who would first represent these things for Padre. In fact, truth be told, none of his other grands would have as close a relationship with him as I did.

Upon learning these things, I initially thought my mother and her siblings' needing foster care was exceptional. However, I later learned that foster care homes were far more commonplace in our culture than I had assumed. Further, they apparently served, in many cases, as an additional source of income for the hosting foster family rather than simply being a gesture of love, as one might hope. Today, some may call that "doing well by doing good." However, this observation has made it clear to me that it is very easy in our culture to view charity as a commodity. There was a great deal of risk involved in the route my mother's father chose. I am sure that Padre had heard many things about the foster care system. But considering the storm he was facing, he simply wanted a better life for his children and this was the best decision he could make at the time… to send them into someone else's care and hope that compassionate hands would receive them.

Eventually, some of the known issues about foster care environments did come to pass. These were things that would unfortunately frame the checkered experiences that my mother and each of her siblings would eventually reveal to me. "It wasn't all bad," my mother would say, "but let's just say that we were made to know our place. When it appeared as though we didn't, there was some form of retaliation—largely from the children of their foster parents." My mother would occasionally make such statements when the subject came up at our seasonal dinners, gatherings, and other outings. I would look around and the silent heads of those present would nod in agreement. They already knew one another's stories, but they were gracious enough to speak judiciously around me. They did not want to mar the unpainted canvas of my experience with the experiences from their youth. And yet this was their subtle way of making me aware, of gently warning me about how people react to us—even those of our own descent who experienced the same bias, etc. Further candidness was reserved for my later teens and beyond, when they thought I could handle weightier details of their revelations. But even then, tact was always important to them. You must understand that I grew up knowing many of the same individuals from these foster families that had taken in my mother and her siblings. They were characters in both of our stories.

At the time of these revelations, I happened to be learning about ancient Greek tragedy in school, wherein the actors could quickly change masks, switching from being a protagonist to an antagonist in the same story. Observing my mother and her siblings as they spoke, sitting in a crescent formation around me, was rather like watching the members of the chorus tell the plot of one of these Attic plays, each speaking about the aspirations and misfortunes of the characters. From these talks, I learned a very poignant but valuable lesson about the duality of people. What my young mind began to register was that our words and actions—not our intentions—are what leave their mark on others. Those marks may impact others we may never know, so we need to be very cautious and thoughtful about the legacy we build. Conversations like these gave me perspective. I decided at that very moment that I wanted to avoid being an antagonist in anyone's story. I would never want an individual, let alone a circle of people, to be sitting around speaking in agreement on how poorly I had treated him, her, others, or them. That realization would not guide me in knowing positively what I should be, but I was happy that it would help me at least to draw the boundaries in terms of what I would not be. I had resolved that I would not be serving as an agent of what I would later understand as mediocrity. I deeply respect the grit and grace and ability of my mother and her siblings to have covered certain matters over with silence and to have spoken of others with such discretion. From what I see in my current generation's desire for convenience and its seeming lack of self-control, we apparently have all but lost this art.

Still, aside from these occasions, my mother never spoke much about this period of her life. As the eldest, it was clear that, from a young age, she became the matriarch *de facto*, and would guard her siblings until they became adults. Sometimes taking unwarranted chastisements to shield the younger, and at numerous times being sent to bed without meals, she may have even kept many, if not all, of these problems of pain from Padre, knowing, as she did, how deeply it all would have upset him. It still bothers me that my mother had to experience many aspects of sacrifice at such a young age. I wish that she could have enjoyed spending more of her youth simply being naïve. But she appreciated how hard Padre was working and trying to cover for everyone, and she didn't want to complicate things for him, or for any of them, it seems. That responsibility that was placed upon her may have exposed her to many things that I think gave her some wisdom, but also aged her prematurely. I think of King Solomon's timeless statement that the knowledge we gain can increase our sorrows.

The same as her siblings experienced her protection in their youngest days, so I would also eventually experience her precious shielding. I would have the honor of seeing my mother's gracious character unfold before me, with each passing year of my life, until hers was no more.

Part Two: Training a Child

"Train up a child in the way he should go; even when he is old he will not depart from it" (Proverbs 22:6). Both my uncle and my grandfather often would tell me, whenever we were alone, things such as: "Jason, your mother loves you. You hear me? She loves you like no one or nothing else… and she's been giving you her all from the day that you were born." I appreciated what they were saying. I knew it was true, I knew my mother loved me and was very committed to me, but at that stage of life, what child comprehends a parent's love? Even now, so many years later, I am still realizing more of this.

I imagine that, like many mothers who are excited to tell their children of their children's arrival, my mother was excited to describe to me the day of my birth. However, it was really Padre's rendition of that special time that I always really enjoyed the most, primarily because it added much more humor. He recounted to me that, when I was born, certain family members and friends made haste, superstitiously, to their local convenience stores to play my birth numbers: 7-11-71. He could not recall if anyone actually won money on those numbers, but it was an interesting way to have your birth recognized—seeing people run out of the room to play the numbers! He'd chuckle and say, "Black folk are real superstitious; they see a sign in almost anything." Something in the way he said that to me always made me think that while others were placing their bets on a ticket, his bets were on that infant that he held in his hands. Looking back at this time, I realize that the state-governed lottery was a new phenomenon then. New York had begun its lottery in the late 1960's, and New Jersey only the year before I was born. Prior to this, people were used to "playing the numbers" and other local forms of gambling. But now BIG money was being put on the table. The claim was that revenues could be used to ease tax burdens and generate funds for schools and cities. However, it doesn't appear that any of that revenue ever really made its way into our parts of town! Nonetheless, they had been promoted as a "yellow-brick road" to comfort. All that was needed was "a dollar and a dream." These gambits have played a huge part in people's hope for a better life. There continued to be significant spending on tickets and raffles, even among those who made very little money. Anytime someone would hit a number, news would travel fast. That windfall, in turn, reinforced people's commitment to playing the odds.

Aside from these stories about the funny world that I entered, the only odd memento that I retained from the days of my infancy is the dent in the top of my head. I was teased incessantly about it during elementary school, and I can remember asking my mother how it happened. The comments of the kids jeering at me had convinced me that there was something wrong with me and that I needed to be fixed, if possible. I had supposed that the dent was possibly a birth defect. My mother explained that it happened when I was a newborn. She had given me to my uncle to hold after I was brought in from the hospital. In his curiosity, he had touched and inadvertently pushed in the soft top of my skull. When everyone saw how deep the impression was, there was real panic and I was rushed back to the hospital. Thankfully, there was no damage to my brain and the indentation would somewhat normalize, although never restore completely.

Although my birth was a time of excitement and celebration for the immediate family, I would later learn that it was not received as good news by everyone. My biological father found the situation damning. My understanding is that he was a friend of my mother's foster family. He was much older than my mother, I believe by at least twenty years. It was their encounter during her youth which caused scandal—a scandal that I was born out of. He was angered by her decision to proceed with the pregnancy. So, as I grew inside my mother's womb, so did her anticipation and his disdain. He subsequently severed ties—save only for the required duration of his making child-support payments. I learned in later years that my mother would periodically send him copies of my photographs, my writings, report cards, academic awards, and other demonstrations of merit. She did so in the hopes that he might consider having a relationship with me one day, but he consistently declined and at some point stopped engaging with her altogether. To this day, I have no words of his in my mind. I have never even seen a photograph of him. My thoughts of my father are like looking into an abyss; I see nothing and don't even hear the sound of wind, just darkness and dead silence—a complete void like a black hole. You know him as much as I do.

Some years ago, I found versions of letters that my mother had either planned to send to him or perhaps had re-written and posted from some earlier versions. Her plea was that she only wanted for me to have a relationship with him, and not one for herself. She believed that I deserved to have a father, or at least to know who he is. I cannot imagine the hurt that his repeated rejections caused her. Even now, as a man myself, I cannot take it in. The simple thought of my doing such a thing turns my stomach.

My mother was deeply concerned about the impact on me of my not having a father. There were too many lures in our environment that might easily fill the void if I didn't have my own constitution. Although my mother was an educator, she was not a chemistry teacher; she could not teach me the chemistry of manhood. But as a specialist in comprehension, she knew that she could help me to identify what qualities a man should have, and how to begin that path to comprehending them. Her hope had been to have a partner in this important process. But that never materialized—at least not in the traditional way she had envisioned.

She did marry a man whom she convinced herself she could help by placing him into our family. Her desire to have a whole family was so intense that it clouded her judgment. She ignored all the warning signs and people's admonitions. He hid it well at first, but shortly after moving in with us, he turned out to be a violent alcoholic, one who became envious of the attention and affection that my mother poured on me. Much in the way that some dogs can become territorial and actually attack their owners' children, competing to lead the pack, my mother's newfound husband would and eventually did attack. This resulted in my being exposed to something in our home that had been unimaginable to my mother.

The school uniform of my private school certainly had drawn lots of unwanted attention, resulting in my almost constant need to defend myself from kids my age. But that was on the street. I had never known violence like that in my own environment, never in a place where I was surrounded by all things that were precious to me. I never knew, until one day in my home, what it felt like to have a grown man's hands wrapped around my throat, and to be pummeled by calloused fists. My mother thankfully arrived home early that day and she literally had to save me. By the time she was done with him, however, and the police and paramedics had arrived, and removed him from the apartment, she had nearly killed him. That experiment had failed with precious consequences. My mother never invited another man into our lives, or into our home, after that. She instead changed her focus from trying to find someone for me, to putting all of her efforts into helping me become the caliber of man she was unable to find. Peace returned to our home and my lesson in manhood could now continue.

Her hope was that the men nearest my life could serve as a reference. She hoped that if she could place me into their hands, their compassion would influence my circumstance. Periodically, she would ask how I felt about not having a traditional family like many of my friends did. Even then I began to notice, however, the steady increase of children, namely boys, who were like me and who did not have a father. When I look back to this time, I find that my closest friendships were with boys who were in similar circumstances. Either they were from single-parent homes or had bonding issues with their fathers. I see now how important it was for us all to have met one another. We didn't realize at the time we played together that we were offering each other comfort, but I know now that that is exactly what occurred.

I found myself studying the behaviors of the men around me a great deal. Assembling what a father was, what a man was, seemed initially like fitting a puzzle while being unsure of what the resulting image should be. There were a handful of men in our family and among my friend's fathers whom I respected and learned from, or in whom I at least discerned respectable qualities—fine qualities that I could put into words. That is one thing I have loved about words; they helped me recognize the qualities that existed in the man that I wanted to become. That is largely how I knew what to look for. Although I maintained a close relationship with Padre, the man that I modeled myself after almost entirely was one whom I called my "Uncle Clyde." Clyde Watkins was of Padre's generation, a hardworking man whose family, like many Black American families, moved out of the South during the Great Migration in hopes of building a better life "up North." He was promoted into management at the company, and there he met my "Aunt Catherine," another manager. She would say: "I was in charge of the girls; Clyde was in charge of the guys." They lived on the first floor, sharing the two-family home of my mother's foster family. That is how I came to know them both. Some of my friends did not understand fictive kin, that it was common to call people who were not relatives "auntie" and "uncle."

In most cases, my mother and her siblings maintained a relationship with their foster families. But Uncle Clyde's awareness of my situation inspired him to waste no time in taking me under his wing. Working in a way similar to the analogy of the infant Moses, this man drew me out of the water with compassion and took me into himself. I have no recollection of ever being introduced to him; he genuinely was always a pillar in my life. I do not know for a certainty, but I would not be surprised if he and Padre made a pact concerning my life. They were very different men, whom I seldom saw together, but in hindsight I have come to glean that their teachings and admonishments seemed flawlessly coordinated. Padre was the first to bring fatherly love to me. After all, in his eyes I was his "blood" and very much to be cared for. From him came many things, including culinary skills, grit, humor, and what most would call "street smarts." Everyone, male or female, in his family was taught to cook, clean, sew, etc. He'd readily tell anyone in our family that was his junior, "If you're going to be around me, you'd better learn something". He had a great respect for God, zero tolerance for hypocrisy, and was, at least judging from my time with him, not a church-goer. His paraphrasing of Christ's sermon in the Gospels about removing the beam out of our own eyes before we seek to remove the splinter from someone else's was just simple and raw: "Even Jesus told people to deal with their own shit before they try to correct other people's." That was Padre!

Uncle Clyde was more of a traditional Christian man (I mean this as the greatest of compliments to him) and a distinct gentleman. He was not stiff, or overly religious by any means, just highly principled. Uncle Clyde was as kind and patient on the inside as he was handsome and poised on the outside—a man of true temperance.

When working in the yard with Uncle Clyde, one noticed that—even there—he managed to dress well. He and his wife would frequently have me stay over in their guest bedroom. I loved sleeping in that room. It always smelled great and was nicely decorated. He would awaken me by pinching me on my nose. Sometimes, I would lie there intentionally and pretend still to be asleep so that he could come in and do that again. They are the little things like that which make children feel loved. If I was still visiting on a Saturday morning, Uncle Clyde and I usually would "shave" together before running errands. Of course, I had no facial hair, but he would remove the blade from one of his butterfly-model razors (the kind where you would turn the knob and both sides of the top would open and then reclose, so that a double-edged blade could be inserted). He showed me how to mix the shaving powder into a rich lather. He also taught me about using all of the men's grooming products, which he kept in his cabinet. If I were getting dressed up for an important event, he'd have me pass by just to ensure I hadn't overdone it with my cologne. His rule of thumb was that if he could smell me before I shook his hand, I was wearing too much. We would drive to local parks, go out to dinner, and attend movies very frequently. He saw that I was hungry for instruction, and he exemplified and taught me so many things that I can no longer distinguish many of the things I know from what he taught me. Such was the depth and breadth of what he modeled and taught; it all permeated my character. The irony of it all is that he and his wife never had children.

During these years, my mother and I lived in an apartment just across the street. Consequently, I would frequently see Uncle Clyde or at least hear his distinct whistle when he drove past me in the neighborhood. We all attended the same church, so on Sunday mornings I would often accompany him on the short walk to the garage where he kept his car. We'd drive up the street to his house and pick up my aunt and mother, Uncle Clyde and I both quickly alighting from the car to open doors and escort both ladies to the vehicle before leaving. That is where I learned to hold open doors, present seating, and perform many other mannerisms of kindness. When I was trusted enough, these cherished adults in my life eventually taught me how to set a table for formal dining. But, in my way, I requested to do so with a ruler so that I could ensure the equidistance of all the objects on the table. The more they exposed me to, the happier I was—and the happier I made them. After meals, we would listen to the radio on the porch or sometimes my aunt would sing; she loved singing gospel songs and I loved listening to them. Sadly, we would not have many more of these times together.

I began developing a deep interest in reading the Bible. My mother's foster parents also served in the church. Certain Sundays were very long if there were special events that I helped with. The Bible was the most vivid book that I had read or would ever read. Its influence was obvious and omnipresent—in our culture at home, in the larger culture, and in the community. I recall how Scripture says that God would speak to Moses as a man does his friend. When I read Scripture, I saw God speaking to me as a father would speak to his son. It is as simple as that. I heard hope speaking from these pages. I hung on the words of kings and wise men because I could do something with them. I discovered, with great pleasure, how the books of Psalms, Proverbs, Ecclesiastes, and the epistles of the Apostle Paul would often contain addresses to "my son." But all of them were a gold mine of wisdom and instruction and spoke very simply of what, to my view, should be in my heart. In my mind, I simply concluded that when I read "My Son...," God was also referring specifically to me. Even among the good men that I knew, no one could tell me all the qualities that I needed to embody—and that was what I had been searching for. I was looking for someone to tell me how I should "BE" as a person, as a human being, and not simply someone who could or would encourage my potential. Scripture answered this question for me—not church, not religion, but Scripture. That was my missing link and it came in the form of words that I needed to believe. So, from my youth, God and Scripture held a very intimate place in my life, and in my character development. Uncle Clyde was very instrumental during this phase of my life, as he was the one who initially pointed me to these sections of practical wisdom in the Bible. Frequently, when it was time to sleep and my mother had shut the lights, I would often have my flashlight under the mattress so that I could finish reading whatever passage I had begun. When I read in Proverbs 22:6 that if a child was trained in how to live properly, such a child would remain that way when growing older, I knew I was "that child" that the Scripture was talking about. I knew I was being trained as a young man, both practically and spiritually.

My mother had been raised in a very strict, religious manner. My experience was unlike hers simply because she decided to do something very radical by not passing on to me the tradition of guilt motivation that she had received from her foster parents. When I asked her why she chose to raise me as she had, she said it was because she never believed that condemnation would ever lead to my having great character. She had too much evidence, in her lived experience, to the contrary.

Part Three: "Them that's got shall get. Them that's not shall lose. So the Bible says..."

"To those who use well what they are given, even more will be given, and they will have an abundance. But from those who do nothing, even what little they have will be taken away" (Matthew 25:29, NLT). When I first heard *God Bless the Child*, it was this lyric that caught my attention because, even as a Bible reader by that time, I was still unsure what passage it came from. That is, until I stumbled upon this passage in Matthew about stewardship.

My mother and everyone around me learned to make do with what they had. They all had a great work ethic. Stewardship was a very important principle in our family. I was polite and expected to thank people for their gifts, but the real thanks was to be shown in how well you cared for the gift you received. The lesson kept being reinforced for me: if I was responsible in the way I handled matters, I would prove that I could be trusted with more. That upbringing eventually did something to shift my perspective on "wants." Like any kid, I wanted lots of things, but wanting things started to feel different the older I became. The more I read the Scriptures, the more I began to see reflected there the very same lessons that I frequently heard. The older I became, the notion of bucking up against the Scriptures (more so than even against my elders) started to become a spiritual issue for me. I could not ignore the source or origin of these statements.

Part Four: "The strong gets more, while the weak ones fade…"

"Then said I, Wisdom is better than strength: nevertheless the poor man's wisdom is despised, and his words are not heard" (King Solomon; Ecclesiastes 9:16). The older I became and matured into my manhood, the more I would be spoken to about strength. Whirling around me constantly were perceptions of what strength was, what it does or does not do, etc. I cannot remember any interaction with others who looked like me where strength was not mentioned. I grew up with many close, multicultural relationships; I began to notice that the emphasis placed upon my being strong was unlike anything I heard with those from other nationalities. There was so much pressure on me to be strong and everyone had a different interpretation of what that meant. Ultimately, the only person's opinion that mattered to me was my mother's. I still find the choices that she made on this topic very interesting. She never repeated phrases such as "act like a man" or "man up" or told me to stop crying when I was hurt, etc. She did her best to raise me to be the man she couldn't find—the kind of man that our society seemed and seems to have plowed salt into the fields of, such that he would never grow, or become a rich crop, or reproduce others like him to nourish, strengthen, love and, if need be, protect, as he might, his community. I know now that true and good manhood cannot be accomplished by simply repeating the same words and themes that are everywhere.

Part Five: Mediocrity and Magnanimity

Padre's choice of New Jersey would prove a benefit for reasons beyond what he could have estimated. I say this because, as a child, my mother loved words and anything that gave her more access to them. She went on to graduate from college and to determine that she wanted to teach reading in the same public school system that she had attended. By this time, New Jersey was one of the best states for those who aspired to become teachers. The 70's were a time of much activism and social reform. My mother decided that teaching would be the platform from which she would change the lives of youth in the town where she had grown up. Her next youngest sister shared similar aspirations, but chose to become a librarian and assist students in finding financial resources to pay for their education. Both sisters found a way to transform their experiences and compassion into careers that would serve as beacons to guide others who did not have what they'd had.

At home I had access, naturally, to many kinds of books and other educational resources. For convenience, I was first enrolled in the school where my mother taught. There, she would easily be able to monitor me. However, the public schools, especially in the minority districts, were inadequately resourced. To have access to the quality of education that my mother wanted me to have, I would need to attend a better school. So, in relatively short order, I was sent to the best one she could afford, which was the only private school in our town. There I spent the remainder of both my elementary and middle school years, enjoying a rich learning environment.

I enjoyed reading poetry, novels, and even reference books. To expand my literacy, my mother started a bit of a game with me. Periodically we'd choose words that were more complex than the ones that I had been learning in my vocabulary classes. This particular year, I was introduced to two words that would cause me to see many things in life differently. "Mediocrity" was the first word. I had overheard its being used in a conversation. It wasn't a word I had ever heard used before. I was excited to bring this to my mother and begin learning about it. But when I approached her, I will never forget my mother's response. She showed me the word in the dictionary and told me that this was not something that I needed to learn. She said that mediocrity was all around us in the society in which we lived, and that it would be easier to spot if I learned the meaning of another word instead. She said, "I want you to learn what the word 'magnanimous' means!" She told me that as I learned that word, I would better understand mediocrity, without being susceptible to it as a term which I was trying to apply to my life.

This was a very different conversation. I could see that she was not speaking of academics. The only way for me to understand what my mother meant was to begin, as I did each time, with the dictionary. But as I did so, I still wondered how this word could be everywhere? What did it mean to be everywhere? Was it something in the environment? Was it as obvious as a billboard advertisement? This was a puzzle that she wanted me to begin figuring out. Once I saw that being magnanimous involved other words I had learned by then, and that it involved themes I had seen others portray throughout my life, I began to understand better. Her charge for me to learn this word was really a charge for me to become, hopefully, what it meant. She was charting a course for me to follow. This stayed with me from that point forward. "Magnanimity" was a decoder that would help me discern when mediocrity was present. The more I chose to apply the meaning of magnanimity, the more I realized that she was correct about how common the other word was.

Where did I see mediocrity? I saw it in what my grandfather told me about how Madre was ridiculed in her youth. I saw it present in the stories of my mother and her siblings during their years in foster care. This concept was becoming clearer to me, but nothing is as real to you as your own experience. One of my first encounters with it, I realize now, occurred very early. I was in kindergarten at the time and was accompanying my mother on errands after she had picked me up from school. Everything took longer than imagined with crowded grocery stores, etc. We stood waiting for our ride home which, also, was unfortunately very much delayed. My mother had reached the point where she needed to use the restroom. As this need became more pressing, she suggested we walk to a nearby pub to ask if she might use their restroom. They refused, even though she offered to buy something. We did this several times with different establishments and all refused. I can remember each time noticing the tone of my dear mother's voice become increasingly desperate. I remember how at each location she hoped they would see that she had a child with her, and did not want to leave the child unattended outside with our groceries while she looked for a restroom. I can remember staring at each of the people as she spoke with them. I couldn't understand why no one would allow her simply to use a restroom. I stared at their not blinking even once; I still remember this. I watched while each person obtusely refused and seemed to speak as if from a script prepared for them—repeating the same unfeeling words. No one listened to reason, no one cared to help in a manner as simple as what was needed. Each person was dismissive. We stood outside and, knowing my mother as a proud woman, I had never sensed embarrassment in her as I did then. But instinctively, I dared not look at her in the face. I didn't say anything. I knew not to speak. I stared straight ahead while a stream of urine flowed on the ground by her foot as we stood there. At that moment, I was introduced to the word that my mother would later tell me I would never need to study. I have come to realize that word in hindsight, as I was not at a place then, at such a tender age, to have understood these things.[1]

But I began to notice its presence elsewhere. After years had passed, with these things looming in the background of my experiences, I was invited to a friend's home to watch the film *Amadeus* with friends. The voice of Salieri, the antagonist who deeply envied Mozart's talent, narrates the story. After showcasing Salieri's much plotting and succeeding in effectuating Mozart's destruction, the film ends with Salieri's referral to himself as the patron saint of mediocrity. Salieri yells out loud: "Mediocrity is everywhere!" That was the first time I had heard someone utter what my mother had said to me years ago. My friends had no idea why I sat transfixed, staring at the screen. Mediocrity was not harmless or passive, as I had initially thought, but rather even in its obtuse numbness it still had the power, the active power, to restrict and to harm.[2] That film in that moment illustrated for me that this was a subject that had been becoming increasingly more conspicuous, aggressive, and intrusive the more I matured into manhood. I would later be surprised to learn not just of its impacts, but also the identity of its agents. I would become, in fact, increasingly shocked at who the agents of mediocrity would or could be.

Even in the midst of all the racial tension of the 80's, it took me a while to twig that the prejudice leading to those events, and to the ones which I had experienced, were actually just licensed forms of mediocrity.[3] There were traps or snares being laid in places where I did not even think to expect them—parks, public pools, and even barbershops. Barbershops? How so? Knowing that many Black and Latino youth would go to a famous barbershop called Astor Place, in Greenwich Village, the police would wait for us outside and offer us money to go with them and stand in line-ups.[4] My friends knew better (some of their parents worked in law enforcement). We knew that it didn't take much for us to look like the suspect, and that was enough to get us caught up and found "guilty" of whatever we, or someone whom we looked like, might have been accused. What judge would accept our saying that we were innocent and just ended up in court or a lineup, for money, particularly if a positive identification was claimed? I shudder to think what happened to scores of young Black and Latino men who did not know better, who thought they were being granted an opportunity for easy money, and who did not have alibis. Thinking back to Padre's barbershop, I found it especially ironic that I would learn such a lesson in that personally meaningful setting. Close shave! These traps would pursue me even there!

No, my mother could not teach me how to be a man, not in matters that men could show me, but she knew—as a teacher of children—what to set in front of me, and she knew—as a good woman and mother—what was good for my heart. She knew the things that would be true and would endure. I realize now that all of the cautionary tales, admonishments, and even humorous stories that I heard as I grew up—these were, all in all, basically just the weavings of a basket of hope. And the lore that was set to song, for me, was not merely about attaining material things and self-sufficiency as evidence of progress. But it was the optimism in my family's conscience that encouraged their sacrifices so that I could be floated into the compassionate hands of hope itself, and benefit from its fantastic change of my circumstances.

ENDNOTES

1   The problem of *misogynoir* is real in American society, as my mother poignantly experienced and as I painfully noticed, on that sad day. This word and concept highlights not simply "misogyny," which is the horrible social problem of "hatred of women"; "misogy*noir*" at the same time highlights the specific hatred of *black* women and black girls, *as* black women and as black girls. See Moya Bailey, *Misogynoir Transformed* (New York: New York University Press, 2021).
2   See Peter Shaffer, *Amadeus: A Play by Peter Shaffer* (New York: Perennial Publishers, 1981).
3   See the cultural, historical, and political insights of former *Village Voice* writer Greg Tate in *Flyboy in the Buttermilk: Essays on Contemporary America* (New York: Simon and Schuster, 1992).
4   For an additional resource on the sometimes hard-edged social, political, and cultural context of my youth, and indeed the New York–New Jersey–Connecticut tri-state world, see: Tricia Rose, *Black Noise: Rap Music and Black Culture in Contemporary America* (Middletown, CT: Wesleyan University Press, 1994). Take specific note, as well, of the heart-wrenching documentary "The Central Park Five" released in 2012 and curated by filmmakers Ken Burns, Sarah Burns and David Mc Mahon. The brutal injustices inflicted upon "The Central Park Five" remains one of the most searing indictments of the U.S criminal justice system to have occurred in my lifetime.

BIBLIOGRAPHY

Bailey, Moya. *Misogynoir Transformed*. New York: New York University Press, 2021.
Rose, Tricia. *Black Noise: Rap Music and Black Culture in Contemporary America*. Middleton, CT: Wesleyan University Press, 1994.
Shaffer, Peter. *Amadeus: A Play by Peter Shaffer*. New York: Perennial, 1981.
Tate, Greg. *Flyboy in the Buttermilk: Essays on Contemporary America*. New York: Simon and Schuster, 1992.
Taylor, Elizabeth Dowling. *The Original Black Elite: Daniel Murray and the Story of a Forgotten Era*. New York: HarperCollins, 2018.

CHAPTER TWELVE
Getting a Handle on Things

Darryl W. Aaron

Getting a Handle on Things

"Sometimes a story arrives complete—a done thing. Usually, though, it comes to me in two parts: first the cup, then the handle. Because the handle may not show up for weeks, months, or even years, you can't go looking for a handle, no matter how beautiful the cup may be; you have to wait for it to appear." This description of the writing process by Stephen King can actually be applied to the life of black people in America. "First the cup, then the handle" is to say first slavery, then "pull yourself up by your bootstraps." The nation became the most wealthy and powerful empire off the backs of black, free labor for hundreds of years, but has refused to distribute the wealth or status equally or equitably. To consider all that a black person encounters daily, he or she is simply trying to get a handle on things. As soon as we think we have experienced the worst, another fire destroys a housing project, another black person is killed, another tweet (in the Trump era) from the President, another legislative policy is rolled back, and life becomes more unstable. There are moments that are so debilitating that no law passed, or promotion granted, or a black person holding even the highest, or near highest, office in the land can comfort us. Constant human troubles such as health challenges, break ups, betrayals, and losses of loved ones can rock our souls so much that we literally lose our grasp. Sometimes it really does take a miracle to get a handle on things. Sometimes it is harder for black people to die than to live; yet daily we attempt to die. We don't go to the doctor, we overspend to mask poverty, we don't vote in numbers the way we should, we drink too much, and we use drugs. Like squeezing out the last bit of toothpaste, we try to squeeze a little more life out of our lives. It seems natural to do those things that will kill us. On the other hand, to be alive in a nation that is structured to keep blacks in an inferior caste system forces one to hold life loosely. What we can handle fluctuates and our techniques for handling life's challenges often must adjust too quickly. Sometimes before we realize it, what we think is working to keep us alive is, in fact, a death practice. Our desire to change to live becomes like when your lips get chapped, and you must stop licking them because it only makes things worse. It is a miracle that we are still alive.

Two Hells

Unfortunately, the miracle of staying alive is, too often, not provided to black people. Every time a black boy or man is killed, I die too. I was not there, yet I was there, on that afternoon while basking in their white power, a dad called his son to go hunt down a black boy. "I was not there, yet I was there," are the words used by Ernest Gaines's character Jefferson in *A Lesson Before Dying*. Jefferson's words speak for all black males who are forever navigating a racist existence. Ahmaud Arbery, of Brunswick, Georgia, was slaughtered for game because America will not claim black males as human beings. In America, it is a cultural norm, like cherry pie contests, for white males to act as predators with black males as their prey. As that spiritual sister, Ella Baker, has proclaimed, "Until the killing of black men, black mother's sons (and daughters), become as important to the rest of the country as the killing of a white mother's sons (and daughters), we who believe in freedom cannot rest until this happens." Every waking moment in these un-united states of America is plagued by the disease of racism for males of the darker hue. Every second my son is not with me, I am in some form of panic. When he leaves the house, when he goes to school, when—yes—he goes for a jog, when he goes to the mailbox, when he goes around the house to the back door, I am afraid he will be slaughtered for game. I don't know how much more or how much longer I can take it. I feel like a cat that has nine lives because I have died so many times.

At the time of this writing, my son is 19 years old; unfortunately, he has been trying to plot a course amid this evil of white people since the day he witnessed and scrutinized the news of Trayvon Martin's death. I never had to inform him what it was like to be a black male in America; instinctively he knew his life was disposable when Trayvon Martin was gunned down by a white man.[1] Like Jefferson, my son was saying, "I was not there, yet I was there." Ahmaud Arbery, a weaponless 25-year-old, was slaughtered at a tender age, but, of course, he had already died multiple times before, because that is what happens to black males who live under the threat of violence. My own father, at the age of 57, exhaled his last breath one cold winter night a week after retirement. The doctors say his troubled heart failed. That is absolutely an understatement. My father had endured a racist military, a racist employer (26 years a postal worker), a racist educational system, a racist healthcare system. Everything he encountered had Jim and Jane Crow's fingerprints upon it. That does not end the litany of assaults on his heart. He also took the blows from divorce, two marriages, and the death of siblings and parents. Without ceasing, he was losing his breath. The night my father's soul wrested itself free of his body, in three heaving breaths, the little engine could not say, "I can" anymore. The late James Cone's trumpet of justice can be heard once again: "Until we can identify Christ with a 'recrucified' black body hanging from a lynching tree, there can be no genuine understanding of Christian identity in America, and no deliverance from the brutal legacy of slavery and white supremacy." America's original sin is forever sliding and slithering, just as it did in the garden of that white middle class neighborhood when dad and son got into their pickup truck to "seek, kill, and destroy" Ahmaud Arbery. Every time an unarmed black male is gunned down, Christ is "recrucified." As I contemplate trying to put a handle around the many mini-deaths of black people, I have concluded that God must give every person who has lived under the whip of white oppression an automatic resurrection. Why? Because it has not been proven that God gives one person two hells. Every time a black male is gunned down, I die too. I was not there and yet I was there.

Tricky Business

This existential crisis of being somewhere and not being there is tricky business. Being black in America is to be acquainted with what Elizabeth Strout, the insightful novelist, calls "big bursts and little bursts," which is "tricky business, really." Strout describes big bursts as "intimacies that keep you afloat" and little bursts as "friendly" gestures that "know how you like" things. I was born on October 31, 1969—at a pivotal juncture, when things had become tricky business for the Civil Rights Movement. The fire in the belly of activists had begun to simmer and whites apparently felt they had made enough gestures for blacks to be pleased with what was keeping them afloat. However, progress is always tricky business. By the time 1969 came around, the nation had witnessed the march on Selma, which propelled President Johnson to sign into law what Congress had presented to him as the Voting Rights Bill. The first black Supreme Court Justice, Thurgood Marshall, had been appointed, interracial marriages were no longer outlawed, and the Civil Rights Act of 1968—an expansion of the 1964 Civil Rights Act—banned discrimination in housing sales and rentals. Of course, none of these monumental acts occurred without a bloodbath. I was there, but I was not there. The number of blacks that died in race riots of the 1960's will only be known when the sea gives up the dead. Within just a few short years prior to my birth, black America had lost Malcolm X and Rev. Dr. Martin Luther King, Jr. The year I came into the world, Richard Nixon was elected the thirty-seventh President of the United States and Neil Armstrong planted his foot on the moon. Among these big bursts, there are many little bursts. In 1968 Richard Nixon had won North Carolina (my home state), the second Republican to do so since Reconstruction. Democrat Hubert Humphrey came in third, behind segregationist George Wallace. Not long thereafter, in 1972, Jesse Helms, who started out in politics working for pro-segregation Democrats, became the first popularly elected Republican senator from North Carolina. Jesse Helms would hold office for 30 years, to span all of my formative years. Racial politics has always impacted my life and, accordingly, has forced me to clinch small bits of community amid much chaos.

Chaos or Community

"In the beginning" was chaos, "without form and void and darkness was over the face of the deep" is how the Biblical drama starts. I have been haunted for some time by one particular morning when my daughter came to my room not to tell me that she loved me, but rather to inform me that President Trump had tweeted, "thugs… shoot….". Since Trump's arrival in the White House, we have awakened to chaos. These unruly mornings remind me of the opening scene of "Blues for Mr. Charlie," given to us by, of course, James Baldwin. Shots are fired, the curtains open, and the "nigger" is dumped like a sack on the ground, by Lyle Britten, a white man. Then Lyle speaks: "And may every nigger like this nigger end like this nigger—face down in the weeds!" Over and over the curtains open to this scene for Americans. There is nothing ambiguous or fictitious about this nation's intent for its black and brown citizens. On a daily basis, black and brown people find themselves face down in the thicket of racism.

Rev. Dr. Martin Luther King asked the profound question, "Where do we go from here: Chaos or Community?" This question was raised just before his assassination, which resulted not only in bloodshed from a martyr, but even more and more blood from others - blood that ran down the streets of a hundred American cities. King's urgent question is before us again: Chaos or Community? I am a preacher, but I will never suggest we simply pray to address our recurring morning chaos. Prayer is essential to the work of community, and for community; however, it can never be used as an excuse not to force the wheels of progress to turn.[2]

In recent years, the fire shut up in the bones of black people has once again heated the nation through the Black Lives Matter movement. And it will be a long time before it dims its flame. As the Biblical character Esther asserted, "too much damage has been done." And may I add, not enough has been done to stop the cruelty upon the black and brown body politic, the black and brown citizenry. We cannot stop protesting. We cannot stop marching. We cannot stop voting. The veneer has been scrubbed off and white people must acknowledge their racist practices. The blame game has lost its potency, and we now know Adam and Eve both wanted to taste the apple. The crafty black-on-black crime arguments must stop because we know that that behavior grew out of the garden of slavery. For maturity to occur, we must admit the truth. In the same way we had to confess the truth about the myth of a white Santa Claus to our children, we must admit that the wrath is upon our nation because our nation is deeply embattled with many of its inhabitants.

America is guilty of nibbling on the fruit of abuse of women and the degradation of black and brown people. The reason we wake up every morning to scorching violence bearing down our necks is because there are not enough good and sane white people. I am more convinced than ever that white people want a "fire the next time." Yes, I am saying, they have wanted the hell of Trump. If America does not want to go to hell, it must stop white people from dumping a "nigger—face down in the weeds!"

Unfortunately, now there is a sentiment screaming from the loudspeaker and whispering under the sheets which declares, like Derrick Bell's "The Space Traders", that Americans want a nation without a black voice. I have lived with Clarence Thomas and Ben Carson at the table of power as representatives of black people. Neither has demonstrated an interest or spine for carrying the burdens of the least and last. Throughout the 2020 election, I heard persons of many persuasions spewing, "Don't be too bold; Stacey Abrams is less intimidating than Kamala Harris," and "Moderate White people will never vote for so and so." Of course, the record is clear that Joe Biden had been written out of the story until the black hero saved the day. Every morning, boldness slaps me in the face with headlines such as, "White police officer shoots and kills another Black man." I am highly persuaded that we need to be bold. In fact, to be black, to vote, and to be a child of God is to be bold.

"In the beginning," our world had to grapple with chaos. The Bible tells us that over that chaos, "the Spirit of God was hovering….". I still believe God is hovering over our mess. The human drama always begins at center stage, God speaking as the main character. The burdens of my heart slightly roll away knowing that God is center stage, projecting justice. The creation story lets us know that chaos leaps to order by the voice of God. In other words, justice is how community is formed. No more "kumbaya" is needed because community has nothing to do with black and white peoples' getting together to say we can do better. When justice is the order of the day, chaos takes a back seat! As the protestors chant, "No justice, no peace", chaos takes a back seat. Community is not some fictitious dream. Instead, it is a reality designed by a just God. God is hovering over our chaos, and soon order will take place. I prayed throughout the 2020 election that all Americans would make a concerted effort to prevent my daughter from tugging on my sheet another morning to inform me of the chaos that had ensued from "four more years" of Trump.

Where Do Black People Go from Here?

On a sweltering August afternoon, a perfect day for an ice cream cone, I drove into the parking lot of a Dairy Queen, the one on Central Avenue in my hometown, where you can get your treat through the window. I am ordering when a frantic white woman runs up, rushes in front of me, and throws her pocketbook through the window. She is indeed disturbed, but no one knows why. Then, the cause of her disturbance appears: a white man, a bricklayer-looking fellow with veins popping out of his head and arms. He walks up and slaps the woman. This is not my problem, yet it is. She is a woman, and I cannot let the man do this in my presence.

I speak, "Hey, you can't be hitting this woman."
He responds, "You want some of this, nigger?"
I retort, "You cannot hit this woman."

The workers at Dairy Queen have by now called the police and almost immediately you can hear the sirens of at least a firetruck in the distance. The man jumps in his car and speeds away.

This is the first time I have been called a nigger. I know trauma can distort one's memory, and to be black in America is to be traumatized daily; therefore, this might not be the first time I had been called a nigger, but it is the first that I can vividly recall.

I believe the recollection is clear because I am an adult who had checked many of the boxes that the politics of respectability had requested of me. At the time, I was a 30-year-old black man with two degrees; and I was a certified teacher, minister, husband, parent, and homeowner. None of these achievements could change America's ideas about me. Nothing prevented me from being a nigger in the white man's eyes. That Dairy Queen scene took place almost 20 years ago, but when a US President daily uses the old Southern Strategy, "Make America Great Again," the man calling me a nigger leaps into the present. What strikes me most about that day at Dairy Queen is the fact that I had believed in the LIE. I am not suggesting that I thought I would be exempt from trouble. I grew up with the "talented-tenth"; life for middle- and upper-middle-class black people was filled with both privileges and burdens. However, the children were closed off from direct contact with white racism, or so we thought. While our white teachers had obvious racial biases, they did not want to be confronted by highly educated black parents. To avoid this confrontation, every year several of the neighborhood kids would become members of the student government. These few privileges warped my thinking to the extent that I believed America would change.

Let us fast forward. Sitting on the couch, watching television with my son, we hear news of Trayvon Martin, a black boy killed by a white man. Obama is the President, yet it cannot prevent another black boy, like Emmett Till, from being murdered by a white man.[3] I hear it all over again: "You want some of this, nigger?" I must warn my son that no talented-tenth ideals can prevent what he is witnessing on the television from happening to him. He was in the ninth grade. Fast forward five years; he is a Yale student, and we are in another house, but in the same place, watching George Floyd's life being snuffed out. No words are uttered between us because we know what each is thinking. If the achievements of blacks will not change America, what will? What good is there to check the boxes when the value gap between blacks and whites will not decrease? We know that Donald Trump is not the exception; rather, he is the dry heartbeat of America. The question that runs up and down the corridors of my heart and mind is: Where do black people go from here?

I am convinced that the answer is in the carnage of America. I find answers from all the people who fought, marched, prayed, and died for a change. Jesus said, "Have you believed because you have seen me? Blessed are those who have not seen and yet have believed" (Jn. 20:29). In the ruins we do not find evidence of change, but we do discover a witness in those who believed and struggled without evidence. Those who bear witness to truth in the midst of lies get my vote. Not only do they get my vote, but they shall receive my sacrifice and belief in a better tomorrow. We are not permitted to check out and give up on a brighter future. To do so is to stain the record. It is to embrace the LIE. The witnesses of truth always die looking beyond what is taking place today. No talented-tenth objectives can prevent America from hating black people, but telling the truth can prevent blacks from living a lie. The question is not, "Does the nigger want some of this?" but rather, "Does the white man want more truth?—as in "You can't hit this woman" nor can you put your knee on my brother's neck.

Only Seeds

The death of George Floyd gave the Black Lives Matter movement its second wind. To be honest, I have drunk deeply from the well of the politics of respectability, therefore, I was not sure what would come of the movement. I was trained to stand up for your rights, but to do it in a way that we all can get along. However, we cannot forget that the face of this movement began with the personalities of Patrisse Khan-Cullors, Alicia Garza, and Opal Tometi, young black women who were pushing black and left, including feminist and queer. The movement did help 96 percent of Black women to vote against Donald Trump, but it did not prevent him from becoming the most powerful man in the free world in 2016. To write that Donald Trump openly campaigned on bigotry, White supremacy, misogyny and misogynoir is not an opinion; I am simply stating the facts. Of course, like the throngs of activists in almost all civil rights movements, black people and vulnerable people who have known a knee upon their necks for a long time wish to obtain equal rights. Too often, when a police officer kills a black person, many white colleagues call and ask: "How can we help?" I have often exclaimed: 1) I hope it does not take another black man to die for someone to help with eradicating racism; and 2) You know more about white people's abuse of power than I do.

The Black Lives Matter movement continues to be criticized by white and black people and we still don't know what will be the lasting legacy of the movement. Nevertheless, I believe it has forced the nation to ask: "What is the movement looking for?" I hate to admit it, but too often I have answered that question with a list of items that will disappear with the slightest drizzle from the sky.

Jesuit priest Anthony de Mello tells a story in *Taking Flight* about a woman who dreamed that Jesus was a salesman in a marketplace. When she asked him what he sold, Jesus told her that she could have whatsoever her heart desired. She eagerly requested things such as freedom from fear, peace of mind and heart, and the end of pain and struggle in her life. When Jesus heard this, he responded to her, "Oh, no you have got me wrong. We don't sell fruits here, only seeds."

As a black man, I have indeed wanted to be free of fear, and to have peace of mind and the end of pain and struggle. Oh, but I have never wanted to be white.[4] And yet, growing up middle class, you are told you must be twice as good and not to be just another black man. Academic excellence was to be your shining armor. With a mother who was also an educator, I was constantly corrected when I put a preposition at the end of a sentence or started a sentence with "Me and...". That was the kind of speech and behavior up with which she would not put. Now that I am a parent of two children, I have begun to question my parents' notions of what we should be looking and sounding like as black people. Asking black children to be twice as good as white people is insidious and harmful. White people should never be the standard of success for any human being. To be your best is simply a noble act which produces authentic peace and contentment. I truly believe my mother was not asking for anything outlandish when she required that I speak "grammatically correct" English, nor do I now believe it imprudent to ask for equal rights and that an oppressor take his or her knee off your neck; rather, these are demands that God secreted in the human soul when He declared we were made in His image. Again, I admit I don't know what the enduring legacy of the Black Lives Matter movement will be, but already America has been given by these brave freedom fighters some seeds such as courage, justice, inclusion, and hope—all of which will, or should, grow and mature in the days, months, and years ahead.

When I consider the seeds that have been planted in my life, I can't help but think of what my mother says about the corn that has been overly processed: "That corn has been messed with and treated in so many ways that you can throw it on cement, and it will still grow." Like the corn we eat, black people often must grow in unfavorable conditions. These unhelpful conditions remind us of Jesus' parable: a sower went out to sow, and as he sowed it chanced that some seed fell on the road, and birds came and ate it up; some other seed fell on stony soil where it had not much earth, and it shot up at once because it had no depth of earth, but when the sun rose it got scorched and withered away, because it had no root; some other seed fell among thorns, and the thorns sprang up and choked it, so it bore no crop; some other seed fell on good soil and bore a crop that sprang up and grew, yielding at the rate of thirty, sixty, and a hundredfold.

The parable is undeniably stating that nothing is wrong with the seed and there are cases where seeds have sprung and shot up in stony places and thorny situations. Black people, often denied our ontology, must continue to remind ourselves that there is nothing wrong with the seed. Blacks are simply forced to grow in rocky and shallow ground. They are the subset of persons growing in unfavorable soil. If C. S. Lewis is correct, unfortunately for most blacks, the crops from good soil "will not happen in a day." The full potential of a black life will yield its full potential "gradually as the tide lifts a grounded ship." And yet we have witnessed many seeds flourish in uncomplimentary and hostile environments despite the conditions.

Somebody's Little Boy

I grew up knowing that I belonged to somebody. Although I was given up for adoption at an early age, my adoptive parents so loved me that it was deeply rooted in the soil of my soul that I had a calling on my life. Howard Thurman wrote in his classic book, *The Inward Journey*, "It is a strange freedom to be adrift in the world of men without a sense of anchor anywhere. Always there is the need of mooring, the need for the firm grip on something that is rooted and will not give. The urge to be accountable to someone, to know that beyond the individual himself there is an answer that must be given, cannot be denied. The deeds a man performs must be weighed in a balance held by another's hand." James Baldwin, author and civil rights activist, writes about his early years of being adrift as a black boy in Harlem. Amid pimps and whores, Baldwin asserts he could see that many of his friends were "headed for the Avenue." When Baldwin was asked by a female pastor "Whose little boy are you?", which were the same words used by the pimps and whores, Baldwin knew he wanted to be somebody's little boy. For that seed to grow amidst hostile conditions, blacks must know, like Baldwin, that we are somebody's little boy or girl!

There is no way of getting around the fact that white supremacy is a powerful disease that seeks to have an entitlement on every facet of our lives.[5] However, we cannot let it claim who we really are. We cannot let the winds of bigotry toss us to and fro and carry us from the foundations of what we know to be real and true. Throughout my life, I have had many ideas and beliefs about who and what I am and can be, become loosened while they were being or had been seemingly bolted. Nevertheless, the underpinning of what was real and true remained because of deeply rooted seeds of love.

Early in my life, I was introduced to songs such as the old negro spiritual, "Somebody is calling my name. Oh, my Lord, what shall I do?". These are the songs that nurtured blacks in America as they were enduring the harsh conditions of segregation. Many years after Rosa Parks' courageous act, she was asked why she refused to move to the back of the bus. Legend has it that she didn't say that she sat down to launch a movement, because her motives were more basic than that. Mrs. Parks said, "I sat down because I was tired." However, she did not mean her feet were tired. She meant that her soul was tired, her heart was tired, and her whole being was tired of being claimed by the racist plague that denied her soul's claim to selfhood. Rosa Parks had grown up in the South under the demeaning and degrading hand of Jim Crow laws. In a place that denied blacks their God-given rights, Rosa Parks continued to hear a voice from within that told her she was somebody. It was in Montgomery, Alabama, riding buses where blacks were demanded by law to stand while whites sat, that Rosa Parks found her place to answer the question: What shall I do? "Somebody's calling my name…what shall I do?" is an ethical echo and the imperative whisper that I have heard throughout my life as I have been forced to grow around the cement of this nation's lack of love and respect for black people.

Being Cool

I began this essay acknowledging that blacks in America are constantly trying to get a handle on things. Relentless human troubles such as sickness, job loss, missteps, mishaps, and betrayals can be volcanic eruptions around which we literally lose our comprehension of living. Sometimes it really does take a miracle to get a handle on things. Throughout this essay I have asked existential questions: Chaos or community? Where do we go from here? What are you looking for? What shall I do? These are, in many ways, age-old inquiries that human beings raise while spiritually tussling with their conditions.

I believe that the challenges and unknowns that blacks have confronted have forced us to grip and grapple with the invisible. Some call the invisible "Mystery." I am unapologetically and unashamedly a person of faith. The Biblical narrative Gen. 32:22-32 has probably been the most influential piece of scripture to shape my life. The setting is between nighttime and morning at the Jabbok River where a wrestling match takes place between Jacob and a mysterious man. Many interpreters of this scriptural passage have declared the man is God; however, the writer of the text does not provide the identity of the mysterious man. All night in this wrestling match, Jacob looks "through a glass darkly." Jacob has questions for this mysterious man. But we must also acknowledge that Jacob has questions for himself. Jacob wants to know who this man is, and he wants to know if he can get a blessing from this mysterious being. Jacob has never met this man, but he seeks a blessing from him. How odd and bewildering is this encounter. And yet, this biblical passage does tell us two unwavering facts about wrestling with Mystery. Number one, you don't ever get a full handle on what and who Mystery is. Number two, you will be changed by Mystery. Because of this wrestling match, Jacob gets a new name and a limp. This is what the Bible is calling a blessing. Jacob is no longer a trickster, but "Israel"—he who has "striven with God and humans."

Growing up, I always wanted to be cool. The cool guys had special names and a special way of walking. They walked with a swagger (it often looked like a limp!) and they received names such as "Kool Moe Dee" and "L.L. Cool J." Someone once provided a wonderful definition for cool:

> Cool means living for more than the next moment. Cool doesn't mean having the latest Dior, knowing people, being on the list, and sitting at Lucien. Cool means you walk the walk. Cool means being a good person. Cool means when you are alone, you can stand to be with yourself. Cool means listening when others speak; cool means holding doors open and smiling. Cool is compassion, understanding, love, and boundaries. Cool is being good.

Blacks in America must wrestle with Mystery, live with not being able to see clearly, see through the glass darkly. We are forced to engage and embrace the invisible. These precarious conditions and spiritual brawls have made me cool, filled with "compassion, understanding, love, and boundaries." Stephen King declared that stories come to him in "two parts, first the cup and then the handle... the handle may not show up for weeks, months, or even years.... no matter how beautiful the cup may be; you have to wait for it to appear." It has been by faith that I have waited on and wrestled with God through many dark nights of the soul, waiting desperately for a handle to help living in such a cruel world. I am indeed blessed to proclaim I have received many cool names and stylish strides. The gospel song lyrics say it best:

> You know I've been born again.
> I started to walk, I had a new walk.
> I started to talk, I had a new talk.
> I looked at my hands, my hands looked new.
> I looked at my feet and they did, too.

ENDNOTES

1   For more detail surrounding this American tragedy, see Tracy Martin and Sybrina Fulton, *Rest in Power: The Enduring Life of Trayvon Martin* (New York: Random House Publishing Group, 2007).
2   See how King's philosophical, spiritual, and very pragmatic outlook reflects his ideological connection to the rich work and thinking of Howard Thuman. See Howard Thurman's *Jesus and the Disinherited* (Boston: Beacon Press, 1976).
3   See, for more social and political context, Barack Obama, *The Audacity of Hope* (New York: Broadway Books, 2007).
4   See, by contrast, the notion of "double consciousness" as articulated in W.E.B. Du Bois's *The Souls of Black Folk* (New York: Norton and Company, 1999).
5   See Frantz Fanon's indicting, anti-racist, anti-colonialist, 1952 classic, *Black Skin, White Masks* (New York: Grove Press, 2008).

BIBLIOGRAPHY

Du Bois, W.E.B. *The Souls of Black Folk*. New York: Norton and Company, 1999.
Fanon, Frantz. *Black Skin, White Masks*. New York: Grove Press, 2008.
Martin, Tracyand Fulton, Sybrina. *Rest in Power: The Enduring Life of Trayvon Martin*. Random House Publishing Group, 2017.
Obama, Barack. *The Audacity of Hope*. New York: Broadway Books, 2007.
Thurman, Howard. *Jesus and the Disinherited*. Boston: Beacon Press, 1976.

CHAPTER THIRTEEN
Once You Are Converted, Strengthen Your Brother

Vernon G. Smith

I was born on April 11, 1944 to Albert J. and Julia E. Smith. My father was a building contractor, and my mom was a housewife and pastor of Our Lady of Perpetual Help Church. I was born at home at 1613 Rhode Island St., Gary, Indiana, the last of ten children. My siblings are Albert J. Smith, James Johnson (adopted), Eddie Smith, Thomas Smith, Donald Smith, Carl Smith, Lucille Smith Samuels, Margaret Smith Ward (all deceased), and Nadine Smith Williams. Albert and Thomas were contractors. Donald and Carl had careers in the Armed Services. Eddie and James were steel mill workers. Lucille was a secretary. Margaret had a career in retail management. Nadine, who is now retired, had a career in public service.

I enjoyed being the youngest. I received a lot of support and, although my siblings did not have a lot of resources when I attended college, they sent small amounts of money to assist me. They thought I was insane to want to be involved in political life, but they nonetheless supported my efforts financially, emotionally, and materially.[1] My aspirations exceeded theirs, but I never felt that they were either jealous or envious of me. Instead, they always demonstrated and voiced how proud they were of me, and for me. Each time I marched in a college graduation, all of them were there with their children to experience my accomplishment. I loved being from a large family; we loved each other, we were close, we were proud Smiths, and we could have a party by ourselves without any guests (smile). As each has made the transition from this life, I have experienced the pain of separation. I understand when John Donne declared "Each man's death diminishes me," but I also feel the warmth of the presence of my departed loved ones when it is needed. I believe in what Apostle Paul wrote to the Hebrews: "Wherefore seeing we also are compassed about with so great a cloud of witnesses...". Perhaps, unlike Paul, I fear being left alone in this side of life. Be that as it may, I, Vernon G. Smith, very much look forward to seeing my departed siblings and other loved ones, all part of that cloud of witnesses, in "that great gettin' up morning." But for now, I am here, in America today.

If asked to describe America today for Black Americans, I would likely begin with a quote from Charles Dickens' *A Tale of Two Cities*: "It was the best of times, it was the worst of times, it was the age of wisdom, it was the age of foolishness, it was the epoch of belief, it was the epoch of incredulity, it was the season of light, it was the season of darkness, it was the spring of hope, it was the winter of despair." Although more than a century-and-a-half old, this description seems to be highly applicable to the US today for Black Americans. How can it be both of these countries at the same time? With an unequal distribution of wealth and access to higher education, how can it be both at the same time? With the negative stigmatization of Black Americans, how can it be both at the same time? With economic problems facing Black Americans, how can it be both at the same time? With racism, prejudice, and discrimination overtly raising their ugly heads again in this Great Democracy, with the fragility of the Black family followed by the lack of racial solidarity, how is it that some rise and others succumb to death and destruction? How is it that some break through the glass ceiling and others are trapped by the ills of negative stigmatization? How do some Black Americans see obstacles and problems as opportunities and others see them as stop signs? Well, I would assert to you that it is a matter of attitude. Charles R. Swindoll, an American clergyman, summed it up: "Life is 10% what happens to you and 90% how you react to it." Collectively as a "race" and especially among our Black male population, we have not been responding well. I offer these ideal and behavioral responses to Black Americans, especially Black males, and I urge you: once you are converted, strengthen your brother.[2]

I direct your attention to Luke 22: 31-32 which reads: And the Lord said, "Simon, Simon, behold, Satan hath desire to have you, that he may sift you as wheat. But I have prayed for thee that thy faith fail not and when thou art converted strengthen thy brethren."[3]

Prior to this divine declaration, Jesus had told the disciples of His pending betrayal. Now Jesus focuses on Peter. It was Peter, the bold, outspoken Peter, who, when Jesus asked who do men say I am, retorted, "Thou art the Christ." This leads Jesus to say, "Upon this rock I shall build my church." It was this Peter, when he saw Christ walking on the water, who said to Christ, "Lord, if it be thou, bid me come unto thee on the water." It was this same Peter who walked on the water to go to Jesus, but when he saw the whipping of the wind, became afraid and began to sink. It was this same Peter who, while in the Garden of Gethsemane during Jesus' betrayal, has the courage to stand up against the multitude. He draws his sword and cuts off the right ear of one of the guards. It is this same Peter to whom Jesus says, "Simon, Simon, behold Satan hath desired to have you that he may sift you as wheat. But I have prayed for thee that thy faith fails not, and when thou art converted strengthen thy brethren."

Peter responds, "Lord, I am ready to go with thee, both into prison, and to death." Jesus, the Christ, in His omniscience, says unto Peter, "I tell thee, Peter, the cock shall not crow this day, before that thou shalt thrice deny that thou knowest me."

As the plot unfolds, Jesus is betrayed, arrested, and placed on trial. Peter follows from afar. A fire is kindled in the midst of the hall and Peter sits down near the fire with the crowd. A maid recognizes him and says, "This man was also with Him." Peter denies Jesus, saying, "Woman, I know Him not." Moments later another sees him and says, "Thou art also of them." And Peter says, "Man, I am not." And in the space of one hour another says, "Of a truth this fellow also was with Him; for he is a Galilean." For the third time, Peter denies Christ and the cock crows. Peter remembers the words of Jesus. He leaves and weeps bitterly. After Jesus' death and resurrection and after the disciples are filled with the Holy Ghost, Peter goes through a conversion. The scripture says, "and they were all filled with the Holy Ghost, and began to speak with other tongues, as the spirit gave them utterance." The scripture tells us that there were men from all different parts of the east who spoke and understood different languages, but every man understood what was being said. Some were amazed. Others mocked saying, "These men are full of new wine."

This time, after receiving the power of the Holy Ghost, Peter is not afraid. He stands up and preaches the gospel and the scripture tells us that on that same day about three thousand souls were saved. Jesus had said to Peter, "When thou art converted, strengthen thy brethren." What am I trying to say? What Peter had gone through was not about him, it was about God's getting him ready for what He had for him to do for others. Peter's mistake, which had a devastating effect on him, makes him strong in his faith. I am sure he said, "I denied him three times, but I'll never deny him again." His mistake empowered him, gave him holy strength. What he went through was to prepare him to have the courage to preach the gospel. His experience was not for his benefit, but for ours. Peter recalled the words of Jesus, "When thou art converted strengthen thy brethren." While racism, discrimination, bigotry, and inequity are embedded not only in the mindsets of too many Americans, but also in legal systems and policies of this great nation, the mission of this chapter is to alert my people, especially my Black brothers, that we do not have to be victims to the ills of the American system. Too often we choose to be victims. It is further the intent of this discourse to motivate the reader to convert any anti-productive thinking and destructive behavior into the positive, productive realm.[4] Finally, it is the aim of this conversation to encourage the reader to commit efforts to strengthen our brothers and to do so in the Ubuntu philosophy: "I am, because we are; and since we are therefore I am." Certainly, there is an umbilical cord that connects us all; therefore, in the words of the singer-songwriter Jeffrey Osborne and, also, the inspirational author Alex Caston, "If my brother is in trouble, so am I."

Know Who You Are—Believe in Yourself

We cannot help anyone if we can't help ourselves. We cannot guide someone if we are lost. We must come to know who we are and believe in ourselves. For a moment, recall the old children's story of the ugly duckling. Here was a swan trying to be a duck. We value swans much more than ducks. We pay money to see swans swimming on bodies of water; however, we take ducks, shoot them, clean them, stuff them, eat them, and excrete them from our bodies. Yet here was a swan trying to be a duck. We have too many Black people who are swans trying to be ducks. We are the descendants of African kings and queens. We are king's kids. And those of us who have taken on the blood of Jesus Christ, we are doubly king's kids. We are overcomers. A West African minister, J.E.K. Aggery, said it best: "My people of Africa, we are created in the image of God, but men have made us think that we are chickens, and we still think we are, but we are eagles. Stretch forth your wings and fly."

Mankind is God's greatest creation. The question is asked in the Bible, "What is man that he was created just a little lower than the angels?" Believing in this quote is empowering. The problem is that far too often we don't know who we are and we don't believe fully in ourselves. The Bible also lets us know that when we accept Jesus in our lives, we become heirs of God and joint heirs of Jesus Christ. The cattle on a thousand hills are ours. The gold and silver in this world are ours. We must come to realize that we are the head, not the tail; the prince, not the pauper; the king, not the pawn; the lion of the jungle, not the mouse.

Knowing who you are leads to believing in yourself. I ask: If we don't believe in ourselves, then who will? Believing in oneself builds self-confidence. The only way to overcome countless barriers is by being confident enough that you can and will. When we create a positive attitude, believing in ourselves, we realize that what separates us from accomplishing our goals is just a matter of time and work. This feeling of being closer to our goals drastically increases our chances of achieving them. We must inspire ourselves to take action. Believing in ourselves does this. When I grow faint in heart, I talk to my spirit. I encourage myself. I tell myself: "I can do all things through Christ which strengthens me." I say, "If God be for me, who can be against me?" I say to myself, "Yea though I walk through the valley of death, I will fear no evil." I tell myself, "The Lord is my light and my salvation, whom shall I fear and what shall I fear?" "Of whom shall I be afraid?" I encourage my spirit and I inspire myself. I believe that I am an overcomer, a doer, an achiever, and I act on those beliefs.

Unfortunately, we have too many among our people who have little to no personal ambition and are victims of "crabism" or the "crab bucket syndrome": they want to stop those who are achievers. They are satisfied sitting on their butts, doing nothing. For them "out" might as well be "in" because they are going nowhere; "up" might as well be "down" because they are going nowhere; "right" might as well be "left" because they are going nowhere; "forward" might as well be "backward" because they are going nowhere; and if they are moving at all, they are stuck in a rocking chair mode—rocking forward and backward, but going nowhere. They are just not going anywhere, yet they want to stop *you*. I am reminded of Jesus when he goes to raise Jairus's daughter from the dead. When He enters, He states, "She is asleep." The mourners burst out in laughter. Jesus has to rid himself of the naysayers—those who will happily ridicule and mock. We can't let ridicule or mockery stop us. Remember that stop signs are for traffic, not for people's spirits, hopes, dreams and ambitions. As a student—even though I was popular and was elected to serve in several leadership positions—I recall the mockery that I was subjected to because I would not do what others did. I didn't do what they did because what they were doing did not mix with my goals, my ambitions. I knew who I was and what my goals were. Even though the ridicule and jokes hurt, I refused to let others define me. We can't let ridicule or mockery stop us. When I received my tenure and promotion to Associate Professor at Indiana University Northwest, I noted while reading my evaluations from the Campus Promotion and Tenure Committee that one evaluator had said in his comments, "He (referring to me) is just a politician. If we give him tenure, he will not achieve anymore. He will discontinue his research." As stated before, I do not allow others to define me. His criticism, his attempt to ridicule me, became the impetus, the motivation, for me to achieve and prove him wrong. As a result, today I am the only Black Full Professor on my campus. We must know who we are and believe in ourselves.

Vision and Goals

Are you aware of the number of promises God has made to mankind? Everek R. Storms[5], a Canadian school teacher, spent an entire year and a half combing through the Bible, counting, for us, the number of promises from God, and he numbered 7,487 promises. We can never claim any significant number of them without a vision. Jesus said that He came to give us life and life more abundantly (hence the promises), but the Scripture also notes that "where there is no vision, the people perish," We will never realize the promises of God without a vision. A vision is an ideal picture of a future state. A vision provides a focal point and gives purpose. Tied to vision are goals. Too many Black Americans have no vision for themselves and are floundering around. When I was a young boy, Melba Brown was the first one in our neighborhood to go off to college. When she left, she was the talk of our community. I wanted people talking about me in that manner, so I envisioned myself in college and set it as a goal. The rest is history. The question is: What do you want and how badly do you want it? I wanted it so badly that I persisted even when my so-called friends taunted me for not doing drugs and other offers that would have prevented me from reaching my goal. I wanted it badly, so I endured and overcame racial "put-downs" and the stigmatization of Black Americans when Dr. Skizoni in a Sociology class gave a lecture on the topic: "Blacks Are Inferior to Whites." I resisted, rebelled against the negative mind-setting and broke through the glass ceiling when Dr. Johnston Karr stated, "If you are a Negro, the best you can get out of my class is a 'D'." I became an overachiever, joining the limited number of Black Americans acquiring a doctorate from a majority White university or college.

Not only must we have a vision or goals, but we must also protect our vision and goals; they are the children of our souls. I am reminded of my first election. I had recently graduated from college and had decided to run for the position of Gary Indiana's 4th District Councilman. When I first began, my college friends laughed at me. They looked at my financial resources. They looked at my political support and they predicted failure. But I held on to my vision and was not only elected, but served 18 years in that capacity. All of this has also led to my serving 31 years as a state representative in the Indiana House of Representatives.

If we have no vision, no goals, we end up just about anywhere; too often it is in prisons and graveyards. Also, we must stay focused on our goals. I am reminded of Peter on the water when he, for a while, was walking on the water towards Jesus. As long as he kept his eyes focused on Jesus, his goal, he was all right. Once he began to focus on the wind and the waves, he began to sink. You must stay focused on your goals. I am reminded of Jesus on the cross. Many of those onlookers at his feet taunted him saying "If you be the Son of God, save yourself. You saved others, save yourself." Certainly, Jesus could have saved Himself; just by speaking, He could have commanded a legion of angels to save Himself, but Jesus stayed focused on His goal, to die so that we might live, to save us from our sins.

Not only is the lack of vision an individual problem, but because of the lack of racial solidarity, collectively as a people, it is also a group problem. We need a vision that provides a focal point that helps to align everyone, all our people, thus ensuring that everyone is working towards a single purpose. Without doubt, and without a doubt, this helps to increase efficiency and productivity of our people. We must ask ourselves, are we a part of the solution or part of the problem? And if you are converted, strengthen your brother.

Our Past Doesn't Dictate Our Future

The film *Freedom Writers* is a stirring depiction of a true story of a committed teacher who believed what Bobby Kennedy echoed so many times: that we can make a difference in the lives of people, that we have an obligation to make the world a better place in which to live. "Mrs. G.," as she was affectionately called, a neophyte teacher, was driven by those who are prisoners of their visions, to educate those who are often forgotten.

As I viewed the movie, I lamented the racial tension among the young people of L.A.—a tension that is not just some distant or ethereal depiction on the screen, but a harsh and expansive reality in this great nation right now. I felt intense pain as I observed the sense of hopelessness among the young—youngsters in a free society, but in a society full of ills, adolescents captured by their environment. And I know from experience that this sense of hopelessness exists. You see, I am a part of a program which mentors nearly 200 African American boys. They express the same sense of hopelessness to me. Believe me, it is heartbreaking. However, Mrs. G. is a change agent, one who is not willing to accept the status quo. She challenges the system and motivates her students to higher heights. She proves what research supports, which is that caring is a quality—and indeed an important attribute—that affects academic achievement. These young people discovered that it doesn't matter where you come from, but where you are going. Our youth, all of our people, must believe the future is so bright that it burns our eyes.

I know of another who came to understand that it doesn't matter where you come from, but where you are going. Well, the Bible tells us of Joseph, the eleventh son of Jacob. As you may recall, Joseph was the one whom Jacob loved the most. Jacob loved Joseph so much that he made him a beautiful, eye-dazzling coat of many colors, a stunner which created a problem for Joseph and envy among his brothers. Joseph had another problem: he was a dreamer. I tell you, protect your dreams; don't let anyone steal your dreams. Joseph dreams of his father and brothers one day bowing down to the earth before him. The dream leads to a rebuke from his father and kindles more hatred in the hearts of his brothers. I can imagine their thoughts; "You little pipsqueak, who in the h--- do you think you are?" But Joseph, who had a meager beginning, was on his way to greatness, to the king's palace. Joseph went from the pit to prison, from prison to the palace. It doesn't matter where you come from, but where you are going.

Many of you, if you are like me, came from humble beginnings. We were not born with a silver spoon in our mouths. We did not have generational wealth passed down to us. We did not have parents with doctoral degrees or, in many instances, even high school diplomas. We were not given the opportunity to choose our beginnings. But life is full of choices. I have made some bad choices in my life, choices that haunt me. But we have to get over the past and refuse to let our past hold our future hostage. We all have the potential to become kings. And consider Esther in the Bible, who became a queen. It doesn't matter where you come from, but where you are going. In our sins we could have been killed, but God spared us. We are still here because God has something for us to do. He has a place or position for us. We must not give up until we get to the place God intended for us—and it's not here in this prison or any other prison. It doesn't matter where you come from, but where you are going. If you haven't done so, now is the time to decide where you are going—and don't let anyone stop you from getting there. Remember, stop signs were made for traffic, not for people. Don't let society program your future. Think for yourself; control your own future. Let the states of this nation continue to build prisons, jail cells, but don't allow them to place your name in or on one of them. It doesn't matter where you come from, but where you are going. And once you are converted, strengthen your brothers...and sisters. Kings and queens, strengthen one another.

Dare to Be Different

The world is inhabited by millions of people, some of whom share similar opinions and values, and some who don't. Diversity of culture, "race," values, politics, body shape and size, sexuality and religion—to name a few—all of these make us individuals.

The Founding Fathers, architects of the US Constitution, recognized the need to build a nation. They recognized the need for acculturation; but they valued our right to be individuals. As this Nation celebrated its 100 Anniversary, France presented America with the famed Statue of Liberty. Inscribed on this Mother of Exiles are these words: "Give me your tired, your poor, your huddled masses yearning to breathe free, the wretched refuse of your teeming shore. Send these, the homeless, the tempest-tossed to me. I lift my lamp beside the golden door!" And the Germans, the Poles, the English, the Irish, the Italians, the Spanish, multiple nationalities came seeking freedom and a better life. Clinging to their ethnic groups, they settled in common neighborhoods; as a result, major cities such as Chicago and New York developed their Little Polands, Little Italies, Little Germanies, etc. These voluntary immigrants had to be socialized into a nation, but the Founders held to their conviction that individuality needed to be respected and preserved.

However, not everyone respects and accepts the differences in others. Some are confused by, scared of, or angered by individual differences. Others are less tolerant and seek to make "others" mimic or become carbon copies of themselves. Peer pressure has become the number one influence on our young, but not only as stemming from our youth. Adults in America use it. Peer pressure is present at the workplace and within the general community, too; there is a constant push for conformity—a coercion, even. It takes courage, real conviction, internal stamina to resist, to be different.

Not only must we dare to be different, we must dare to make a difference. We must have the courage to defend the down-trodden, the least of the least, to proclaim the Word, to do what is right and not what is popular, to become the change we want to see.

Think Not of Yourself

When we enter the world, we are born with a mindset of "me-ism." It is all about me. I cry when I am wet. I cry when I want to be held. I cry when I want to eat. I cry when I want you to walk with me. I cry when I want you to hold me on your shoulders. I cry when I want you to cradle me. As a baby it is all about me. As we mature, we find that it is not all about "me"; the world does not revolve around "me." We discover that there is something called "we-ism." We discover that no man is an island entire unto himself. However, some people never make the transition. They never learn to share, to give, to help. They continue to look for what they can get out of life, instead of what they can contribute to life. They never learn that it is not about "me," but about "others." You see, God blesses us so that we can be a blessing to others.

The Scripture tells us the story of Esther, an orphaned Jewish girl who had been raised by her cousin Mordecai, who had an office in the household of Ahasuerus. According to the Book of Esther, when Vashti was dismissed from being queen, all the most beautiful virgins of the kingdom were brought before Ahasuerus. Unaware of her background and parentage, Ahasuerus chose Esther to be his queen. Later, because Mordecai refused to pay homage to Haman, a man in the Persian government, Haman influenced the King to issue a decree calling for the extermination of the Jews. Mordecai persuaded Esther to intervene on the Jews' behalf, at the risk of her life. Esther is afraid to appear before the King. Mordecai tells her not to think of herself, but of her people. He tells her that she may have come into the kingdom for such a time as this.

Unfortunately, most people in general tend to think of themselves rather than others. Admittedly, if people do not take care of themselves first, they may suffer negative consequences; they have to provide for their own needs, protect their own lives, and reach their own goals. While this is true, some are selfish by nature; they often refuse to help, or are reluctant to give or to serve even out of their abundance. However, to build and maintain a healthy community, we need those who care about and are concerned with the wellbeing of others. As a people, we need to understand that we are only as strong as our weakest link. We are the sum total of all our parts, all of the ones who make up our "race." If we strengthen our brothers, our sisters, we become a stronger people. None of us are as rich as all of us. None of us are as smart as all of us. None of us are as strong as all of us. We need to develop a spirit of lifting while we climb. Without small efforts from all, nothing will ever change. Touching the life of another in a positive way is the simplest way of improving the plight of our "race." Giving hope is like lighting a fire that cannot be extinguished. And remember the future of our "race": our children are watching.

Save Those Whom We Can

The Bible tells us that one day Apostle Paul is preaching in an upper room of a building. Allow me to paraphrase the story. There is a lad sitting on the windowsill. As Apostle Paul preaches, the young lad falls asleep and as he drifts further into slumber, he falls backwards and out of the window. The parishioners run down, pick the boy up, and pronounce him dead. Paul follows along the steps, takes the lad in his arms, prays for him, and brings him back to life. When I read this episode in Christian history, I sometimes think, "Wouldn't it be great if I had this power? With the rate of homicide among young Blacks in urban communities, I would be the first one on the scene, picking up our young, praying for them, and restoring their lives—but sadly, I don't have enough faith". Even though Jesus said that the things He did, we could do and witness even greater things, the truth of the matter is that I do not have enough faith; and before you criticize me, let me assert that neither do you. But the one thing that I got from this story is the point that, if someone had paid attention to the young man sitting on the window sill in the first place, or had taken the initiative to wake him up or catch him before he fell, he would not have died. Wouldn't it be great if each of us felt it our responsibility to wake up a Black child who doesn't value his education, who is not trying, who doesn't want to learn, and who is caught up only in the "education" that these mean streets have to offer?

One day I was ill and confined to my bed. I decided to watch a movie that normally I would not have had time for. The movie, *The Neverending Story*, immediately drew me in. In the film, a young boy, Bastian, takes an old book and begins to read it. He is drawn into the plot of the book and soon finds himself in a place called Fantasia, a land where anything that a child could possibly imagine could happen. He rides the back of a flying dog or racing snail. Eventually, Fantasia is threatened by a terrible force called "The Nothing"—a horrendous entity that consumes everything. As I thought and thought while watching the movie, I became convinced that this very same disease, "The Nothing," is the one that is affecting our Black youth. We have too many Black youth who want to stand on corners and do nothing, who want jobs but once they get them want to do nothing, who go to school and want to do nothing, who father children and then do nothing.

As people who derived from Africa, we were the first mathematicians, the first botanists, the first chemists, the first physicists, the first astrologers and the first zoologists. Our ancestors developed languages and the arts. Yet too many of our people are failing—failing because of a negative mindset. They have accepted the mentality that they cannot achieve academically. Their cry is that math is too hard. I do not understand geometry. Algebra makes no sense. Physics is too difficult.

The truth of the matter is that they do not understand that, without pain, there is no gain. So the achievement gap persists when we should be first among all peoples academically. The truth of the matter is that, as a people, too many of us do not have the right attitude. We simply have some terrible attitudes. Some do not want help. They do not want anybody touching them, saying anything to them, or even looking at them. They have what I call the "C" Attitude; they are just *seeing* their way through one situation until they find themselves in another situation. They also have what I call the "B" Attitude. When we ask them how they are doing, the response we may get is: "You know me; I *be* chillin'." The odds are so against us as a people that we do not have time to be chillin'. We must run twice as fast, three times as fast, to stay in the same place. Simply put, some of us need an attitude adjustment.

I also believe that we will not be able to save all our young, but we must work diligently to save those whom we can. Think with me, if you will, upon the story of a man who is walking on the beach. He sees a young lad tossing things into the water. Curious, he moves closer to the boy, and observes that the young lad is picking up starfish and flinging them back into the ocean. He asks the boy, "What are you doing?" The young one replies, "You see, the morning tide washed these starfish up on the beach and I am trying to toss them back into the ocean before the noonday sun dries them out and kills them." The man glances out at the very large number of starfish on the sand and responds, "How can you possibly save all of these starfish?" The young boy, continuing to fling the starfish back into the beautiful waters, reaches down and—without missing a beat—picks up yet another. "I might not be able to get to all of them," he says, tossing yet another into the water, "but I saved that one." He picks up another one and says, "And I have saved that one." The man is so impressed he joins the boy in tossing the starfish back into the ocean. We will not be able to save all our youth, but we must do our level best to save all those whom we can.

I recall another aquatic story. Two men are fishing on a lake. They notice that periodically something is being thrown over the bridge into the water. They decide to row over to see what on earth is being thrown off the bridge. As they row closer, they notice that the object is a baby. One of the men frantically jumps out of the boat and speedily swims over to the baby, brings the child into the boat, applies CPR, and ultimately revives the child. Just as he completes this heroic task, he notices that yet another baby has been thrown off the bridge. The man jumps again out of the boat and swims over to the baby, bringing this child into the boat, applies CPR, and revives this child, too. Just as he has finished doing so, he is aghast to see that another baby has been thrown into the water. This time he starts swimming, but in the opposite direction, towards the bridge. His friend in the boat yells out, "Where are you going? Why aren't you going after the baby?" The man in the water shouts out, "I'm going up onto the bridge to see who is throwing these babies off of that bridge!" This man knew he had to get to the root of the problem.

In getting to the source of the problem, we must look at the parents of our young. Those of us who are of the Baby Boomer Generation were, as a whole, taught to value education, but this is not the case today. We have too many parents who do not value education and thus have transferred their lack of appreciation of education to their children. While they transfer values, too many parents do not transfer positive, societally acceptable values. They do not teach their children compassion, patience, love, honesty, a work ethic, and an appreciation of delayed gratification. Values are like a rudder on a ship; they provide direction in life's journey. In addition, parents have not always taught their children their role in school. They need to know that they are the child, the student, not the adult and not the teacher. Too many parents instruct their children to call them if the teacher puts her/his hands on you. Some even tell their children if the teacher hits you, hit him/her back. This sends out a message to students that they can cross the line with adults. Our parents were supportive of teachers. If we got in trouble in school, we prayed that our teachers would not call home. Today too many parents do not come to school to ask questions to find out what happened. Instead, they come over to jump on the teacher. There are too many parents living their lives through their children. They are so busy giving their young what they did not have that they have forgotten to give them what they did have. They have failed to put structure in the lives of their children and hold their children accountable for their behavior.

Not to place the blame totally on parents—and without my telling you, we already know that we have far too many teachers who contribute to the problem. There are some who just do not care, who are a part of the problem. William Purkey, considered the father of invitational education, identifies four kinds of teachers. The first kind are those who are intentionally disinviting. They are nasty individuals. They intentionally turn off students. They see their classrooms as their domains. They are intentionally dis-inviting. Next, he identifies a group of teachers who are unintentionally disinviting. These teachers want to connect with students, they want to motivate students, but they do not know how. They are unintentionally disinviting. The next group that Purkey identifies are those who are unintentionally inviting. They have good days with students, and they want to replicate the days, but they cannot. They are unintentionally inviting. The last group he identifies are those who are intentionally inviting. They connect with students. They motivate students to learn, and they can consistently do so. They are intentionally inviting. The truth of the matter is that we have a few too many teachers who are in categories one and two and not enough in the latter, by far the better half of this quadrant.

It is also true that we have incompetent teachers in our urban classrooms. We have teachers who do not care, who do not like children, and who often are uninviting in their dispositions. They turn off children, rather than motivate them. They escalate conflicts rather than de-escalate them. Let me remind you that it is criminal not to teach. I firmly believe that if there is no learning, there is no teaching. Teachers do not just affect the thirty or so students within an assigned class, but they affect generations and generations who are the offspring of that thirty.

I admit that I do not have all the answers, but I do know that we cannot afford to lose another generation of Blacks. I implore you to join me—join the many others and me—who care to seek out the answers and to make a difference in the lives and futures of our people, our young, and especially—these days—our Black men. For our people are our greatest natural resource, not the rolling water of the Midwest, not the coal we extract from the ground, not the trees of our forests, not the gold we store in depositories. Our people, our children, our boys and girls, are our greatest natural resources. Let us save all those whom we can.

Once you are converted, strengthen your brother!

ENDNOTES

1   For a broader view of the political landscape of that time and place, see two very useful resources: Emma Lou Thornbrough and Lana Ruegamer, *Indiana Blacks in the Twentieth Century* (Bloomington: Indiana University Press, 2000); and Richard G. Hatcher, *Black Power, Gary Style: The Making of Mayor Richard Gordon Hatcher* (Chicago: Johnson Publishing Co., 1970).

2   See Elliot Liebow's classic text and sociological study, *Tally's Corner: A Study of Negro Streetcorner Men* (Boston: Little, Brown and Company, 1967).

3   Theologian and scholar Peter J. Paris underscores how the "black church" tradition, a "surrogate world" for many blacks in the United States, is deeply rooted in faith-focused social teachings. See Peter J. Paris, *The Social Teachings of the Black Churches* (Philadelphia: Fortress, 1985).

4   See, for example, the inspirational messages of Hill Harper, *Letters to a Young Brother: MANifest Your Destiny* (New York: Gotham Books, 2006).

5   See Journal Review article, "The Promises of God". Site: www.journalreview.com. 17October 2020.

BIBLIOGRAPHY

Carter, R.K., Schultz, C., and Landers, A. "Religion: Promises: Standing on the Promises of God." *TIME Magazine*, December 24, 1956.

Harper, Hill. *Letters to a Young Brother: MANifest Your Destiny*. New York: Gotham Books, 2006.

Hatcher, Richard G. *Black Power, Gary Style: The Making of Mayor Richard Gordon Hatcher*. Chicago: Johnson Publishing Co., 1970.

Liebow, Elliot. *Tally's Corner: A Study of Negro Streetcorner Men*. Boston: Little, Brown and Company, 1967.

Paris, Peter J. *The Social Teachings of the Black Churches*. Philadelphia: Fortress Press, 1985.

Thornbrough, Emma Lou (ed.), Lana Ruegamer. *Indiana Blacks in the Twentieth Century*. Bloomington: Indiana University Press, 2000.

CHAPTER FOURTEEN
Faith has Prepared Us for this Moment

Askia Davis

To be an African American man is to traverse an internal mindset, an internal monologue, laden with contradictions. I am American. Really, I am! Yet, there are many definitions of "American" and most seek to reject or define me as either "other" or an anomaly.

Faith Captures Me

I was born in 1950 in Swainsboro, a small intensely segregated town in rural Georgia with a population of 4,300. The schools were segregated. The white school was well-funded, while the Black school was dramatically underfunded. The schools were profoundly Plessyian—separate and unequal in defiance of the 1954 *Brown v. Board of Education* Supreme Court decision. The good, white conservative Christians across town who controlled local government, and those in state government, were intent upon maintaining that status quo. I remained in our segregated school from September of 1956 until May of 1965.

Now, nearly seventy years since *Brown*, many good, white Christian evangelicals in Georgia and throughout America are preaching the same blasphemous theology of white supremacy as God's manifest destiny for America.

To get to school in 1956, my schoolmates and I had to walk across a little wooden bridge that lay above a large, open sewer. The bridge was about two hundred yards south of my home in the then recently constructed housing projects. Beneath the wooden planks, the waste water from various neighborhoods flowed constantly, having first flowed through various conduits in the adjacent Black neighborhood. Near the school for whites across town, as one might suspect, there was no open sewer to greet the students on their walk or ride to school.

While the details may be startling or new, the narrative itself is tragically past and present. Today throughout Black neighborhoods across America, most notably Flint, Michigan, Blacks are leading the struggle to remove toxic sites that undermine their health. There is a clarion call for environmental justice in many communities where the health and longevity of citizens have been diminished by the deliberate nearby placement of toxic sites. Lead paint in dilapidated housing has had numerous deleterious effects upon children in terms of their physical, social, and even cognitive development. The battle to grow and protect excellence in black children is a multi-pronged, generations-old effort. Like democracy, it requires constant vigilance.

I learned to read at the age of three. This was a time-honored, communal tradition in my family. It was expected that the older siblings would teach the younger ones to read by that age. I was taught by my sister Gloria, who was a few years my senior. When I was five, I taught my sister Lillie, who was three.[1]

Along with learning to read, I was also conditioned in faith—faith in excellence and faith in my ability to achieve great things even in the face of great challenges. The expectation was that one would push through difficult circumstances, whatever they were. When I started school at age six, there were nights when I would go to bed hungry. However, I awakened each morning eager to go to school even if my breakfast was only grits and butter.

The effort mattered and paid off. My older brothers and sisters were known for being "very" smart. At age six, I was known for being "exceptionally" smart, even among the friends of my older siblings. Some would offer me a nickel to demonstrate my spelling and math skills to them. A nickel was a powerful motivator because it was sufficient to buy ten ginger snap cookies, my favorite.

Despite my zeal for reading, my access to books, broadly speaking, was extremely limited. My family's income was quite low, so purchasing books was out of the question. However, at home I did have regular access to my older siblings' school books; these were the enriched resources to which I had easy access for more reading, math, and studying of history. Every day my little eyes were in their books.

I benefited as a result. In Mrs. Lawrence's second grade class, I became something of a co-teacher. On days when she might be called to the principal's office for special assignments, I would often be instructed to continue to lead my classmates through the reading and math lessons. Such responsibilities grew. For many years, starting in my fourth-grade year, the principal or testing coordinator would pull me from class and place me alone in an empty office to score the California Achievement Test which had been taken by all students from grades one through twelve. It would take me two to three days to complete scoring and organizing data for presentation to the principal. The testing coordinator, a teacher, of course had her own methodology for ensuring the accuracy of scoring and data reporting. Even so, I learned, grew, and was trusted in the world of formal education.

I loved my school. Emanuel County Elementary and High School, its teachers, and the teaching profession were held in the highest esteem among Blacks in Swainsboro, as has been the case for similarly situated schools and Black communities across America. Our teachers were the stars of the community. If a student ever had a problem with a teacher, he or she would soon have a problem with his or her parents after arriving home. Blacks from my generation know exactly what that sentence means.

Education was a communal undertaking, long before the phrase "It takes a village" became an overused cliché. At Emanuel County, all of my teachers from grades one through nine—literally all of them—were devoted and outstanding educators. Teaching was a calling for them, and back then it was also the beginning of a calling for me. The teachers of Emanuel County had long internalized another African American proverb: "keep your eyes on the prize." This sage call to action reflected an ever-increasing movement towards collective self-determination and the fullest expression of our ability to shape not only our reality, but also America's. Our long-suffering, enslaved ancestors had kept their eyes on the prize. Moreover, they nursed an ever-increasing faith that one day our people would walk fully and righteously in the light of that prize. Black people knew that if America were to achieve its highest ideals as a true democracy, we had to persist as the vanguard that pushed America forward, as we have always done.

With their eyes on me as an important part of the bigger prize, my mother, uncles, aunts, teachers, and my neighbors in general nurtured in me a deep faith in my ability to achieve academic excellence. Through them I came to understand that one key avenue toward self-determination would be my ability to contribute to establishing the America that our ancestors could only dream of. I had to keep working hard, looking up, and believing.

Once, when I was six and coming back home from downtown, a really small commercial district with a few stores in the white part of town, an elderly woman named Mrs. Ocela called me over to sit on her porch for a few minutes. Mrs. Ocela would customarily sit on her porch in her rocking chair after sundown. When I sat on the concrete porch, she rocked and pointed at a star. She at once queried and proclaimed, "See that star? It tells me things about you! It tells me you are going to do great things." It was my first time hearing that stars could tell stories, even of the future.

I later told my mom what Mrs. Ocela had said to me, and my mother affirmed that I would do great things. Well, if my mom said it, then it must come true! After all, she is love and wisdom personified. I would later learn that Mom was also sharing that belief within the family and throughout the community—with our friends and neighbors.

I am equally as confident, however, that I was no exception. Black mothers and fathers throughout Georgia and, no doubt, all over America were dreaming aloud, envisioning and projecting greatness for their sons and daughters. After all, there was a powerful Civil Rights movement afoot, gaining steam. The Great Migration, towards what was seen as more promising lands of self-determination and economic opportunity, had been taking place for about forty years. Aspirations were real. By the age of ten, I was anxious to join three of my older brothers who had left Georgia for New York City after graduating high school. I was, of course, too young, but as an alternative, I grabbed every school book available to help me learn all I could about New York City, the Big Apple, the City That Never Sleeps, the Great White Way.

My mother would not let me leave for New York City until I was 15, and only after I told her if she didn't relent I would continue to be a good son—yes—but I would not be a happy son. Eventually consenting, Mom wisely informed me nonetheless "everything that glitters ain't gold." Still, she had faith that I would overcome the obstacles that New York would invariably present. My opportunity to join the Great Migration thus would come in the summer of 1965. With that amazing opportunity would come many things—including books! A few months after joining the Great Migration to New York City, I had access, for the very first time, to a public library.

From Faith to Passion

When I arrived in New York on May 31, 1965, my new home was in the Bronx with my oldest brother, Willie. It would be my first New York stomping ground, but not my last. Around mid-June I decided to take a trip to see a family friend to whom another brother of mine had previously been engaged. When I emerged from the subway at Eastern Parkway and set eyes for the first time upon the trifecta of the Brooklyn Museum of Art, the Brooklyn Public Library on Eastern Parkway, and Grand Army Plaza, I knew deep within myself that this slice of New York was precisely where I was meant to be.

The vista of Eastern Parkway from the museum to the library was stunning and remains today, to my mind, one of the most beautiful blocks in New York City. The family friend whom I visited lived two blocks south of the library, and on the day I arrived I found myself actively trying to convince her to let me live with her—and her new husband and son—in Brooklyn. Of course, my brother was rightfully upset, but I always had a passion for knowing what I wanted, and usually getting it.

My first job in New York City, in September of 1965, was an after-school position cataloging books at the beautiful and grand Brooklyn Public Library at Grand Army Plaza, quite the contrast to my first job in Georgia, which had been picking cotton from the time I was age five to ten. In the South, I had also worked prior to the age of fourteen cropping tobacco, clearing demolished housing sites, climbing tall pines to get pine cones to sell, climbing pecan trees to get pecans, harvesting peanuts, washing dishes at Keys Café, logging pines, cleaning the office of the local draft board, and even digging a grave. I never looked down on those jobs in Georgia, of course, for they provided income which my family had desperately needed. However, I was keenly aware, in Brooklyn, that this new employment which provided me with a high measure of autonomy in a library that held more than one million books was definitely, for me, more than a step up.

In September I also began tenth grade at John Jay High School in Park Slope, about a mile from my apartment. John Jay was a predominantly white high school of more than four thousand students, a massive population which was greater than that of my entire hometown. I had my first exposure to integrated schooling, however, within a largely segregated enclave at John Jay reserved for "honor students." (More than 55 years later, the phenomenon of tracking or segregating "gifted" students from the general population persists across New York City. For decades a controversial test has been used to identify four-year-olds who would enter gifted and talented programs.) I was placed in the honors enclave at John Jay, the only Black student to reap that so-called honor.

The homeroom classes at John Jay were typically integrated, but not the subject area classes. In my homeroom class I sat eyeing beautiful Black girls that I would see only for the ten minutes that homeroom lasted. Then it was off to the segregated honors classes before I could even say hello to them!

My first geometry teacher at John Jay High School was what teenagers back in the day would call a "trip." She was not interested in explaining anything to anyone. I had been placed in her class about two weeks after it began, and I sat there clueless. But my family and earlier teachers back home had prepared me for that moment. I went to the white principal and, with my deep southern accent, insisted that he not only remove me from the class but also review my school records "from Georgie." He then placed me in the honors class of Mrs. Montemarano, an Italian American teacher who would eventually become my chief advocate and protector throughout my three years at John Jay.

Also, by dint of my own personality, I would not be Ralph Ellison's "Invisible Man" while at John Jay. I was outspoken and developed a high profile among the honors students and within the general population—white, Black, Puerto Rican, and Asian. I developed friendships in each group, but it was with my Black and Puerto Rican male friends that I attended basement parties and played basketball after school.

I don't know if Tuskegee Airman Dr. Roscoe Brown had dreams as a child of being a soldier in the United States Armed Forces, but as a young child, from around age six, I routinely dreamt that I was a general in America's army. I would ride a white horse leading tanks and infantry into battle! Some nights I would awaken in the middle of a dream and would command myself back to sleep to continue a particular dream. I had absorbed the distorted myths of American military chivalry, from the genocide and removal of Native Americans, through the Alamo and the "conquering" of Mexico. Hollywood had been my educator.

I first picked up *The Autobiography of Malcolm X* in the spring of 1966 at the Grand Army Plaza public library. A student had left it on a table in my area thinking that I would return it to the stacks. When I picked up the book, Malcolm X's right index finger was pointing at the center of my forehead. The front cover had a statement from him foretelling his death prior to the book's publication. I checked out the book at the close of my shift.[2]

The book was not on the reading lists of my English classes at John Jay. Those lists included instead *The Great Gatsby*, *Death of a Salesman*, *Julius Caesar*, and other "great books" or "classics" written by white men. One white woman was on the reading lists: Pearl S. Buck, and her novel *The Good Earth*. I enjoyed reading each one, and each was useful, but they were not what decades later Dr. Yvette Jackson, author of the award-winning book *The Pedagogy of Confidence*, would identify as particularly "culturally relevant" texts for a young Black student.

Until I had read *The Autobiography of Malcolm X*, no other book had awakened within me a deeper passion for learning the truth about the history of Africa, America, and African Americans; furthermore, no other book had served more greatly as the educational foundation for the man and the professional I would become. I didn't know that Malcolm X had existed until the day his index finger pointed at my forehead. I was from rural Georgia. We knew of Dr. King, but Malcolm X had been off the radar.

I recall reading the book within twenty-four hours. As I read it, America's distorted white supremacist myths about Africa and America, which had been with me since childhood, were all washed away: wanting to be the cowboy instead of the Indian when playing cowboys and Indians; imagining saving Custer and his cavalry instead of riding as a warrior with Sitting Bull; wanting to enter the screen while watching "The Alamo" to fight alongside Davy Crockett and Jim Bowie against Santa Anna and his "invading" Mexican troops; playing Tarzan with my friend Charles where we pretended to beat up the naked African who only shouted gibberish while jumping up and down!

America's media had hoodwinked and bamboozled Charles and me; it had led astray tens of millions of other American children, of every description, with its many distorted myths. Charles and I were not the only misadventured cowboys killing Indians. He and I were, tragically and most assuredly, not the only miscast, self-cast "Tarzans" beating up and dehumanizing the "Africans" while we swung from tree to tree on vines and ropes in the woods near the projects.[3]

After reading *The Autobiography of Malcolm X*, the next day at John Jay I began, as a student, to discuss and focus on Malcolm X's teaching in my social studies and history classes. This was not part of the curriculum, but I persisted in classes where I was the only Black student. One day, in Social Studies, Betty, a popular blonde and the head of the cheerleaders, couldn't take it anymore. She blurted out in frustration, "If you are so proud of Africa, why don't you go back and swing like monkeys from a tree!?" I calmly announced to my classmates that Blacks in Africa had built pyramids and great centers of education in Egypt and Nubia when Europe was devoid of great architecture and centers of learning.

Reading about Malcolm X gave me power, resolve, and enabled me to understand that one could be brilliant in one area and in another "super dumb" (using the vernacular of the 60s). After my exposure to Malcolm, I read Carter G. Woodson's *The Miseducation of The Negro* and became even more fiercely determined to fight for the emancipation of the minds of Black students. In 1966 I was passionately determined to change the course of my education, and to do so almost overnight.

Malcolm X was then the North Star of my teen years. Muhammad Ali would soon join him as a twin star. As I continued to take Malcolm and Black history books, including Lerone Bennett Jr.'s *Before the Mayflower*, into the classrooms, I dropped the term "Negro." I dressed in long black leather coats and wore my black leather cap backwards inside the building. I "bopped" when walking down the hallways. I did not want to try fitting in with the other Black and Puerto Rican students because they were largely unaware of Malcolm X. I was carving out my own space for self-expression, pushing John Jay to meet my expectations.

I was on my way to becoming valedictorian. My family, especially my mom, and my teachers in that little segregated school with limited resources back in Georgia, had prepared me for that moment. I had internalized faith in my ability to achieve academic excellence even in an unwelcoming environment. Furthermore, my mother, my aunts, and my teachers had imparted invaluable folk wisdom through their conversations and lived examples. African American folk wisdom sustains us through the ups and downs and through deep internal and external challenges to our faith. Its foundation is the Emotional Intelligence of our African American ancestors, an intelligence that existed long before the students of Travis Bradberry and Jean Greaves in 2009 began to bring the concept into the training of corporate and educational leaders. In fact, our ancestors brought "Emotional Intelligence" with themselves across the Atlantic and in so doing made it possible for 200 million people of African descent to stand in the Americas and Caribbean today.

From Faith to Passion to Perception

I am sure the white principal of John Jay wasn't happy with either my image or me, but I had two white "ethnic" female teachers looking out for me, Mrs. Montemarano, the Italian, and Mrs. Fitzgerald, who was Irish American. I was going to be John Jay's first Black valedictorian. I was going to be valedictorian of a school where it was not uncommon for white students of various ethnic backgrounds to gather in large groups on Seventh Avenue after school to initiate large-scale battles against Black and Puerto Rican students. Park Slope was a white neighborhood where, quite frankly, Blacks and Puerto Ricans were largely unwelcome. The riots would take place around 2:20 pm after general dismissal, while I would be in honors classes, which were not dismissed until 50 minutes later.

Thankfully, I was never harassed while often walking home alone through Park Slope. Maybe It was because Gus, this huge and popular Italian student, was friendly towards me in gym class and the hallways. Or maybe all the white students who were looking to fight had had their fill and were, as I walked home, by then at community playgrounds or somewhere else at or near Prospect Park.

By September of 1967, I had made up my mind to graduate a semester early, in January of 1968. I had begun to show up late for certain classes although I was physically in the school building. The classes were not interesting. I enrolled at Brooklyn College and started classes in February of 1968. I had been living alone for a year. My brother Willie had been drafted into the army in 1967. Rather than return to Georgia, as he had insisted since I was 16, I knew that I was prepared to keep his apartment in the Bronx while continuing my education at John Jay.

Soon after enrolling at Brooklyn College, I was sitting outside my apartment building in the Bronx when I saw Sekou Odinga walking past in his Black Panther attire. Within that week, I had joined the Harlem Branch of the Black Panther Party. I was 17. Lumumba Shakur, the branch commander, made the biggest impression on me. He was a Pan-Africanist, as was his wife Afeni Shakur and his brother Zayd Shakur. I admired Dhoruba Bin-Wahid because he exemplified confidence and courage and had a speaking voice that was a unique blend of the voice of the university, or academia, and what we would call the university of the streetwise. Jamal Eddie Joseph was a 15-year-old Harlem Panther, as was Nile Rogers.

Within a few months after joining the Black Panther Party, I was selected as Lieutenant of Education for the Harlem branch. As I led in Harlem, I also organized at Brooklyn College and was selected as one of two top leaders of the Brooklyn League of Afro American Collegians. I was attending classes at Brooklyn College in my Panther uniform. I did not give any thought to what the white professors thought of my activities. My eyes were on the prize. At Brooklyn College, the prize was the creation of the African American Studies Department, the Puerto Rican Studies Department, and opening enrollment to the tens of thousands of Black and Puerto Rican high school graduates who had been denied entry into Brooklyn College and City University of New York.

In the spring of 1968, the Black and Puerto Rican students began rallies and sit-ins demanding the policies we desired. Nineteen Black and Puerto Rican students, including me, were secretly indicted in May of 1969 and on May 13th we were arrested. I was arrested at the hands of a small squad of cops who invaded my apartment. One detective placed a .357 Smith and Wesson Magnum to my temple as some others proceeded to search my apartment for weapons. They found none.

My male comrades and I were taken to notorious Rikers Island prison where we learned through news accounts that each of us was facing the possibility of a sentence of 228 years for riot, arson, and other charges. Three Black female comrades were held at a different detention center for women. Apparently, the charges had been fabricated with the assistance of a Black undercover cop, Mel Beatty, posing as a Brooklyn College student.

However, the Brooklyn College administration, the district attorney, Mel Beatty, and the New York City Police Department apparently did not anticipate the anger that the arrests would generate broadly, even within the largely white student population and among many who did not agree with all the objectives and methods of our struggle. The day following our arrests, thousands of students boycotted classes and held rallies demanding that charges against us be dropped and that the police force that occupied the campus be removed.

Congresswoman Shirley Chisholm, a past graduate of Brooklyn College, immediately began to organize the Black community following our arrest. She secured financial assistance from prominent Black clergy and business leaders to bail us out of prison. Four days after our arrests, we were released on bail.

While in prison facing the possibility of a life sentence, I thought that either my passion could shrink or that I could rise up, draw upon my faith, and realize that I was indeed prepared for the moment. My perception of the systems that America uses to oppress Black people and suppress any attempt by Blacks to strive for self-determination and equal opportunity became even clearer. After all, I was locked up in one such system and therein surrounded by young Black men who were victims of miseducation and the "schools-to-prison pipeline." I became determined not to let prison break my spirit. If indeed America could seek to sentence a group of college teens to life in prison, simply for demanding that Blacks and Puerto Ricans have fair access to a tax-financed public college, what would it not do to other Blacks demanding justice and opportunity?[4]

Within a few months of our release from prison, an agreement was reached between our lawyers and the district attorney to drop all charges. Brooklyn College and City University relented to our principal demands and similar demands on other campuses and enacted an Open Admissions policy. Since that policy was implemented, hundreds of thousands of students who would have otherwise been shut out have entered and graduated from Brooklyn College and the other senior colleges of City University of New York.

In the spring semester of 1970, while serving as president of the Black Student Organization at Brooklyn College, I led the organization to assume a deeper focus on community and youth development. Scores of Black students joined me in spending more time in the communities of Brownsville and East New York rather than on campus. We opened the largest free breakfast program for children in Brooklyn. We organized tenants to demand housing improvements from landlords. We developed cultural and educational after-school activities and a summer program at Ralph Community Center. In Brownsville, we operated in the "territory" of the Tomahawks, a street gang of thousands that would hold assemblies in the park near the center. Some members attended our events. There was never a fight within Ralph Center or even along its perimeter during the nearly three years of our presence there.

We were more than college students; we were community developers and "servants of the people!" My perception about the need for this dramatic change, from being solely campus revolutionaries to also being community developers, began to emerge shortly after my release from Rikers Island. In the fall of 1970, I took a semester off from Brooklyn College to enhance the foundation of our community development activities.

When I graduated in the summer of 1972, the President of Brooklyn College sent a highly regarded Black professor to me as a messenger, offering me a position as a counselor at Brooklyn College with a high salary and future opportunities. It was August of 1972, and I had no prospects for another job. In fact, after taking that earlier semester off, I had no time to focus on job searches because I had a heavy load of classes and coursework to complete. I had professors writing an "A" on my papers then drawing a line through the "A" and writing a "C." Nevertheless, I graduated cum laude.

I did not have $500 in the bank when the professor, the President's messenger, approached me. My beloved daughter Ife was one month away from birth. I knew that the offer was to bring me over to the "white" side, to use my influence among the students as a future suppressor of any student revolutionary action on campus. My faith said "No!" How could I betray my ancestors, my mother, the legacy of Malcolm X, and my own faithful spirit by becoming a tool of oppression and suppression?

Within three weeks, or just one week before Ife's birth, I secured a position as a "street worker" or counselor at Haaren High School. I had to go to playgrounds, parks, pool halls, alleyways, and neighborhood hangouts in Harlem to encourage young men to return to school. It was as if Providence knew where I needed to be. It was hard work, and I put in long hours every day in "after school" tutoring of the young men. I loved every minute, or all but two minutes during my two years at Haaren. My position paid far less and would be considered less prestigious than the position at Brooklyn College. However, I was working in a school for thousands of young Black and Latino boys who had generally been miseducated and cast aside by the City of New York and its school system. Who could ask for more?

From Faith to Passion to Perception to Ever-Increasing Faith
What is greatness?

When my beloved son Akhenaton was resting in his mother's womb in 1992, I would whisper to him daily: "You are destined for greatness. Greatness is living in a manner that helps to enable others to prosper!" That is the lesson of our African ancestors. It is the lesson that is shut up inside our bones, that flows through our spirit.[5]

Examine the African Americans who were most revered by African Americans during and after their journey in America. Harriet Tubman. Nat Turner. David Walker. Frederick Douglass. Sojourner Truth! 54th Massachusetts Infantry Regiment. George W. Carter. Ida B. Wells. Jack Johnson. Joe Louis. Jesse Owens. W.E.B. Dubois. Marcus Garvey. Booker T. Washington. The Harlem Hellfighters. The Tuskegee Airmen. Malcolm X. Martin Luther King, Jr. Medgar Evers. Fannie Lou Hamer. Muhammad Ali. John Lewis. Barack Obama. Michelle Obama. Alice Walker. Stacey Abrams. LeBron James. The list could continue.[6]

Everyone on the list has had more than a cheering squad. Most have had the vast majority of African Americans wishing for their success and viewing their efforts and success as a testament to the strength, vision, and wisdom of our people in a collective effort to establish a more just America.

In January of 1974, while still at Haaren, I decided that I would enroll in Teachers College Columbia University to pursue a doctoral degree. I had begun to realize that if I were to ultimately be in a position of leadership to effect real change in schools, a doctoral degree from the nation's leading school of education would be an invaluable asset. I had $1,000 saved, and I took $594 to enroll for six credits. With a second beloved daughter, Kakuna, on the way, my wife asked how could we afford Columbia. I told her: "God has placed someone at Columbia to take care of me."

Later, on a cold January morning, I paid my fees and went up to the office of the chairman of my department. I introduced myself to Professor Anne Lieberman, who entered from a different office. In a few months, by March, Dr. Lieberman had secured a one-year paid internship (equivalent to a teacher's salary) and a full scholarship that would pay all of my tuition and fees throughout my doctoral studies.

While at Columbia, I read Benjamin Mays' autobiography, *Born To Rebel*. The book became a guidepost for my future work as an educator. I internalized the concept of not just being excellent in accomplishing big things, but rather striving for excellence in establishing and implementing transformative initiatives.

I graduated from Columbia in May of 1983. By December of 1985, I had founded and built a multimillion-dollar, state-of-the-art professional development conference center in one of the wealthiest communities in New York City. The Center for Educational Leadership (CEL) was located in the Tribeca section of Manhattan. With its cutting-edge practices, it became the most prominent professional development site for teachers and principals in more than 120 schools.

Due to CEL's success, Chancellor Joseph Fernandez, then the nation's most celebrated proponent of School-Based Management (SBM), asked me to lead that initiative. The initiative in New York had been floundering for many months since his arrival from Miami, where he had established his reputation as America's leading visionary educator. The resistance from principals was formidable. The initiative could only be implemented in a school if the principal, teachers, and parent leaders voluntarily agreed.

When I arrived as Senior Assistant to the Chancellor around October of 1990, approximately 30 principals and their schools had voluntarily entered the initiative. Within 15 months, more than 330 principals and their schools, with a combined student population of more than 300,000, had voluntarily entered. The success of our initiative and a similar one in Philadelphia prompted the federal government to re-conceptualize the multibillion-dollar Title I programs to reflect the best educational practices from our initiatives.[7]

I would go on to become Senior Assistant to the next two Chancellors, having a responsibility for leadership in conceptualizing and implementing their principal educational initiatives. In 1993, Chancellor Ramon Cortines asked me to examine a math and science initiative that he had implemented as superintendent in San Francisco—with an eye toward establishing a similar one in New York. The initiative had been a small-scale tutoring program for Black and Latino students to prepare them to compete to enter San Francisco's most competitive high school. With Benjamin Mays in mind, I took the initiative to collect data on math and science classes throughout the 250 high schools and presented a plan that would eliminate all of the math and science courses in all of our high schools that were not college preparatory. New York City became the first major urban district to retrain its teachers while eliminating all such math and science courses. Such courses had been largely populated by low-income Black and Latino students due to low expectations of their academic potential.

In 1995 I wrote and negotiated the nation's first Redesign Plan for Low Performing Schools, for Chancellor Rudy Crew. I later became superintendent in Harlem and Deputy Regional Superintendent for 120 schools in the Bronx, all on a mission of transformation.

As you might expect, none of my accomplishments came easily. First of all, there exists a deeply rooted natural resistance to change in the culture of schools. That resistance is so powerful that even when change occurs, its effects are often eroded over time. That reality has led some researchers of school culture to confirm, with data, yet another cliché: "The more things change, the more they remain the same!"

I was also a young Black man in the Chancellor's Office dealing with more senior department and division leaders, and longstanding superintendents who were all territorial. However, my faith in my excellence and the Emotional Intelligence passed down to me by ancestors and mentors enabled me to help them to see themselves as winners in the transformational initiatives.

In 2016, in Dubai, a few years after retiring from the school system, I first presented an Emotional Intelligence course I had developed to senior corporate executives after thoroughly examining the strategies I had employed. The course was entitled "The Application of Emotional Intelligence in the Strategic Transformation of Organizations." Within the course we examined what I had identified as "Twelve Attributes" of the Emotional Intelligent leader.

During all my years as an educational leader, I drew inspiration from Black men and women in the school system who had often been "change agents" long before I had gotten started. They were often my mentors. I also drew inspiration from certain contemporaries. We were Blacks of the same generation who had transformational visions which were enhanced through our time together in studying, planning, and implementing. As had happened to me, some were punished by the "gatekeepers" of the system, the guardians of the status quo—

and indeed punished in the prime of their careers—for being transformational leaders with new visions, philosophies, and strategies.

Today I can only imagine how much more advanced economically and socially America would be if it had faithfully drawn upon the excellence of Blacks, rather than having sought at almost every turn to suppress, subvert, or nullify it. Nevertheless, our own faith in our excellence is not, and has not been, diminished. Rather, our faith increases. While it might frighten the white supremacists, we will always be ready for the moment. We, too, sing America, and our song carries a more beautiful melody, a more fruitful vision, for all.

ENDNOTES

1   The idea that we should "let each one teach one" is a time-honored concept in many of our families and broader kinship communities. See the powerful biography of Ron Casanova, *Each One Teach One* (Willimantic, CT: Curbstone Books, 1996).

2   See Alex Haley, Malcolm X, *The Autobiography of Malcolm X*. (New York: Ballantine Books, Random House Publishing Group, 1964).

3   See Fanon's classic discussion of the deleterious impact of racism and colonialism on the self-perception of black and brown peoples of the world, and his call for revolution in Frantz Fanon, *Black Skin, White Masks* (New York: Grove Press, 1991). See also Carter G. Woodson, *The Mis-Education of the Negro* (Washington, DC: The Associated Publishers, 1933).

4   See Angela Y. Davis (ed.), *If They Come in the Morning...: Voices of Resistance* (New York: Verso, 2016).

5   See now his book: Askia Akhenaton Davis, *Coming of Age in the Hip Hop Generation: Warrior of the Void* (New York: Askia Davis, 2012).

6   See, for example, the commanding reporting, research, and editing of Myrlie Evers-Williams and Manning Marable, *The Autobiography of Medgar Evers: A Hero's Life and Legacy Revealed Through His Writings, Letters, and Speeches* (New York: Basic Civitas Books, 2005). See also, the important work of Kate Clifford Larson, *Walk With Me: A Biography of Fannie Lou Hamer* (New York: Oxford University Press, 2021).

7   In the sociological work of DuBois, and the American tradition, Philadelphia represents, of course, something of a "ground zero" in terms of researching the profound challenges, educational and otherwise, historically facing African Americans in urban areas. See the classic study by W.E.B. DuBois, *The Philadelphia Negro* (Philadelphia, PA :University of Pennsylvania Press, 1899).

BIBLIOGRAPHY

Casanova, Ron. *Each One Teach One*. Willimantle, CT: Curbstone Books, 1996.

Davis, Angela Y. (ed). *If They Come in the Morning...: Voices of Resistance*. New York: Verso, 2016. First published by The Third Press, 1971.

Davis, Askia Akhenaton. *Coming of Age in the Hip Hop Generation: Warrior of the Void*. Brooklyn, NY: Askia Davis Publishing, 2012.

Ever-Williams, Myrlie and Marable, Manning (eds). *The Autobiography of Medgar Evers: A Hero's Life and Legacy Revealed Through His Writings, Letters, and Speeches*. New York: Basic Civitas Books, 2005.

Fanon, Frantz. *Black Skin, White Masks*. New York: Grove Press, 1991.

Haley, Alex and Malcolm X. *The Autobiography of Malcolm X*. New York: Ballantine Books, Random House Publishing Group, 1964.

Larson, Kate Clifford. *Walk With Me: A Biography of Fannie Lou Hamer*. Oxford, England: Oxford University Press, 2021.

CHAPTER FIFTEEN
When I Was a Boy

Daniel Black

There will be no children to surround my death bed, no grandchildren to reminisce of holidays with Pawpaw, no great grandchildren to carry my name into eternity. But that's not why I came. I came to reproduce ideas—not people. I came to show the world what God looks like in the flesh. To remind black people of their majesty. To figure out why Africans had to be dispersed throughout a world that still doesn't know who they are.

I spent years longing and begging and pleading and hoping to fall in love when, according to my people, I was unlovable. God had not made me what I was. Somehow, I had sneaked into this realm, unsanctioned by the angels, and thus undivine. This is what the people said. They even agreed that, if I didn't change, Hell would be my home. Only the Devil would know me in eternity. I had no choice but to believe them. There was no other God to pray to, no other deity who would plead my case. I asked about other gods and people told me that there was only one. All these people in the world and only one God to pray to? If only I'd been free enough to know better.

I lived in bondage then. My people came in chains. Everything about us was enslaved, including our imaginations. We were duped into leaving our own gods behind and bowing before entities that had no power at all. Not over our lives. But, over time, our belief in them empowered them to capture our minds and rearrange our belief in ourselves. Now, when we close our eyes and pray, whiteness cloaks our ethereal space. There is hardly any blackness at all. They took our names, our tongues... so small wonder our gods couldn't follow us.

Yet here I am. Black, male, queer... and clear that God looks like me. Can't you see it? A fine, bronze, black form sitting proudly upon a throne, overseeing a kingdom of wingless angels. Can't you hear the bangles jingle in the wind? Don't you see the countless *ilekes* draped around the throat? Aren't you just a little envious of the ropes of locks tangled the way black people must've been enmeshed in the belly of those ships? Maybe if you close your eyes you could see my blackness and then you might understand why my people keep singing about a place called Heaven. Don't nobody want the blackness here; but you can't get over there without it.[1]

As a boy, I wasn't sure I wanted to be a man. The men I knew weren't upstanding or virtuous. They didn't love God; they thought they were God. They were drunk with power and shrouded in arrogance. Their joy was others' subservience. They belittled because they could. Violence was the blood of their being. Whipping, beating, lashing, criticizing was the signature of their identity. Women wondered why God gave them seed if they hated to plant. Children dreaded their coming, as if something monstrous was on the way. I didn't want to be feared to be followed. I didn't want control without consciousness. I didn't want privilege without honor. I wanted love unspeakable and nurturing immeasurable and kindness inconceivable. I wanted the praise of women without the use of their bodies. I wanted the warmth of boys' hands because they felt like mine.[2] I wanted the braiding of girls' hair because their joy gave me joy. And I wanted a father who could see not only God in me, but God as me. Yet I didn't get any of these things. Afterall, I was a boy.

Girls laughed at me. They wanted my governing, my inherited authority, my precious slave name. They dreamed of sharing my right to oppress, my God-given headship, my influence to tell God what to do. They waited with bated breath for me to age and take my place and thus save the world. But I didn't want to save the world. I wanted to change it. But no one supported me. After all, I was a boy.

In high school, I read books and pieced quilts and baked cakes and wrote in diaries. I scratched my grandma's scalp and danced around her living room like Baryshnikov and Gene Anthony Ray. I learned to knit and crochet when other boys were coon hunting and chewing tobacco. I sang lead in the church choir and cried when Nettie and Celie reunited. I took French and Home Ec instead of shop and engineering. But I could've done engineering. Math came easily for me. It just didn't invite the sharing of my heart, so I abandoned it—the way the world had abandoned me. I painted my nails once, just to see what they would look like, then, not knowing of fingernail polish remover, I soaked my hands in gasoline before my father could justify my death. My brothers showed me *Hustler* and *Playboy* pictures that didn't elicit my erection. I was a failure. No wet dreams, no masturbation, no jokes about boobs and ass. I was a weirdo. A fuckin' freak. A nobody. A disappointment to a nation of men.

Yet I insisted on living. I don't know why. Death had no appeal for me. I didn't want an after-life if I hadn't had a this-life. So I got busy living.

I joined church, thinking I was following the King of kings, the Man among men. The saints called God He. They said God wasn't a man, but clearly God had preferred pronouns. When I called God she, trying to imagine the full divinity of an omnipotent savior, preachers said I should read my Bible and see that God is spoken of in the masculine. Of course God is, I said, since men wrote the book and thus named all the characters. Yet what was the harm, the danger, the cost of considering God female? What did we lose by conceptualizing God as a woman? My grandmother was far more righteous than my grandfather. Bulging eyes and agape mouths told me to shut up, so I did. But I didn't stop thinking.[3]

I learned that people wanted unenlightened black boys. Unkind black boys. Weed-smoking black boys. Half-drunk, baby-producing black boys. Girl-chasing black boys. People applauded black boys with faded cuts and cascading locks—not mounds of nappy hair resting atop an uneven head. They celebrated boys with mediocre grades and unexceptional character. Boys who solicited cheerleaders but never themselves cheered for anyone. Those were the boys who made mothers smile and fathers boast. Those were the boys girls gave themselves to. The boys other boys privately desired. These boys became preachers and pastors, civil rights leaders and college professors, news anchors and coveted mechanics. Not novelists and philosophers or moaners and healers or painters and sculptors. No. Black people in my day wanted black boys whose gifts they could commodify, boys whose talents might one day elicit millions. I was a cheap writer. Nothing to be proud of. Not yet.

But something about language buttressed my self-worth. In words, I heard the timbre of God's voice, the frantic fluttering of angel's wings, and I knew that if I could gather words into my mouth I could speak my own value. I could mix subjects and objects and verbs and phrases and unspeak what the world had said about me. I knew instinctively that if I could master the word, I could reconstruct the heart I had grown to hate. So I read books and pamphlets and TV Guides and Reader's Digests and flyers and obituaries and church anniversary programs and automobile manuals and the parts of the Bible I liked and newspapers and coupons and grocery store receipts and junk mail and birth certificates and birthday party announcements. I read recipes and cereal boxes and encyclopedias and church hymnals and Sunday School primers and shopping advertisements and, of course, library books. Yet those boys who received all that praise were never in the library. They were out in the world somewhere, being what I could never be.

With all that reading came questions no one could answer. Like why would God put people in paradise then tempt them to ruin it? Or why couldn't humans eat from the tree of good and evil and be all-knowing? Why was that a bad idea? Or why did women take men's last names although no men took theirs? Or what personal satisfaction did white people get from watching black bodies swing from trees? Isn't that kind of pleasure sadistic and evidence of a soulless people? Or why didn't men wear dresses, especially in the summer? Lord knows it was hot enough. Or why didn't men accompany each other to the bathroom like women? And why do men stand up to pee? Isn't sitting far more comfortable? Every time I asked these questions, people said I was too smart for my own good. Whatever that meant. Some said I thought I was high and mighty, better than other folks. Funny thing… I actually thought I was far less. They thought I was better. None of us was anything, really, except ex-slaves trying to get the master's attention.

Since many sexy, desirable black men sang, I tried that route as a way to acceptance and celebration. But something went wrong. I think my range was too high. I sang a natural-voice soprano so loud and strong that most turned away when I performed. My flailing arms didn't help. Nor did my trembling vibrato, which I thought people loved. And they did—but not in a boy. They wanted Barry White or Marvin Gaye or Luther Vandross. Those were not my idols. When I practiced in the barn, I sang along with Patti LaBelle and Vanessa Bell Armstrong and Chaka Khan and Natalie Cole. If I could hit their notes—and often I did—I felt accomplished. Of course I could sing with the men; that was nothing extraordinary. Yet singing with the divas, in their exultant range, was a triumph.

And, still, no praise. I couldn't figure it out. What did people want? I had straight A's, no criminal record, no illegitimate children. Then I admitted what I already knew: they wanted a man.

So I gave them one.

I started smoking weed and hanging out in bars and alleys where masculinity was free for the taking. I started flirting with girls—well, women by now—and having sex to prove my prowess. I started pimp walking like Denzel and holding my head like Will Smith. I cut my hair down to a smooth fade and straightened the top naps with a nylon wave cap. I threw away those form-fitting jeans, the ones I liked so well, and began sagging along with all the other homeboys. My grandmother said she didn't recognize me anymore. My father said it's about time. I didn't like what I was becoming, but I was becoming, and that was the goal. His goal. My goal. The world's goal. I was a man in the making.

In exchange for masculinity, I stopped reading. I stopped analyzing movies. I stopped dancing before full-length mirrors. I stopped playing for the choir. Stopped scratching Grandma's scalp. Stopped crying at others' abuse. Stopped caring about women's issues. Stopped cooking, especially baking. Stopped going to church. I guess I stopped acting like a faggot. Boys were relieved. Daddy told his friends, "I know what I raised!" Momma thanked God that prayer changes things.

Yet when I got to college, I dropped the charade. It just didn't make sense anymore. Life-changing books found me and restored my senses. Herman Hess's *Siddhartha* and Zora Neale Hurston's *Their Eyes Were Watching God*. Chinua Achebe's *Things Fall Apart* and Ann Petry's *The Street*. We read essays by Joan Didion, Langston Hughes, Alain Locke, and Audre Lorde. Poems by Paul Laurence Dunbar, Sonia Sanchez, John Milton, and Shakespeare. My chains fell off (as Baldwin might say). I discovered the depth of my self-imposed incarceration. Each work summoned the unashamed expression of my authenticity. I think I wept to be reunited with myself.[4] One short story in particular set me free. It's Arna Bontemps's "A Summer Tragedy." The story is about black agency in a time when black people weren't supposed to have it. The narrative centers on an old, poor, disenfranchised black couple who decides how and when they're going to die. They don't wait for Death to come and snatch their lives away. Instead, they dress in their Sunday best and intentionally drive off a steep cliff, thus meeting Death on their own terms. I had never read anything so empowering, so liberating. And that's what I wanted: freedom. From others' opinions and desires for me. From the confines of gender expectations and religious piety. From the need to be something I had no desire to be. Through knowledge, I found my autonomy. I finally accepted who I was. It was a beautiful thing.

But was I a man?

One night on the quad, I met a brother who forced my clarity. It was after midnight. He sauntered easily, going nowhere really, and found me drowning for attention. I spoke first. Or maybe he did. I don't remember. But our conversation changed me forever. We shot the breeze for a minute or two, then he sat next to me on a bench beneath a lamppost and asked, "Who are you?"

I told him my name, where I'm from, stuff like that.

He said, "Naw, man. I'm askin who are you?"

I didn't understand. He shook his head.

"Your name is what we call you. Your home is your place of origin. I want to know who you are, why you exist."

I couldn't answer him. Everywhere I searched within, I found only vacant spaces where consciousness should've been.

He chuckled and said, "I'll see you around, man. Next time, have an answer."

I sat there, by myself, until the sun rose the next morning. I'd never known such turmoil, such spiritual anxiety. All night long I turned his question over in my mind until realizing this was what I'd come to college for. It was my job to decide who I was—not someone else's privilege to define me. That was the error I'd made my whole life—waiting for others to confirm my right to exist. I understood now.

Several nights later, that brother and I met again on the same bench. It felt like time had returned us to the earlier moment, since, once again, it was only him and me.

He approached with a smile and a warm demeanor. Then, without hesitation or self-consciousness, he touched my hand briefly, like a compassionate lover, and I knew we'd be friends forever.

"Well?" he said.

And I said confidently, "I'm a spirit, come to show people how to love."

He nodded. "There you go. Now you got it." Then he left.

And I never saw him again.

ENDNOTES

1   See Baldwin's brilliant reflections on God, religion, and the United States in *The Fire Next Time* (New York: The Modern Library, 1962).
2   See also James Baldwin's classic and beautiful novel, *Giovanni's Room* (New York: Alfred A. Knopf, 1956).
3   See Audre Lorde, *Your Silence Will Not Protect You* (London: Silver Press, 2007).
4   Consider the thoughtful and poetic works of Julian J. Walker, *A Year Without You* (Scotts Valley, CA: CreateSpace Independent Publishing Platform, 2018).

BIBLIOGRAPHY

Baldwin, James. *Giovanni's Room*. New York: Alfred A. Knopf, 1956.
Baldwin, James. *The Fire Next Time*. New York: The Modern Library, 1962.
Lorde, Audre. *Your Silence Will Not Protect You*. London: Silver Press, 2017.
Walker, Julian J. *A Year Without You*. CreateSpace Independent Publishing Platform, 2018.

CHAPTER SIXTEEN

Miguel Se Fue

Tony Medina

Death(s) always force me to reassess myself. I get sad and melancholy and nostalgic. Even with those I do not know personally, but culturally. The last few months of our pandemic year, 2020, we lost a lot of Poets: Diane di Prima, Naomi Long Madgett, Aldo Tambellini—and, ultimately, as December was fast approaching, Dr. Miguel Algarín, Poet, Playwright, Shakespearean scholar and Founding Father of the Nuyorican Poets Café. For me, personally, to pay homage to Algarín is not to speak so much about the importance of the Nuyorican Poets Café or the poetry movement that precedes it; a movement, by the way, that bridges the Beat and Black Arts movements—and encompasses all others within its tent.[1]

To pay homage to Algarín is to talk about my beginnings as a poet, writer, literary artist—my halcyon days of coming up in New York back in the day when back in the day was back in the day. It most likely begins with me ETSing out of the Army to find that James Baldwin had passed and seeing his funeral on Gil Noble's *Like It Is*.

Around that time, I was an undergraduate at Baruch College, City University of New York, majoring in English. It was at Baruch where I met the great Addison Gayle, Jr., who was my African American Literature professor. From there I remember finding out about the Black Writers Conference that Larry Robin threw taking place in Philly. Being a writer, I felt compelled to join the school paper, *The Ticker*, at Baruch. I told the staff I was going to a Black Writers Conference in Philly, and that I would cover it for my first story. They agreed, and so I made it out to Philly where one of the first poets I met was Lamont Steptoe in Larry Robin's legendary bookstore.

During the culmination of the writer's conference, I found myself at a museum, I believe, where the last event was being held. I spotted an older brother with a graying beard and short 'fro speaking to a taller woman who I learned later was Paula Giddings. I walked up to the brother and asked him if he was Amiri Baraka. The brother and Paula Giddings both chuckled and he said, "No. I'm Junius Williams. But I know Amiri." Junius was a lawyer and an activist. He took out his card and wrote Baraka's address on the back. He told me that Baraka throws poetry readings there once a month in his basement called Kimako's Blues People, named after his younger sister who was slain by a homeless man she befriended and tried to help. June Jordan was a very close friend of hers and even has a poem praising Kimako Baraka.[2]

So, one Saturday night, I found myself making the trek from the Bronx to *NewArk* by myself. That night, the featured poet was Martin Espada. He had just won an NEA grant and Baraka threw a celebration for him. There was an open mic, and although I had never read publicly and was nervous as all hell, I took the stage and read one of my anti-capitalism poems (I was reading Karl Marx's *Communist Manifesto* in the Army while stationed in Wildflecken, West Germany, before the wall came down). I was so nervous that I used the page I was reading from as my crutch from looking at the audience. After I read, Amiri chuckled and said, "Sounds like somebody I know!" Martin stepped to me and said, "Hey, Amiri really likes your work" and handed me his card and said, "Send me some poems!"

Fast forward to the summer and I was at Central Park to listen to Amiri Baraka and Jayne Cortez read. After they blew up the spot, I headed to the stage to say what's up to Amiri. It was then I met Jayne Cortez, this cat my age, Dave Mills, a poet and an actor, and Rashidah Ismaili (of Umbra) who was at the stage level, and befriended Dave and me, and invited us backstage. When Rashidah found out we were poets, she invited us to come with her, Amiri, and Amina to Sekou Sundiata's crib to a party. We all jumped in Baraka's small red car where he was playing Fela, with Amina in the front seat and Rashidah sandwiched between me and Dave Mills. Amiri cut across upper Manhattan and into the South Bronx where Sekou lived on the Grand Concourse walking distance from the courthouse. As we went into Sekou's where the joint was jumping, Amina said to Amiri and me, "Oh, we have to take Tony to meet Miguel!" So they snatched me up and rang the elevator, which we took to the penthouse where Miguel Algarín lived with his sister. They had a patio view into the outfield of Yankee Stadium!!! As Miguel's sister let us in, Amiri and Amina bum-rushed Miguel's bedroom, opening the door, but keeping the lights off. Amiri sat on the edge of Miguel's bed teasing him and cracking jokes while Amina said, "Miguel, you gotta get up and meet this poet, Tony Medina!" Miguel was sprawled out on a heap of clothes, and rolled over to look at me. He busted out in a big-ass ghetto Santa Claus laugh and said, "HAHAHAHAHA! I had a dream about you!" Amiri and Amina got Miguel to throw on some clothes and head down to Sekou's party. It was at Miguel's penthouse that Dave Mills and me would read at a benefit for Lenora Fulani's political campaign. I remember mentioning it to my father and him telling me he dated Lenora Fulani! Small world!

Shortly after, I remember hanging with Miguel, riding around in his big-ass baby blue Chevy, headed to various places: 116th Street between Fifth and Madison, where I ironically would get an apartment I had for 15 years and so many books ago; the Puerto Rican Day Parade (led by Tito Puente) in the Bronx; and to the 2nd version of the Nuyorican Poets Café while under construction as he read poems about him and Miguel Pinero (at what would become the bar) that would subsequently be in his book, *Love Is Hard Work*.

Subsequently, Lamont Steptoe got me my first paid poetry gig reading with Ishmael Reed at The Painted Bride in Philly. Ever since I met Lamont he was constantly saying—after I would crack a joke or something—"You gotta meet Ishmael! You gotta meet Ishmael! You two are kindred spirits!" Part of Lamont's genius was his pairings at The Bride. Lamont hosted the joint for several years and created a venue featuring an established poet with an up-and-coming poet. Ntozake Shange lived across the street from The Bride; and Major Jackson took over as host after Lamont. Lamont arranged for Miguel Algarín to introduce me and Sonia Sanchez to introduce Ishmael. If I'm not mistaken, Miguel either picked me up at my crib on 148th and St. Nicholas or at the Schomburg where there was a Black publishers festival where people like Louis Reyes Rivera, Gary Johnston, Layding Kaliba and a whole crew of other artists were selling books and other cultural items with various programming throughout the day. I was there with Kevin Powell and when Miguel came to get me, with Nancy Mercado driving shotgun (the first time we met), Kevin wanted to go. So, we all hopped in the car headed to Philly. When we got there, we were early and the crowd was just filing in. I was a nervous wreck. Miguel said, "I know what you need." He took us around the corner to a bar and got me two dry martinis to calm my nerves and get me straight for the reading. When we got back Miguel told me he asked Kevin to introduce me since he was my peer and knew my work. (My first anthology credit was in his and Ras Baraka's *In the Tradition*, published by the late, great Glen Thompson of Writers and Readers/Harlem River Press.) I opened the show and remember being relaxed and in the zone. The Bride had a real intimate feel and the lighting and the mic were perfect. It was a packed house and the audience was hype. Ishmael stood in the wings watching me read. After I got off, he said, "That's good stuff, man!" I remember Miguel coming up to me after the reading mimicking my reading style by cranking his right leg up and down like a dog. He was making fun at me getting into it and damn near levitating off the ground as I read. He was hilarious as usual. And true! I did read like a nut!

One summer, me, Miguel, and Lamont Steptoe went to Coney Island to the beach and to ride the rollercoaster. It was there on the boardwalk where a miracle occurred. A homeless woman named Rhudine I had met some years back in Queens when I worked for New York City Transit, and who I immortalized in a poem on the back of my clipboard as she limped off to the women's homeless shelter which was an armory, cradling a bottle of beer under her arm, suddenly appeared in Coney Island, hauling a shopping cart full of empty cans and bottles. I screamed, "Lamont! That's Rhudine!!!" He took a picture of us with my arm around her carrying a beer and a boombox.

But the last couple of times I saw Miguel were probably attached to Amiri, ironically. At the Schomburg, where the poet Ted Wilson celebrated Amiri's birthday. Miguel performed and mesmerized the whole audience, as usual, with his salsa scatting and Yoruba funk. And perhaps at Amiri's wake the January he passed back in 2013. Before I met Miguel in person through Amiri and Amina, I was already blown away by his and Miguel Pinero's seminal Nuyorican Poets anthology. The original one before the publication of *Aloud*. That book was a live wire in my hands, electrifying me to the possibilities of what poetry could be—soapbox and Salsa jam. Timbales crashing across my skull. A lyrical attack against capitalism in praise of the everlasting 'hoods of the world! It was afros and congas. The Red White & Blue Rice and Beans aesthetics with a star for an asterisk! Miguel's vision was to merge academia with the streets. The page and the stage. The Nuyorican Poets Café—in all its various formations from Miguel's very own crib to a bar to an all-out building bum-rushed by poets—took all comers and midnight crawlers. When I started going there, making my trek from the Boogie Down, then Harlem all the way down to Alphabet City with those long-ass treacherous blocks from A to B to C to whatthehell?!!!, I met poets like Ron Cephas Jones and Titor Lespier and a whole host of other cats who'd poet and party to the small hours of the night. After the endless open mic was always the dance floor. Tables and chairs pushed aside for dancing Salsa feet.

Miguel Algarín's importance is immense. Every poet, no matter how high and mighty would roll through. On any given night you were bound to run into Allen Ginsberg, Robert Creely, Amiri Baraka, Ntozake Shange, and an endless all-star parade of others. Some reading, some just listening and chilling hard. With Steve Cannon holding court. And Julio at the door and Lois Elaine Griffith at the bar with a shrine to Miguel (Mikey) Pinero.

This is my little way of paying Miguel Algarín homage for the role he played in my narrative as an emerging poet navigating through the landscape of the giants who paved the way for me and my generation of poets finding our voices and a home to be true to art and the beautiful struggle. Miguel Algarín was gregarious and a big personality who was generous and loved by many and influenced us all. But he was also a Shakespearean scholar, an institution builder in the vein of Arthur Arturo Alfonso Schomburg. He was a working poet and professor who published many books of his own poetry as well as seminal anthologies and a translation of one of my favorite Pablo Neruda books, *Song of Protest*. (At that Lenora Fulani shindig fundraiser at Miguel and his sister's penthouse on the Grand Concourse, I recall whipping the book out and Dave Mills talking about critiquing/"improving" on Neruda's poetry. Me and Miguel fell the fuck out!!!). Miguel was also a survivor of HIV. I remember when we all found out about it. A number of us poets made it out to, I believe, Joe Overstreet's gallery to check out Quincy Troupe's reading. He was back from Cali on a book tour, so all us poets came out for him. Jayne Cortez was there mentioning how she's always checking on me and Paul Beatty. (Paul would later hook me up with a gig to go to Berlin where I was paired with Pamela Sneed in a three-day series featuring six poets from New York.) When she asked me what I was up to (code for what's up with my work), I told her I was working on a couple of anthologies and I'd love to feature some of her poems, she said, "Tony, anthologies are all well and good, but don't get caught up with other peoples' work. You need to focus on getting your work out." I never forgot those words. (Jayne was a big supporter of my work. She had me and Suheir Hammad read with Dennis Brutus at NYU when she was curating a poetry series as Artist-in-Residence.) It was then that Miguel let us know his status. But like Magic Johnson, Miguel beat HIV's ass and lived on to poet and produce. His books, which I have in my Nuyo section in the crib, are: *Mongo Affair, Body Bee Calling from the Twenty-First Century, Time's Now/Ya Es Tiempo, On Call, Love Is Hard Work* (my fave), *Survival Supervivencia*, and anthologies such as *Nuyorican Poetry* with Miguel Pinero, *Aloud: Voices from the Nuyorican Poets Café* with Bob Holman, and *Action: The Nuyorican Poets Café Theater Festival* with Lois Griffith. Read them. Treasure them. Pass them around like a blunt (post-Rona!).[3]

I can go on and talk about meeting Jesus Papoleto Melendez (back from years of being in Cali), Gaston Neal, and Hettie Jones all in the same night (not at the café, but some place in the Village we read at) or my many other adventures. But in thinking about a major death—of a major literary and cultural figure who has factored in my beginnings as an artist—I thought it'd be best to remember my own personal Miguel connections. Like the blues song says (and Cornelius Eady's book tells us): You don't miss your water till your well runs dry. Hey, man. Miguel se fue! Algarín as Ancestor!

ENDNOTES

1   See, for more background, Roger Bonair, *Burning Down the House: Selected Poems from the Nuyorican Poets Cafe National Poetry Slam Competition* (Berkeley: Counterpoint Press, 2001).
2   See "3 for Kimako" in Jan Heller Levi and Sara Miles (eds.), *Directed by Desire: The Collected Poems of June Jordan* (Port Townsend, WA: Copper Canyon Press, 2007). See also June Jordan, *Things That I Do in the Dark: Selected Poetry* (New York: Random House, 1977) and Patricia Herrera, *Nuyorican Feminist Performance: From the Cafe to Hip Hop Theater* (Ann Arbor: University of Michigan Press, 2020).
3   See Miguel Algarin, *Action: The Nuyorican Poets Cafe Theater Festival* (New York: Touchstone Books, Simon and Schuster, 1997); Miguel Algarin, *Mongo Affair* (New York: Nuyorican Press, 1978); and, also, Miguel Algarin, *Love Is Hard Work* (New York: Scribner, 1997), among others.

BIBLIOGRAPHY

Algarin, Miguel. *Action: The Nuyorican Poets Cafe Theater Festival*. New York: Touchstone Books / Simon & Schuster, 1997.
Algarin, Miguel. *Mongo Affair*. New York: Nuyorican Press, 1978.
Algarin, Miguel. *Love Is Hard Work*. New York: Scribner, 1997.
Blackman, Nicole. *Aloud: Voices from the Nuyorican Poets Cafe*. Henry Holt and Company, 1994.
Bonair-Agard, Roger et al. *Burning Down the House: Selected Poems from the Nuyorican Poets Cafe National Poetry Slam Competition*. Counterpoint Press, 2001.
Herrera, Patricia. *Nuyorican Feminist Performance: From the Cafe to Hip Hop Theater*. University of Michigan Press, 2020.

CHAPTER SEVENTEEN
For You...I Give

Taroue W. Brooks

In the Beginning

God speaks to us all. However, he tends to share a bit more with me at times. His words are so powerful and, sometimes, overwhelming that I had a difficult time expressing myself when using words while growing up. Most called it stuttering, but I'd like to think that this difficulty gave me a way to express myself more creatively while navigating and processing the complex world around me. No matter what speech therapy was tried, or the particular patience extended by my mom, stuttering is where it all began for me. Although viewed as something negative and a problem for most, stuttering was, for me, an opportunity to strengthen my creativity, my writing, and my compassion for others who were as different from me as I was from them. Some of my family and friends would mock and tease me about stuttering. You know kids play "the dozens" nearly every chance they get, especially about things and people who are different from them. While I wouldn't dare participate or respond, this experience helped me to not allow others' words or opinions to disrupt my focus or my plans. Stuttering was a challenge for me in the beginning, but who doesn't have challenges that must be confronted and hopefully overcome?

In school, stuttering would remain a constant companion and challenge. I was once even given an assignment to read aloud the poem "In the Morning" by Paul Laurence Dunbar. This caused my mother great concern and rightfully so. If I stuttered when asking for milk or lunch money, how was I ever going to accomplish this task? Despite her concern, this recitation assignment proved to be the first of many opportunities I had to sever ties with my lifelong companion. To everyone's surprise, I was able to recite the poem without stuttering. My mom was so relieved and thrilled for me that to this day, every once in a while, she'll ask me to recite the poem in front of someone. In 2018, while on vacation in Martha's Vineyard, after having an amazing breakfast with friends, Mom asked me out of the blue to recite "In the Morning." My friends cackled in amusement at our interaction and exchange with each other as Mom leaned on me to get me to comply with her request. I didn't recall the poem in its entirety, of course, but I recited what I could. That was enough for Mom; she was overjoyed and—truth be told—whenever or wherever Mom makes her special request, I acquiesce with a smile and proceed to do my best.

14th Avenue

My name is "Taroue" and since my young adulthood, my friends have called me "Roue." With a nickname such as that, I've always thought of my life, naturally, as somewhat akin to a pot of gumbo, one made with love and ingredients that are chock full of flavor and spice and is all simmered to perfection. Any good gumbo must start with a good "roux" or a strong base. For me, that base began on 14th Avenue. Having grown up in Gary, Indiana on 14th Avenue taught me a lot of life lessons and skills that still serve me well to this day. It has long been said, of course, that it takes a village to raise a child. For me, that village consisted of many elders who were also my neighbors and who took the time to invest in me, aiming always to help me to hone my skills and make the best use of my talents. And with each passing decade, it becomes more evident that it will take more than a village to protect and steer the next generation in the right direction. I'm thankful that my village was strong and ready to answer the call of duty.[1]

One of the first lessons I learned on my path to entrepreneurship occurred when the late Reverend Dr. Robert J. Lowery engaged my mom about the possibility of my cutting his lawn. Prior to having me cut and care for his lawn, Reverend Lowery expressed that he would compensate me. I asked him the meaning of "compensation," to which he replied: "I am gonna put some money in your pocket, slide you some bread for your service." Thank you, Reverend Lowery!

While most of my childhood neighbors are deceased, Ruth Strong is still living across the street from our house. Mrs. Strong and the late Mrs. Sharon Blake would always notice that I was different from the other kids on the block. Constantly saying that I would grow up to be successful, they were very encouraging along the way. The funny thing is they would express that I shouldn't forget the "little people" on 14th Avenue. Ruth Strong has traveled to attend my events and to be my guest at the National Museum of African American History and Culture, where I am a donor. Like the Jacksons, who loved 2300 Jackson Street, I love 14th Avenue, always home.

The Thickening

The key to any good gumbo is the thickener, which is used to maintain the viscosity of the roux. Although seemingly simple, making the roux is crucial because it is heavily based on a capacity of the creation to withstand stress that could otherwise potentially lead to a deformation or other unintended, altered state of its original properties. If handled incorrectly, a roux can go awry. If you use the incorrect measurements, it might be too runny or too thick. If you use too much heat, it may scorch and be ruined, forcing you to start again. Finally, you must be patient, allowing it to cool so that when added to hot liquid or vice-versa, it won't clump. Either way, care must be taken when crafting a roux.

Undoubtedly, our childhood experiences are likely, on the whole, not all that different from the other; our respective villages serve as the "thickener" to help build our fortitude in preparation for the world that lies ahead. This is true for the children within my family as well. I recall a conversation I had with my mother about why my siblings and I had to wash dishes. Like most children, we all had chores and I really despised doing the dishes. When I voiced my concerns and inquired about why this was something we had to do, my mother sat me down and said: "I may not wake up tomorrow and I need to know that my boys can take care of themselves." Now I can hem my pants (this would serve me well later in life), replace a button, change a tire, and take care of the home. Who knew these things would also serve me well even in my professional life. Thanks, Mom!

There is much to be appreciated about having "thick" skin and it is quite beneficial for children to learn early on how to deal with peer pressure and societal expectations. A thick skin can help you better navigate life. As an active child and student, I grew quite interested in tap dancing and continued taking lessons through high school—until I began to get challenged about tap dancing versus playing basketball. I gave up tap dancing because, as black boys, my peers and I had been conditioned to participate in stereotypical sports that have befallen black boys for decades. I didn't understand or appreciate the pressure and attention that my tap dancing brought, but I knew it made me seem different from other boys. I remember telling my mom after she had purchased my next pair of tap shoes that I no longer wanted to tap dance. Although disappointed, she respected my choice. More significantly, however, I later determined never to deny myself something that I enjoyed based on the opinion of someone else.

Key Ingredients

Like the cook who's tasked with utilizing his or her talents to create a meal that both blesses and nourishes the body, I have found that—as the saying goes—"To whom much is given, much shall be required." As a result of enriched exposure in my childhood, coupled with my innate or acquired creative abilities which have been developed ever since, I do a lot of different things well and am viewed as something of a Renaissance Man. At the time, I had not always realized how the ingredients I'd chosen to add to my own life were being cooked to perfection and would one day benefit others.

Being the oldest child, I was proud, and determined to do anything I could to help my mother. That is why I learned to cook. Whether it was making pizzas from scratch or cutting potatoes to make french fries to cook in our Grand Daddy Fryer—(fries remain one of my favorite foods)—or putting ribs on the grill, I love to cook. My neighbor and fireman, the late Jerone T. Blake, Sr., taught me how to grill. I also learned another skill that would further the entrepreneurial spirit that Reverend Lowery had sparked in me earlier. In my Home Economics class, I learned how to bake, which allowed me to make desserts such as pound cakes and cheesecakes for my neighbors who took them to church or to their social gatherings. There I was again, getting compensated and "putting more bread" in my pocket for my skills and talents.

I expanded my skills by learning about horticulture while observing my neighbors mulch and plant their rose gardens and various flowers such as peonies, marigolds, and so much more. I internalized that knowledge and began manicuring our lawn with the same meticulous detail, watering and fertilizing the entire yard. There was edging, trimming of the shrubs, and raking leaves, all to ensure that my masterpiece was perfect. This attention to detail, this ensuring that everything reached its full potential, was arduous but would serve me well in my future endeavors as both an event planner and publicist.

Stirring Slowly with Purpose

Ensuring that I was well prepared for the next stage in life (like a good gumbo in process), I moved on to an opportunity that required attention and could not be rushed. In high school, I found myself at Indiana University Northwest (I.U.N.) as the result of a partnership which the university had established at that time with Theodore Roosevelt High School, my much-celebrated secondary school (also known as "'Velt" or "The 'Velt"). The innovative program allowed high school seniors to enroll in college, taking freshman English classes while still earning the high school diploma. It was there that I learned to stand out while standing alone. My professor at the time, Dr. Ralph Powell, was straightforward and intimidating. The class was given the assignment to submit a term paper. This was my first time writing a 10-page paper and Dr. Powell had given us very strict guidelines for review and submission of the paper. While I followed the guidelines, I also submitted my paper weeks early, an approach which Dr. Powell had discouraged me from taking. Still, this paper was my best work. Of course, my peers thought that I had lost my mind and, after submitting it, I couldn't help but wonder if perhaps I had made a mistake by turning it in early. Anxiety got the best of me and I began to worry and think about what my mom would say if I didn't get a good grade. The following week, at the beginning of class, Dr. Powell summoned me to the front of the class and reiterated both the seriousness of this paper and how he had warned us about taking the time to ensure that we had submitted our best work. He turned to me and handed me my paper. I received an A- and he stated that I didn't have to return to class. Dr. Powell was, no doubt, an intimidating man and, when making gumbo, due to all of the rules that go into cooking, it can be intimidating as well. If you stick to your recipe and the fundamentals of cooking, you will be okay. I trusted myself and knew that I already had within me the fundamentals of life, from home, thanks to my village, and didn't allow myself to get discouraged by either the task at hand or what others thought about me with regard to it. This experience exercised my faith, as it showed me to trust my abilities. I knew beforehand that I had already done my best and that I'm always in God's hands. Flying solo would also be one of the varied attributes that made me different.

Dark Brown Roux

There are different colors to roux, and that is a direct result of how long the roux is cooked. White and blond roux are considered the most common, while dark brown roux (which is cooked the longest) is considered hearty and perfect for the richest recipes. While attending Texas Southern University, I watched a news story about two women, one black and one white, who occupied dilapidated homes. The white woman received a new home and other luxury items, but no mention was made about the black woman or the upshot related to her well-being. I reached out to the news station to inquire about this woman. They expressed that local citizens had helped the white woman and they weren't under any obligation to help the black woman. I was given, off the record, the address of the woman who had been ignored and decided to get in contact with her. After our visit, I was determined to help her and spent weeks contacting social services to assist. I also engaged the late Hanq Neal, Minister of Music at Windsor Village United Methodist Church, about hosting a gospel concert that would benefit this woman. He agreed, and the "If I Can Help Somebody" concert was a successful blessing that featured gospel artists Yolanda Adams, Kathy Taylor, and the church choir. To my surprise, social services also came through with resources to help as well. All glory be to God! This experience brought me joy and represented the evolution of my passion and purpose to help others.[2]

Most people don't think or believe that they can be anything they want to be when they grow up, but when my mom told me this, I was crazy enough to believe her. While most may dismiss it as some cheesy cliché or platitude, I was empowered by these words. Keeping these words close was ultimately how I ascended to success within my own career. I am grateful to my mother for allowing me to dream without limits and for not impressing or projecting any fears or insecurities that she may have had onto either my brothers or me. As I look back over my journey, I realize that one of the great blessings of my life has been my ability to connect with my passions and to turn them into my purpose. This speaks to the personal intentionality in the work that I do, the boards on which I serve, and even the friends who are in my life. I am always determined to live by enjoying whatever interests me along my life's journey—whether it be art, exquisite cuisine, theater, travel, or cooking.

Chocolate City USA

Who would have known that, upon entering college, I would find that all roads would lead me to our nation's capital and, in that important place, set the stage for the next phase of my career? While a student at Texas Southern University, I interned with the A. Philip Randolph Institute, working on the 30th Anniversary of the March on Washington. This opportunity allowed me to work with civil rights leaders such as Reverend Jesse Jackson, the late Coretta Scott King, and others. This experience also confirmed what I knew all along about how this country has viewed African Americans and has overlooked the level of sacrifice and contributions made by those who came before us. Once in DC, I also worked on Capitol Hill in the office of the first female African American US Senator, Carol Mosley Braun, an experience that added significantly to my overall professional skill set. It showed me the inner workings of the government. I was empowered to do more. Braun was also, of course, the first African American US Senator since Reconstruction.

If you've ever made gumbo, you know that making gumbo takes the better part of a day to cook and, before that, you must make sure you have everything, from the right-size pot, the prepped ingredients, and any accouterments necessary for serving this celebrated Southern dish. In my life, all of the planning and prepping started coming together; the flavors began to marry together while slow-cooking into a gumbo. As life would have it, I ended up working as a production assistant with Black Entertainment Television in the Special Projects for Syndication Division. Our first show was, "A Tribute to Black Music Legends," paying homage to Louis Armstrong, Josephine Baker, Billie Holiday, and Marvin Gaye. The show received an Emmy nomination. As I gained more traction and ventured into the world of entrepreneurship, I started planning charity events and worked on projects with a host of notable people and celebrities. The network I've built is an extension of the continuous empowerment received every time I work with someone, and the relationships developed during my time on Capitol Hill.

Throughout my career, I have been privileged to work with wonderful clients such as Lynn Whitfield, someone for whom I have great admiration and respect. She invited me one day to attend the ESPY Awards with her at the last minute. I immediately caught a flight to New York City. I arrived at her home to enjoy cocktails with a host of celebrity friends such as Samuel L. Jackson, Jackée Harry, and others. Curious as to why she invited me at the last minute, I asked her why she thought that I would be ready to come at a moment's notice. She looked into my eyes and said, "You are always ready." My heart smiled at the beauty of that compliment, although it didn't register fully for some time. Ms. Whitfield's comment was a testament to my upbringing and the talents and skills that had been honed in my childhood.

Having been an event planner and publicist for two decades, I have developed a different perspective on how people with some level of acclaim are viewed and treated. This reality has given me pause in being public with my life, making it sometimes difficult to share my accomplishments and success. Understanding the power you possess, how to control it, and having a supportive cast of close confidants are essential elements in navigating any career, whether you are on the frontlines or whether you prefer working behind the scenes, like me.

In life we will have storms, but when you move and step out on faith, God blesses you when you least expect it. I am reminded of the time I was faced with Hurricane Katrina in Miami. It was at the MTV Video Music Awards and I was planning one of the events. Because the storm was looming, we had to move quickly to modify or adjust events and plans. Imagine having a three-day setup arranged for an event that is now scheduled for less than 24 hours and involves transforming the historic Lyric Theater! To add to my already distressed state, many of the items needed to transform the venue for the event were stuck at the shipping companies and wouldn't be delivered for the event in time. Additionally, Hill Harper, one of my guests for the event, finally made it to Miami after multiple flight delays. Upon his arrival, he wanted to go out. With only 24 hours to get this event done, I was beyond stressed and wasn't in the best state to drive around Miami. Despite the new time constraints for the pending event that still needed planning, I took a couple of hours to roll with Harper, and boy am I glad I did! Harper had me at the private listening party for Mariah Carey. I must share my love for the wonderful woman in show business known as the incomparable Mariah Carey. She is one of my all-time favorite vocalists and someone for whom I have great respect; her craft and talent are amazing. I am eternally grateful to Hill Harper for that opportunity.

Still, the reality of planning a major event began to set in, so back to work I went, laboring to transform the venue space. The outdoor space was transformed into a "juke joint." An art gallery was set up in the newly renovated wing of the theater and we removed the seats in the theater, and built a dance floor. The stage was the VIP area and the DJ was on the balcony. Whenever an event is set before me, a moment in time is created, offering you an experience that you will never forget. I received so much positive feedback from this event that it rivaled Diddy's memorable party that was going on at the same time. This event is by far my most memorable. It is the culmination of these experiences, both good and bad, that gave me numerous opportunities and allowed me the ability to ramp up how I wanted to express myself to the world. In the coming days, the whole world would be transfixed by the unspeakable horrors and devastation of "Katrina." Too often we are unaware of how very blessed we are.

Global Impact

Beyond my career and accomplishments, I have increasingly come to realize how profoundly my humanity is connected to and impacted by the world. As I stepped further into my purpose, things began to move at an accelerated pace.

As might be expected in most major planning events, moments behind the scenes can get heated. Liken this, if you will, to precisely what the cayenne pepper does for the perfect gumbo. I have been able to work with phenomenal people and have planned numerous events. From reaching my first career milestone in securing international press with the planning of a fundraiser for Haiti in the wake of the devastating 2010 hurricanes, to working with Africare and TransAfrica, where I was blessed to meet the late Nelson Mandela, to my having been given the opportunity to plan the African American Inaugural Ball for President Bill Clinton, I have truly been challenged, tested, and blessed. Planning high-profiled events such as these led to the opening up of more opportunities for me to work with living legends.

I was fortunate to meet Nelson Mandela on three separate occasions. While vacationing in Africa with Doug E. Doug, I received a call that provided me with two tickets to attend the state dinner for Mr. Mandela in Cape Town.[3] The event was to occur the following day, so I rushed to the mall and purchased a black suit and hemmed the pants to fit appropriately. This was yet another "full circle" moment as I recall the comments of my friend, Ms. Lynn Whitfield. Indeed, I had to be ready at a moment's notice.

When Haiti was devastated by the hurricane in 2010, I planned a fundraiser for Hollywood Unites for Haiti. Actor/Ambassador to Haiti, Jimmy Jean-Louis, is the founder of this organization. Much like my dedication to helping others, his commitment to the people of Haiti is extraordinary. The former Ambassador Raymond Joseph, Danny Glover, and former Governor Douglas Wilder were featured guests. This is another example of how God works through us to help others. As we grow older and step out into the world, we must press on, in the company of good people. Yes, there may be people, places, and things that will attempt to hinder us or strive to dim our light, or even separate us further from our dreams and goals. Stay on fire. Navigating these things can be difficult, especially when you have left the supportive comforts of home. I have learned not to give up.

As a creative, driven, and loving individual, I have gained confidence in knowing that my gifts and talents had to be refined and perfected, even tested by fire, over time. To add to my soup, God blessed me to meet John and Dorothy Davis, who are as revered as the salt of the earth. They have been extraordinary in sharing their love, wisdom, and support of me. They, too, have a special prayer line like my mom's, which also keeps me covered. Major Lewis has also been a remarkable part of my journey as an adult. He has shared his wisdom, both personally and professionally. His brotherhood keeps me focused and full of laughter like nothing else I've ever experienced. Because of Major Lewis, I remain unbothered when the negativity and challenges of life rear their ugly heads.

That HBCU Life

Because of my respect for education and my desire to give back to my community, I developed an interest in serving as a board member for an HBCU. The opportunity presented itself while I was attending the honorees' luncheon for the NAACP Image Awards. During a conversation with Donald Comer, the question was posed about my interest in serving on the board of an HBCU. Later, I was introduced to Dr. Cynthia Warrick, the first female president of Stillman College. Today, I am most proud to serve as a Trustee for Stillman College, committed to exposing students to and preparing them for the world.

The classroom has a special place, as do our lived experiences. I am blessed to share my expertise with the college and to offer access to additional resources. As I work to help transform the institution and improve Stillman overall, the best thing I can do to effect a difference is to provide new exposures to a demographic that might not otherwise have the opportunity to experience them. God has also allowed me to help very many people by my sitting on the board of directors and special committees. Serving in these roles has further allowed me to share my offerings of gifts and talents and, in so doing, support the organization in fulfilling its mission to serve the people.

As an avid art collector, I believe art breathes life into people and continues to give much to us all. It is my intention to have a positive impact in whatever I do and, as such, as a board member, I want to help to tell the story of Stillman. The unique idea to collaborate with students and gather their input to commission and gift a mural was recently born. After I had the pleasure of speaking with Dr. Warrick about creating the mural for the campus, the decision was made to move forward with it. Collaborating with the students who inspired the vision for the mural was both motivating and empowering for them; it brought much energy to the campus. The artist Shawn Perkins, "SP The Plug," was tapped for the opportunity to share his talent and to paint this mural that will forever be part of the rich history at Stillman College. A series of giclees were created and sold as part of a fundraiser to commemorate the mural. Having developed a deep appreciation for art, I am delighted to have learned of and to have been invited to the ZuCot Gallery. It is the largest African American–owned art gallery in the southeastern region of the country. This gallery is a family-owned business wherein the father, Aaron Henderson, is the artist and sons Omari and Onaje, along with a friend Troy, create the total gallery experience, and represent artists nationwide. Since meeting Omari, we have moved forward as brothers and work together to highlight the careers of African American artists such as Charly "Carlos" Palmer, Chukes, Steve Prince, and Charlotte Riley-Webb. This relationship also has led to my becoming the publicist for ZuCot Gallery as well as to the welcome expansion and enhancement of my art collection. To further feature their offerings, a coffee-table book titled "*Fight On* was published by the gallery. In the book, there are various highlights of "Negro Spirituals" paired with paintings by Aaron Henderson, depicting the meaning of the particular spiritual in question.

The Path Forward

For the most part, I have been very clear about what I have wanted in life. Even if it wasn't always clear what I wanted, I knew what I didn't want. There was a time when I wondered why God gifted me with so many talents and blessed me to do so many different things at an elevated level. Well, almost everything. With the exception of the gift of song, I have excelled at everything that I attempted. At the same time, *Ebony*, *Jet*, *GQ*, *The Robb Report*, and *Esquire* have proved to be the written soundtrack of my childhood. These publications took me on a journey and exposed me to the world of sartorial splendor and varied lifestyles of people who had achieved a certain level of success and access. These publications proved to be sheer music to me. They are a major part of my motivation and vision.

The choices we make and our accountability for them are important because our decisions directly impact the trajectory of our lives. One of the primary benefits of having a strong support system and a robust network is that they help you to develop your skills and talents, keep you grounded, offer different perspectives and exposure, and help you gain access to new opportunities. One time, on a return flight from Oakland, I had the pleasure of meeting James Ferguson, the former Executive Director of the National Coalition on Black Civic Participation, Inc. (NCBCP). Having recently quit my job and being unclear about what I wanted to do, I volunteered to help plan a fundraiser with the NCBCP. To my surprise, Mr. Ferguson compensated me for my services and forwarded two contacts that also needed help with their events.

It's important to note that, as we evolve, what we want will change, and having a network is essential to navigating the new world around us. As such, we should look at our network as the wonderful seasoning to our gumbo—full of flavor and aromatics. Another important factor that has helped me in my growth is establishing and maintaining standards, especially when I was in the early days of my career. According to any valid or respectable recipe for gumbo, there are standard ingredients that are needed in order for the final product to be considered a "gumbo." Even so, some recipes call for ingredients that you may not necessarily choose or prefer because you dislike the taste.

The Man I Am

As a Black man in America, I know that life is rife with layers and levels that confront, present obstacles to us, and are meant to disable us. But, much like my stuttering, it is how we process and navigate these obstacles that will determine how we fare in life. While it seems that the hate towards Black men is more prevalent now than ever, there really hasn't been a time when our country truly valued or protected us.

As a Black man in America, I have presented and been perceived differently, and my presence alone has always been in direct opposition to the stereotypical narrative that permeates society regarding Black men in America. God blesses us through one another, and I am committed to helping as many people as possible. I have intentionally created space for us to be seen in a different light, to challenge the existing narrative about Black men.

As an African American male, I believe that exposure is the main ingredient for liberation. For centuries, African American males have endured trauma with no help. It is clear how Black men are viewed in America and, as time moves forward, the media has become progressively dogmatic about how we are presented. "Entertainers," "Athletes," and "Criminals" are the top three categories of how we are portrayed. While that is part of who we are, African American men show up in so many other ways. Before my current endeavors, as the oldest of five children, I had the desire to create opportunities to expose my brothers and other young people to different narratives about our community in general and Black men in particular.[4]

One of these efforts was a calendar project entitled, "When I Grow Up, I Want To Be...." This calendar featured African American men based on their occupations, along with historical facts on the achievements of African American men. Given the negative and longstanding social and political climate, it was evident that content to combat the persistently limited narrative of Black men in America needed to be created. The first calendar was being designed when the 9/11 attack occurred on the World Trade Center, where the graphic designer worked. Long before "Katrina", that is, my professional life had significantly been swept up in the horrors of a national catastrophe. Many in the world were left numb, as was I.

While the graphic designer in the World Trade Center was safe, all of our files and images were destroyed, leaving me feeling all the more numb and defeated. But God! With encouragement from my village, I picked up the pieces and ultimately produced the much needed, inspirational 2002 calendar. This experience took a lot from me and, to be quite honest, had discouraged me temporarily. As life would have it, people continued inquiring about the next calendar. After much contemplation and prayer, the 2005 calendar was subsequently also produced. This time around, the calendar was sold in Borders Bookstores. The collective of young men who participated in the production of this project earned more than a million dollars annually. No athletes. No entertainers. No criminals. This project also took care to highlight these successful men by properly profiling and recognizing them for their hard work and evident success. Imagine twelve African American men in tuxedos standing before an audience to be celebrated for their achievements.

The men from the calendar became more empowered by the encouragement and acknowledgment from the community.

Today, social media has exposed thousands of situations in which African American males were harassed and killed by the police. Some say that these are modern-day lynchings of Black males. While hard to watch, these videos go viral, forcing the hand of justice to confront the blatant brutality, racism, and injustice. The wounds inflicted when a black man encounters police officers often leaves him, and those closest to him, traumatized. Until we are humanized, we will never be treated fairly.

Gumbo is a life-giving and life-sustaining dish that requires time, patience, fresh ingredients, and love. I have been fortunate enough to have had all of these and more. As human beings and as Black men, we all require the same. America's racial reckoning requires multiple resources. It also requires key players to be on deck as we try to find the way forward. In many ways, the plight to change this monolithic narrative has just begun. My hope is to be a part of the solution, and to offer alternatives to the pervasive stereotypes that govern how Black males are perceived in this country.[5]

It was two years ago that I grew even more frustrated with how the media was pushing the limited view of who we are as Black men. With the help of my friends and noteworthy executive producers D. John Jackson and Darryl Pitts, I was able to launch the "What About Me?" documentary. It revealed how African American men are viewed in America, but from *our* perspective. The documentary gave the world an opportunity to hear what African American men have to say about our contributions to society, about police brutality, about being convicted of a crime for something we did not do, about fatherhood, voting, and much more. These men and I created several "social media live" events to host deep conversations with the public about issues and themes such as "Trauma of a Black Man" and "Brother 2 Brother: The Legacy Continues." This documentary was aired in syndication nationally and is available now on Amazon Prime. It has garnered great recognition, provoking dialog in high schools, colleges, corporations, and throughout communities nationwide. Most viewers and discussants expressed that they rarely ever get to see and hear what African American men think or feel.

We can't change what the media has done to misrepresent African American men. However, we can create content that speaks to our truth—content that can be consumed like a very, very good soup, and that provides true nourishment for us completely—reaching even to our minds and souls. We must control the narrative. Carefully....

ENDNOTES

1   See Angelise M. Rouse, *The King Inside: Practical Advice for Young African-American Males* (Philadelphia, PA: Especially4Me Publishing, 2016).
2   A certain deep kind of joy comes from not simply achieving success, but also from giving. See Reginald F. Lewis and Blair Walker, *Why Should White Guys Have All the Fun? How Reginald Lewis Created A Billion Dollar Enterprise* (New York: Wiley, 1995).
3   For more on his extraordinary life, see, of course, Nelson Mandela, *A Long Walk to Freedom: An Autobiography of Nelson Mandela* (London: Time Warner Books, U.K., 1995).
4   For an extraordinary discussion of this important topic and other critical and related themes, see: bell hooks, *We Real Cool: Black Men and Masculinity* (New York and London: Routledge, 2004).
5   For a very useful, broad, thoughtful, and historical analysis, see J. Fred MacDonald, *Blacks and White TV: Afro-Americans in Television Since 1948* (Lanham, MD: Rowman and Littlefield, 1983).

BIBLIOGRAPHY

hooks, bell. *We Real Cool: Black Men and Masculinity*. New York and London: Routledge, 2004.
Lewis, Reginald F. and Walker, Blair S. *Why Should White Guys Have All the Fun? How Reginald Lewis Created A Billion-Dollar Enterprise*. New York: Wiley, 1995.
Rouse, Angelise M. *The King Inside: Practical Advice for Young African-American Males*. Philadelphia, PA: Especially 4Me Publishing, 2016.
MacDonald, J. Fred. *Blacks and White TV: Afro-Americans in Television Since 1948*. Rowman and Littlefield, 1983.
Mandela, Nelson. *A Long Walk to Freedom: An Autobiography of Nelson Mandela*. London: Time Warner Books, U.K., 1995.

CHAPTER EIGHTEEN
My Sardonic Self

Hank Grimes

I am, at once, incredulous and thankful to be starting my seventh decade as a denizen of a small oblate spheroid spinning around its nearest stellar orb. While neither of these bodies is particularly remarkable in the greater, known-universe-sized scheme of things, this petrous little ball and its life-supporting star are the be-all and end-all for the flora and fauna that coexist here in the Goldilocks zone. As luck would have it, I, too, reside here in the form of a sentient, self-aware, modern human being.

Ironically, the very possibility of my terrestrial debut was set in motion some 300,000 years ago by none other than climate change that forced my prehistoric ancestors to behave in ways that would help them survive the challenges of newly unstable environments. We've come full circle and are confronted with a similar dichotomy: adapt and thrive or persist and perish. This time, however, things are not at all the same. Our ancestors responded to climate change by doing what they had to do with nothing more than a modest array of stone tools fashioned to meet their everyday needs and, apparently, an abundance of good sense. Today, we so-called modern humans are responding to environmental upheavals with denial, suspicion, finger-pointing, and inaction before a backdrop of technology of heretofore unfathomable complexity. In other words, we are swimming in a sea of knowhow without even getting wet. This is especially true of some extremely powerful individuals who are uniquely positioned to effect the very changes needed to prolong our survival. I am dismayed by such intransigence, as it is we, the citizens of the Divided States of America, who are the second largest producers of carbon dioxide—the main cause of modern climate change. Yet "alarum" bells, red flags, and disaster warnings notwithstanding, our citizenry is behaving like fractious adolescents who have pledged largely emotional allegiances to a host of identities far too plenteous to unpack here.

I, too, have pledged allegiance to a personal identity which, over time, has not been forged from rancorous disagreements but, rather, has been shaped by personal change, life-altering situations, and eye-opening epiphanies. So, tongue-in-cheek jabs at the prevailing 21st-century zeitgeist aside, I shall unapologetically state for the record that I am a black, gay, non-theist who hails from the United States of America and, lest anyone get it twisted, I have written a disclaimer for everyone's careful consideration:

The following is a work of non-fiction and does, indeed, depict a living person and a series of events that are not to be construed as anything other than my "I", my truth, my reactions to that which life has done to and for me as well as that which I have done to and for myself.

Life is less about the things that happen to you than it is about your reactions to them and how you choose to deal with those things. I've been cursed, mocked, praised, derided, cheated, and richly rewarded and, through it all, I've managed to beat out the dents, right the ship, set the train squarely back on its tracks, and survive the slings and arrows of the naysayers and the smattering of haters who derived no joy from seeing me forge ahead in life while following an agenda that had little, if anything, to do with them.[1]

The adult phase of my life began, in earnest, the day I took my place on a raised dais before the bright smiling faces of 30 or so Chinese undergraduates who were there to learn all there was to know about English conversation and composition from me, the Foreign Expert, as we expatriate teachers were called in those days. But more about that later. First, I'd like to back up a little—well, a lot—to tell you about my first "I-been-shook" moments. Mercifully, these occurred a long time ago, but I'm here to tell the tale.

One day, as my kindergarten teacher, Mrs. M, held up an eggbeater that didn't turn properly, she excitedly asked the class, "Now children, would you find this inside the house or outside the house?" My hand went up like a shot and, because it was the only hand in the air, she knew she would have looked real silly if she had ignored me as she was often wont to do. So, with her permission, I matter-of-factly explained that her eggbeater would be outside in the trash can at my house because we had a new one in our kitchen that actually worked. I realized that I'd either gotten the answer very right or very wrong by the way she pursed her lips and got that tell-tale squint in those steely blue eyes of hers, and she proceeded to let me have it. "Get out! Just get out of my classroom, and don't come back without your mother, you hear me?!" Well, I may have been in kindergarten, but I knew darn well that I hadn't done anything wrong, so I seized the opportunity—as if I had a choice—to get away from her icy stare and that breath that smelled like thunder sounded. The next day, mama came, mama saw, mama politely put Mrs. M. in her place by letting her know that, in our house, my education did not end with the last bell of the school day.

My mother taught 3rd grade for many years and, for obvious reasons, wherever she taught, I attended school, so you can imagine the insights I gleaned from her conversations with the other teachers, the office personnel, and the janitorial staff. I'm not sure where it came from but, in my early years, I had a competitive streak a mile wide, and any student who garnered praise in private landed on my to-outdo list in the classroom. With the exception of mathematics, I liked doing anything that the teachers said my classmates did so well—only better. In hindsight, it was my version of insider trading to gain a competitive edge. The SEC would have been proud.

Early on, I became smitten with cursive writing and, one day, as a 2nd grader, I was at the board in my mother's classroom, diligently practicing my loops that went above and below the line. My teacher came in to tell my mother something, and I called her attention to what I had been doing—pretty loops and all. Without missing a beat, she took a perfunctory glance at the board and said, "We're not there yet." Undaunted, I retorted, "Yes, I know, but I am." With that, the line was drawn; I officially did not like my 2nd-grade teacher, not that it would have taken much more than such a brief slight to dislike that woman. She had a snowball's chance of making my Top-10, anyway.

A few weeks later, I hit upon the perfect plan. I decided to write my entire assignment backwards in the hopes of sending a not-so-subtle message and costing her a considerable amount of extra time in reading the whole thing. I waited and waited and waited, but I never heard another word about the matter. Of course, I didn't dare check with mama about some stunt I had no business pulling in the first place, and I eventually forgot that it had even happened. It wasn't until a few years later that my mother finally told me that the very next day, my teacher had rushed into her classroom with my assignment in hand, and she simply gushed and giggled about that assignment. All she had done was hold my paper up to a mirror, and she read it without much effort. She also told my mother that she was going to keep it forever. "No child has ever done such a cute thing," she chortled. Luckily, that was all I had in my arsenal at such a young age. I had no interest in raising the stakes, as it would have meant doing something I would regret had I been more determined to vex this woman without probable cause. I didn't fully develop my vindictive chops until quite a few years later.

In the early grades, my facility with language outpaced that of my classmates, and language arts classes bored me to tears. In 3rd grade, we were reading about Dick, Jane, their dog Flip, and some friggin' red ball, but I was hopelessly caught up in the pages of the World Book Encyclopedia. I had no time for Dick or Jane!

Where I had failed in 2nd grade, I succeeded the next year with Mrs. O. and another of my stunts to relieve my boredom. After reading about the antics of Flip and his red ball for way more pages than was necessary, we then had to answer workbook questions to check our understanding. I was, like, are you kidding me right now? I read it! I got it! Let's keep the train moving, shall we?

Unfortunately, my classroom comportment grade was riding on my proving my understanding. So, I answered the questions, but not to Mrs. O's liking. After she finished grading our work, she shot me a look that said, "Mission accomplished," and she marched me straight down the hall to my mother's room to show her what I had done.

> Q: Why did Dick and Jane go to the park with Flip?
> A: Because they were sick of sitting in the house.
> Q: Why did Flip run with the red ball?
> A: Because that's what dogs do.
> Q: What type of day was it?
> A: Like any other day, I guess. (without the comma, of course.)

Well, you get the idea. I was not feeling the book, the workbook, or the assignment, so I added a dash of "Hank stank" to my answers to punctuate the morning with a smidge of drama. Well, leave it to my mother to put things in perspective for me. After Mrs. O., her beet-red face, quivering bottom lip, and shaking hands left the room, my mother sat me down and started dropping truth bombs on me. "I don't care how smart you think you are," she said. "If you don't show it, no one will know it. You can read whatever you want at home but, if a teacher asks you to do something, you better do it, or I will warm your butt, you hear me?" All the while I'm thinking, "Uh, duh, loud and clear," but I simply answered, "Yes, ma'am." I mean, no one could warm you up like mama could.[2]

These incidents all occurred in the earliest years of my life, so it would be downright hyperbolic to characterize them as life-altering, epiphanic, or causing anything close to an upheaval. Instead, I'll say that they were irritants that made a lasting impression on me. After all, they all happened over 50 years ago, but I remember them as though they happened yesterday, and I've managed to move on without nary a scar, therapist's bill, or juvenile record and, today, I'm none the worse for wear.

Boy, what a difference a few months can make. Somewhere between the Dick & Jane episode and the middle of my 4th-grade year, my focus shifted from my teachers to my classmates. The boys began wondering out loud if the girls stuffed, and I was at a complete loss as to what this meant. I didn't dare tell on myself by asking, "Stuff what?" so I pretended to be as curious as the rest. Hell, I thought they were wondering if the girls could make stuffing—dressing, as it was called in my house. Anyway, I knew that someone would eventually fill in the blanks. A few days later, a classmate began asking, "Do you think (insert girl's name) stuffs?" and I had just about enough with that stupid question when another classmate piped up and said, "Hell no, she don't stuff. She don't even wear a bra yet!" You could have knocked me over with a feather to find out that there was no connection between our female classmates and a much-loved Thanksgiving side dish. I'm thinking about food, but all they could think about was the size of the girls' breasts. In my defense, I tipped the scales at 170 pounds at that time, and food was never far from my mind. Suddenly, my intel was of precious little value to me, as it raised more questions than it answered. Why the sudden interest in the girls in the class? Why didn't I care about their bras or the size and contour of their budding womanhood? All the other boys were straight trippin' about something that didn't interest me in the least, and this caused me to attempt a deeper dive into a pool that had no depth. I had never cared about my classmates on such a personal level but, when I finally took a little time to think about it, I realized that I was way more interested in the other boys than the girls, and I spent many a playground hour staring at the boys and the girls because I just had to make the bra thing make sense.[3]

There I was at a school assembly one day with my arm around my then girlfriend's chair, not because I was genuinely feeling any type of way toward her but because that's what I'd seen other boys do. So, I followed suit in the hopes that they'd all get the message that I was one of them. At the same time, I knew that nothing could be farther from the truth, especially when I was sitting next to my girl and wishing like hell that I could sit next to my boy, Tony, who was four rows in front of us. There was nothing overtly sexual about my interest in my male classmates, either. All I knew was that I had begun to wonder quite often what it would be like just to touch them, hug them, or peck one of them on the cheek, especially Tony—OMG! Then the doubt crept in, and I couldn't help wondering if there was something "wrong" with me. All of the boys seemed so taken with the girls, but they never lit up my board. Suddenly, I stopped caring, one way or the other, and resigned myself to the fact that I was just different from them.

Late in the summer of 1968, James Brown was on the radio rocking the house with "Say it loud, I'm black and I'm proud" and I remember feeling a real sense of pride because we "colored" folk had finally come up with a name for ourselves. The term colored never cut it for me because there were no transparent people around, which meant, technically, that everyone was colored. But black? That was different,and, judging by the reaction of those around me, we'd apparently hit upon something real, something right, something to be truly proud of. I remember being on the playground thinking, I'm black, and you (white folks) didn't have anything to do with it. I also knew that I wasn't really black, but "Say it loud, I'm brown and I'm proud" or "Say it loud, I'm darker than white people and I'm proud" were hardly acceptable alternatives. So, it was settled, I would henceforth and forevermore identify as "black."

In 1988, Jesse Jackson and several other very famous, very well-positioned black people began calling for yet another name change. This time and, supposedly, for the last time, we were to stop calling ourselves black and start using the term African American. This, to me, had a dissonant, almost cacophonous ring to it, as I'd been black for just about as long as I could remember. White people were happily white, and I refused to be anything other than happily black. Not to mention the fact that I preferred to take my Americanism straight with no chasers or hyphens, thank you very much. I couldn't have felt more strongly that Jesse and his gang needed to get back in their lane and keep their well-heeled opinions off my identity. To this day, I feel that the urgency of this name-change campaign and the ensuing media blitz surrounding the new moniker was more about social segregation than reunification, but I've never had a problem standing arm-in-arm with those who were somehow different from me.

Best estimates place the number of languages spoken on the continent of Africa somewhere close to 2,000 which, mathematically, is fully one-third of the languages in use today. There are 54 sovereign nations in Africa and I shudder to even think about slicing and dicing that geopolitical pie into digestible bits. Nigeria alone is home to 503 languages and dialects, and, in South Africa, there are 11 official languages that are recognized by law. As if those numbers weren't staggering enough, there are also over 3,000 distinct African ethnic groups in existence today. In simplest terms, religion in Africa can be seen as a three-part puzzle comprised of African traditional religions, Christianity, and Islam. But religious affiliation is anything but simple, and it must be pointed out that Christian and Islamic beliefs are relative newcomers to the party, as indigenous traditions antedate these two religions by multiple centuries. So, where do I, the lowly individual end and the grandiloquence of the African continent begin? Africa overstates me by a few orders of magnitude, and I woefully understate Africa, especially if my brown skin is my only qualification.

I'm an educator by training and, for the past 30 or so years, I've taught English as a foreign/second language, American culture; critical thinking, reading, writing, and developmental academic skills among other things.[4] By the eighth month after arriving in Mainland China and stepping foot onto that raised dais I mentioned earlier, I had learned enough Mandarin to begin sharing certain details about my life in passable Chinese. It was exciting to be speaking a language that most of the world considered so exceedingly difficult. Turns out, listening and speaking are pretty easy skills to acquire once you get that song in your head. Reading and writing, however, were next-level difficult if you failed to put in the time.

I remember talking to a friend when I casually referred to myself as (一个黑种人) "a black person." The guy had a surprised look on his face, and he quickly corrected me, saying, (但你一点也不黑) "But you're not at all black!" That's when I told him that, for me, black was not my color, it was my group, my people. He seemed satisfied with this, and the topic never came up again. This brief exchange piqued my interest in the local perceptions of black people, and I got a glimpse of the insight I was seeking during a conversation about a Rwandan acquaintance, Bahizi Umulisa, whom I'd met at a dance a few weeks earlier. I ran into Bahizi in the parking lot next to the international student dorm, and our exchange was quite surreal. We'd only shared a few words since we first met, and I didn't remember his English being as limited as it was. So, there we were, face-to-face and keen to converse, but Bahizi spoke precious little English, and I was 7 years removed from my last French class, so our conversation was very strained until he switched into Chinese, and I followed suit. A black American and a Rwandan communicating in Mandarin Chinese! All the while, the refrain "If They Could See Me Now" kept muscling in on the conversation, and it just made sense. If the folks back home could have seen me, indeed. I was anxious to tell another Chinese friend about this conversation and how smoking hot I thought Bahizi was, but he ruined the mood when he said, (他只是太黑了) "He's just too black!" I went from zero to white hot in a matter of seconds, and I asked, "too black for what?" Is he too black to hold a passport and travel the world? Is he too black to spend weekends in other countries just for fun? Is he too black to dress like he just stepped out of a fashion magazine? Is he too black to learn your language? I mean, your French is non-existent, you can't get a passport, you've never been on a plane, you ride your sister's bicycle, and your clothes are hand-me-downs, so, please, tell me what Bahizi is too black to do besides wind up in your bed?

On another occasion, two of my students had dropped by for a visit and it just so happened that there was a Discovery Channel–style show on television. The program was all about the Maasai people of Kenya. One of the students had distinguished himself as one of the dullest knives in the drawer, but I was more than willing to overlook this cognitive shortfall, as he was an affable young man who tried mightily to rise above his lack of academic and linguistic prowess. I liked him right fine, but when he dismissed the beauty of the Maasai people by saying, (他只太傻了) "They're just stupid," I painted a bullseye on his chest and the grilling began.

Stupid, I demanded? Too stupid for what? Aren't you the one who was just complaining about life in China? Aren't you the one wishing you could be anywhere but China? Well, look at those people. They're celebrating, smiling, and dancing. So, are you saying that they are too stupid to be as miserable as you are? He had no response that was worth sharing here, and I never heard him juxtapose the words African and stupid in the same sentence again. And when this kid excused himself to take a bathroom break, his friend thanked me for calling him out so quickly.

For the Chinese government, granting international students access to a tertiary-level education was all about forging alliances and winning friendships. Unfortunately, large swaths of the Chinese population didn't get it. That's because most international students from Africa south of the Sahara had come to China on scholarship and were the sons of government officials and powerful businessmen. So, the scholarship perks they received were much more valuable than those of the Chinese nationals, including the hefty stipend they collected each month. The Chinese resented this, and bad blood had been running through their veins since the late 60s. Then, when these rich Africans began cavorting with Chinese women, it was seen as a personal affront that could not go unanswered. While many Chinese men were known to fight, riot, and burn the African students' dorms to protect their women's honor, it was business as usual for me. The locals were loath to even acknowledge the existence of men interested in forming intimate friendships with other men, so I never had to worry about angry mobs showing up at my door with torches or pitchforks. No one felt the need to protect the honor of Chinese men from me and those who shared my proclivities.

One Friday, a good friend of mine and I were somewhat desperate for a change of pace, so we boarded a train for Beijing and a much-deserved chance to relax. Little did I know that a popular political reformist by the name of Hu Yao Bang had died and by the time we got to Beijing, his funeral was in full swing. There were throngs and throngs of people as far as the eye could see. The extent of my interest in the proceedings was simply marveling at the sight of so many people gathered in one place. Turns out, Hu Yao Bang was an icon of Chinese reform and countless thousands of students had gathered to mourn the loss of the man they believed was their last hope for real change. Well, the students refused to let Hu Yao Bang's funeral mark the end of the matter and things blew up into the infamous student protests of 1989. Had I known that I was witnessing the early days of the Democracy Movement, I would have paid closer attention. But, by the time our entire student body left the classroom to join a city-wide strike till the end of the semester, the movement had my undivided attention. I didn't know it then, but I had also landed on the radar of the Public Security Bureau (GongAn Ju), and they watched me as I watched the students by day and the local male population by night. I also found out that the GongAn were discussing my expulsion because I knew too much about "that" side of Chinese society. In the end, I was spared such an indignity.

From the outset, I knew that this struggle was not my struggle, and the students' anger was not my anger.[5] The best I could do was take a seat on the sidelines to watch things develop. I wound up back in Beijing on June 4, 1989, and I had the distinct displeasure of ducking and running with the rest of the crowd as members of the People's Army delivered warning shots above our heads as they slowly retreated to the west. Tensions ran high as the extent of the killing became clear. For a brief period, even the local police were nowhere to be seen, and I was told that they were staging their own mini-strike as they stepped aside to let the army do whatever it was that they were going to do. As for me, while the cats were away, this mouse chose to play. No prowling eyes of the GongAn Ju, no local police force making the rounds to ensure that public decency remained intact, no police presence at all. Everywhere I turned, the streets were empty for the next few days, but the hookup spots were jumpin' like juke joints. Everyone was emboldened, albeit rather briefly, by the diminished threat of police intervention and harassment. I remained in China for three more years, experiencing first-hand the pall of fear and disbelief that hung heavily in the air for months and months after the attack on TianAn Men. Saddest of all were the loss of faith in the party's willingness to live up to their egalitarian rhetoric and the realization that dissent and social upheaval would not sully the party's idealized version of a Democratic Socialist Dictatorship with Chinese characteristics. Whatever the hell that gobbledygook was supposed to mean.

Little boxes began popping up like mushrooms on campus and around town. They'd actually been there all along, but with a fresh coat of green paint and conspicuous white lettering, the citizenry was reminded that information leading to the arrest of anyone involved in the upheaval could earn them up to 20,000 RMB—100 times the average salary of the day. The times had changed and people were angry, but they expressed their anger in hushed tones well out of earshot of teachers, colleagues, classmates, and family members. 20,000 RMB was a LOT of money, and no one was to be trusted entirely. With neither Shibboleth nor flaming hoop, I continued to earn people's trust because, to my knowledge, there were no black Americans working with or for the Chinese Communist Party. So, people continued to open up in ways they would never have done with their compatriots.[6]

Meanwhile, this brown skin continued to hold a definite allure and, while relieving myself, on more than one occasion, men would walk right up to me, lean over, and take a good look at my junk. Those uninvited stares at my genitalia either confirmed or disconfirmed certain popular rumors about black men. This certainly would have been grounds for a knock-down-drag-out in middle America, but I'd long since become desensitized to such invasions of privacy because I knew they were nothing more than innocent attempts at conducting informal research. Had sex been the desired outcome, most guys would have been much more circumspect in conveying their intentions.

Eventually, the student-loan people began calling about their money, and I had no answers for them, not on my salary of $250/month which, by the way, was the highest salary on campus, second only to a PhD holder, who earned 150 more RMB than I did. To this day, I remember my time in China as one of the most satisfying and enlightening periods of my entire life. Living there was like buying a new car without the fancy accoutrement. No, such embellishments came in dribs and drabs over the years of my stay. The more I learned, the more tricked out my imaginary ride became. My metaphorical vehicle never reached fully loaded status, as there was so much left to learn by the time of my departure. Sadly, I wound up fleeing, in a sense, to a better paying job and the ability to keep the loan people at bay. So, in the spring of 1991, I left China for a new adventure and more money in Nagoya, Japan.

At the risk of waxing negative at best and vituperatively disparaging at worst, I'll simply say that I was not ready for Japan. I met up with a group of students who had been studying Chinese at the university where I taught and I was looking forward to having a built-in group of friends to soften my landing in my new environment, but that never happened. It was early August, and the Bon Odori festival had begun. There were six students in the group, and we had plans to go to dinner and then take in some of the sights of the festival. Much to my chagrin, everyone had their hearts set on Italian food, and all I could think was, eeewww, why would I come all the way to Japan to eat Italian food? My mother, sister, and I went to Europe between my 7th- and 8th-grade year, and we were in Italy for 12 days. The food wasn't just good, it was clean off the hook, so I wasn't interested in partaking of Italian food made to suit the Japanese palate.

So, in quintessential American fashion, I suggested that they go get their Italian while I took a sushi break, and we could meet up a little later to enjoy the festivities. We parted ways, and it was as though someone just "genie blinked" the whole group out of existence. I never heard from any of those guys again. Turns out that they never contacted me because I had gone against the wishes of the group. In other words, I did not "qualify" for inclusion because the individual, the few, were expected to defer to the wishes of the many. I don't mean to inflict any cultural harm here, but this episode immediately called to mind the 1987 film, *Invasion of the Body Snatchers*, and I had no stomach for becoming one of the pod people, not after spending so many years carving out my niche of individuality. So, I let 'em all kick rocks, and I proceeded to do my thing in my own way. Within two weeks of landing in Japan, I had lost an entire group of potential friends and, thanks to a couple of knowledgeable expats who'd lived in Nagoya for some years, found all the male companionship I could have hoped for. I was supposed to be in Nagoya for two years, but I left after barely a year with precious few good memories and only one sentence in my linguistic arsenal: 私は英語の先生です。(*Watashi wa eigo no senseidesu*): "I am an English teacher."

Before leaving Japan, I managed to track down a promising job opportunity at a local junior college. I thought I would be a shoo-in with my MA in Applied Linguistics and my teaching experience. Unfortunately, neither I nor the head of Academic Programs had counted on a buxom blond from Australia with no teaching experience and a BA in Health, Physical Education, and Recreation scooping me. The Dean of the school was a horny little goat who got hopelessly stuck on the booty, the beauty, and that blond hair while failing to give a passing thought to the needs of the students who had paid good money for the chance to learn from experienced educators. Instead, he saw fit to grill me about company loyalty, asking, "If you're willing to leave your current employers, what guarantees do I have that you won't leave us, too?" Sometimes, I just can't help myself when confronted with such tissue-thin crap masquerading as genuine concern, so I chose not to bite my tongue, and I told him that there were no guarantees but, if this truly turned out to be a college as the name implied, chances were good that I'd be there a while. And with that, the interview ended, and his final decision was of precious little importance to me. I was ready to go.

I was too experienced a traveler to ever think that I was leaving China for some Japanese version of the same—China 2.0, if you will—but I was ill-prepared for the ensuing culture shock, from which I never fully recovered. Instead, I sought refuge in the comfort of Mainlander Chinese, Taiwanese, and Singaporean friendships with the odd American expat thrown in for good measure. Becoming Chinese or Japanese was never my goal, but I remained open to any changes that these cultures may have made upon my being, so long as they were positive and transferable changes. I went to both countries to teach English, but, the more I thought about my successes in China, the more my life in Japan disgusted me, and I knew I had to leave before my disappointment affected other important facets of my life, namely, my personal relationships and, most importantly, my ability to just be nice to other people. So, I left at my earliest convenience.

I quickly turned the page and made a beeline for the east coast of the Arabian Gulf. I was giddy with anticipation of the bump in salary but burdened with trepidation given the conservatism that was part and parcel of the regional culture. I soon found out, however, that things weren't going to be so bad. It was the end of the holy month of Ramadan, and the Eid al-Fitr had begun by the time I landed. I wasn't allowed to travel because I hadn't passed my 90-day probation period, so, there I was, stuck in a quiet room in an empty building with nary a neighbor in sight. Fortunately, our living quarters were built close enough to the shore for me to gaze at a stunning flamboyance of flamingos every morning and, far beyond this gathering of avian beauties, I watched the slow comings and goings of many a cargo ship on the horizon.

As my new surroundings were uncharted territory for me, I chose to remain close to home until I found someone, anyone, to venture into the nearest town with me. It was sometime between 21:00 and 22:00 in the evening of the fourth day when I'd simply had enough. I went out on the balcony to search for signs of life when I spotted a lone soldier standing guard at the east gate. I slowly made my way to street level, and I greeted the young man with a very jet-lagged "hello." He waved back and I remember thinking, "Dayum, he fine as silk." He didn't speak a word of English, and my Arabic was non-existent, but I still tried exchanging pleasantries. Once I'd run out of hellos and how-do-you dos, I asked, "What time do you get off?" He didn't understand, and I resorted to pantomime to get my message across. I pointed at him then at my watch then I formed an X across my chest, and he quickly nodded in the affirmative. He immediately responded with an unintelligible الساعة الحادية عشر (*alsaaeat alhadiat etshar*), or eleven o'clock. He saw the confusion on my face, so he drew a big eleven in the sand. I was only there to make small talk, but that little question got a big response—the guy began pinching and rubbing his nether regions, much to my surprise and approval. Turns out he was as bored as I was, and he was more than willing to meet under the stairs after his shift to find a way for us to help each other break the boredom. I got back to my room thinking, "I knew life would be hard here, but that wasn't quite what I meant. I ain't mad at him, though." I know I kept that stupid grin on my face until I finally drifted into a very restful sleep.

The next morning, I awoke wondering if the previous night had been an anomaly or something I could count on happening again. Well, I didn't have to wait very long to find out. Apparently, my new friend couldn't hold water, and he had shared the news with a quickness. For the next few weeks, I couldn't leave the base without the guards pinching, rubbing, or touching themselves and staring at me with an I-know-what-time-it-is look on their faces. Talk about your mixed feelings; I was scared to death that the news would work its way up the food chain and I would eventually lose my job, but I was also too excited and flattered to let any of that stop me. I was in my early 30s, and it had been a minute since I'd had 18-, 19-, and 20-year-olds looking at me in that kind of way. The only thing hotter, I mused, was the midday sun that saw temperatures rise to 115° in the shade.

I guess time really does fly when you're having fun. Thanks to that unexpected rendezvous and the guard's loose lips, I got to "know" many of his fellow guards, a chief petty officer, and two commanding officers in fairly short order. I could only marvel at how life in my new home was, well, like shooting fish in a barrel. And it became clear to me that my survival, i.e., avoidance of the military police or members of the Society for the Promotion of Virtue and the Prevention of Vice, depended entirely on my discreetly indulging in the love that dare not speak its name. Categories like *gay*, *straight*, *bi*, and *trans* had NO meaning in the Gulf and Middle East regions at that time. If you pitched, you were a man; if you caught, you weren't, because you'd "chosen" to play the role of the woman in the encounter/relationship. But, depending on the time, the place, and the individual, these roles were not set in stone; fluidity was the norm, and the locals would switch things up in a heartbeat, especially if they felt sufficiently safe in the knowledge that you weren't going to run your mouth off to anyone who might use such knowledge against them. Oh, the double standard of it all!

But there was a certain freedom to be found amidst the conservatism and prevailing piety of the day. Perception drove reality, and I took my cues from the locals when it came to doing what I wanted to do. I never was a fan of the American penchant for pigeonholing, labeling, and compartmentalizing people for the sake of cognitive clarity, and I was mercifully spared the homophobic offense that was feigned so adroitly by guys in the US. In fact, even if I hit on the "wrong" guy, I was often pleasantly surprised by most Arabs' offer to call a friend or a relative to pinch hit. And guess what—the bullpen was always full of willing participants. In the US, the go-to reaction among men was to proudly announce that they were not gay, so they couldn't take me up on the offer, or play a little. Not without a little cajoling and a couple drinks, at least. Whenever I got that tired "I'm-not-gay" reaction, I liked to counter with, "I know, that's why I'm trying to talk to you. I like men who like girls, not men who act like girls." So, on balance, their spilling my "T" and my offering to share my "T" were pretty much the same thing in the Middle Eastern mind.

After eight years of the same old same old, I was ready for a break from the region. To be sure, I hadn't learned all that I could have, but I had learned all that I cared to by the time I went back home. In research parlance, I had reached cultural (theoretical) saturation. Each new encounter, each new conversation was disappointingly similar to the last. Our class discussions, and I use the word loosely, had become an exercise in pod-peopleism that was eerily reminiscent of the situations I'd encountered elsewhere, and no one wanted to offend the religiously-minded class monitors who were never openly identified until the proverbial fecal material was about to hit the oscillating ventilation machine; but, by then, it was too late. Any discussions focusing on democracy, life (á-la-USA), liberty, and the pursuit of happiness tinged with drugs, sex, or rock and roll were frowned upon and were immediately brought to the attention of the school administrators, and that rarely ended well for the errant teacher and the defiant/brave student alike. Apropos of summarizing my time in the Gulf/Middle East,

I'll say that Michael Jackson hit the nail on the head when he advised us all to just "Keep it in the closet." It was understood that no one was going to peek through your curtains, and you were better off not peeking through your neighbors' curtains. If you ever made the mistake of swinging from the nearest chandelier in the town square within clear view of a pious (often pretentiously so) public, you were toast! For Americans and Europeans, this meant expulsion from the country. For fellow Muslims and workers who hailed from much poorer countries, it meant a Friday morning visit to chop-chop square—an open area near the larger mosques in the city reserved for public beheadings, floggings, and the removal of the hands of incorrigible thieves.

This cake has been in the oven for just a smidge over 60 years and, mercifully, it's still a bit jiggly in the middle, which means it's still a work in progress; I still have a lot to learn, and I'm looking forward to the process. In the meantime, though, the black, gay, non-theist part of me has survived intact. If anything, this infrastructure of my identity is stronger than ever and, I reiterate, life is less about the things that happen to you than it is about your reactions and how you choose to deal with those things. When I say a lot has happened in my life, I do mean a LOT, and my reactions have run the gamut from sagacious adult-like stoicism to impetuous adolescent fragility. I'll admit that it hasn't been easy playing the wise one in every situation, and even when I had to leave a dollop of dignity on the dance floor, I always managed to get my point across, which was usually well worth it. Sometimes you have to teach people how to treat you, and those lessons can get rather messy.

Soon after my return from Saudi Arabia, a younger relative managed to find that very last tingly ass nerve that I kept hidden for special occasions somewhere on the left, and he stomped on it! So, I proceeded to read the beads clean off of his rosary. Smack in the middle of this serious dressing down, I remember telling him that I couldn't care less about family and that he wasn't going to get an automatic pass from me just because we shared a few genes. Of course, he heard what he wanted to hear and made the mistake of reminding me some months later that I was the one who said that I didn't give a damn about family. To that I responded, "Look, boy, I'm not gonna put up with your mess just because we're family, and I don't ever want to hear you misquote me again. I've already told you that I did not mean that I didn't care about you as a person. So, this time, I'll speak more slowly and use smaller words so even you can understand me. I meant only that I didn't care about the family part because you're acting just like all the other miscreants in the neighborhood and, at this point, family ties mean nothing to me. I'm your elder, and I don't just want your respect; I demand it! You ought to know that I'm not about to start kissing an ass that I used to wipe! If you act like family, I'll embrace you like family, but if you act like the next thug auditioning for three hots and a cot on the county's dime, I'll ignore you like a canceled check."

This scenario has played out, on some level, more times than I care to remember, and it just goes to show that consanguinity (blood ties) and matrimony are no substitute for good behavior. I've got a list of relatives that's about as long as I am tall who no longer interest me, and I won't be contacting them anytime soon—So let it be written, so let it be done. I've got another, much shorter list of individuals who've landed in my pantheon of fictive kin whom I'll treasure till the day I die. I don't love these short-listers because they can be found somewhere on the family tree or because they married someone hanging listlessly on some hidden branch of the family tree. On the contrary, I love them because they're genuine, they're in my corner, and they aren't going anywhere anytime soon. These are the folks who have looked clean through me and have still enjoyed the view, warts and all. One of the more recent additions to my list of family members who have no ties based on blood or marriage is a cool breeze of a man I had the pleasure of meeting a little over twenty years ago. Yes, a full twenty years ago. I don't open that door to just anybody.

I am far too long in the tooth to get away with wanting to be Charles R. Frederick, Jr. when I grow up, so I'll just settle for the possibility of being very much more like him in my next incarnation. Charles Frederick, or Chip, as he is widely known to the Indiana University (IU) community, is the Director of the IU Student Academic Center, my former boss, professor, and much appreciated mentor. This is one of the most supportive and most scary individuals I've come to know. I'll let the word "supportive" speak for itself but, when I say he's kinda scary, I don't mean it in a dangerous, damnit-I'll-bite-ya sort of way. I mean that Chip had this calm, collected, Obi-Wan Kenobi thing going on, and try as I might, I've never quite gotten the hang of doing things as he does. He is a master at "getting you off the ledge" in a way that makes you forget that you were ever up there whoopin' and hollerin' in the first place. Once, someone mentioned Rosa Parks and, of course, they called her the mother of the Civil Rights Movement, and my hair caught on fire. I'm a huge fan of Ida B. Wells-Barnett and all that she accomplished a half a century before Ms. Parks rose to prominence. Just as I was preparing to launch headlong into an explanation of why I was so over Ms. Parks, Chip looked at me and quietly announced that there would be no kicking of sacred cows that day. So, I took off my boots, put my street shoes back on, and quickly dropped the matter.

Yes, he's scary, as his understanding of emotional intelligence is positively next-level, and it is always a pleasure to watch him work. People are good at carrying out business-as-usual when they're around the people they admire the most and heaping praise on them when they're not around, which I don't mind, but I'd really like to hear more of the good stuff before I die; at least, that way, I'd be able to enjoy it. I hope everyone has a list of fictive kin whom they treasure as much as I do mine. And I'm even more hopeful that everyone is able to let these people know how much they are appreciated. Chip's name bears mentioning because he has always made me a better person by making me want to improve even when I didn't realize that I needed to do so. When we meet, I can always depend on becoming ever so much wiser.

I returned from a four-year stint in Saudi Arabia two months before COVID-19 hermetically sealed everyone off from each other for our own good. I got back with some very well-laid work plans that would give me a break from ESL/EFL and stop me from dipping into my savings. But each of these opportunities vanished like so much smoke in a stiff breeze as the deadly nature of the coronavirus became clear. Until now, I and mine have survived unscathed, and I'm willing to stay home and hide my comorbidities from an organism that can take its toll like few others. The pessimist in me is ever ready to bemoan the challenges of this new global reality. My inner optimist/opportunist, however, is thankful for the lull in the action, and I welcome the chance to think about my next step toward my goals. I also welcome the chance to think long and hard about who I've become, how I got here, and which point on the compass I want to follow toward my next new normal.

Socrates once said that an unexamined life is not worth living. So, from this point on, I will certainly be examining my life through the lens of purposeful goals and objectives. If I do wind up taking to the friendly skies again, I will have asked all the right questions and found all the right reasons to do so, as I've still got traveling on the brain; but the pragmatist in me is going to need some very good reasons to keep schlepping through cavernous airports, putting up with touchy-feely security agents, once again taking a seat on the low end of the learning curve, peeling back the layers of someone else's culture, and deciding if it will be worth it to try my hand at cracking the code of yet another foreign language. We'll see.

In the meantime, I've pieced together memory after memory from the height of my adventures and wanderlust, and the picture is clear: regardless of citizenship, native language, or dominant cultural norms, people are people, and they are doing their best with what they've got. They're also managing to make the beast with two backs in whatever manner pleases them most. I had the pleasure of working in seven countries and visiting 33 others, thus bringing the total to 40 and counting. There are 3 billion genetic building blocks in our bodies, and a paltry 1% of these are responsible for our differences in eye, hair, and skin color and a host of other characteristics, even our shared risk for getting certain diseases. With these facts in mind, it should stand to reason that the same expressions of sexual desire are also shared the world over. Heterosexuality, homosexuality, heteroflexibility, onanism, fetishism, etc., are part of every society known to man- and womankind. A little parlor trick of a question asks, "If a tree falls in the woods but there is no one around to hear it, does it still make a sound?" Yes, damnit, it still makes a sound; just ask the animals of the forest, if you don't believe me. By the same token, just because you're not standing in the presence of strangers while they're going at it, it certainly does not mean that these encounters do not or cannot take place in your neck of the woods! I've said all of this to draw the thinnest line possible under the fact that McDonald's will run out of hamburgers before I visit a country where I can't get a good "meal." It may take a hot minute to find the right restaurant, but I've never gone hungry for very long. The Chinese have their public baths, aka 钓鱼池 ("fishing ponds"), and a plethora of alternative meeting spots. The Japanese have their Love Hotels, although I don't know how much "love" is going on. Arabs are famous for the eyebrow twitch while walking through a mall and scratching your palm during a handshake, but online apps have ruined this hunt-and-chase method of meeting new people. On the streets of San Ya, the southernmost city on the southernmost island in China, I was asked if I wanted some "big sisters." Of course, I asked if big brothers were on the menu. Lo and behold, the pimp dropped everything, took me to a friend's house, and he threw caution to the wind. Nothing like doing something strange to make a little change, huh?

A good many of my international friends who loudly extolled the virtues of their respective belief systems were more than willing to get very busy, then head straight for the shower with the intention of purging their souls as they watched their sins circle the drain with the bath water. I was unmoved by this, as it was their struggle, not mine. You see, they could tell me who and what they were till they were blue in the face, but the minute they *showed* me who they were, especially while dressed in their birthday suits, I always believed them the first time!

And it is here that my sexual identity dovetails nicely with my religious identity or lack thereof. My dear mother was fond of reminding us (my sister and me) that love was not a feeling; it was an action. So, if we truly loved her, we would have no problem showing her. The same holds true for one's religiosity, if I may use that word. If you talk about it more often than you live it, God ain't in ya. How do you treat those who have nothing to give you? How do you speak of others when they're not in your presence? Do you only speak ill of another man's shoes, or do you also make plans to buy him a new pair? In other words, what, exactly is your heart made of, and is there room in there for anybody else?

At one point in my life, the specter of Hell loomed quite large until we began studying exponents and scientific notation in Algebra and Chemistry and, suddenly, "eternal" damnation no longer made any sense. How could anyone with a lifespan of 60, 70, or maybe 80 years do anything so wrong that they deserved to be punished for more years than they ever had a chance of living? Forever is a helluva long time. Besides, I figured that it was not my job to square this threat with my reality. In my experience, if I did something wrong, and my mother got wind of it, I got a whoopin', and that was the end of the matter. Divine retribution by the loving God of biblical lore was seemingly okay with giving me a whoopin' every day all day till I was no more, and that would only be the beginning of things. But, after learning that this threat was the brainchild of long-dead, first-century bishops who didn't even know how to make soap or brush their teeth, my 20th-century ears weren't trying to hear any more of it.

I much prefer a kind spirit to a well-placed word. Your gift of gab is no gift of mine. I do not subscribe to any religious beliefs, organized or otherwise, but I know that God is not Santa Claus, our fairy godmother, or the tooth fairy, for that matter. I also know that nothing will ever change in our lives until something changes. So, whence all the prayers for things and bling and something as mundane as a good grade on a test? Show me the individual who collects a check without going to work or applying for benefits, and I'll show you where I like to sit while singing, swinging, and banging the tambourine every Sunday morning. Again, nothing changes until something changes—a change that invariably begins with human action, not prayer and prestidigitation. Simply put, I don't believe as religious adherents do, and I am confident that God, if the deity exists, is infinitely wise and forgiving enough to understand my persistent skepticism.

Last but not least, I remain steadfastly opposed to identifying as an African American because the term carries little meaning or reason for inclusion in the very warp and weft of my being. In 2001, my best friend and I made our way to Egypt for a two-week vacation. There we were, strolling through one of the oldest parts of Cairo, known as Khan el-Khalili, when the proprietor of a coffee shop caught sight of us and rushed to the door to greet us with an ebullient, "Hello, my niggerrrrz." He was a fetching young man with pearl-white teeth, ruddy red skin, deep-set brown eyes, thick curly hair, pouty lips, and . . . wait a minute . . . where was I going with this? Oh, yeah, "my niggerrrrz." Anyway, he stopped my friend and me dead in our tracks, and we turned to ask each other, "Did we really come all the way to Egypt for someone to call us niggahs?" It was so unexpected that we just burst out laughing at the improbability of it all. We approached the young man, explained the error of his ways, and we got free tea and snacks for our trouble. Once, at the end of my first teaching day at a school in Saudi Arabia, a student rushed to my desk to ask with great urgency, "Teacherrr, what is the nigger man?" Some years before this, a student in China just point-blank asked me if I was a nigger. Back in the US, black people continue to struggle mightily to be taken seriously as productive members of society, to not be followed by store security, and to not get stopped by traffic police because black men and nice cars are disquieting and oxymoronic in the minds of morons. African Americanism does precious little to mitigate these indignities, and I won't pretend that this term is intended to send an unequivocal message to our white counterparts, letting them know that we are somebody. The whites in my life who matter already know who I am and they need no convincing. Those who do still need proof aren't listening anyway and aren't worth the effort.

Beyond the realms of sports, entertainment, and newsworthy political pieces, black America continues to be terra incognita for the rest of the world and, I might add, for those who really should know better. From 2000 to 2005, I taught for the Indiana University School of Education while completing my course work for my doctorate degree. I was on my way across campus with two of my classmates when one of them asked me, with the most inquisitive tone, "Where did you learn your English?" I was temporarily nonplussed, but I recovered quickly and I said, "I'm an American citizen. I was born and raised right here in Indiana. I attended 12 years of compulsory education in the public school system. I hold a BA, an MA, and an MS degree. Now which part of that story has made you question my language skills. I mean, is it the language or the color of the vessel from which the language flows?" So, please, step back while I stay black, as a self-ascribed Africanism is hardly an effective unguent for the thousand little cuts inflicted over time by other people's stupidity.

ENDNOTES

1   For some additional, thoughtful reading on identity and its related themes, see: Devon Carbado, *Black Men on Race, Gender and Sexuality: A Critical Reader* (New York: New York University Press, 1996).

2   See Mortimer J. Adler and Charles Van Doren, *How to Read a Book* (New York: Simon and Schuster, 1972).

3   For an interesting global, or diasporic, treatment of sexual identity issues, see the creative work of Nigerian-American writer Tope Folarin, *A Particular Kind of Black Man: A Novel* (New York: Simon and Schuster, 2019).

4   See Tim Marr and Fiona English, *Do Not Shake Bridge! Rethinking TESOL in Diverse Global Settings, The Language and the Teacher in a Time of Change* (London: Bloomsbury Academic, 2019).

5   It is fascinating to note how people define their particular struggle(s) and even their chosen, or allotted, physical place within such work. Those who become "expats" are often working from very complicated understandings, definitions, and motivations. See, for example, the powerful book by Randall Robinson, *Quitting America: The Departure of a Black Man from His Native Land* (New York: Plume, 2004).

6   For some authoritative and truly thought-provoking readings regarding the political buildup and fallout surrounding the April 1989 democracy demands in China, see: Rowena Xiaoqing He, *Tiananmen Exiles: Voices of the Struggle for Democracy in China* (New York: Palgrave Macmillan, 2014). See also Louisa Lim, *The People's Republic of Amnesia: Tiananmen Revisited* (Oxford, England: Oxford University Press, 2014).

BIBLIOGRAPHY

Adler, Mortimer A. and Van Doren, Charles. *How to Read a Book*. New York: Simon and Schuster, 1972.
Carbado, Devon. *Black Men on Race, Gender, and Sexuality: A Critical Reader*. New York: New York University Press, 1996.
Marr, Tim and English, Fiona. *Do Not Shake Bridge! Rethinking TESOL in Diverse Global Settings, The Language and the Teacher in a Time of Change*. London, England: Bloomsbury Academic, 2019.
Folarin, Tope. *A Particular Kind of Black Man: A Novel*. New York: Simon and Schuster, 2019.
He, Rowena Xiaoqin. *Tiananmen Exiles: Voices of the Struggle for Democracy in China*. New York: Palgrave Macmillan, 2014.
Lim, Louisa. *The People's Republic of Amnesia: Tiananmen Revisited*. Oxford, England: Oxford University Press, 2014.
Robinson, Randall. *Quitting America: The Departure of a Black Man from His Native Land*. New York: Plume Publishing Company, 2004.

CHAPTER NINETEEN

Ancestral Calling: An Afro-Rican "WandaVision" Novela: A True Barrio Story

Jaime "Shaggy" Flores

Family history, spoken truths can become complicated depending upon who delivers the message and the willingness of the receiver to critically analyze the communication. The truth is contextual and it can evade us as we pursue it. Without full access to information, the truths we hold dear may actually be the view of the world that someone wished to be real. Without knowing it, like in a Marvel television sci-fi TV series, we may be living in someone else's "WandaVision." In the spring of 2021, during the COVID pandemic, I inadvertently discovered information that challenged everything I knew about my origin story. In the end, the ancestors placed something in my life right when I needed it, even though I did not know that it was missing.

In January of 2021, my friend, cultural documentarian and genealogist Melanie Maldonado, wanted to include my family history in a research project that she was conducting. Melanie is a Chi-Rican (Chicago-bred or -born Puerto Rican) with a passion for community work and the recognition and preservation of Afro–Puerto Rican culture. As the founder of PROPA (Puerto Rican Organization for the Performing Arts) and the creator of the International Bomba Conference, Melanie lives and breathes the preservation of Borinquen history. Melanie's work focuses heavily on studying African ancestry and how that ancestry has informed the work and lives of cultural workers, community activists, and artists. This common passion made us fast friends.

Melanie's recent research project and Spring 2021 online video series focused on uncovering the African lineage in the families of three Nuyorican poets and discussing the impact of that history on their individual identities and poetry within the African Diaspora construct. Her research findings would culminate in an online panel discussion with the poets. In preparation, all of the poets, including myself, were asked to provide their family history and to complete one or two of the popular DNA tests available on the market. I chose to take both tests—23andMe and AncestryDNA. I expected to affirm my African ancestry, confirm my family's oral history, and connect with my father's Jewish paternal lineage.

A Tale of Two Pauls

I was born in the early 70s in El Barrio (Spanish Harlem) and raised in the slums of Shaolin (Staten Island), Puerto Rico (Guaynabo and Cupey), and, for the majority of my youth, Springfield, Massachusetts. Similar to many children experiencing their youth in the 80s, my parents' self-indulgence and absence meant that I would teach myself essential life skills; I was a latchkey kid in the very essence of that word. Essential components of this self-education included voraciously consuming history books, music (House, Latin Freestyle, Salsa, Yacht Rock, and Hip-Hop), and nerd pop culture locked behind closed doors.

My parents separated while I was still developing in my mother's womb. The family story is that one day my father, Paul Lopez, left to buy milk and never came back home. As a child, I can recall encountering Paul fewer than 10 times. I only knew him to be my father because my mother told me so. During the few, lucid conversations that I had with Paul, I observed him to be an astute critical thinker with a profound interest in the human condition. Paul has other children, most notably my brother Paulito, who is a few months younger than I. This means that even before he left for milk that day, Paul was involved with someone other than my mother. Paul's physical absence was compounded by an emotional absence—a byproduct of his struggle with a heroin-fueled substance use disorder.

I am the fourth of my mother's five biological children. With the exception of a few short years, my mother was a single parent. Although my siblings, like me, did not have their fathers present in the home, unlike me, they had relationships with their dads. Periodically, gifts and cash would arrive from their fathers' families while I watched their joy empty-handed. Our lives existed where poverty, substance abuse, mental and emotional health disorders, and housing instability collided. These conditions left my siblings and me vulnerable to the whims of our mother's dreams and nightmares.

Everyone in our home was subjected to my mother's physical, emotional, and mental abuse, but I was a particularly vulnerable target. While she was abusive to the others, my familial isolation meant that her violence towards me could be exacted without the potential of recourse or consequence. I was her favorite punching bag. Any household item became a weapon and any action or inaction became a justifiable reason for the bodily harm. In addition to the physical attacks, my mother employed intentional efforts to increase my social isolation by encouraging my siblings to participate in my abuse. Isolated and alone, I became self-reliant at an early age and adopted the belief that my current condition would not limit my future. I was convinced that somewhere, in some universe, someone had made a mistake and placed me with the wrong family.

My first childhood memories were formed in Puerto Rico. I can recall the warmth of the sun, the songs of coquis filling the air, playing with geckos, and walking to kindergarten. Along with these memories, I also recall the horrors of living in the projects in Puerto Rico. There was the danger that lurked and the stench that lingered in the elevators; the spiders and giant roaches that invaded our space as though we were guests in their homes; as well as the occasional dead bodies found hanging from trees or just out in the streets.

In 1979, when my mother and 3 of 5 of her children boarded the plane to move to Springfield, Massachusetts, we believed the opportunities would abound. We would be safe from random violence, free of poverty, and able to live in a beautiful home tucked away in a friendly neighborhood. Quickly, my siblings and I learned that none of our wishes were true. In Springfield we had all of the poverty, violence, and insecurities that we experienced in Puerto Rico, compounded with a language barrier and systemic racism.

My kindergarten curriculum included repeating words in English. Mother, father, and family were the first words we learned. In my six year-old mind, having mastered those words made me a fluent English speaker. My response to all of the questions I encountered in the English language world were "mother, father, family." "Hey kid! What's your name?" My response: "mother, father, family." As you can imagine, this did not always end well.

I was determined to learn English. To teach myself rather quickly, I stopped speaking Spanish and used television as a tool to learn English. Within a short time, I was able to speak and read in English fluently. Books became my friend and my escape. I discovered the neighborhood library and participated in all the children's free activities they hosted. This space allowed me to avoid my mother's fits of anger and improve my academic performance. Places such as the Pine Point and Main Street libraries became my own personal educational oases.

Historically, Springfield was/is a city of migrants and immigrants—Italian, Portuguese, French Canadian, Greek, and Irish immigrants, and African-American Southern migrants to be precise. Politics, neighborhoods, educational opportunities, and socializing fell neatly along these tribal lines. In the late 70s, Puerto Ricans began to move to the city in significant numbers. Simultaneously, white families—and Black families with means—began to abandon the city for the surrounding suburbs. Previously well-groomed, grand Victorian homes and neighborhoods started to deteriorate. House fires reached epidemic proportions due to negligence or intentional efforts. The "City of Homes" was entering decline. The social and political tensions that arise from limited resources and opportunities permeated the city. This is the Springfield that I came to know in 1979.

In Springfield public schools, the city's social problems were magnified. The majority of students were Black and Brown while the majority of teachers were white. A growing student population spoke English not as their primary language, but as a second language in classes that were severely lacking. Increasingly, the students were experiencing trauma induced by poverty, housing insecurity, and drug abuse, but the schools failed to offer sufficient mental health and social supports to ensure their success.

Without a context to understand the mechanics of poverty and how it was shaping the city and, by extension, my life, I confronted the symptoms of poverty on a regular basis. White teachers questioned my capacity to learn and excel academically. Time and again I was forced to demonstrate that I had actually read the books I said I read or that I had written the essays that I submitted. It was a struggle to gain admittance to advanced classes or to participate in certain extracurricular activities. While I explicitly addressed the constraints that white teachers and administrators placed upon me, the more pervasive influencer of my academic success remained largely unseen—lack of familial support and an abusive home environment.

In my mother's "WandaVision" world, Springfield was perfect and she wasted little time enticing the people she wanted to populate her fantasy to come to the city. She spun tales of abundant jobs, affordable housing, and Puerto Rican–centered social supports. Over time, she was successful in attracting my father, my sister's father, and members of their extended families to move to Springfield. At some point or another, most of the connected Springfield transplants lived with us. My grandmother Carmen was one of the people who relocated to Springfield.

Carmen was my father's mother. When she relocated to Springfield from New York City, she brought her children and her grandchildren (my siblings), too. This move provided me with an opportunity to develop relationships with my aunt, my uncles, my cousins, and my grandmother. My grandmother lived in close proximity to us when she was in Springfield. She and my cousins gave me an actual family where I felt loved and included. They did not shun me and, with the exception of my aunt and one of my uncles, they did not adopt my mother's abusive stance toward me. My grandmother's house became somewhere I could go to escape my mother's beatings. While there, I also learned about my family history.

My father Paul was named after his father. According to my grandmother, Paul's father was named Paul Schiff. She described Paul Schiff as a middle-class, hardworking Jewish textile merchant from New York. My grandmother met him while working as a maid for his family. Because she was Puerto Rican and they were of Jewish faith, my father was told that he could never receive their last name. My father's existence was a secret and only two people from the Schiff family knew of his existence—his namesake, Paul Schiff, and his grandmother, Frida.

The country entered into the Second World War just after my father's birth. My grandmother was rushed to Puerto Rico, along with her one-year-old child, to hide his existence. After the War, Carmen returned to New York with her son. He was reconnected with his father. The two would have regular visits at the senior Paul's office.

Carmen married another man and the senior Paul married another woman, but Carmen continued to receive monthly financial support for her son. The family story recalls that as my father grew into his teenage years and developed some bravado, he became tired of meeting his father in private. He demanded to be recognized and to carry his father's last name. After an afternoon of shopping and at lunch, Paul asked his father for his last name. Paul Schiff reiterated that this was not possible. My father overturned the lunch table full of food and told the senior Paul that he would never see him again.

Carmen continued to receive monthly financial support for five more years following this incident. Paul never saw his father again and he developed a deep distrust of Jewish people. He felt as though he was disposable to the Schiff family. This sense of abandonment may have fueled his future drug use.

Prior to his death, I was able to speak with my father about his experiences. He provided me with very specific names, addresses, and dates when it came to his father. In pursuit of the genealogical research I was conducting with Melanie, I pieced together my family's oral history, my mother's research, and historical documentation to identify Paul's father as Paul Felix Warburg. The Schiffs and Warburgs were the closest thing to Jewish aristocracy that we have in this country! The family owned banks, railroads, textiles, and much more. Paul Felix Warburg's mother was named Frida (*née* Schiff). She was one of the wealthiest socialites in Manhattan history. She donated her mansion and it eventually became The Jewish Museum of New York City.

Paul, my father, was denied his birthright and, like me, he was dealt a life far crueler than what he deserved. I sat with this knowledge as I grew up, knowing that perhaps the ancestors were keeping me alive and surviving my circumstances to do more with my life. That I had ancestors who had accomplished great things, and that perhaps my mother knew this and responded to my father's abandonment by inflicting physical harm upon me, was revealing.

Who's Gonna Take the Weight

In 1992 I graduated high school and, through the Bilingual Collegiate Program, a special program created to improve racial parity in state colleges and universities, I found myself studying at the University of Massachusetts at Amherst. I am the only one of my mother's children to graduate high school and I was the first to attend a four-year college. With a few dollars in my pocket, a few outfits in my bag, and without any financial or emotional support from my mother, in 1993 I began my lifelong dream of escaping the world she created.

On my first day on campus, I nearly died when I discovered that the dining commons had an "all you can eat" policy. As someone who knew poverty and hunger, often standing with my mother in long lines at open food pantries, the whole university felt unreal. It would take almost 7 years, intermittently taking time off as a full-time student to attend to emotional or financial barriers that presented themselves, before I completed my undergraduate degree in 2000.

At UMass I began in-depth exploration into African Diaspora studies. I had the privilege to study under scholars such as Sonia Nieto, Manuel Frau, John Bracey, Martin Espada, William Strickland, Agustin Lao, and Carlene Edie. My cultural work also allowed me to become a mentee of Nuyorican poet and scholar Louis Reyes Rivera.[1] My cultural studies were not limited to the classroom. I believe in activating academic endeavors. As a student, I helped establish the Puerto Rican Student Organization; began my involvement with Black and Latino Greek life; resurrected the Black Student Union; resurrected the famed DRUM journal, then renamed NOMMO; and started a Zulu Nation chapter in Western Massachusetts.

I always had a gift for writing stories, but it was at the university, under challenge of the false narratives about Puerto Rican identity being perpetuated by students from the island, that I began writing to ensure that my experiences and the experiences of those like me were on the record. UMass in the 90s was a hotbed of student political activism and, in many ways, part of the 90s Latino cultural renaissance that was occurring on campuses throughout the country. These studies and my activism would culminate in my becoming a founder of the largest African Diaspora concert in the five-college community, *Voices for the Voiceless*. For 13 years, *Voices* would host some of the most respected Black, Latino, Native American, and Asian American poets from across the nation. The evening would close with the distribution of the Louis Reyes Rivera award, given to persons who used their art to empower local communities.

I realized that my formal education had roots in the world my mother created. Although the men in my mother's life suffered from substance use disorders, they were educated men. None of them finished college, but they were passionate about their intellectual pursuits. As young men, all of them were community organizers fighting for Puerto Rican rights. Inadvertently, these men taught me history and helped to cultivate my deep reverence for the work of my Black and Puerto Rican ancestors.[2]

Racially, these men, my first history teachers, emphasized to my siblings and me that we were not only Puerto Rican, but also Black.[3] We were an Afro-Taino people, eating African food, listening to African-based music, moving like African people but speaking Spanish or more often Spanglish. These lessons were etched into my memory. In Springfield, I lived in the same neighborhoods, attended the same schools, fought in the same street rumbles against white racist kids as did my Black brothers, sisters, and aunties. Also, we spent days at each other's housing units. We did not see each other as separate entities.

The 90s at UMASS was not the current Black Lives Matter movement we see today. Back then, it was not cool to be Black and even rarer for Blaxk Puerto Ricans to claim their Black identity; but my upbringing taught me who and what I was. This meant that, even though I was less melanated, most likely due to Paul's Jewish ancestry, I was still Black in all of its manifestations. This identity did not make me popular amongst the *mestizaje* crowd in our community who did not accept their Black identity. The work of scholars such as Arturo Schomburg, Dr. Antonia Pantoja, Juan Flores, and Marta Moreno Vega influenced me to use history to challenge these false perceptions.

After I obtained my degree in African Diaspora Studies, I married my wife La'Keisha (a respected health-care activist and scholar in her own right) and moved to the Washington, DC metro area. There, I began work as a communications and marketing professional committed to organizing and addressing disparities in civil and human rights. I was fortunate to receive professional mentoring from David Santiago and Ida Castro, community organizing icons in New York and DC. I also worked under respected labor leader Oscar Sanchez at the Labor Council for Latin American Advancement and eventually my work was recognized/praised by AFL-CIO executive Linda Chavez Thompson. In addition to my daytime work, I also published two books, appeared in national poetry slams, and lectured at colleges and universities around the country. My personal and professional life dovetailed to reflect my passion for history and sensibilities about injustice and abuse.

In 2008, I obtained my Master's in History, with a concentration in Afro-Caribbean History and Culture, from Virginia State University. My thesis, *Breaking Beats Creating Cultural Revolutions*, reflected my research on the formation of Hip-Hop culture before 1979. It was presented at the Puerto Rican Studies Conference.

This that Maury "That Baby Ain't Yours" Section

So, in January of 2021, when Melanie contacted me for her genealogy project, I thought I was ready to learn more about my past. I had transitioned from a past that included abuse, fear, and insecurity into my role as husband, father, author, executive, and community activist. I was the proud father of two beautiful girls, Orixa and Lelolai, and understood the importance of creating special family moments and being there for your children. The physical and emotional distance from my childhood would allow me to understand how my family story shaped the person I became. While we waited for the DNA results, my wife and I began to create my family tree on Ancestry.com. We were able to match the addresses Paul, my father, mentioned to me with the business address associated with the Schiffs and the Warburgs. We confirmed that Paul Warburg used both last names in his business dealings.

In a book titled *The Warburgs*, we discovered that there was a clause in Paul Warburg's father's will stipulating that if any of his children married or had children outside of the Jewish faith, they would lose access to their inheritance. All of these years my father believed that his family discarded him randomly, not knowing that his father risked a lot by having a relationship with him and his mother. We also noticed that the time when my father stopped receiving monthly support payments aligned with the deaths of both his father and grandmother. The two people in the family who knew of my father's existence passed away and my father was denied his birthright. The irony is that when my father died, he was one of the last heirs of Paul Felix Warburg still living. I truly wished that he were still alive to discover these historical truths. My hope was that when the DNA results arrived, I would verify my African ancestry as well as my Jewish ancestry.

When I finally received my highly anticipated results from 23andMe, my African, Native American, and European ancestry was present as expected. But my Jewish ancestry was missing. This was startling. Were the results wrong? Did they have the wrong person? In place of my expected Jewish ancestry was an unexpected half-sister living in North Carolina. What?!? I thought I knew all of my brothers and sisters. There was never anyone from North Carolina. Was this a mistake? Paul was a rolling stone, as the Temptations would sing, but he claimed all of his children. This one in North Carolina was a mystery. Neither my mother nor my siblings ever mentioned her. I reached out to the woman through email, not expecting to receive a response.

The absence of Jewish ancestry in my DNA results meant one of three things:

(1) Paul and my grandmother recalled his origin story incorrectly. I strongly disputed this scenario because I knew my abuela Carmen to be many things, but a liar was not one of them.
(2) Paul's father was not Jewish. Perhaps Carmen was involved with a friend of the Warburg family and not a Warburg. This scenario was questionable as well because Paul was named after his father and his resemblance to the family was uncanny.
(3) Paul was not my father, and my mother had lied to me about my origins. I was stunned that this could be possible. I picked up the phone, called my sister Tania, and had her relay the newly found information to our mother. My mother vehemently denied that anyone other than Paul could be my father.

A few days passed and I received a response to my message from my newly found half-sister. I told her my story, how I found her, and that perhaps we shared the same father. She stated with certainty that her father's name was John and he lived in Florida. She was positive that Paul was not her father. She described a man that is a free spirit who lived a fast, hippie life and toured with the Grateful Dead family and the Carnival circuit in the 70s and 90s. She sent me photos of John and they sent chills down my back. The photos of John in his early 30s and 40s looked exactly like me. It was like looking at a clone of myself. She believed that John had five children, but she could not be certain because he was involved with a lot of women. A few days later, we connected again and she mentioned that John would like to speak to me, but he was not open to taking a DNA test.

I spent the next few days in a fog. Paul was probably not my father, my mother had lied, and a man named John living in Daytona was my father! Perhaps 23andMe was wrong and the AncestryDNA results would be clearer. Perhaps the AncestryDNA tests would show the Jewish ancestry and dispel what the half-sister told me. I was confused, but knew that speaking to John would be the beginning of answering my questions.

We on an Award Tour

John Sanchez is an interesting man who has lived a carefree life. A lightly melanated brown man with long flowing hair, he can appear to be Middle Eastern or Native American. John traveled the world and ran his own business. A proprietor of one of the most respected smoke and T-Shirt stores on the Daytona strip, his name is synonymous with Daytona Bike Week. Thousands make an annual pilgrimage to his store, which is dedicated to the Rock and Harley Davidson lifestyles. Only at his store can enthusiasts purchase the limited-edition Grateful Dead brand items that he and his brother Manny created. He is an avid biker who, even in his late 70s, still rides a Harley Davidson motorcycle on long trips with his local Latin American bike club.

A Vietnam vet, John was one of the few Puerto Ricans to serve on his ship in the BT Division during the late 60s and early 70s. He served his time, but left the military because of the racism he encountered. He hired a lawyer and threatened to sue the military because he was exposed to uranium-filled shell casings and was not provided protection for his ears. He received an honorable discharge.

Following his discharge, John became one of the first Puerto Ricans to enter a prestigious Wall Street training program/school. With his wife at the time, John was raising a son named John Jr. and working hard to move quickly through the Wall Street program. He completed the program while simultaneously enrolled in Bronx Community College. Before he could become a broker, the firm that sponsored him let him know that as a Puerto Rican he could never hold the position to which he aspired.

Motivated in part by his experience at a Grateful Dead concert, John took the money he collected from his side hustle as a popular marijuana dealer serving city college students, quit the Wall Street job, and walked away from everything. He decided that he would no longer work for anyone but himself. He recruited his brother Manny, divorced his wife, packed his things, and began a 20-year journey touring the country and riding his Harley, performing some stints internationally. His travels took him to England, France, Germany, and even Thailand, where he lived for several years. In Thailand, he created the largest Harley Davidson rally in that country. By the time John opened his store in Daytona, he had created a mystique in the biker community. In Daytona, John and his "Daytona Indian," a large Native American wooden carving that stands in front of his store, are a mainstay of Daytona Bike Week.

On the day we spoke, John acknowledged that he could be my father, but he was not certain. Age and his past promiscuity blurred the names of the many women he met in the 70s. John said that my mother's name was vaguely familiar and my father's name sounded like someone he knew in the Bronx. In hindsight, my mother would have had the opportunity to meet John at one of his parties in 1972. It is also likely that Paul strongly suspected that I was not his son.

John and I talked a few more times over the next few days. He provided more details about his life, including other children he had. He believed that there were probably 6 of us in total, but he could not be sure. He shared his regret that he did not have a good rapport with any of them. After much discussion, John agreed to take the DNA tests, 23andMe and AncestryDNA, to close this chapter in his life. He knew that, at his age, he might not get another chance to meet or know about all his children and grandchildren, so the test would be a way to start that process. I paid for both tests and walked him through the first one through a video call.

As we waited for John's results, I was still hesitant to acknowledge that perhaps he was my father. My mother did not recall him and was adamant that Paul was my father. Even though I was the only one of Paul's children that did not have his last name and that he abandoned, my mother still denied that anyone else could be my father. My mother and I had a strained relationship, but I needed answers and she was not willing or able to provide them. The lack of Jewish ancestry in my results and the half-sister in North Carolina gave me the gut feeling that the truth I was seeking was staring me in the face.

The impact that Black fathers have on their children is a much-researched topic. Frequently, the discussion does not continue to include the psychological turmoil (PTSD) that is created for children when their father is not a presence in their lives. On one hand, my willingness to fight against the childhood abuse caused by my mother inspired me to do better. That past informs my poetry and my community activism. But it also left gaping wounds that this ancestry research exposed. My siblings and I were isolated from my mother's family. They had their fathers, but I had none. As a result, I felt disconnected from my family history and lacking an appreciation of where I came from. Ancestry is extremely important in the African Diaspora. Such a lack of familial connections can be devastating to a child.

Our People Once Had Mana

A month after I received the 23andMe results, the AncestryDNA results arrived. The ping from the phone app woke me up and informed me that the results were processed. My DNA not only matched what 23andMe showed, but it also showed that I had another half-sister. This half-sister resided in Pennsylvania and, as I had done with the other half-sister, I proceeded to send this one an email. Two days later she responded and, just like the first, she mentioned that her father was a man named "John" whom her mother met on the Carnival circuit. Unfortunately, she had been told by her mother, who had since passed away, that John was dead. This half-sister had been trying for years to learn more about him. I informed her that I was genetically her brother and that her father was still alive and living in Florida. After a flurry of emails and phone calls, she was able to connect with John a few days later. During that time, we also connected with another half-sister living in Germany.

I found myself talking to John every day and learning more about the similar traits we shared, as well as and his love for and desire to learn more about Puerto Rican history. My two stateside siblings and I decided to visit John in Florida over the Memorial Day weekend. John has an annual block party on Memorial Day in support of his local business association. He asked me to DJ the event.

A few weeks passed and we all met for the first time at the Hard Rock Café. To the backdrop of a concert featuring Latin Freestyle artists from the 90s, we shot selfies, talked about our families, and laughed over stories from John and his adventures. Although John was not without his flaws, the three of us were grateful that we were able to meet and to know that we had a shared lineage. Before leaving Daytona, I interviewed John and helped him to take the second DNA test from AncestryDNA.

While I was in Daytona, John's 23andMe results arrived. The results listed him as my father. It also linked him to my half-sister from North Carolina. At that time, it became conclusive: he was my father. The ancestors connected us at a time when I could help him to develop relationships with his children and he could help me connect to my family history.

Surviving Africanisms

That Memorial Day weekend closed with my web discussion with Melanie. Broadcasting from the back of the store owned by the father she helped me to find, we discussed my ancestral journey. For her Nuyorican Poets episode, Melanie focused on the side of my family who resided in Cupey, Trujillo Alto Y Bajo, and San Juan. Through researching the archives, she discovered that my ancestors, prior to the abolition of slavery in Puerto Rico, were categorized racially as Black and were members/influencers of the oldest Black free town in Puerto Rico. The area of San Juan from Santurce to Cupey was known as San Mateo De Cangrejos. This area had been a hotbed of free Black activity and abolitionist gatherings. Not only that, but my DNA results showed that I was also related to many of the same Puerto Rican scholars I had met early in life, including Melanie! Wow! That ancestral calling, that "Black identity that was previously misunderstood" lore, was proven to be true and was perhaps another reason why I had a disposition to preserve and advocate for the Black and Puerto Rican communities.

In his work, the late scholar Sterling Stuckey spoke of Surviving Africanisms and how the Trans-Atlantic slave trade did not completely erase our traditions or cultures. Our black ancestors were able to not only persevere through, but also to preserve those things, that essence which made them what they were. Our "Soul" from the ancestors speaks through their descendants! In the 90s, most in the Nuyorican community knew me as an Urban Griot, an Afro-Taino, lightly melanated storyteller who was part of a lineage of Afro-diasporic poets of different complexion who played an important role in archiving our history. That Melanie's research would further solidify that I had an ancestral predisposition to this work was not only surprising, but helpful to answering questions about what drives me as an activist and someone who loves history and culture.

In the late 90s, I was initiated into the IFA faith by my aunt (my sister's biological aunt). My aunt, Ifalade (Jenny Curbelo), and her husband, Ogun Ogodemi (Rudolfo Curbelo), were highly respected *Santeros* (priests) on the island of Puerto Rico. As some of the old-school generation of Santeros, Ifa practitioners, whose lineage goes all the way back to Cuba and their Madrina (Godmother), Mercedes Nobles, I was initiated into the ways of my ancestors by hands I trusted. My *titi* (aunt) would often sit me as a child growing up in her *ile orisha* (saints' holy room) and tell me Pataki, Orisha origin stories dating back thousands of years ago in what is known today as Nigeria. I was often drawn to that room when I lived in Puerto Rico, not just to steal the candy and food left for the saints, but because I felt a familial spirit, a calmness in that space. Titi would often tell me "Our religion, our spirituality, is one of the stone, and one that predates the others. These Pataki go far back into Africa and they are yours to preserve and remember. They are your roots, never forget your heritage."

Years later, after meeting my father and learning more about my ancestors in Puerto Rico, I would remember the teachings of my *titi* and thank whatever ancestors and *orishas* guided me in my journey of discovery. I believe the ancestors are always calling; we just have to be willing and ready to listen when they do. *Punto.*

Three-Card Monte at the Georgia 12/6/20 Debate

for Truth Thomas, Tony Medina, Carlos Ramos, and Hector Perez

Repeating
Radical
Right-wing
Robots
Reminiscing
Of Making
America Great Again

Of Making
Segregation divide again
Of Making
Lynchings entertainment again
Of Making
Affordable Healthcare a myth again
Of Making
Whiteness popular again
Of Making
Black lives not matter again
Of Making
Farm workers field slaves again
Of Making
Asians be excluded again
Of Making
Native Americans extinct and reserved again
Of Making
Women not have a voice/a right again
Of Making
Immigrants criminals again
Of Making
Overseers hunt again
Of Making
Education a privilege again
Of Making
The Melanated be on Display in zoo's again
Of Making
Freedoms a dream again
Of Making
Heaven's Gate, NXVIM, Cults, Scientology,
Poverty Prosperity Ministries profitable again
Of Making
Repeating
Radical
Right-wing
Robots
Rule the earth
Again
And
Again

And
Again
And
Again
And
Again...
Punto.

Lessons Learned from Don Gabino, the Local Wino on Bay Street Poem #15

for La'Keisha, Orixa, Lelolai, and Melanie M.

There
Are no such things
As Policemen
In the inner-city
Only Overseers
Whether
They are Foe
Or friend
Abuser or Savior
Is dependent
On your
Tax bracket
Punto.

ENDNOTES

1   See Fernando E.E. Correa Gonzalez, *The Emergence of a New Identity: The Nuyorican Afro-Boricua as Presented in Selected Works by Poets Louis Reyes Rivera and Jaime "Shaggy" Flores.* (Mayaguez, PR: University of Puerto Rico Mayaguez, 2020).
2   See, for example, Urayoán Noel, *In Visible Movement: Nuyorican Poetry from the Sixties to Slam* (New York: Contemporary North American, 2014).
3   While seemingly new to some, this idea and reality have been advanced by some Puerto Ricans for decades and can be found in rich, canonical texts such as the classic autobiographical novel written by former New York–based author Piri Thomas, *Down These Mean Streets* (New York: Knopf Doubleday Publishing Group, 1974).

BIBLIOGRAPHY

Correa Gonzalez, Fernando E.E. *The Emergence of a New Identity: The Nuyorican Afro-Boricua as Presented in Selected Works by Poets Louis Reyes Rivera and Jaime "Shaggy" Flores*. Mayaguez, PR: University of Puerto Rico Mayaguez, 2020.

Noel, Urayoán. *In Visible Movement: Nuyorican Poetry from the Sixties to Slam*. New York: Contemporary North American, 2014.

Sartre, Jean-Paul. *The Anti-Semite and the Jew: An Exploration of the Etiology of Hate*. New York: Schocken Books, 1948.

Thomas, Piri. *Down These Mean Streets*. New York: Knopf Doubleday Publishing Group, 1974.

CHAPTER TWENTY
Becoming Lazarus

Lazarus Louis Baptiste

"The Pledge"

I was born Louis Handral Jean-Baptiste, and unless you speak French, you just butchered my name. To say "Louis Handral Jean-Baptiste" just right, you have to put a piece of candy in your mouth, to weigh your tongue down just right so your French can flow as sweet as the Merovingian cursing in *The Matrix Reloaded*. I've often found my name a bit pretentious, the kind of name Anne Rice would give to a tall, lanky, golden-locked, French aristocrat vampire. I am the opposite of that. I am short, bald and dark-skinned enough to have been called "Crispy Critter," "African Booty Scratcher," and "Darkness" at different stages of my life, and though I'm known as "The Nightographer," I don't suck blood.

I was born in Port-au-Prince, Haiti, on January 9th, 1970, nine pounds and twelve ounces of chocolate with an Afro. My mother, Esther Milord, named me "Louis" because it was her father's name. Louis Milord, also known as "Papa Louis," was a legend of a man—a farmer, a businessman, a great friend to many, a philanthropist, a three-term congressman, a husband (once), a father (at least 22 times), and my mother's lifelong hero. As I'm sure you've surmised when you read "at least 22 times," my granddad was a rake who raked more than the fields of coffee, cacao, and yam on his farms. Unlike most Lotharios on a quest to populate the earth, Papa Louis took care of his kids. Louis started having kids as soon as possible and by the time he had his first baby girl in September of 1932, my mom was his fourth child. Two years later, Louis Milord married Louise Belizaire, affectionately known as "Loulouze." Loulouze would, with her husband, raise her children alongside his children from outside of their marriage, with no discrimination. My Mom became the Lil' Mama of the bunch, and the bond between her, Loulouze, and her father's other children was unbreakable. Mom and Loulouze loved each other so much that, when she moved to New York to seek opportunity and a better life for herself and me, Mom entrusted my care to Loulouze and her sister Maa Ca (also known as Josephine). I was three months old.

I lived with Loulouze and Maa Ca till I was three. To this day Maa Ca, now 102, delights in telling me little stories themed always on how fat and ravenous a baby I was, how smart a child I was, and how much everyone loved me. Writing these words now reminds me just how fortunate I am. I cannot remember a time when I wasn't told I was smart. How different would my life have been if I had never, or only seldom, heard those words? To be frank, being told you're smart and believing it can also be a little tricky to navigate. In understanding the unusual family structure in which my mother was raised, I can see why she was such a giver, a caretaker, and the most compassionately selfless person I ever met.

The Boarding House

Between my third and fourth birthdays, I moved to a boarding house in one of those historic Haitian gingerbread-style houses in the Bois Verna section of Port-au-Prince. Many of my fondest, earliest memories of Haiti are from my time there.

I remember watching the older boys making *cerf-volant* kites with five skinned twigs, a clear plastic bag, some string, and a bit of shredded fabric for the tail. The skies were full of *cerf-volants*, all different sizes and colors, humming overhead like tiny biplanes doing battle. These kites would be considered "Welfare Kites" by American standards, but, to us, they were the very best anywhere. Some mornings the kids and I were organized into hunting parties. Whatever chickens we could catch, we could eat. The chickens could see the posse of kids coming round the bend and they knew we weren't there to play catch-and-release. Even when we tried to "head them off at the pass," we had no chance against the big, juicy, Usain Bolt chickens. We ate a lot of the slow scrawny ones. I remember sneaking into the kitchen daily and stealing a handful of rock salt that I would hide in my right pants pocket. Throughout the day I would pop a piece in my mouth and enjoy the taste and feel of the salt melting on my tongue. I had convinced myself that rock salt for me was what spinach was for Popeye.

I had many highlights during my time at that boarding house, but my worst memory was the Cherry Tree incident. A group of us were tasked with picking cherries from the cherry tree in the yard. We were ecstatic! Picking cherries meant that the staff would be making cherry confiture the next day. There was a little girl in our group whose limbs were too short to reach the branches. In a show of gallantry, I got her a broom stick and lowered a branch for her to take a swing. With one swing, Mighty Mouse knocked out four of my teeth. There was blood and Chiclets everywhere! It took a couple of years for my teeth to come in and when they did, they were adult-sized in a mouth full of baby teeth. Two sets of braces and four veneers later, I still have an overbite. And, unfortunately, I was one of those kids who wet the bed long after most other kids had stopped. I wonder if the sound of boarding school kids singing "pisannit, pisannit, pisannit" will be as traumatic when, in the not-too-distant future, in my second childhood, I start wetting the bed again?

My best memories by far were of the times my father would steal over to see me. As a result of the complicated circumstances of my birth, and through no fault of his own, my father and I spent very little time together. He had no right to pick me up at the boarding house, but my godmother Tati Julia could. Every Saturday morning, my father Napoleon Aubourg, would pick up my godmother and drive to the boarding house to get me. While at the boarding house I had to pretend he was my godfather, and as soon as I got in the car and we drove off, I could call him "Papi" again. We then dropped my godmother back at her house and my father and I would go to his house in Petion Ville. At his house, I would have fun, learn, and play with my sisters Judith and Meredith and my baby brother Alain. Dad was a smoker and one afternoon, I watched him throw a cigarette butt on the floor and stomp it out. I tried to pick it up and that butt burned me right on the tip of my finger. I never told anyone, but I still have that burn mark today. Every Sunday evening, we reenacted Saturday morning in reverse.

Those years at the boarding house were some of the happiest of my childhood. I didn't know I was in a "Third World country" or in "the poorest country in the Western Hemisphere".[1] My life was simple, structured, stable, and wonderful. There were no material luxuries of any kind. We made our own toys with our hands and our imaginations. We learned, we studied, we grew and somehow we understood that, although our parents were somewhere else, they for sure loved us. Wherever they were, they loved us enough to work, and to send money for us to be educated, fed, happy, and together.

Proper French Education

By 1974, what had become in vogue among the Haitian Diaspora in the United States with kids in Haiti was the idea of their children getting a "proper" French education. The diaspora didn't think much of the American educational system, so they would only have their kids come to the United States during summer vacation where they would hopefully pick up a little English.[2] In step with the new fashion, and much to my father's chagrin, my mother removed me from the boarding house in Haiti and sent me to be "properly" educated at a boarding school run by nuns in Montreal, Canada. While I lived in Canada, my Tati Rene was my primary caregiver.[3] Just as I had lived in the boarding house in Haiti, I also lived at the boarding school in Canada during the week, and on the weekends Tati Rene and I would spend time together.

I remember all of us pretending to sleep after our nightly prayers and lights out. We would have to stay super quiet for about 30 minutes till the nuns fell asleep. Once they did, we started partying "up in here, up in here" like a bunch of wet Mogwai. I hated the cold, but I loved everything about snow—playing in snow, snowball fights, making snowmen, making snow angels, eating snow, and learning the secret formula for yellow snow. Best Canada memory by far? Seeing indigenous Canadians, or "Indians from the cowboys and Indians" movies, as I innocently referred to them at the time, on horseback riding through the streets. From that day on, I didn't want to be a cowboy anymore. The "Indians" were more relatable. I had never seen a cowboy in real life anyway, so they could kick rocks.

For financial and other unfortunate reasons, my "proper" French education only lasted about nine months.[4] Even though she worked three jobs, my mother could not afford to keep me in Canada.

Proper Haitian Education

When I returned to Haiti I was about five, and the plan was to get me the best education available in Haiti. A dollar went a lot further in Port-au-Prince than it did in Montreal. I was quickly enrolled at the dopest, most happening kindergarten in all of Port-au-Prince, the Jardin Fleuri (flower garden) de Yolaine. I moved in with Tati Daniella, Tati Carmen, their mother Memere, and my cousin Lesly. Lesly was about six years older than I. I loved being back home in my warm little country. "Haiti Cherie" playing on the radio meant so much more. I missed snow terribly, but that's about it. Commuting to school every day was unusual. At both boarding houses, school was always downstairs from where the other kids and I slept. The bond I shared with the other "Princes of Maine and Kings of New England" was gone, and I had to get used to living in a house with only one other kid. The house was quiet, unless my cousin and I were laughing; no other children were.

School was my element and I thrived at Yolaine's. The classrooms were basic but clean, with rows of neatly positioned two-person wooden desks with connected benches. I remember the red and yellow swing set where kids waited their turn to get queasy. I remember the little yard where we would play tag, the smiles on the faces of the teachers, and the shrill sound of the whistle that would signal the end of recess. I have a few pictures of my time at that school, and they get me every time. I was the mayor of that little garden of flowers. Come Christmastime I played Joseph in the televised Christmas Pageant, and the year I graduated I was valedictorian.

After being graduated from Yolaine's, I had two options to consider for an all-in-one primary and secondary school: College Roger Anglade and Institution Saint-Louis de Gonzague. I took the entrance exam at College Roger Anglade and, based on my results, they decided that I would skip a grade. After that evaluation, I never bothered to take the exam at Saint Louis. One less year of school was an offer I couldn't refuse. Frankly, I never quite understood how I could have done so well on that exam. I remember being terrified because, for reasons I couldn't understand, I didn't remember which way the number three was supposed to face. I guess I guessed right.

College Roger Anglade was often abbreviated CRA, and those letters were stitched into the left pocket of the light grey uniform shirt or blouse all the students wore. In 1980, we would joke that CRA stood for Carter, Reagan, Anderson, the three US presidential candidates that year. The school system in Haiti was completely different from that in the States. The grading and how they handled report cards seemed specifically designed to create competition between the students. At the end of each marking period every student's grade-point average and ranking first of 20, second of 20 etc., was posted in the classroom for all to see. I still remember all of us crowding around the ordinance to see who was who. The top five students were always vying for supremacy, and nobody wanted to be in last place or bringing up the rear. Academics in CRA was a Game of Thrones and feelings were not spared. If you were in the top five, you were royalty; if you were in the bottom five, you were a court jester; six to ten, you were nobility. Everyone else was a commoner.

Weekday mornings, Tati Carmen and I would take a Tap Tap taxi bus that would wind its way through what seemed to me like every single street in Port-au-Prince to pick up every other person and finally let us off right in front of Anglade's green gate. On the other side of that green gate was a courtyard with a long cement staircase. At the bottom of the staircase were two statues, one on either side, of Greek women. We would take a lot of our class pictures in front of that staircase flanked by the two peculiar Greeks.

During my years growing up in Haiti, I understood my schooling to be my job. My singular responsibility was to get good grades. Good grades meant that you could get a good job; a good job meant that you would have money and influence; money and influence meant that you made it. "Making it" meant that you could leave the country if you wanted to and see the world.

Moon Landing

Setting foot on the tarmac at John F. Kennedy International Airport on July 1, 1981, was my moon landing! Without the money and influence, without the good job, I went from good grades straight to "Made it Ma, top of the world!" I was going to live in New York City and be an actual New Yorker (*You can't tell me nothin'*). To me, New York *was* the United States, or at least its capital. I was eleven then, and even at fifty-one, I still write love poems to the City of New York.

I was finally going to get to know my mother. She wasn't working three jobs anymore; she wasn't living with four other family members in a one-bedroom; she wasn't working in a factory; she was a keypunch operator in an office. She had her own one-bedroom apartment in East Flatbush Brooklyn, between Avenue D and Clarendon Road. She had made it, too!

Up until this point in my life, I saw my mom every two years when she would save enough to have me come and visit her for a month during summer vacation. Every two years, we would try to get to know each other. Every two years, we would leave each other broken-hearted. One month every two years just wasn't enough time together. I asked her if I could stay with her, and she said yes. I had zero idea how much more difficult that decision would make my mother's life.

"The Turn"

The English I had picked up over the summer visits was very Tarzan. I had a big decision to make: Should I go to a bilingual school where I would learn English along with my other studies or should I go full immersion at a normal school and be set back two years because of my lack of English? I chose option two. I didn't want the help of the bilingual school. I was smart. I had skipped a grade anyway, so I was only really losing one year. Effective immediately, I was going to learn English at a breakneck pace, and they were going to give me back my two years. My mother got me the 16-volume *Compton's Precyclopedia* set to get things started and then the 26-volume *Compton's Encyclopedia*. It took my mom a while to pay those books off, but "What my baby wants, my baby gets." I read them all cover-to-cover. To help with my verbal skills I sat in front of the television and parroted everything I heard. During that time in my life, I could hardly discern accents at all. British, Australian, or American, it was all English to me. I stayed true to my word, but I never got back the two years. The system just didn't work that way.

I enrolled at St. Stephen's Lutheran School located just a block away from our apartment, and that September I started the fifth grade. My homeroom teacher was Mr. Chang. Contrary to what you just assumed, Mr. Chang was a kindhearted, smooth-voiced, brown-skinned Caribbean man. All the mothers had a crush on him, including mine. Mr. Chang was Obama before Obama was Obama. The staff at St. Stephen's, with rare exceptions, were pretty awesome. Unfortunately, many of the students were merciless.

School was my thing, but I don't know that it was for my fellow students, at least not in the same way. I was awkward. I didn't get the jokes. I didn't get the culture. I struggled with English. I found out I was a nerd, and for the life of me, I couldn't understand why that wasn't great. I thought I was cute; I found out I was wrong about that, too. In pre–Wesley Snipes America, dark-skinned was not the thing to be. Unfortunately for me, I had a small face with big manga eyes and in 1982 I got the nickname that would stick with me till I left for high school: "E.T." I couldn't tell you how many times kids would point their index finger at me and say "E.T. phone home." I also couldn't tell you why that was so funny for so long.

Things were rough during those years, but they were about to get worse. The horrible HIV-AIDS epidemic was being partly blamed on Haitians. This was the kill shot for so many of us living in the United States and, indeed, all over the world. I thought, I finally got to the top of the world, and it blew right up in my face.

With my living with her now, Mom had to get a second job on the weekends. When I wasn't at school, I was home alone, a bona fide latchkey kid. I quickly went from extrovert to introvert. At St. Stephens, there were a handful of kids who were kind to me, and their kindness kept me sane. My confidence had been shattered, but my self-esteem survived. Through it all, I had one great friend, my buddy Ashmore. We were inseparable in school and after school we were on the phone for hours on end, mostly watching TV together. I was a huge television junkie, with good reason: 80s TV rocks! There was *Battle of the Planets* before school; *He-Man*, *Voltron*, *G.I. Joe*, *Inhumanoids*, *Inspector Gadget*, *Jem and the Holograms*, and *Transformers* after school. *Manimal*, *Street Hawk*, *The Greatest American Hero*, *Bosom Buddies*, *Benny Hill*. And that was just weekdays. TV was my therapy and Ashmore was my therapist.

I was graduated from St. Stephen's in the spring of 1985 and I could not wait to get out of there. Back at home, things had changed, too. Our little duo had become a trio when my grandmother, my mom's mom, came to the US and moved in with us. And we were about to become a quartet. In a stroke of great fortune, my cousin Junior would be moving in that July. As I was losing Ashmore, I was gaining Junior.

What I didn't understand back then was just how opportunity and popular culture affected everything. In Haiti, there were just a few broadly accepted ways to "make it." Most commonly, either you were born into the right family, or you were fortunate enough to get access to a good education—you competed, and you succeeded. Your lineage was up to chance, but the educational system was a meritocracy. A good education was not a common thing and was therefore seen as something to be desired and cherished because it could make a giant difference in the quality of life enjoyed by you and yours. In the United States, there were various ways of achieving a success level not even fathomed in Haiti. You could be a success in comedy, singing, dancing, boxing, basketball, football, movies, and/or television, among many other things, none of which were necessarily related to your GPA. And the American appetite for the latest and greatest continually fed the matrix with new, more disposable talent. In Haitian society there were far fewer has-beens; once you were popular, your fans stuck by you for life. In "Third World" Haiti, getting a good job made you relatively extraordinary; in the "First World" United States of America, not so much. All of this and other factors fundamentally led to the American student rallying cry: "Nerd! Get 'em!"

The Renaissance

I met Junior (also known as "Francisque Milord Junior") while I lived with my aunts in Port-au-Prince. Lesly and I would visit his sister Choumi (also known as Marie-Denise) and him on the weekends. Junior was five years older, so at the time he moved in I was fifteen and he was twenty. He and I were inseparable, like Batman and Robin, and I desperately needed a big brother. Junior got me out of my shell and out of the house. He was a classic alpha male—a barrel-chested, dark-skinned, athletic mesomorph. He was a couple of inches taller than I, supersmart, and the kind of guy you knew nobody ever picked on. He was "my bodyguard" and determined to make a man out of me. No more spending the day sitting in front of the TV. We were broke, so we walked everywhere. It took forty minutes to get to Flatbush Comics and Books. It was a proper comic book store where we would spend a couple of hours rummaging through the rows of issues you couldn't get at the local Te-Amo. A couple of times a year, we would go on a pilgrimage to Forbidden Planet, the legendary science fiction and comic book shop.

The first summer Junior moved in, we walked an hour to Prospect Park just for something to do and ran into a crew playing proper volleyball. Junior was already a damn good player, but I had never played the game. I wasn't allowed to get on the court, but the guys would teach me and let me pass the ball around during their warmups. There were at least three teams each time, so somebody always needed a warmup. Volleyball at Prospect Park became our weekend thing.[5] Every Saturday and Sunday we walked one hour there, had six hours of play, and walked an hour and fifteen back. I had a lot of fun and found that I had some natural athletic talent. An athletic nerd, who'd a thunk it?

I had always been a big fan of martial arts movies. It all started with Bruce Lee when I was in kindergarten; then, when I was television binging, during my St. Stephen's years, it was Drive-in Movie on Saturdays at 3 o'clock on Channel Five. Shaw Brothers Studios changed my life! Junior and I would go to the pre-Disney 42nd Street and buy throwing stars, knives, and ninja slippers. I would ninja-walk all over the house trying to sneak up on people. I would like to officially apologize to all the trees my ninja stars and I traumatized in East Flatbush. I was young, dumb, and didn't know better.

As much as I loved martial arts movies, I couldn't fight. Once again, Junior came to the rescue. He taught me how to handle myself in a street fight. I learned how to make a fist and throw a proper strike. More importantly, he taught me not to fear getting hit. He would have me stand in front of him as he punched me dead in the gut, the solar plexus, and kidney. He said, "Never be afraid of pain; it hurts more when you're scared. If someone hurts you, make him hurt worse!" Later in my youth, my self-defense skills were properly developed when I took classes with Professor Pierre Renee.

Learning to Think

I started at Xaverian in September of 1985. At the time it was a private, all boys, college prep school in the heart of Bay Ridge, Brooklyn. I was the only kid from my class at St. Stephens to go there that year, and that was fine by me. St. Stephen's had only been a block away from my apartment, but to get to Xaverian I had to take two public buses which could take from an hour to an hour and thirty minutes, depending on how the buses were running or whether I caught the connecting bus on time. What all of this meant is that I had to be at the bus stop weekday mornings by six a.m.

I remember arriving at school on the very first day. There to greet us at the bus stop in front of the school's side door was Mr. Murack. Murack was the retired drill-instructor type, the kind of guy that would call a marine "Private Pyle." After exiting the bus, the group of us made our way to the entrance where there were two sets of double doors, one open, the other closed. A bottleneck formed as students waited in line to go through the open doors. "Open the other double doors, you bunch of geniuses! Oh my God!... we got the cream of the crop this year!" Murack exclaimed.

Whereas St. Stephen's had been an all-black-student school, Xaverian was practically an all-white-student school. I imagine there were no more than fifty black students out of the eleven hundred or so in attendance. "Race" aside, a nerd was a nerd. But, fortunately, there were a lot more of us nerds at Xaverian. My particular blend of discrimination—part racism, part nerdism—was more subtle and bearable than the blatant rejection I had endured previously. "Herb, Herb, step aside please" after the Wendy's and Burger King commercials, was the running gag about me. They teased me, but I didn't let it get to me. I didn't care to be a part of their circle; I was going to make my own.

First chance I got, I tried out for the volleyball team and, thanks to my time with Junior and the guys at the park, I made the junior varsity team. Coach Raftery recognized my natural athleticism and quickly set out to Professor X my latent mutant power. Put this kid on a leg intensive workout routine . . . This little froggy can jump. Before long, I could leg press the whole Nautilus machine and calf press the entire rack on that machine, too. By the middle of freshman year, I would rotate in with the varsity team during practices. By sophomore year, I was on the varsity team full time. The track team came after me for both the high jump and the hurdles. The basketball team tried to recruit me, too (did I mention I'm five foot, eight?). I didn't want to play any of those sports, so I declined and stuck with volleyball. It's amazing what a forty-two inch vertical leap can do for your "residual self-image."

Doctor Giordano was my favorite teacher. He taught English and he was completely outside the box. I had him my sophomore year and, just walking into his classroom, he had our attention. There were comic book posters all over the walls! How awesome was that! Once class started, he began "I know that many of you sitting here think I'm fat!" Laughter erupted in the class. He continued: "My goal, gentlemen, is that by the end of our time together you will think I'm corpulent, obese, burly, portly, broad or even rotund. Anything but fat." Game, set, match, Giordano! Dr. G. was the one who introduced me to Sherlock Holmes. I was fascinated with Holmes's ability to solve a murder he had not even witnessed. Critical thinking, attention to detail, and deductive reasoning transformed my mind.

As I mentioned before, Junior was a very smart guy, a "day walker," a rare hybrid with both street and book smarts. I remember his infatuation with Eric Van Lustbader books, Doc Savage, Sun Tzu, Asimov, and others. At a point in our relationship, he set out to motivate, cultivate, and engage my mind. For example: If we watched a movie together, he would ask me what I thought. "I liked it" or "It was all right" or "I didn't like it" were never satisfactory answers. I was expected to explain what I liked, what I didn't like, what plot hole, if any, I found in the story, and how I felt it could have been improved. As I fell into these thought patterns more naturally, the quality and effectiveness of my communication improved dramatically. The quality of the conversations between Junior and me had become more mature and more nuanced. What Junior did for me in the three critical years we lived together was to show me that the quality of my life and the quality of my thoughts were acutely related. I think of the Bible verse, "As a man thinketh in his heart, so is he" (Proverbs 23:7).

If I think of my heart as the innermost part of my mind, then what I allow myself to consider inevitably seeps into its inner chamber and impacts my behavior. When I had allowed myself to consider constantly the abuse and ostracization that I had suffered from my classmates, I had begun to ostracize myself and become a shut-in. Once I no longer gave those thoughts mental space, I was able to make my own safe haven with more like-minded people. Junior set the foundation for a confidence, work ethic, mindset, and will power that have been instrumental in every aspect of my life to this day.

"The Prestige"

The summer of my junior year, Junior moved out. What should have been a sad occasion wasn't. I would miss his presence in the house, but I didn't need it. He knew I was ready to stand on my own two feet, and I did, too.

I wasn't the guy people picked on anymore; everyone knew that I could handle myself in a fight. I was finally comfortable in my skin. As a matter of fact, I became the one who protected other nerds from bullies and became the Pied Piper of underclassmen. I was co-captain of the volleyball team, a fierce hitter from the front and the backline with a patented Vulcan floating serve. I was elected to the Student Coordinating Council, became an editor of *The X-Press*, did original oratory on the speech team, was a founding member of the African American Club, won second place in our Halloween window art competition, got into AP classes, and could straight leg my own pants. I did not realize I had so much to give, but you can only give what you've received. My unsolicited advice, reader, is to get, get as much as you can, so you can give as much as you have. Just like my mentor, I became a reader: (*Flowers for Algernon, Silas Marner, Native Son, Sherlock Holmes and The Hound of the Baskervilles, The Autobiography of Malcolm X*, and anything Anne Rice. I read the book version of any movie I particularly enjoyed: *Nine and a Half Weeks, The Godfather, Platoon,* and *Dangerous Liaisons,* among others. All these books and all these movies were more than just entertainment, they were data: lessons, observations, examples, experiments. I was seeking to acquire wisdom from lifetimes I had not lived.

I did not then nor do I now care to conform to culture. I'd rather be transformed by the renewing of my mind. During my early life, things happened to me and all I did was lament and react. A better way is to foresee, adjust, and respond appropriately. The summer that Junior left, I decided to be the man I would have loved to have had raise me. In the absence of that man, I had to raise myself and become him, my own Franken Father. That man was part King David, part Malcolm X, part Solomon, part Neo, part Apostle Paul, part Francisque Milord Junior, part Napoleon Aubourg, part Forrest Gump, and all me. The particulars of my journey may be unique, but its arc, its essence, is familiar to scores of immigrants, expatriates, and refugees seeking what is advertised to be self-evident and unalienable. That summer, I began my pursuit of happiness and the lifelong quest to come forth as the ultimate manifestation of myself. I called the man I was called to become: "Lazarus."

I was born Louis Handral Jean-Baptiste. Now my name is Lazarus Louis Baptiste, and that suits me just fine.

ENDNOTES

1   See the discussion of Haitian history and the critiques of Haiti's critics offered by Laurent Dubois, *Haiti: The Aftershocks of History* (New York: Metropolitan Books, 2012).

2   For a well-founded and brilliantly conceptualized discussion of the "African Diaspora" and the possible implications of this concept of the Caribbean, the globe, and for "modernity," see Patrick Manning, *African Diaspora: A History Through Culture* (New York: Columbia University Press, 2009).

3   For a broader context of what life in Canada could have offered a person such as me, see Jonathan Vance, *A History of Canadian Culture* (Oxford, England: Oxford University Press, 2009).

4   Haiti's deep cultural connection to France and the powerful implications of its having defeated Napoleon and his imperial rule are matters that run deeply in the Haitian outlook, consciousness and identity. See C.L.R. James, *The Black Jacobins: Toussaint L'Ouverture and the San Domingo Revolution* (New York: Vintage Books, 1989).

5   For an engaging pictorial glimpse and backdrop into the rich history of energetic "youth culture" in Brooklyn, see Larry Racioppo, *Brooklyn Before: Photographs, 1971-1983* (Ithaca, New York: Cornell University Press, 2018).

BIBLIOGRAPHY

Dubois, Laurent. *Haiti: The Aftershocks of History*. New York: Metropolitan Books, 2012.

James, C.L.R. *The Black Jacobins: Toussaint L'Ouverture and the San Domingo Revolution*. New York: Vintage Books, 1989.

Manning, Patrick. *African Diaspora: A History Through Culture*. New York: Columbia University Press, 2009.

Racioppo, Larry. *Brooklyn Before: Photographs, 1971-1983*. Ithaca, New York: Cornell University Press, 2018.

Vance, Jonathan. *A History of Canadian Culture*. Oxford, England: Oxford University Press, 2009.

Afterword

Yohuru Williams

My first encounter with "Mannish Water" came while I was a graduate student at Howard University in Washington, DC. A West Indian friend of mine insisted that we have lunch at a Jamaican Restaurant not too far from campus. We were taking a class in Caribbean History and she and the professor, who was also West Indian, would often engage in repartee about the delights of Caribbean Cuisine. Their verbal jousting would often leave the class not only entertained, but hungry—curious to sample the glorious "Yard food" they boasted loudly about in a mocking, cartoonish vernacular, so familiar to me.

I remember the first wave of West Indian Immigrants that arrived in my hometown of Bridgeport, Connecticut when I was a pre-teen. Like the one mentioned by Jaime "Shaggy" Flores, my community was a tapestry of diverse cultures. The Jamaicans' rich music and culture added to the broad spectrum of blackness and masculinity that defined my youth, embodied by the mumchance proprietor of a large, white bodega that suddenly appeared on the corner of Stratford Avenue, our neighborhood's main thoroughfare. The store was called Jocelyn's—so my friends and I called him "Jocelyn". Entering his domain was like entering another world—one which first presented itself in the odiferous glories of the golden baked pastries that lay warming in a glass case near the front of the store. Soon we were saving our nickels and rushing home from school to purchase the Patties and Coco Bread.

The neighborhood youth and I were often cruel to Jocelyn—the Black immigrant businessman—in the way that children can often be cruel from a lack of understanding. We mocked his speech and his dress, his meekness and his mannerism. We, I now imagine, were a big part of his thickening.

It certainly was not a result of his singularity. Ours was a neighborhood where Black businesses thrived. The Jackson brothers owned two bodegas and a liquor store along Stratford Avenue. There were also Black hairdressers and barbers, restaurant owners and barkeepers. At one point there was even a clothing store, an ice cream Parlor, and a Record shop—all black owned or Latin (Puerto-Rican) owned and patronized by the hodgepodge of teachers, factory workers, civil servants, doctors, nurses, and domestics who, along with the more familiar pimps, drug pushers, and addicts, made up our community.

Our story, as my father told us many times, was James Baldwin's story, Amiri Baraka's story, Muhammad Ali's story, and Charlie Parker's story; to survive, like them, we had to become bad motherfuckers.

Taroue W. Brooks describes this as a key ingredient in the process of becoming a "Black Man"—the hardening that is necessary to weather the challenges of being Black in America. Over the years, I witnessed a hardening in Jocelyn's eyes, which, at the time, I misread as bitterness. It was what I now would characterize as a bitter acceptance.

Through adolescent eyes, it seemed that whatever Jocelyn had come to the United States in general, and Bridgeport in particular, to pursue had somehow eluded him. As our city and community slowly disintegrated in the late 1980s, pulled apart by a combination of urban renewal, deindustrialization, and the raging crack epidemic, I imagined that everyone felt as trapped in our six-block universe, *sans* the tunnel and the train, as Ntozake Shange found Harlem to be: condemned to faded dreams shattered on broken city blocks.

I nevertheless admired his resilience. I did even moreso one afternoon as I watched him tutoring his son at a little table near the back of the store. The meekness that we had known was nowhere to be found that day. He seemed to be a cruel taskmaster, barking instructions to the boy who, while complying, looked wistfully off in the distance.

I can only imagine what his son was thinking. I imagine I shared the same thoughts about my own father, the teacher and musician. He both awakened, nourished, and ultimately crushed my interest in music with a similar style of instruction. He taught my siblings and me African History and African drums, but killed my desire to "play" music by making it work. We needed to practice long hours, we needed to focus, good was never good enough, we needed to be two times better, youth was wasted on dreaming, we needed to learn how to be men, to practice like men, to play like men, to be professional like men, to act like men.

I held a grudge against him for nearly a year once, because he made us miss the season finale of our favorite television show—after an especially rocky performance. We practiced for five hours that night, and, in an age before VCRs and streaming services, this guaranteed that we would never know how the season ended.

I can't even remember now what the show was, but I remember the power and the importance of the seasoning he put us through. What I never applied toward becoming a musician became the blueprint and foundation for me to achieve in other areas. The journey contained in it, however, the bitter stew of another type of Mannish Water, delivered raw and unfiltered, through the experiences of the men in my life, especially my father. Wounds produce narratives—both of sadness and of joy, of triumph and of loss.

Like the pasture of youth terminating in a cliff described in J.D. Salinger's *Catcher in the Rye*, I saw the men in my community as catchers, returned from their own plunge to guide and protect us from the inevitable encounter with the barriers imposed by life and racial injustice. In this regard, the men in my community fell into three broad categories: the Totems, the Anansi, and the Griots. Each had a story and a talent to share. The Totems, represented by the pimps, pushers, and addicts, the jaw jerkers and hustlers, testified silently—through the witness of their despair—to the not-so-hidden dangers lurking in the field. The Anansi, the professionals and teachers, business leaders, and preachers, like the protagonist in Afro-Caribbean folklore, modeled strength and wisdom, and the key to success for navigating, if not totally overcoming, those challenges. Finally, there were the Griots—the artists and musicians, poets and theoreticians who narrated their stories, with a dash of flavor from their own lives. They offered a cup of hearty life stew, filled to the brim with the accumulated experience of the elders and a path to much more than just survival, namely, enlightenment.

The contents of the unique ingredients of one's serving, of course, were invariably influenced by remnants of portions shared out by those who did the serving.

The ingredients from my father's portion—the free flowing and creative spirit of Jazz embodied in the musical stylings of his hero Charlie Parker, tempered by the teachings of Black thinkers and intellectuals such as James Baldwin, Marcus Garvey, and Malcolm X—eventually found their way into my soup: an epigenic record of the struggle of being a black man in America expressed not only in terms of what food I put in my body, but the very genetic code of my body itself. Taroue W. Brooks writes that "God speaks to us all," but rightfully acknowledges that those messages land differently according to how our bodies and minds are attuned, and according to who did the tuning. Some, like Jaime "Shaggy" Flores, realize this in time enough to ask for the recipe—the recipe that is not only expressed in markers of our genetic code, but also in the worlds in which they were made.

* * *

Walking into the restaurant in DC, my friend counseled me about what I should order. "Have you ever had Mannish Water?" she teased, at the same time providing a vivid description of its components, preparation, and supposed medicinal benefits. "It will put some hair on your chest," a patron standing behind us joked as he witnessed my skittish reaction to the ingredients—goat's head and belly mixed with yams, green banana, taro root and other "delights." "That's why they call it Mannish," he explained. I laughed nervously and ordered a cup.

As we sat down, it felt like all eyes were on me as I lifted the cup for my first taste. Before I could register my reaction, I felt a distinct warmth—much stronger than the tepid liquid traveling down my throat. It was an outpouring of warmth and camaraderie delivered in English, Spanglish, and Patois by the diverse group of strangers and brothers who shared space with us that day. Some laughed, several congratulated me loudly, and one patted me firmly on my back. Tasting the soup was a rite of passage that invited both the warmth of other suns—represented by the many shades of Black present in the small restaurant that afternoon— and the warmth of other *sons*, the unspoken acknowledgment of having taken another step in the diasporic journey toward becoming a man.

This is the unifying theme of this volume.

In the brewing of Mannish Water, nothing is wasted. Mannish Water is composed of remnants, or "offal"—but I want to be clear to distinguish between remnants and waste. Western Society often celebrates indigenous peoples for thrift in using every part of the creatures they slaughter. I believe this backward. Instead of making use of "wasted things," they found value in all parts, and in all experiences.

The thrift masks the utility, creativity, knowledge, and skill of the preparer—and the lesson such an experience holds for the consumer. There is, of course, a price. The first sip of Mannish Water can be bitter, but if one endures the discomfort and vulnerability of the sampling, the hopes of the miraculous gifts it promises to bestow—health, vitality, virility—are evident in its lesser advertised benefits: knowledge and experience.

The stories, or truths, that the scholars have shared in this volume are both a celebration and affirmation of the accumulated knowledge and experience of Black Scholarly men. The personal is indeed the political. It is also spiritual. From these personal testimonies emerge themes of faith, spiritual awakening, and the overcoming of obstacles. A reflection of goodness abounds in this volume, affirming not only the human instinct toward survival, but also the strong desire to give back.

Epilogue

By their very nature, autoethnographic essays provide subjective insights by challenging writers to investigate and reflect upon the interior spaces of their lives, and to connect those lives to broader contexts: past, present, future, and recurring.

The mission in the Mannish Water anthology project was, in some respects, simple: to have Black, scholarly men in 21st century America to tell their truths. As the editors, we (Femi and Carlton), provided general guidelines, explicitly inviting the essayists to speak out on childhood, youth, dreams, pain, love, struggle and life, in general, in America. In short, we craved forays into epistemology and ontology. We asked the writers to bring the world into greater knowledge of their existence in America, including the meaning that the essayists perceived as attached to their own lives.

Significantly, we did not know what was going to be returned to us. We remain grateful, however, that we trusted the process. These brave men returned true slices of life in America, veritable glimpses – soil samples, as it were – into the complicated journeys of men who were "raced" and raised as Black.

In Mannish Water, four generations of Black men remind us that life in America has been, in summary, "no crystal stair". Serving as almost the hype men for Tricia Rose's new book (Metaracism: How Systemic Racism Devastates Black Lives – and How We Break Free), these men bear witness to the knock-on, compounding, and often confounding, effects of the "race" function in America. The essayists in Mannish Water at the same time boldly center their own perspectives, experiences and interpretations, irrespective of the labels and attitudes that exterior persons and systems direct at or project upon them.

Consequently, the voices that ultimately emerge in Mannish Water dynamically converge and diverge, mirroring fantastically (literally fantastically) the outside world, and refusing in each moment to be muzzled, muted or silenced.

We, the editors, are all the more grateful that we, from the very start, provided these varied men a tremendous amount of berth for the sharing of their contextualized life stories. As the individual essays were returned to us, we explored the pages in appreciation, awe, and surprise -- in much the same way, perhaps, as you have done.

We heartily thank Peniel and Yohuru for their eloquent framing of this ambitious project. We also thank you, of course, for reading the lives of the Mannish Water men, whom we thank, but profoundly, for the sharing.

~Carlton and Femi

About the Authors

Carlton Long. Co-editor of the *Mannish Water* anthology, Carlton Long is a former Rhodes Scholar whose graduate research at Oxford University focused on the reification and social construction of "race" as well as the application of "affirmative action" (US) and "positive action" (UK) principles in the development of supplementary educational programs and schools in the communities of Brixton (South London) and Harlem (New York). Dr. Long received his undergraduate degree from Columbia University, where he later taught political science and was a Chamberlain Fellow and a multi-year nominee for the Mark Van Doren Teaching Award. He received a D.Min. degree from the Morehouse School of Religion, Interdenominational Theological Center (ITC), in Atlanta, Georgia, and was subsequently certified to preach within the Baptist polity. Aside from having taught at Columbia University, at London University (Goldsmiths College), and in a wide variety of college, university, and K-12 enrichment programs, he worked as an international and national staff developer, executive vice-president and CEO in the world of professional staff development. For over a decade, he has focused on enhancing honors programs within a wide range of private and state colleges and universities in the United States, including the brokering of opportunities for students at Yale University and Oxford University. Carlton Long was also an Associate Professor, Dean of the Graduate College and Director of the Freddye T. Davy Honors College at Hampton University. With his wife, Monique, he has also prepared generations of college students to embrace the "Leadership Creation Process," their unique model for pursuing prestigious scholarships and fellowships (Rhodes, Marshall, Fulbright, Schwarzman and more) with a view to becoming effective global leaders grounded in community-mindedness, service and grace.

Olufemi Vaughan. Co-editor of the *Mannish Water* anthology, Olufemi ("Femi") Vaughan was raised in Ibadan, Nigeria and received his D.Phil. in politics from Oxford University. A 2022 Guggenheim Fellow, Dr. Vaughan is also the Alfred Sargent Lee & Mary Farley Ames Lee Professor and Chair of Black Studies at Amherst College. Vaughan's scholarship interrogates major themes in African studies, notably, state–society relations in Africa, religion and state formation in Africa, and globalization and migration in Africa. He is the author of four books and editor/co-editor of eleven other volumes, including *Religion and the Making of Nigeria* (Duke University Press, 2016), *Nigerian Chiefs: Traditional Power in Modern Politics* (Rochester Press, 2000), and *Oxford Encyclopedia of African Historiography: Methods and Sources* (editor-in-chief, Thomas Spear; Oxford Press, 2019),; winner of the Nigerian Studies Association Prize; winner of the Cecil Currey Prize (Association of Global Studies); winner of the Waldo Leland Prize (American Historical Association). Professor Vaughan is also the author of about eighty scholarly articles and reviews. Aside from the current Guggenheim award, his research has been supported by a Woodrow Wilson Fellowship and a Ford Foundation Fellowship. Vaughan was Professor of Africana Studies & History at Stony Brook University and the Geoffrey Canada Professor of Africana Studies & History at Bowdoin College.

Peniel Joseph. Dr. Peniel Joseph authored the foreword to the *Mannish Water* anthology. He holds a joint professorship appointment at the LBJ School of Public Affairs and the History Department in the College of Liberal Arts at The University of Texas at Austin. He is also the founding director of the LBJ School's Center for the Study of Race and Democracy (CSRD). His career focus has been on "Black Power Studies," which encompasses interdisciplinary fields such as Africana studies, law and society, women's and ethnic studies, and political science.

Prior to joining the UT faculty, Dr. Joseph was a professor at Tufts University, where he founded the school's Center for the Study of Race and Democracy to promote engaged research and scholarship focused on the ways issues of race and democracy affect people's lives.

In addition to being a frequent commentator on issues of race, democracy, and civil rights, Dr. Joseph's most recent book is The Sword and the Shield: The Revolutionary Lives of Malcolm X and Martin Luther King, Jr. He also wrote the award-winning books *Waiting 'Til the Midnight Hour: A Narrative History of Black Power in America* and *Dark Days, Bright Nights: From Black Power to Barack Obama*. His book *Stokely: A Life* has been called the definitive biography of Stokely Carmichael, the man who popularized the phrase "black power." Included among Joseph's other book credits is the editing of *The Black Power Movement: Rethinking the Civil Rights-Black Power Era* and Neighborhood Rebels: Black Power at the Local Level.

Yohuru Williams. Dr. Yohuru Williams penned the afterword to the *Mannish Water* anthology. He is Distinguished University Chair and Professor of History, as well as the Founding Director of the Racial Justice Initiative, at the University of St. Thomas, in St. Paul, Minnesota. He received his PhD from Howard University in 1998 and is the author of: *Black Politics/White Power: Civil Rights, Black Power, and Black Panthers in New Haven* (Blackwell, 2006); *Rethinking the Black*

Freedom Movement (Routledge, 2015); and *Teaching Beyond the Textbook: Six Investigative Strategies* (Corwin Press, 2008).

He is the editor of *A Constant Struggle: African-American History from 1865 to the Present, Documents and Essays* (Kendall Hunt, 2002) and is co-editor of *The Black Panthers: Portraits of an Unfinished Revolution* (Nation Books, 2016); *In Search of the Black Panther Party: New Perspectives on a Revolutionary Movement* (Duke University Pess, 2006); and *Liberated Territory: Toward a Local History of the Black Panther Party* (Duke University Press, 2008).

Dr. Williams also served as general editor for the Association for the Study of African American Life and History's 2002 and 2003 Black History Month publications, *The Color Line Revisited* (Tapestry Press, 2002) and *The Souls of Black Folk: Centennial Reflections* (Africa World Press, 2003). He served as an advisor on the popular civil rights reader, *Putting the Movement Back into Teaching Civil Rights.*

Dr. Yohuru Williams has appeared on a variety of local and national television programs, most notably on ABC, CNN, MSNBC, Aljazeera America, BET, CSPAN, EBRU Today, Fox Business News, Fresh Outlook, HuffPost Live, and NPR. He was featured in the Ken Burns PBS Documentary "Jackie Robinson" and the Stanley Nelson PBS Documentary "The Black Panthers." Williams is also one of the hosts of the History Channel's Web show "Sound Smart." A regular commentator on the Cliff Kelly Show on WVON, Chicago, Dr. Williams also blogs regularly for the Huffington Post and is a contributor to *The Progressive Magazine.*

His scholarly articles have appeared in the American Bar Association's *Insights on Law and Society*, The Organization of American Historians Magazine of History, *The Black Scholar, The Journal of Black Studies, Pennsylvania History, Delaware History, The Journal of Civil and Human Rights,* and *The Black History Bulletin.*

Dr. Williams is presently completing a new book, titled *In the Shadow of the Whipping Post: Lynching, Capital Punishment, and Jim Crow Justice in Delaware 1865-1965,* under contract with Cambridge University Press.

Darryl W. Aaron. Rev. Dr. Darryl Warren Aaron teaches at Wake Forest Divinity School and is the Pastor of the historic Providence Baptist Church in Greensboro, North Carolina, an institution established over 150 years ago by formerly enslaved Africans. His B.A. degree in Dramatic Literature is from North Carolina Central University; his Master of Divinity degree is from the Samuel Dewitt Proctor School of Theology at Virginia Union University; and his Doctor of Ministry degree is from Drew University. He has served as a guest lecturer and preacher at many universities, including as an ISGAP Fellow at Oxford University, and has participated in a broad variety of mission trips to Africa, Israel, and Romania. The Rev. Dr. Aaron belongs to many civic organizations and serves on several important public and private sector boards in the State of North Carolina.

Lazarus Louis Baptiste. "The Nightographer," Lazarus Louis Baptiste is an internationally acclaimed celebrity makeup artist and beauty brand ambassador turned world-class cityscape photographer. He has declared: "Makeup taught me to previsualize and photography taught me to see." Lazarus is a specialist in super high resolution panoramic night cityscapes, and he prints BIG. His image of the New York skyline, "Twilight Light," featured in Vienna, Austria, is a world-record contender for the largest exhibition quality print ever mounted and framed in one piece. "Twilight Light" was printed by Stefan Fiedler at an astounding 8.2 x 31.8 feet with a resolution of 1200 dpi. His other works have been presented by Chromaluxe at Photokina in Cologne, Germany, at a more modest 4 x 8 feet. Lazarus was born in Port-au-Prince, Haiti and immigrated to Brooklyn, New York at age 11. He notes: "I started makeup in 1994 and photography in '96. For a while, I did both but when I was offered the opportunity to co-design the Philippe Prive' cosmetics line, I chose to focus on makeup and put my Minolta away." Once Lazarus did everything he wanted to do in makeup, it was time to pick up the camera again. Lazarus' first project, "NYCANDI," is a 7-year photographic love poem to the city of New York. He has taken on the moniker "The Nightographer" because of his love of night photography and the unique challenges it presents. Lazarus lists Fan Ho, Gordon Parks, William Klein, Brassai, Hugh Bell, and Ansel Adams among his photography heroes.

Danny Black. Dr. Daniel Omotosho Black is the author of several critically acclaimed novels published by St. Martin's Publishers, including *They Tell Me of a Home*; *Listen to the Lambs*; *The Coming*; and *Twelve Gates to the City*, amongst others. As an undergraduate honors student and English major, Black received a full scholarship to Clark College (now Clark Atlanta University). He subsequently was awarded the Oxford Modern British Studies Scholarship to study at Oxford University. After graduating magna cum laude from Clark College, Black was granted a full graduate fellowship to Temple University, where famed poet and writer Sonia Sanchez was one of his dissertation advisers and where he earned a PhD in African-American Studies. Dr. Black is currently a tenured associate professor at Clark Atlanta University (CAU), his undergraduate alma mater.

Taroue W. Brooks. Taroue W. Brooks is a dynamic communications and marketing professional, executive producer, event planner, and lifestyle architect. Whether representing a high-profile client or planning a presidential event, he is a modern-day Renaissance man. Brooks has a proven track record delivering results that leaves an indelible impression on all who encounter him. Brooks currently serves on the boards for Social Change and Stillman College. He is passionate about human rights, educational issues, and supporting future generations. Brooks has recently channeled his vast experience to create "What About Me," a documentary that allows the world to see what black men think and feel about how they are viewed in America.

Askia Davis. Dr. Askia Davis is a social entrepreneur, executive volunteer, and co-founder of the Executive Service Network of Nigeria, which is focused on enhancing the organizational capacity and impact of social development enterprises and institutions in Nigeria through the deployment of tens of thousands of volunteers who are active and retired professionals. A trailblazing leader with significant accomplishments in transforming educational institutions and outcomes in the USA, he received his doctorate from Columbia University and has served as an educational consultant and policy consultant nationally and internationally. Dr. Davis is an inspirational speaker and master of executive leadership training, strategic planning, team building, organization development, and proposal development/writing.

Jaime "Shaggy" Flores. Mr. Jaime "Shaggy" Flores is a Nuyorican poet, writer, and African Diaspora scholar who forms part of the Nuyorical literary movement. Born and raised in Spanish Harlem, New York City, as well as in Puerto Rico and Springfield, Massachusetts, he received his primary and secondary education in Puerto Rico and in Massachusetts. As a child, growing up in Robinson Gardens Housing Projects, he was heavily exposed to the work of the early Nuyorican poets, his mother being a poet herself. Later, in junior high and high school, he showed a proficiency for writing and for creating short stories that depicted the Puerto Rican experience. He graduated from the High School of Commerce and eventually met a recruiter from the University of Massachusetts Amherst's Bilingual Collegiate Program, who helped him continue his studies. An active spoken word artist and extensively published poet, he also studied at Virginia State University. During the early nineties, he was heavily involved with student politics at the University of Massachusetts, resurrecting old student organizations and creating new ones in the process. It was during this period that his work as a Nuyorican poet became known and he began to find "elder" Nuyorican poets who could serve as mentors.

Hank Grimes. Milburn Earl ("Hank") Grimes received the moniker "Hank" at age four from his grandfather, whose last name was "Hankins." Born and raised in Indianapolis, Indiana, Hank has traveled the world extensively and is currently a semi-retired EFL teacher and program administrator. His undergraduate and graduate degrees are from Indiana University, Bloomington, Indiana. His skills and expertise include foreign languages (Spanish, Mandarin, and Hijazi Arabic), Excel, and Data Analysis and Visualization, as well as "pretty much anything I set my mind to mastering." He was voted most popular teacher two years in a row (2007/2008) by the student governance of the Academic Bridge Program under the auspices of the Qatar Foundation for Education, Science, and Community Development. His hobbies include traveling, reading, foreign languages, statistics, critical thinking, and studying MS Office Production Suite.

James Henry Harris. James Henry Harris is distinguished Professor of Preaching and Senior Research Scholar in Religion and Humanities at Virginia Union University and Pastor of Second Baptist Church, Idlewood Avenue, both in Richmond, Virginia.

Thomas M. Jackson. Thomas Matthew ("Thom") Jackson is an American educational entrepreneur. CEO and Owner of EdisonLearning, he has an extensive background in issues of educational access, equity, and rights. He received his undergraduate degree in Political Science at DePauw University in Greencastle, Indiana, with an emphasis on economics and international relations. He then proceeded to receive his Juris Doctor degree from the University of Cincinnati College of Law. Jackson initially joined EdisonLearning as General Counsel, and later assumed the role of Chief Operating and Legal Officer. Prior to his leadership at EdisonLearning, Jackson served as Chief Regulatory Counsel for Prudential Financial.

Norm J. Jones. Dr. Norm J. Jones is a productive organization development professional and higher education administrator with prior professional experience in K-12 public school administration. He received his PhD in Workforce Education and Development (emphasis in Organization Development) from Pennsylvania State University in 2011. He received a Masters in Public Administration from Pennsylvania, and his undergraduate degree from Morehouse College, where he majored in English with an emphasis in Linguistics. Dr. Norm J. Jones aspires to the development of a theory- and application-based approach to leadership development, institutional diversity, change management, and organization development work. He possesses strong research interests in male student-of-color access and achievement; systems thinking among senior leaders; and executive/leadership development and change management.

Jason Scott Manuel. Jason Manuel was born in Jersey City, New Jersey in 1971. He was born the only son to Lauren Delores Manuel, a long-time educator in the local public school system, who instilled in him a deep love of his Christian faith, multidisciplinary learning, and the arts. Following his collegiate fine art and business studies, Jason first took interest working in the burgeoning nightclub culture of Manhattan in the 80's and 90's, during one of the most prolific and pivotal cultural periods in the history of New York City and beyond. Jason was exposed to an amalgam of new trends and rising talents across technology, fashion, music, culinary, and other art forms, which would eventually echo globally. There, at a young age, Jason became a nightlife personality and eventually worked in management of some of New York City's most celebrated establishments and entertainment industry events. Eventually, Jason brought his business and management prowess into corporate culture, where he would achieve senior management positions across several industries for Fortune 100 and 500 companies. During this phase of his experience and tenure, Jason would play key roles in transitioning legacy organizations to future-forward operational models; in helping major educational publishers produce educational programs to redefine the traditional meaning of literacy across the United States; in operationalizing cutting-edge methods to optimize healthcare in leading BioPharma organizations; and more. Having developed a love of food culture in his youth, Jason would also have the privilege extended to him to hold business development and leadership roles in the culinary and lifestyle sectors, working on projects with culinary luminaries such as Jacques Pepin, Julia Child, Anthony Bourdain, and Anne Willen. Jason is also a published food writer in his home state of New Jersey. Desiring to combine the inspirations of his faith with his passion for the arts and education, in 2008, Jason founded the faith-based lifestyle brand ANOTHEN.com, for which he serves as President.

Tony Medina. Tony Medina is the author/editor of 24 award-winning books for adults and young people, the most recent of which are *Che Che Colé; Death, With Occasional Smiling; Thirteen Ways of Looking at a Black Boy; I Am Alfonso Jones; Resisting Arrest: Poems to Stretch the Sky;* and the recent poetry chapbook, *Breathing in the Ruins* (Floodgate/Stay Thirsty, 2022). Medina's poetry, fiction, and essays appear in over 100 anthologies and literary journals, including *Revising the Elegy in the Black Lives Matter Era; Show Us Your Papers; Carving Our Rights; African American Poetry: 250 Years of Struggle & Song; The Future of Black; Where We Stand;* and *Obsidian's* "Heirloom: Preserving HBCU Futures" (issue 47.2). Medina's *I and I, Bob Marley* audiobook, narrated by actor Jaime Lincoln Smith and produced by Live Oak Media, received the 2022 Audie Award in the Young Listeners category. The first Professor of Creative Writing at Howard University, Medina holds a master's and PhD from Binghamton University, SUNY. His poetry collection *Serious Trouble* and his anthology *Everywhere Drums: Poetry from the Black Arts to Black Lives Matter* are forthcoming from Third World Press. Medina has presented his work all over the United States, as well as in Germany, France, Poland, the Bahamas, Puerto Rico, and the Netherlands.

Oral Moses. Born in South Carolina, Professor Oral Moses began his singing career as a member of the United States Seventh Army Soldiers Chorus in Heidelberg, Germany and as a member of the famed Fisk Jubilee Singers while attending Fisk University following his military career. As a T. J. Watson Fellow, he studied in Germany and Austria and, upon his return to the United States, he earned a Masters of Music and a Doctorate of Musical Arts Degree in Vocal Performance and Opera from the University of Michigan. A scholar of music and a bass-baritone, Dr. Moses performs regularly throughout the United States and Europe, singing oratorio and recitals with special emphases on Negro Spirituals and Art Song repertoire by African-American composers. In 1986, as a recipient of a National Endowment for the Humanities Grant, he co-authored a book titled *Feel The Spirit—Studies in Nineteenth Century Afro-American Music*, published by Greenwood Press. He is a contributing author in both the third edition of *Notable Black American Women* and the second edition of *Notable Black American Men*, published by Gale Press. He is a frequent guest lecturer and clinician for Gospel and Spiritual music workshops and conferences. Dr. Moses has had numerous successes in oratorio and opera, performing major roles in *Le Nozze di Figaro*, *Regina*, *La Bohème*, *Albert Herring*, *Treemonisha*, *Rigoletto*, and *Die Zauberflöte*, among many others. Symphonic engagements have included works with the Nashville Symphony, the Jackson Symphony, the Detroit Symphony, the Lansing Symphony, the Tacoma Symphony, and the Atlanta Symphony.

Hugh Price. Hugh Bernard Price, civil rights activist and past president of the National Urban League, was born in 1941 into a middle-class home in Washington, DC. He began his schooling in a segregated elementary school and graduated from an integrated high school. His parents, Charlotte Schuster and Kline Price, were involved in the early litigation that would lead to the historic and groundbreaking *Brown v. Board of Education* decision of 1954. Mr. Price graduated with a BA from Amherst College in 1963 and married Marilyn Lloyd that same year. He entered law school at Yale University, graduating in 1966. Mr. Price has been an advocate for the urban poor for decades. In 1977, he moved to New York City, where he was hired as an editorial writer for *The New York Times*. His editorials focused primarily on issues concerning race and poverty. In 1982, Price became the senior vice-president and director of production for WNET-TV in New York City. Six years later, in 1988, he became vice-president of the Rockefeller Foundation, which funded projects to better the communities and lives of disadvantaged people. His experience at the Rockefeller Foundation led the National Urban

League to recruit him as president. In 1994, when Price became president and CEO of the National Urban League, he quickly began to play a crucial role in revitalizing the League, making it, once again, a leading organization in social justice activism. Until Price's presidency, the National Urban League had focused primarily on preparing rural African Americans for life in the cities. Recognizing that the Great Migration of southern blacks to northern cities was over, Price reoriented the goals of the organization. He focused on three principal initiatives: education and youth development programs; economic empowerment; and inclusionary programs. These initiatives, in turn, promoted the League's new priority, addressing intergenerational urban poverty and aiding the urban underclass.

Rodney J. Reynolds. Magazine publisher Rodney J. Reynolds was born in Cleveland, Ohio. He attended the University of Cincinnati, where he studied graphic design and advertising. Reynolds undertook his first publishing venture with a national, general purpose publication targeted toward African American men, *Spectrum Magazine*.

In 1992, Reynolds and *Corporate Cleveland Magazine* developed *Minority Business*, a quarterly publication where he served as publisher and editor. He went on to publish *New Visions* and *Renaissance Magazine*. He also developed *Today*, a magazine that focused on African American families. Reynolds founded RJR Communications, Inc. in 1992. In 1995, Reynolds, along with Forbes, Inc., began publishing *American Legacy Magazine*, which centers on African American history and culture. In February of 2001, RJR Communications and New Millennium Studios, founded by entertainer Timothy Reid, launched American Legacy Television, a nationally syndicated television program. Reynolds has served on the board of directors for the Mount Vernon Public Library, the Young Men's Christian Association (YMCA) of Central and Northern Westchester, the Harriet Tubman Home, and the Rye Country Day School. He was appointed as the diversity chairperson for the New York Blood Center–Westchester Region. In addition, Reynolds is a member of Kappa Alpha Psi Fraternity, Inc. In 1998, Reynolds received the "Forty Under 40 Award" from *The Network Journal*. In addition, Delta Sigma Theta Sorority, Inc. honored his work with the Lillian Award. He received the Percy E. Sutton Award from the Harlem Business Alliance; the Visionary Award from the African American Men of Westchester; the National Business Leader of the Year Award from the African American Chamber of Commerce of Westchester and Rockland County; and the 2002 Triangle of Service Award from the Southeast Regional African American Preservation Alliance. In 2004, Reynolds received the inaugural Earl G. Graves Entrepreneurial Award; and in 2005 he was the recipient of the W.O. Walker Community Excellence Award.

Austin L. Scott. Dr. Austin L. Scott is an experienced missionary, entrepreneur, and human services professional with a demonstrated history of working in the education, international development, workforce development, and healthcare industries. Salutatorian of his graduating class at Livingstone College, where he majored in Elementary Education, Dr. Scott believes that, per the Booker T. Washington tradition, knowledge ought to lead to action, unity, and racial uplift. Author of various academic books and articles, Dr. Scott received a Master of Arts, with a focus on Liberal Studies, from the University of North Carolina at Wilmington. He received the Doctor of Arts Degree from Harrison-Middleton University, with a special focus on Great Books in the Western Tradition. A chess champion, experienced classroom teacher, and certified nursing/health/residence counselor, Dr. Scott has devoted much of his time to educating young people, many of whom have been at-risk teenagers. He has also worked with the aged and infirm. Trained in theology, teaching, public speaking, career counseling, workforce development, and cross-cultural relationship building, Dr. Scott seeks to apply the Gospel of Christ to his everyday work and service. He has participated in Christian missions in diverse areas around the world, including in Europe, Central America, and West Africa.

F. Keith Slaughter. Keith Slaughter is a graduate of Tuskegee University with a B.S. in History (1991) and master's studies in Counseling and Student Development (1992), an honors graduate of the Morehouse School of Religion/The ITC with a Master of Divinity in the Psychology of Religion/Pastoral Care and minor work in Homiletics (2003); he earned the Doctor of Theology degree in Pastoral Counseling from the ITC (2009). He has served as a chaplain and counselor for many troubled souls and, as a clinically trained helping professional, in the capacity of pastoral psychotherapist and pastoral counselor. He holds the rank of assistant professor at the Interdenominational Theological Center in the Psychology of Religion/Pastoral Care department and has worked as a researcher at the ITC's Institute for Faith-Health Leadership. Dr. Slaughter was the founding Faculty Chair of the Master of Pastoral Studies Program at American Baptist College in Nashville, Tennessee (2010-12), and is the former President-Dean of Morehouse School of Religion at the ITC (2012-2016). He is Senior Servant of the BeLOVEd CommUNITY Development Corporation. Dr. Slaughter is former host of "The Movement" radio show on CBS Radio (WAOK-Atlanta) (2015-2020) and currently hosts "The Movement Raw & Uncut" podcast. He is the author of the monograph *Therapeutic Dimensions of Black Preaching* (2009) and several published essays and articles. He lives in Atlanta with his wife, Arnetta. They are parents of four adult children.

Vernon G. Smith. State Representative Dr. Vernon G. Smith became a member of the Indiana House of Representatives in the 1990s and represents Indiana House District 14 at the Statehouse in Indianapolis. Prior to his election to the Indiana House of Representatives, Smith had served on the Gary City Council since 1972. Dr. Smith is currently a professor of education at Indiana University Northwest (IUN), where he has won every teaching award offered on the Northwest Campus. He has served as the interim dean of IUN's School of Education. Representative Smith serves as a ranking minority member of the Education Committee. He is also a member of the Judiciary Committee and the Local Government Committee. Smith's professional background also includes experience at several public schools in Gary. He was the principal of Williams School from 1985 to 1992, principal of Nobel School from 1978 to 1985, and assistant principal of Ivanhoe School from 1972 to 1978. Smith taught in Gary Public Schools between 1966 and 1971. He graduated from Froebel High School; earned his bachelor of science, master of science, and doctorate in education degrees from Indiana University; and has undertaken post-doctoral work at Indiana University and Purdue University. Smith serves as a deacon and a Sunday School teacher at New Hope Missionary Baptist Church. He is the author of multiple refereed journal articles and several books, including *Against All Odds; The Power of the Tongue*; and *Creating Excellence: Becoming an A+ School*. He is the recipient of more than 200 awards and citations. Smith has served in a wide range of civic and community leadership positions, including: founder and board president of the African-American Achievers Youth Corps, Inc.; past chair of the Indiana Commission on the Social Status of Black Males, which was created through a bill he authored in the state legislature; founder and chair of the Gary City–Wide Festival Committee; founder and president of I.U. Dons, Inc.; founder and member of the Northern Indiana Association of Black School Educators; founder and sponsor of the Vernon Stars; national chair of the African-American Male National Council; sponsor of the Annual Spirit of Christmas Dinner on Christmas Day for the needy, homeless, and lonely; and sponsor of the Annual Harvest Feast, which feeds the less fortunate during the Thanksgiving season. Smith is a member of the Indiana University Alumni Association and is a life member of the NAACP. He has been involved in the work of the Omega Psi Phi Fraternity; the Faculty Colloquium on Excellence in Teaching; International Council of Professors of Educational Leadership; the Gary Reading Council/Indiana State Reading Association; the Indiana Association of School Principals; Phi Delta Kappa; Katie Hall Educational Foundation; African American Achievers Youth Corps, Inc; I.U. Dons, Inc.; Brothers' Keeper shelter for homeless men; the Indiana Commission on the Social Status of Black Males; and Handgun Control, Inc.

Shannon Travis. A former reporter for CNN, Shannon Travis is the Emmy-winning founder and CEO of Higher Glyphs Content Group, a Washington DC–based firm specializing in Marketing, Strategic Communications, Brand Management, Content Creation, and Corporate Solutions. In four years, Travis has grown the company from startup to $1 million annual revenue. As Chief Executive, he is responsible for meeting revised revenue targets and overall budget management; expanding the company's client base; reducing customer acquisition costs; finding and managing resources and talent; and maintaining the company's high visibility by serving as chief spokesman. Among his responsibilities as Chief Creative Officer are creating and managing original content; safeguarding clients' brand identity and corporate reputation; leading brand equity building campaigns; overseeing the creative vision for individual client brands; and devising and executing creative and media campaigns that ultimately attract and engage desired audiences. Travis relies on 20+ years of experience to also make deals toward strategic partnerships and to brainstorm new products, services, and customized solutions. Higher Glyphs clients come from sports, entertainment, music, finance, private corporations, nonprofits, and government and professional staffing organizations, among others. Under Travis' direction, Higher Glyphs led a rebranding campaign for AARP's employee resource groups that serve its 10,000+ members.

Cecil J. Williams. Cecil J. Williams is an American photographer, publisher, author, and investor best known for his photography documenting the Civil Rights Movement in South Carolina, beginning in the 1950s.

Mr. Williams began his career at an early age, photographing weddings and family parties. He studied at Claflin University, in Orangeburg, South Carolina, while also serving as a photographer for the university.

His photography has been published in hundreds of books, newspapers, and television documentaries. His work has also been exhibited in galleries in the Southeastern United States. The Cecil Williams South Carolina Civil Rights Museum in his hometown of Orangeburg, South Carolina features hundreds of his civil rights photographs, including the famous image of his drinking from a "Whites Only" water fountain in the Jim Crow South (a copy of this image can be found in the present *Mannish Water* volume). The Cecil Williams South Carolina Civil Rights Museum serves as an ongoing historical testament to the moral challenge posed by racial hatred and racial discrimination in the United States.

Index

Aaron, Darryl W., 10
Abrams, Stacey, 183
abundance, 172–173
abuse, 126
   alcohol, 131
   curb, 66
   drug, 131
   of women, 183
academics, 174–175
   analysis, 4
   excellence, 186, 207, 211
   skills, 252
Academy for Educational
   Development (AED), 54
Accra, Ghana, 29–30
acculturation, 198
activism, 45, 174, 272, 277
adolescent fragility, 260
AED. *see* Academy for Educational
   Development (AED)
affirmative action, 66
African-Americans, 94, 96, 98, 101, 145,
   149, 215, 242, 244–245, 252, 264
African diaspora, 160, 267, 272–274, 277
African ethnic groups, 252
The Afro American (newspaper), 41–42
Afro-Christian ancestors, 126
Aggery, J.E. K., 194
aggression, passive, 124
airport trans system, 154
Alamo, 210
alcohol abuse, 131
Algarin, Miguel, 12, 227–231

Alpha Phi Alpha, 47–48
America/American, 27–28
   Board of Urology, 39
   democracy, 113
   for Democratic Action, 39
   educational system, 285
   mainstream, 40
   race relations, 36
   revolutionary change in, 112
American Legacy magazine, 148
Amherst College, 36, 41, 44, 46
AncestryDNA, 267–268, 275–278
anger, 78
anti-capitalism poems, 228
Anti-Defamation League, 55
Antioch Baptist Church in
   Cleveland, 149
anti-slavery movements, 67–68
A. Philip Randolph Institute, 238
Arbery, Ahmaud, 3, 86, 180–181
army (US), 28
Ashanti people/palace/king, 30
Atlanta, Georgia, 105–106
Atlanta Journal Constitution, 143
Atlanta University Center (AUC), 154
The Autobiography of Malcolm X, 210–211
autonomy, 108
awakening, 100

Baby Boomer, 107, 202
"backsliding" democracy, 1
Baker, Ella, 180
Baldwin, James, 70, 78, 182, 188, 227

Baptiste, Lazarus Louis, 14–15
Baraka, Amina, 228
Baraka, Amiri, 228, 230
Baruch College, City University of New York, 227
Bay Area Urban League, 55
behavior, 261
beliefs, 63, 70, 158–160
    acknowledgment of, 112
    Christian and Islamic, 252
    systems, 263
believe in yourself, 194–195
Bell, Alexander Graham, 37
Bell, Derrick, 183
Beloved Community, 105
Benjamin, Walter, 74
Bible/biblical, 132–133, 171–173, 183, 194–195, 197–198, 200, 223, 293
    character, 182
    grounds, 62
    lore, 264
    narrative, 189
    practical wisdom in, 172
    story, 163
    supported racism, 63
Biden, Joe, 83, 113–114, 183
bigotry, 186, 188, 193
Bin-Wahid, Dhornba, 212
bisexuality, 96
bitterness, 78
Black
    Christianity, 125
    community, 40, 90, 96, 125, 127, 129, 143, 160, 207, 213
    empowerment, 129
    equity, 65
    genocide, 110
    inventors, 37
    K-12 school, 128
    male exceptionalism, 2
    Nationalist, 137
    neighborhoods, 64–65, 128, 164, 205
    physician, 39
    preaching, 109
    school, 41
    self-consciousness, 106
    students, 44–45
    truth and reality, 114
    valedictorian, 212
    youth, 176, 201
Black, Daniel, 12
Black Americans, 119, 192
    families, 170
    negative stigmatization of, 192
    stigmatization of, 196
    vision and goals, 195–197
Black Coalition, 47–48
    of New Haven, 46–47
Black Lives Matter movement, 83, 103, 182–183, 185–187, 273
blackness, 3, 221–222
Black Panther Party, 212–213
Black people, 1, 55, 184–185
    police murders of, 113
Black Writers Conference, 227
boarding house, 284–285
Bon Odori festival, 256
Bontemps, Arna, 225
boycott, 213
Brazil, 104
Bridgeport, Connecticut, 25
Brooklyn, 208–209, 212–215, 291
Brooks, Taroue W., 11
Brown, James, 251
Brown Penn Recreation Center, 123
Brownsville, 214
Brown v. Board of Education, 42–43, 205
Buck, Pearl S., 210

Burgess, Henry, 24
Bush, George W., 95–96
business, 105–106, 116, 147–148

California Achievement Test, 206
Calloway, Cab, 50
Campus Promotion and Tenure Committee, 195
Cape Coast, Ghana, 30–31
Capitol Hill, 238–239
Carson, Ben, 183
Carver, George Washington, 29
Center for Educational Leadership (CEL), 216
chaos, 182–184, 189
Charlotte, 130–131
    Schuster Price, 39
Chauvin, Derrick, 108
Chesnutt, Charles W., 140, 142
Chicago, 90–92, 100, 199
child/children, 151, 164–165, 222
    financial responsibility for, 151
    memories, 137, 269
    training, 167–172
China/Chinese, 248, 253–257, 262, 264
Chinese Communist Party, 255
Chisholm, Robert, 146
Chisholm, Shirley, 213
Christianity/Christian, 62, 80, 82, 93, 125, 127, 129, 133, 170, 181, 200, 252
    activity, 131
    community, 25
    identity, 181
    ingenuity, 125
    missionary, 126
    practice of, 82
    repentance and faith in, 133
    traditional, 170

church services, 25
citizens, health and longevity of, 206
City University of New York, 213–214
civil liberties, 54
civil rights, 45, 61, 67, 69, 89
    for Black Americans, 69–70
    marches, 61
    organizations, 54
Civil Rights Acts, 67–69, 181
Civil Rights Movement, 44, 66–67, 120, 181, 208, 261
Civil War, 65–66
class/classrooms, 2, 249–250, 286–287
Cleveland, Ohio, 137–138, 140, 143–144, 147–149, 151
Cleveland Browns, 141, 144
Cleveland Business League, 147
Cleveland Indians, 138
Clinton, Bill, 46, 240–241
Clinton, Hillary, 46
C. M. E. Methodist Church, 26
CNN, 93–95, 97, 99
Cobb, Montague, 41
cognitive development, 206
Coleman, Lonnie, 147–148
college
    curriculum, 26
    education, 28
College Roger Anglade (CRA), 287
Collins, Charles, 55
Columbia University, 97, 215–216
Comer, James, 47, 49
commonsense, 5
communitarian
    goal, 2
    totality of black women, 4
community, 2, 21, 24–25, 45, 78–79, 107, 116, 123–124, 128, 182–184, 189, 196, 199, 214

activities, 23
  disparities in, 134
  drug dealers of, 126
  playgrounds, 212
  stagnation and degradation of, 127
  wealth of, 125
Community Progress Incorporated (CPI), 46
Comprehensive Employment Training Act (CETA), 66–67
congregation, 106
Connecticut, 26, 28
conservatism, 257
Continental Army, 36
cool, 188–190
Cooper, Anderson, 94
coronavirus (COVID-19), 73, 78–80, 83, 86, 104–109, 113–114, 116–117, 119, 262, 267
  cure for, 107
  immunity, 108
  midst of, 109
Cottin, John R., 28–29
Coward, South Carolina, 19, 23
CPR, 202
crab bucket syndrome, 195
crabism, 195
credentials, 153
criminal injustice system, 54
Critical Race Theory, 88, 117
Crow, Jane, 180
Crow, Jim, 180
cultural/culture, 129
  diversity of, 198–199
  harm, 256
  shock, 257
  victims and perpetrators of, 128
  wars, 1
curb abuses, 66

curriculum, 107, 269. *see* educational system/education
  college, 26
  school, 25–26

dandy, 164
Darling-Hammond, Linda, 51–52
The Dash (Ellis), 160
Davis, Asa, 37
Davis, Kelvin, 93
Davis, Sr., Askia, 14
death, 22, 116, 227, 231
The Deep South, 25, 40, 119
delayed gratification, 202
de Mello, Anthony, 186
democracy, 1
Democracy Movement, 254
Dickens, Charles
  A Tale of Two Cities, 192
digital imaging, 120
Dionne Jr., E. J., 53
diplomacy, 95
Discovery Channel-style show, 253
discrimination, 41, 67–68, 193, 283
disparities, structural power and presence of, 76
diversity of culture, 198–199
Douglass, Frederick, 37, 70, 82
Dr. Comer's School Development Program, 49, 52
Drew, Charles, 41
drug
  abuse, 131
  addiction, 91
Du Bois, W.E.B., 29
Dunbar, Paul Laurence, 233
Durden, Bill, 157
Durden, William, 157
dying, level of, 22

economic crisis, 81
educational system/education, 28, 38, 153, 164, 174, 180, 201–203, 206–207, 210–214, 217, 241, 248, 254, 265, 269, 272, 280, 286, 290
    appreciation of, 202
    college, 28
    French, 285–286
    Haitian, 286–287
    quality of, 174
    settings, 155
egoism, 81
Egypt, 157, 211, 264
Ellis, Linda
    The Dash, 160
Elmina Castle, 31
Emancipation Proclamation, 40, 67–68
Emancipation Speech, 56
embarrassment, 175
emotional/emotions, 44
    health disorders, 268
    intelligence, 211–212, 217, 261–262
empowerment, 129, 139
Enforcement Acts of 1870 and 1871, 69
entertainment, 3, 93, 113, 159, 239, 265
Entrepreneur Magazine, 99
environments, 128, 175, 247, 256
epiphanies, 247–248
equality, transitive property of, 63–64
Eskridge, Brian, 143
ethnic
    cleansing, 63
    groups, 198–199
    infiltration, 63
ethno-biographical conceptual lens, 5
European NATO countries, 27–28

faith, 59–62, 79, 189, 205–208, 218
    to passion, 208–218
Falmouth Historical Society, 40
family
    dissection, limits for, 90
    structure, 284
    traditional, 169
Fanon, Frantz, 4–5, 8
fatherhood, 11, 149–151, 245
federal programs, 59–60
fictive kin, 60
Fisk University, 28–29
Flint, Michigan, 205
Flores, Jaime "Shaggy," 13
Florida Education Fund, 54
Floyd, George, 86–87, 108–109, 112, 185
flu pandemic 1918, 79
food
    chain, 258
    sharing, 105–106
Food Stamp Program, 59–60
forgive, 150–151, 156–157
foster
    care environments, 165
    family, 165, 168
"four track" system, 25–26
fragmented genealogy, 61
Frankel, Max, 48
fraternity, 155–156
Freedom Writers (movie), 197
Freeman, Henry, 148
French education, 285–286
friendships, 155–156
    intimate, 254

Gaines, Ernest, 180
Garrison, William Lloyd, 37
Gary, Indiana, 234
Gayle, Jr., Addison, 227

gay/queer, 248, 259
gender, 2
    orientation, 63
generation
    differences, 153
    wealth, 125
Generation X, 107
genocide, 110, 114
George, Mel, 50
Georgia, 84, 106, 109, 208–209, 211
Georgie, 212
Germans/Germany, 27–29, 32
"Get Global" program, 129
Ghana, 29–32
Giddings, Paula, 227–228
gingerbread-style houses, 284
global
    impact, 240–241
    pandemic, 74
    reality, 262
God, 111
    omnipresence, 109
    protective hand of, 124
Goldmark, Peter, 51
Gordon, Edmund W., 55
Gould, Stephen Jay, 55
    The Mismeasure of Man (Jay), 98
gratification, delayed, 202
Gray, James, 36
Great Migration, 35, 170, 208
greed, 81
Grimes, Hank, 13–14
Gulf/Middle East, 259
Gunnell, Robert, 37–38

Haiti/Haitian, 240–241, 283–287, 289–290
    diaspora, 285–286
    education, 286–287
Hall, Blanche, 22

Hampton, Henry, 50, 75, 154
Harlem, 212–213, 215, 217, 268
Harris, James Henry, 8–9
Harris, Kan1ala, 183
Hawley, Daniel, 36
HBCU, 241–242
hedonistic pleasure, 87–88
Helms, Jesse, 182
Heron, Gil Scott, 114
Hickory, North Carolina, 123–124, 126–127, 130
higher education, 159, 192. *see also* educational system/education
His Majesty the King, Otumfuo Osei Tutu II, 30
Hispanic Americans, 104
Hitler, Adolph, 63
Holy Ghost, 27
Holy Spirit, 78
homelessness, 133
homeroom classes, 209
Honduras, 129–130, 132
    internationalization experience in, 132–133
hope/hopelessness, 74, 76–78, 80–82, 163–164, 245
Houston, Charles Hamilton, 41, 46, 52, 55
Howard University, 39–41
human/humanity, 160
    behavior, 123
    capital, 129
    nature, principle of, 62
    rationalizations, 62
    rights, 1
    trafficking, 62
Hurricane Katrina, 239–240
Hussein, Saddam, 95
hyperbolic excursions, 104

IFA faith, 279
immoral behavior, 127–128
incredulity, 192
Indiana House of Representatives, 196
Indianapolis, Indiana, 35, 140
Indiana University Northwest (I.U.N.), 195, 236–237, 261, 265
inequity, 193
"inflection" moment, 2
information, 94, 103
ingredients, 236
institutionalized racism, 61, 69
institutional racism, 44, 63
Insurrection of January 6, 2021, 81
intellectual/intellectualism, 153, 158–159
interconnectedness of life, 156
International Institute for Democracy and Electoral Assistance (IDEA), 1
internationalization, idea and realities of, 129
intersectionality, 3, 63
The Inward Journey (Thurman), 187–188
Iraq, 95–96
Islam/Islamic, 252
Ismaili, Rashidah, 228
Ivy League universities, 44

Jackson, Jesse, 252
Jackson, Thom, 7
Jacob, John, 48, 52
January 6, 2021, 113
Japan/Japanese, 256–257, 262
Jefferson, Thomas, 68
Jeremiah, Rodney, 150
Jesus, 111–112
    death and resurrection, 193
Jewish, 55, 271, 274–275
    community, 55

Jim Crow laws, 66, 119, 188
Johnson, Harry, 48, 59
    War on Poverty, 60–61
Johnson, James Weldon, 29
Johnson, Lyndon B., 59–60
Jones, Norm, 11
Jordan, Vernon, 35, 48, 51
Joshua, Richard, 150
journalism, 89, 93
joy, 74

K-12, 159
Kappa Alpha Psi Fraternity, Inc., 145, 150
Kennedy, John F., 45, 119–120, 144
Kidd, Roye, 145–146
killings, 69
Kimball, Harold, 146
kindness, mannerisms of, 171
King, Jr., Martin Luther, 28, 45, 47, 56, 64–65, 67, 73, 137–138, 181–182
King, Stephen, 179
King Solomon, 125, 166, 173
kinship, 4
    network, 55
klansmen, 124
Kline A. Price, Sr., 38
knowledge of family origins, 124
Korazim Plateau, 111
Ku Klux Klan, 33, 38, 124–125, 134n2
Kumasi, Ghana, 30

Lancelot, 137–139
languages, 201, 249, 252
Latimer, George W., 36–37
Latimer, Lewis, 37
Lawn, Butler, 94
leadership, 155

responsibility for, 216–217
League of Women Voters, 39
League's Campaign for African American Achievement, 53
learning, 157, 165–166
    to think, 291–293
Le Droit Park, 38, 41
Lewis, John, 48
LGBTQ community, 101
LIE, 184–185
life, 248
    adult phase of, 248
    fundamentals of, 237
lockdowns, 74
Locke, Alain, 29
Louisville, Kentucky, 153, 155
love, 82–84, 163–164
    embodiment of, 85
    obedience, 84–86
Lowery, Robert J., 234, 236

magnanimity, 174–177
Mainland China/Chinese, 252
Maldonado, Melanie, 267, 278–279
maleness, 3
Mandela, Nelson, 240–241
manhood, 4, 10, 12, 126, 168–169, 173, 176
mankind, 194
mannerisms of kindness, 171
Mannish Water anthology, 2
mantric syllogism, 64
Manuel, Jason Scott, 10
March on Washington, 45
marriage, 151, 261, 283
    institution of, 156
Marshall, Thurgood, 46
Martin, Trayvon, 69, 180, 185
masculinity, 224
Mason Dixon Line, 44

masonic/masons, 22–23
matriarch, 22, 160, 166
Mays, Benjamin, 216–217
media, 210–211
medications, 116, 158
Medina, Tony, 12
mediocrity, 166, 174–177
meditations, form of, 164
me-ism, 199
mental asylums, 164
mercy, 77
metaphor, 133
Metropolitan Museum of Art, 50
Miami, 239–240
Miami Dolphins, 141, 144
Miles, George, 49–50
Mills, Dave, 228, 231
Milord, Louis, 283
Ming, Melvin, 49–50
"ministry of presence" in crisis, 106
minority sexual identity, 3
miseducation, victims of, 213–214
The Miseducation of The Negro (Woodson), 211
The Mismeasure of Man (Jay), 98
misogynoir, 177, 186
mission/missionary, 130–131
Mississippi River, 44
MLK National Memorial Project Foundation, 47–48
Montreal, Canada, 286
moon landing, 288
Morehouse College Glee Club, 155–156
Morrison, Toni, 1–2
Morrow, E. Frederic, 41
mortality, 107
Moses, Oral, 6–7, 30
multicultural relationships, 173
murders of Black people, 87

mutual love, 86
My Town USAs, 129

N95 masks, 106
Nagoya, Japan, 256
Narcotics Anonymous, 91
National Achievers Society (NAS), 54
National Association for the Advancement of Colored People (NAACP), 41–43, 48
    Image Awards, 241–242
    Legal Defense Fund, 43
National Coalition on Black Civic Participation, Inc. (NCBCP), 243
National Commission on Teaching and America's Future, 51
national pandemic disaster, 82
national security, 89
National Urban League, 35–36, 48, 52–53, 55–56
Native Americans, genocide and removal of, 210
The Neverending Story (movie), 201
New Haven, Connecticut, 47–48
"New Hope" community, 19
New Jersey, 164, 167, 174
new world order, 77–78
New York City, 47, 49–50, 56, 93, 97, 101, 167, 199, 208, 214–217, 230–231, 239, 270–271, 288
The New York Times, 48–49, 53–54
9/11 attack, 244
Nixon, Richard, 181–182
non-fiction anthology, 3
Nuyorican Poets Cafe, 227, 229–231, 272

Obama, Barack, 99, 185, 289
Olive Grove Baptist Church, 23, 25
Olive Grove Community, 19, 23

Open Admissions policy, 214
"Open Air Worship" service, 106
Operations Research Office (ORO), 43–44, 46
oppression, White, 89
ORO. *see* Operations Research Office (ORO)

Palgrave Macmillan, 5
Pan-Africanist, 212
pandemic, 74–76, 81, 83, 103, 112, 115
parent's love, 167
Paris, France, 75
Parker, Henry, 47
Parks, Gordon, 48
Park Street Congregational Church, 26
Paul, Apostle, 172, 191, 200
PBS, 49–50
peer pressure, 199, 235
perception, 259
    of progress, 70
pernicious reality, 65
personal
    consequences, 89
    identity, 247–248
    indulgence, 90
    insecurity, 128
physical
    distancing, 79
    harm, 271
    mobility, 20
Pittsburgh community, 106
pod-peopleism, 259
poetry readings, 228
Poitier, Sidney, 50
police
    brutality, 245
    intervention and harassment, 255
    killings, 54

lynching, 87
political power, 62
popular entertainment, 3–4
post-Reconstruction, violence and degradation of, 40
poverty, 127
Powell, Kevin, 229
Powell, Ralph, 237
power, 81, 107, 200
    of Holy Ghost, 193
prayer, 182
    band, 27
prejudice, 176, 192
press coverage, 53
Price, Hugh, 7
Price, Robert, 38
privacy, invasions of, 255
proverbial glass ceiling, 51
psychological baggage, 132
public
    library, 123
    schools, 105
    television history, 49
Puerto Rico/Puerto Rican, 209, 211–214, 268–273, 276, 278–279
    Day Parade, 229
    Organization for the Performing Arts (PROPA), 267
Purkey, William, 203

quarantine, 106
queer, 12, 186, 221

race/racist, 2, 89, 200
    behavior, 124
    healthcare system, 180–181
    pedestrian concept of, 5
racial/racism, 56, 63, 67, 193
    conversations about, 60
    pandemic of, 83
    reckoning, 2–3
    solidarity, 196–197
    violence, 69
    white, 184–185
racing, 5
Ragland, Kenneth, 146–147
Ralph Community Center, 214
Raspberry, William, 53
rationalizations, 62
Reagan, Ronald, 61, 67
realization, 166
reconstruction/post-reconstruction, 40
recovered memories, 90
redneck speed trap, 24
Reed, Ishmael, 229
regret, 158
relationship, 90, 113, 151, 155, 168, 170, 259
    multicultural, 173
    with the property management, 131
relaxation, 159
religious
    adherence, 101
    beliefs, 264
    bias, 63
    experience, 25
    services, 38
renaissance, 290–291
respectability, politics of, 184
Reynolds, Rodney J., 9–10
righteousness, 110–111
riots, 87
risk, 163–164
Rivera, Louis Reyes, 272
Rockefeller Foundation, 51
Roosevelt, Theodore, 107
Rosa Parks, 188, 261
rubber gloves, 106

sacrifice/sacrificing, 95, 163–164, 166
salvation, 79–80
Sanders Memorial, 22
sanitizer, 106
Sarah, Grandmama, 22
Saudi Arabia, 260, 262, 264
school, 175, 202–203
    culture of, 217
    curriculum, 25–26
    funds for, 167
    Greek tragedy in, 165–166
    system, 217
    uniform, 169
School-Based Management (SBM), 216
"schools-to-prison pipeline," 214
Scott, Austin L., 8
scripture, 77–80, 82–83, 85, 87–88, 172–173, 193, 195–196, 199
Second World War, 6, 271
segregation, 19, 23, 25–26, 35, 37, 39–43, 45, 65–66, 119–120, 129, 188, 205, 209, 211, 252, 280
self-actualization, 6
self-affirmation, 6
self-confidence, 194
self-consciousness, 226
self-destruction, 114
self-education, essential components of, 268
self-medication, 113
sense
    of "freedom," 115
    of hopelessness, 127, 197
    of inferiority, 127
separation, 191
September 11, 2001, 150
sex/sexism, 2, 63
    partners, 131
Shakur, Afeni, 212
Shakur, Lumumba, 212

shame, 93, 158
Slaughter, F. Keith, 9
slaves/slavery, 111, 132, 183
    in America, 117
slavocracy, 87–88
Smith, Vernon G., 10–11, 191
social
    anxiety, 128
    distancing, 79
    gatherings, 236
    media, 245
    work, 153
    worker, 157
societal expectations, 235
Society for the Study of Black Religion, 75
sorrow, 74
The South, 19, 45, 73, 124
South Carolina, 26, 119–120
South Center Street, 124–125, 127
special assignments, 206
spiritual transformation, 110
sports, 265
Springfield, Massachusetts, 268–270
status quo, 205, 217–218
Steptoe, Lamont, 229–230
stereotypes, 3
stewardship, 173
stigmatization, 192
    of Black Americans, 196
Stillman College, 241–242
Strout, Elizabeth, 181
structural racism, 63
St. Stephens, 291–292
Student Nonviolent Coordinating Committee (SNCC), 45
students, 159
Students for a Democratic Society, 45
stuttering, 233
suffering, 74, 126

Sunday Times, 53
Sundiata, Sekou, 228
Sviridoff, Mike, 48
Swainsboro, Georgia, 205, 207

A Tale of Two Cities (Dickens), 192
Taylor, Breonna, 86
Teachers College Columbia University, 215–216
teachers/teaching, 159, 207
Texas Southern University, 237–238
13th Amendment, 68
Thomas, Clarence, 183
Thomas, Franklin, 48, 51
Thomas J. Watshon Fellowship, 29
Thurgood Marshall, 181
Thurman, Howard, 187
    The Inward Journey, 187–188
Till, Emmett, 24, 73, 185
The Times, 49
Tindall, Al, 47
traditional family, 169
transformation, 127
    visions, 217–218
transportation, 29–30
Travis, Shannon, 9
Tribble, Israel, 54
Trumbull, Connecticut, 36
Trump, Donald, 74, 76, 81, 83, 103–104, 107, 113, 117, 179, 182–186
truth, 201
Turrentine, Stanley, 146–147
23andMe, 267–268, 274–278
2020 election, 184

Ubuntu philosophy, 193–194
Umulisa, Bahizi, 253
United States
    Army, 27
    Constitution, 68–69, 198
    Defense Department's Operations Research Office (ORO), 43
    political leaders, 95
    racial reckoning in, 2
University of Cape Coast, 31
University of Massachusetts at Amherst, 272–273
University of Michigan in 1922, 28–29
Urban League movement, 35
Urban Leaguers, 38–39

vacations, 154
vaccine, 74, 76, 114–115
Vance, Cyrus, 46
Vietnam, 28
violence, 180, 269
vision, 195–197

Wade, James "Jimmy," 143
Wall Street Journal, 53
Walton, Jon, 94
Wampanoag Native American tribe, 40
Warfield, Paul, 141, 144–145
War on Poverty, 66
Warrick, Cynthia, 241–242
war stories, 55
Washington Post, 106–107
Washington's Black community, 40
Watkins, Clyde, 170–172
wealth, 127, 192
we-ism, 199
Welfare Queen, 61
Wharton, Clifton, 51
white
    Americans, 104
    nationalist, 113

oppression, 89
oppressors, 110
privilege, 113
racism, 184–185
supremacists, 103, 210, 218
supremacy, 56, 83, 181, 186, 188, 205
Whitfield, James Monroe, 65–66
Wilde, Oscar, 61
William Penn Foundation, 55
Williams, Cecil, 7–8
Williams, Junius, 228
Winston, Wayne, 138
Wittgenstein, Ludwig, 74
WNET, 50–51
women/womanism, 4, 23
Woods Hole Historical Museum, 40
Woodson, Carter G.
   The Miseducation of The Negro, 211

Woolworth, 69
World Book Encyclopedia, 249–250
World Trade Center, 244
World War II., 27–28
wrangling, 78
wrath, 78
Wright, Bobby, 113
Wright, Richard, 75

X, Malcolm, 45, 181, 210–211, 215
xenophobia, 62

Yale, 47, 52
Yale University, 46
Young, Whitney, 48
youth development, 214

Zoom, 107

Praise For The Book

"Mannish Water bears witness to the power that comes from writing heartfelt truths. The Black men contributing to this volume write as individuals and as community, willing to offer, through the Word, a space for revelation and healing much in the way our womanist writers and scholars have done with their work."

Dr. Valerie Ann Johnson
Dean - School of Arts, Sciences, and Humanities
and Professor of Sociology,
Shaw University

"This mosaic of Black intellectual thought is as bold as it is impressive. In an age where society's noise often cancels out the needs and concerns of minority voices, Mannish Water unapologetically interjects the clear and booming voice of America's Black men into the national discourse of social and political thought.
Black livelihood is constantly at risk in America, and the voices here demonstrate the imminent threat Black families face if no one dares to address the situation with careful thought and analysis. The effort here is monumental. We owe this group of scholars our gratitude."

A. Hannibal Hamdallahi, Ph.D.
Associate Professor, Political Science
Director, African American Studies,
Fisk University

www.ingramcontent.com/pod-product-compliance
Lightning Source LLC
Chambersburg PA
CBHW020330240426
43665CB00043B/194